# The American Class Structure

# The American Class Structure

Joseph A. Kahl

WASHINGTON UNIVERSITY

*with an Introduction by*

KINGSLEY DAVIS

UNIVERSITY OF CALIFORNIA

Holt, Rinehart and Winston

New York - Chicago - San Francisco
Toronto - London

FEBRUARY, 1967

SBN: 03–008815–1

Library of Congress Catalog Card Number: 57-6451

1234  090  15141312

# Introduction

AMONG THE MYRIAD BOOKS on American society, few if any resemble the present one. Professor Kahl's treatment is at once sound and lucid (a rare combination), and his topic is one that has seldom if ever been handled in such a comprehensive and yet empirical manner. The book brings together in a well-organized way the research findings, increasingly numerous in the last thirty years, which have illuminated the American class structure. There is scarcely a topic in social science more deserving of such a synthesis.

That the class structure forms a fundamental feature of any society has often been recognized. Historians of the Middle Ages, for example, whatever their theoretical predilections may be, invariably find it necessary in analyzing Medieval society to deal with the clergy, the nobility, the bourgeoisie, and the peasantry. Students of indigenous India generally make reference to the caste system, just as observers of precommunist China must usually refer to the gentry. As in these societies, so in the United States. To understand ourselves we must be aware of the various strata, of the determinants of membership in these strata, of the motives and attitudes that go with social position and with changes in position. These are realities which affect every aspect of life, and which cannot be understood exclusively in economic or political terms. To look at our system of stratification is to look at ourselves in a way that cuts across the traditional disciplines and brings out new perspectives otherwise missed.

Curiously, however, there has sometimes been a tendency in historical, economic, or political writing to avoid coming to grips directly with class phenomena. It almost seems as if the facts of human inequality are too unpleasant to the social scientist, so that he loses his objectivity or his courage. Even the Marxians, who have used the class struggle tenaciously as their point of departure, have comforted themselves with the thought that inequality could ultimately be eliminated.

Nowhere has this proclivity to evade the subject of class been more apparent than in the United States up to thirty years ago. In part this was due to the open and unfettered nature of our economy and, with the westward expansion, to the growth of grass-roots democracy. If class barriers were weak, if talent and industry were rewarded, and if the majority ruled by ballot, recall, and referendum, the view could be truthfully held that our society was almost, and should be entirely, without classes in the sense of fixed inherited strata. It became almost taboo to think of ourselves in "class" terms, but since the word "class" included both the idea of inherited strata and the idea of achieved inequalities, this restriction led to the slighting of important realities in American life by American scholars. In addition, the traditional speculation about social classes was European in origin and in its frame of reference, and was therefore plainly inapplicable in detail to the United States. The traditional literature on the subject, furthermore, was so tinged with Marxism and hence with ethical and political controversy that American social scientists tended to avoid the subject. True, Sumner, Veblen, and Cooley dealt with class phenomena, as did others more casually or indirectly, but they did so more in the vein of interpretive speculation than in that of scientific investigation.

Not until the 1930's and 1940's, when the great depression forced us to re-examine our precepts, did serious study of social stratification begin in this country. Since then the subject has quickly emerged as a field of specialized study; and though it reached this point later than such related topics as "race relations" and "labor economics," its progress has been so fast that by now a large and varied assortment of empirical investigations are available, perhaps more here than in any other land. A number of young sociologists, including Professor Kahl, are now concentrating in this field and advancing our knowledge of it by original research; and college curricula are increasingly including courses on the subject. Only recently has it become possible for a genuine textbook to be written on the American class structure, a fact which contributes to the novelty and significance of the present volume.

The author has wisely set as his task the sifting, evaluation, and organization of the principal findings revealed by empirical studies. He has not undertaken a philosophic or propagandistic interpretation, but rather a disinterested, well-organized synthesis of what the research investigations show. He has ordered his material in terms of six dimensions of class position, and he has dealt in a clear and original fashion with the crucial matter of class mobility, seeking to ascertain not only the degree to which gradations in our society are open to recruitment from above or below but also the degree to which different factors contribute to such interclass movement. Also, his scientific integrity has made him unwilling merely to set forth the conclusions reached but to try instead to give the reader a knowledge of *how* the conclusions were reached.

The focus of the book is entirely on the United States. Although studies made elsewhere, particularly in Europe, are occasionally used to elucidate or supplement the American findings, the volume is clearly not a weighty treatise on stratification in general but rather a brief analysis of our own system. The truth is, of course, that our class order is not, at least in general outline, unique. It is a product of our urban-industrial stage of economic development, of our west-European cultural heritage, and of the circumstances of settlement in a new continent. Although one cannot measure the relative influence of such broad and intertwined variables, much weight must be given to the stage of development. Our class system is probably more similar to that of the Soviet Union or that of Japan today than it is to the class system of Medieval Europe. Professor Kahl's book is therefore an analysis of one type of class structure through the medium of one case, or country—a type which tends to go with an urban-industrial technology and economy regardless of cultural background. If and when similar analyses are written for other countries, we shall be able to see more clearly what is common to this type and what is variable.

Needless to say, the type of social stratification found in a country is not the same thing as the type of political structure found there. Social autocracy or democracy is not identical with political autocracy or democracy. The political order concerns those who govern, their relations with others and among themselves. Though the governing group obviously plays an important role in the system of stratification, the class structure as a whole is much wider; for it includes all the strata and all of their modes of interdependence, nonpolitical as well as political. In other words, the framework of a society is more fully described by its class organization than by its political organization. The author of the present volume, by giving us a clear and ingenious delineation of our class system, has written not only a unique textbook in sociology but has made a distinguished contribution to American self-understanding.

KINGSLEY DAVIS

*University of California*
*December, 1956*

# Preface

A GREAT DEAL OF RESEARCH has been done on the class system of the United States; indeed, this field of inquiry is a favorite among American sociologists. One reason for its popularity is the fact that the stratification system ties together many different facets of society. Thus a study of a particular American community, or even American society as a whole, that uses stratification as its focus provides an integrated and comprehensible view of social life.

Most research that has used social class as its unifying theme has been confined to small communities. From "Middletown" to "Jonesville," one American town after another has revealed to the investigator a pattern of integration via its class system, a pattern somewhat analagous to that of kinship and clan which is so well known in ethnological research. However, there is also a substantial amount of knowledge available about stratification on a national scope, particularly concerning occupation and income.

It is the purpose of this book to organize the two bodies of research —local and national—into a unified portrait of the class system of present-day America. The emphasis throughout is on verified knowledge based on systematic research. But systematic research is, for many areas of stratification behavior, as much an ideal as an accomplishment. Consequently, the student of the subject must be aware of the differences between verified knowledge, suggestive but inconclusive evidence, and speculation. He needs to know how the supposed facts were discovered and measured. In this book, research results will be accompanied in each instance by a critical review of the methods used by the investigator. It is my hope that the reader who learns something of these methods will then be able to evaluate for himself various popular pronouncements about American social class. Insofar as such pronouncements appear regularly in newspapers and magazines, and lie behind much debate about political affairs, an ability to judge their validity is of more than academic interest.

Because the central aim of this book is a description of the realities of the American class system, emphasis is always on the available facts and not on the competing theories about stratification. Nevertheless, theory is important to the present task. From traditional theory I have derived a six-factor conceptual scheme which serves as a framework for organizing the research data. A separate chapter is devoted to each of the factors: prestige, occupation, possessions, interaction, class consciousness, and value orientations. Those researches which are primarily concerned with a given factor are analyzed in the appropriate chapter. Throughout the book, but particularly in Chapter VII, interrelations among the factors are also explored. Finally, two additional topics are analyzed: the barriers faced by ethnic groups and the question of social mobility.

The conceptual scheme serves to isolate the most important aspects of class behavior and to indicate some of the ways in which they influence one another, but it is not presented as a causative theory that fully explains how and why the stratification system got to be the way it is. I do not believe we have a theory adequate to that task, and certainly any approach to such a theory would have to be based on detailed comparisons of the American class system with others, as well as a minute study of the histories of various class systems, and neither is the purpose of this book (although occasional comparative and historical illustrations are presented).

The book is written primarily for college students of sociology, but others might find it of use. All social scientists must deal with stratification. Psychologists find that class position influences personality test response; economists know that class position influences consumer behavior and work attitudes; political scientists realize the close connection between stratification and political debate and voting behavior. And specialists in other fields, such as journalism and education, find social class to be basic to the American life they seek to understand. In order to make the book useful to these various specialists, sociological terminology is kept to a minimum and is defined wherever it has to be introduced as a tool of scientific communication.

I have had important help in writing this book. To begin with, I have benefited from experience doing research relevant to stratification under the wise guidance of Professors Florence R. Kluckhohn, Talcott Parsons, Samuel A. Stouffer, W. Lloyd Warner, and William F. Whyte. My first experience in teaching stratification was a course in Harvard College taught jointly for two years with Professor Peter H. Rossi; from him I learned a great deal that appears here. Various drafts of the manuscript, in whole or part, have been read and criticized by the following persons; I am grateful for the many important suggestions they offered and apologize for those I was unable to accept: John D. Campbell, Stuart Cleveland, Kingsley Davis, George C. Homans, Clyde Kluckhohn, Kurt B. Mayer, William Petersen, Renato Tagiuri. Professor Davis was particularly helpful; his interest in the book and the time he devoted to it went beyond what an author has a right to expect from an editor.

A textbook leans on the creative research of many men. The references at the end of each chapter indicate the sources of material used. They are designed to support the statements made in the text and to indicate the major additional references for the student who wishes to explore further. Thus, they make up a selective and annotated bibliography rather than an exhaustive one. Complete bibliographies are available elsewhere, as indicated in the references of the first chapter.

The following authors and publishers graciously permitted quotation from their works:

Yale University Press: W. Lloyd Warner and Paul S. Lunt, *The Social Life of a Modern Community*. Copyright 1941 by Yale University Press (quoted in Chapters II, IV, and V).

University of Chicago Press: Allison Davis, Burleigh B. Gardner and Mary R. Gardner, *Deep South: A Social-Anthropological Study of Caste and Class*. Copyright 1941 by The University of Chicago (quoted in Chapters II and VIII).

John Wiley & Sons: August B. Hollingshead, *Elmtown's Youth*. Copyright 1947 by John Wiley & Sons (quoted in Chapters II, V, and VII).

Harcourt, Brace & Company: Robert S. Lynd and Helen Merrell Lynd, *Middletown*. Copyright 1929 by Harcourt, Brace & Company (quoted in Chapter III). Robert S. Lynd and Helen Merrell Lynd, *Middletown in Transition*. Copyright 1937 by Harcourt, Brace & Company (quoted in Chapter III). St. Clair Drake and Horace R. Cayton, *Black Metropolis*. Copyright 1945 by St. Clair Drake and Horace R. Cayton (quoted in Chapter VIII).

Princeton University Press: Richard Centers, *The Psychology of Social Classes*. Copyright 1949 by Princeton University Press (quoted in Chapters III and VI).

Harvard University Press: Oscar Handlin, *The American People in the Twentieth Century*. Copyright 1954 by The President and Fellows of Harvard College (quoted in Chapter VIII).

Harvard Educational Review: Joseph A. Kahl, "Educational and Occupational Aspirations of 'Common Man' Boys," Volume XXIII, Number 3. Copyright 1953 by The President and Fellows of Harvard College (quoted in Chapter X).

JOSEPH A. KAHL

*Washington University*
*St. Louis*
*November, 1956*

# Contents

# Tables

# Figures

# The American Class Structure

# I

# The Dimensions of Class

ALL COMMUNITIES DIVIDE THEMSELVES INTO THE FEW AND THE MANY. THE FIRST ARE THE RICH AND WELL-BORN, THE OTHER THE MASS OF THE PEOPLE. . . . THE PEOPLE ARE TURBULENT AND CHANGING; THEY SELDOM JUDGE OR DETERMINE RIGHT. . . . GIVE, THEREFORE, TO THE FIRST CLASS A DISTINCT, PERMANENT SHARE IN THE GOVERNMENT. THEY WILL CHECK THE UNSTEADINESS OF THE SECOND, AND, AS THEY CANNOT RECEIVE ANY ADVANTAGE BY A CHANGE, THEY THEREFORE WILL EVER MAINTAIN GOOD GOVERNMENT.

*Alexander Hamilton* [1]

THOUGHTFUL MEN have recognized the importance of social classes since the beginnings of Western philosophy. They knew that in every society men were unequal: some had more money or more influence or more prestige than their neighbors. And the philosophers realized that the differences between men were more than personal, for they created a stratification hierarchy. In it large groups or classes of people shared certain positions that gave them interests in common with their equals but different from groups who were above them or below them. Finally, it was clear that many of the acts of men in society were consequences of their class interests. As Hamilton said, the rich sought social stability to preserve their advantages, but the poor worked for social change that would bring them more of the world's rewards.

This book is an analysis of the class structure of the United States today. It examines the distribution of money, prestige, and the other stratification variables among the different classes in the country. It will point out the ways in which the variables react upon one another; how, for instance, a man's income affects his beliefs about social policy, or how his job affects his choice of friends or a wife. And it will explore the question of movement from one class to another; for a society can have classes and still permit individuals to rise or fall among them.

In order to measure the several dimensions of the class structure— and we cannot understand how they influence one another if we cannot measure what we are talking about—it is necessary to define them with precision. The way to do that is to take a backward glance at the

I

history of stratification theory in order to identify the major facets of the subject.

## KARL MARX

Although the discussion of stratification is ancient, it was not until the nineteenth century that Karl Marx formulated the systematic theory of class differences that has been so influential on modern thought. In his intellectual work Marx followed Hegel and Ricardo. From the former he borrowed a theory of historical change which taught that each stage of social life contained the seeds of the next, that life was constantly developing in a way that could be comprehended through the abstractions of the philosophical intellect. From the latter he borrowed many tools of technical economic analysis which he thought were sufficient to allow him to build a complete theory of the operations of capitalism. Marx believed that the shape of a society was determined by its economic foundations and that social classes formed the key link between economic facts and social facts. Thus he said that an understanding of social classes was basic to a comprehension of society and history.

Marx maintained that every productive system established a limited number of types of work roles—a man could raise food, make tools, be a merchant who traded goods, or perhaps be an owner of land or other property. Each group of men who stood in the same relationship to the means of production formed a class. They not only did the same kind of work, but had basic interests in common which often put them in conflict with other classes. Their interests were created by their position in the productive system and were expressed in the legal rules of property.

A given type of productive system, or mode of production, would continue to exist as long as the various classes remained in equilibrium despite their contradictory interests. This often meant that the most powerful class, the one that controlled the most important means of production, had gained power over the entire society and used the organs of government to keep the other classes under control. The ruling class, through law and propaganda, would create a whole superstructure of community life that would further its class interests. Thus the rules of property, the laws of family life and inheritance, the schools, and even the churches, were shaped for the benefit of the few who had power. Naked economic interest need not always be in evidence, for the rationalizations of men are devious and wondrous. Through their power even a slave can be made to accept slavery and fight for his master.

Adam Smith elaborated the consequences of an economic market in which people trade as individuals; Marx elaborated the consequences of the social controls that govern economic behavior. He stressed the fact that men do not behave only as individuals, but as members of groups, and that each group has institutional interests in common.

Historical change was explained by Marx as the unfolding of the class struggle. As new means of production are developed, new class interests arise that upset the old balance of power. Sometimes readjustments in power and in the various social institutions in which it is embedded are made slowly and peacefully, as was the case in Great Britain when it industrialized in the eighteenth and nineteenth centuries. But sometimes the conflict of interests is so great, and the rigidity of the society so firm, that only revolution can overthrow the grip of the old ruling class and permit the new productive forces to expand. Thus, France had a revolution that was promoted by the rising merchants to free them from the grip of the landowners and their agent, the King. For Marx the French propagandists may have been talking about the "Rights of Man," but they really meant the "Rights of the Bourgeoisie."

This "historical materialism," or the belief that the primary force in social change is economic interest, was first elaborated by Marx and Engels in the *Communist Manifesto* of 1848. Its second page reads as follows [2]:

The history of all hitherto existing society is the history of class struggles.

Freeman and slave, patrician and plebeian, lord and serf, guild-master and journeyman, in a word, oppressor and oppressed, stood in constant opposition to one another, carried on an uninterrupted, now hidden, now open fight, a fight that each time ended either in a revolutionary reconstitution of society at large, or in the common ruin of the contending classes.

In the earlier epochs of history, we find almost everywhere a complicated arrangement of society into various orders, a manifold gradation of social rank. In ancient Rome, we have patricians, knights, plebeians, slaves; in the Middle Ages, feudal lords, vassals, guild-masters, journeymen, apprentices, serfs; in almost all of these classes, again, subordinate gradations. . . .

Our epoch, the epoch of the bourgeoisie, possesses, however, this distinctive feature; it has simplified the class antagonisms. Society as a whole is more and more splitting up into two great hostile camps, into two great classes directly facing each other—bourgeoisie and proletariat.

There follow several pages of striking analysis of the disintegration of late medieval society in Europe by the new economic forces of modern capitalism.

For Marx modern capitalism was a form of society that was based on the private ownership of fluid industrial capital and the availability of free labor (not tied to the land by vestiges of feudal law). When medieval society began to disintegrate, the opportunity was opened for some men to amass substantial amounts of money and credit that could be put to work in the production and exchange of salable goods. The force of this system was explosive: eventually most traces of the old order based on feudal custom, local loyalties, and integrated communities disappeared before the superior productive power of free capitalism. Marx claimed that the old distinctions among men, dividing them into lords, gentry, serfs, artisans, were displaced by a single fundamental distinction: those who owned capital and those who did not. The capitalists or bourgeoisie were united by interests that transcended local or even national boundaries, for they wanted to maintain this system which brought them so much profit, and they wanted to keep under control the mass of proletarians who worked in their factories. According to Marx, the proletariat might occasionally get a temporary increase in their standard of living out of this new system, but in the long run they would be reduced to complete impoverishment and misery. Furthermore, they would be molded into a single homogeneous body, for gradations of skill would be eliminated by machine production.

Marx believed that a capitalist gained his profit from the "surplus value" of the work of his laborers. The price of labor was determined not by the value of the products that a laborer could produce, but by the cost of supplying him, that is, by the minimum cost of living for the laborers and their families. Under ordinary circumstances a worker could produce goods that were worth more than the cost of his wages, and the difference between his wages (plus overhead) and the sale price of the goods went into the pocket of the owner of the factory. Thus, as long as production was carried on under capitalist rules, the worker would be exploited out of part of the value of his labor.

The reasons why the capitalists would grow ever richer and the proletariat ever poorer were deduced by Marx from technical theorems that only economists and communists claim to understand. But in the middle of the nineteenth century, when Marx wrote, there seemed to be much confirmation in fact for those deductions. As all readers of Dickens know, the conditions of life in the factories and workingmen's homes in the most advanced capitalistic country, Great Britain, were miserable. Many contemporary observers believed that the previous social order had contained an equilibrium between the various grades of society that offered them all a modicum of contentment, whereas this new order was reducing the vast bulk of society to an animal level at the same time that plutocrats of uncountable wealth were created by their sweat and agony.

Marx used most of his pages to discuss the details of the capitalistic order. Only occasionally did he offer a hint of things to come. He said that certain internal forces within capitalism would lead to its downfall.

As the workers would be concentrated more and more within a few large factories, they would become increasingly aware of their common misery and common destiny. Communist leaders who understood the "scientific inevitability" of their condition would circulate among them and teach them the economic facts of life. Eventually their growing interaction with one another and expanding understanding of their position would lead them to join together and revolt against their masters. Then a new order would be established under which the proletariat would seize the state and own the means of production; classes would disappear, for all men would stand in the same relationship to the means of production—they would all be workers. Like most practical propagandists, Marx was much more detailed in his descriptions of the evils of the existing system than in the mechanics of the millennium.

This materialistic conception of history was a grand feat of imagination; it stands today as one of the few great abstract ideas that gives a semblance of order to the confusing pages of history. But it always turns out that history is too complex for any such unifying abstraction. Especially when the theory was tested by the events of history after Marx's time did its inadequacies appear: peasant countries have gone communist, and the most advanced capitalistic country has the richest and most contented proletariat the world has ever known. However, the fact that the theory will not stand as a perfect scheme does not deny that it contains some truth and points our minds to some interesting problems. *The dynamic relationships between economic fact, class membership, and cultural institutions are well worth studying even if all have reciprocal influences on each other instead of merely flowing automatically from the first.*

### MAX WEBER

Marx was glib and superficial when he spoke of the processes that created the cultural superstructure [3]. He simply said that the bourgeoisie had seized the state and used it to oppress the masses. It remained for the sociologists who came after him to study empirically the effects of economic differences on social life. One of them, the great Max Weber of Germany, who wrote in the early years of the twentieth century, spent most of his life doing historical research on the reciprocal influences between ideology, social structure, and economic processes.

Weber made a crucial distinction between three orders of stratification: *class*, *status*, and *party*. The first refers to groupings of people according to their market position; it is the same concept as the class of Marx, but it is narrowed to its economic core and stripped of most aspects of the social superstructure. For Weber class situation or mem-

bership refers to the economic opportunities an individual has in the labor
or commodity markets. These opportunities for worldly success or "life
chances" are determined mainly by a man's skills in an occupation or
his supply of monetary capital.

A class then becomes a group of people who share the same life
chances. Notice that this way of defining a class does not imply that
the individuals in it are aware of their common situation. It simply defines a category of people who are, from the point of view of the
market, similar to each other. Only under certain circumstances do
they become aware of their common fate, begin to think of each other
as equals, and develop institutions of joint action to further their interests—in Weber's words, become a "community."

By contrast, writes Weber [4]:

. . . *status groups* are normally communities. They are, however, often of an
amorphous kind. In contrast to the purely economically determined "class
situation" we wish to designate as "status situation" every typical component
of the life fate of men that is determined by a specific, positive or negative,
social estimation of *honor*. . . .

In content, status honor is normally expressed by the fact that above all
else a specific *style of life* can be expected from all those who wish to belong
to the circle. Linked with this expectation are restrictions on "social" intercourse (that is, intercourse which is not subservient to economic or any
other of business's "functional" purposes). These restrictions may confine
normal marriages to within the status circle and may lead to complete
endogamous closure. . . .

Of course, material monopolies provide the most effective motives for
the exclusiveness of a status group. . . . With an increased inclosure of the
status group, the conventional preferential opportunities for special employment grow into a legal monopoly of special offices for the members. . . .

With some over-simplification, one might thus say that "classes" are
stratified according to their relations to the production and acquisition of
goods; whereas "status groups" are stratified according to the principles of
their *consumption* of goods as represented by special "styles of life."

In those passages Weber specifies many of the interrelations between
class and status, between economy and society. Because of one's class
position he earns a certain income. That income allows him to live in
a certain style, and he soon makes friends with other people who live
the same way. As they interact with one another, they begin to conceive
of themselves as a special type of person. They restrict interaction with
outsiders who seem too different (they may be too poor, too uneducated, too clumsy to live graciously enough for acceptance as worthy
companions). Marriage partners are chosen from similar groups, for
once people follow a certain style of life, they find it difficult to be

comfortable with people who live differently. Thus the status group becomes an ingrown circle. It earns a position in the local community that entitles its members to social honor or prestige from inferiors.

Status groups develop the conventions or customs of the community. Through time they evolve appropriate ways of dressing, of eating, of living that are somewhat different from the ways of other groups. Eventually these distinctions react on the market place; in order to preserve their advantages, high-status groups attempt to monopolize those goods which symbolize their style of life—they pass consumption laws prohibiting the lower orders from wearing lace, or they band together to keep Negroes from moving into exclusive residential sections, or they keep Jewish boys out of the better colleges.

A status order tends to restrict the freedom of the market not only in the monopolization of certain types of consumption goods, but also in the monopolization of the opportunities to earn money. If they can get the power, status groups often restrict entry into the more lucrative professions or trades, giving the son of a bricklayer more chance of gaining a union card than the son of a farmer. And even without such formal restriction, birth into a high-status family gives a boy great advantages of education and of personal contacts that help his career. Weber indicates that in its pure form the class or economic order is impersonal; it knows no distinctions, and operates solely on the basis of competitive skill. But the status order is exactly the opposite; it is based on distinctions among men that make some "better" than others, and thus tends to restrict freedom of competition in both production and consumption. Thus, although in the long run the status order is created by the class order, for consumption is based on production, yet the status order in turn reacts upon and deeply influences the class order.

Finally, Weber wrote of the third order of stratification—parties, which are groups whose "action is oriented toward the acquisition of social 'power,' that is to say, toward influencing a communal action no matter what its content may be [5]." In short, Marx maintained that parties were always mere reflections of economic classes, whereas for Weber they might also represent status or other groupings in society.

Weber took Marx's notion of class and broke it into three components. He showed how they tended to coalesce, but not in any mechanical and automatic way. The status order and the party or power order were not merely appendages to the economic order; they had an existence of their own, grew and changed according to the totality of local circumstances, and in fact had great influence on the economic order itself. At any period of history the economic order was organized according to traditions and laws that defined the legitimate areas

for individual competition, and these rules were in part determined by
the status and power orders of the society, albeit they in turn had grown
up from an earlier stage of economic development. Weber's analysis,
partly logical, partly an inductive conclusion from the meticulous study
of history, demonstrated that the stratification system of a society was
a complex phenomenon of many dimensions [6].

## THE SIX VARIABLES

Empirical sociology in the United States is a product of the past
thirty years. In that time a great deal of knowledge has accumulated
about American society in general and the stratification order in particular [7]. Unfortunately, the facts are described from numerous points
of view and in terms of different conceptual frameworks. However,
when this mass of data is viewed from the perspective of the history of
stratification theory, it becomes more orderly. What the researchers
have done is to develop measuring tools that apply to the phenomena
described by Marx and Weber, but in smaller scale. Sociological research
finds it difficult to handle with precision anything as complicated as a
"class order" or a "status order." The empiricist knows that each of
those concepts is in turn composed of several variables, and to study the
real world around him, he needs devices that measure only one thing
at a time.

It is possible to combine the knowledge from these many empirical
researches (and that is the task of this book) if we use six variables
which are further refinements of the scheme of Max Weber. Each of
these variables can be defined "operationally," or in terms of the procedures used by a research man when he measures them. Let us briefly
define here the six basic variables, and then in subsequent chapters
examine each one in detail both as a concept and as a body of verified
information about the United States.

The first variable we deal with is the most obvious one; if we study
a local community we notice immediately that some people have higher
*personal prestige* than others. An individual has high prestige when his
neighbors, in general, have an attitude of respect toward him. Another
word that is often used for this attitude is deference, or the granting of
social honor. Prestige is a sentiment in the minds of men, although they
do not always know that it is there. The shrewd observer can often
notice deference behavior that is not recognized by the participants.
Consequently, it is necessary to study prestige in two ways: by asking
people about their attitudes of respect toward others, and by watching
their behavior.

Secondly, we can stratify a population according to *occupation*. An occupation is a social role which describes the major work that a person does, and most men work directly in the production, sale, and service of material goods. However, most women work at home as housewives, and some men are engaged in occupations that are not directly concerned with economic production, such as political and religious leaders.

People grant prestige not only to persons known to them in a local community, but also to abstract occupational titles. They believe that some occupations are "higher" than others, partly because they are more important to the welfare of the community, partly because it takes special talents to be in them, partly because they pay high rewards. And societies vary in the prestige they grant to different spheres of occupations, thus reflecting their values about what they consider important. Thus, we are a people primarily devoted to business, and with the exception of a few top statesmen, give highest prestige to successful business and professional men. But Sparta honored its soldiers, ancient China its wise men, and medieval Europe its bishops.

Occupational activities cannot be performed without tools and instruments. Furthermore, people who work get rewards in tangible form: in modern society, negotiable money. Consequently, we need another variable called *possessions* to cover capital and consumer goods. Perhaps the easiest way to study stratification in the United States is by money income, and we know that people with high incomes can afford an elegant style of life in consumption behavior, have contacts with people of note, are granted considerable prestige, and, through the workings of capital investment, can multiply their incomes.

People who share a given style of life tend to have more personal contact or *interaction* with one another than with those who live diffently. In a large society everyone cannot interact with everyone else; there must arise patterns of differential contact, and people feel most comfortable when they are with "their own kind." Scholars who emphasize this fact as the key to community stratification are sometimes called the "who-invites-whom-to-dinner" school.

Interaction is a variable which directs our attention to process, to everyday social behavior. It is only in recent years that scientific sociology has found ways of studying it directly instead of only speculating about it. Now we count its frequency, measure its duration, classify its quality, see who initiates and who follows.

The degree to which people, at a given stratification level according to one or more of the other variables, are explicitly aware of themselves as a distinctive social grouping is called their degree of *class consciousness*. In some circumstances similar people do not have much contact with one another, and think primarily in individualistic rather than in group terms. In other circumstances they become highly group-conscious, and then they are likely to organize political parties to advance their group interests. In general, Americans are less class-conscious than Europeans; our traditions of equality lead many of us to deny that classes exist. But the traditions concern more what "ought to be" than "what is," and the differential distribution of the other variables creates a class system whether we recognize it or not.

Finally, we must consider *value orientations*. Values are convictions shared by people in a given culture or subculture about the things they consider good, important, or beautiful. Values define the ends of life and the approved means of approaching them. They tend to become organized into systems, and when a group of people share a limited number of abstract values which organize and relate a large number of specific values, we call them value orientations.

It was stated above that values indicate which occupational activities are considered important and thus worthy of high prestige. But values operate in still another way: the people who perform the same activities or who occupy a given prestige level in a stratification system evolve a set of value orientations distinctive to themselves. Consequently, if we measure values, we measure stratification position. For example, businessmen glorify individual initiative and ambition, factory workers stress group cooperation and manual skill, and college professors idealize intellectual thought and independence from commercialism.

We shall not speak of power as a separate dimension, although many authors prefer to do so [8]. The reason is a pragmatic one: power is difficult to measure, and it is difficult to observe. Weber defines power (the end desired by parties) as the probability of being able to control the actions of other people. It is thus a potentiality that is important in social behavior, but because it is potential, it is usually impossible to see. Furthermore, where it exists, it tends to be deliberately hidden; those who sit among the mighty do not invite sociologists to watch them make their decisions about how to control the behavior of others. Consequently, we shall treat power as a latent factor in all behavior, and discuss it at several points in the chapters that follow, most particularly in the one on interaction, where we shall show that one practical approach to the study of power is the delineation of the cliques of important men in a community, and in the chapter on possessions, where we shall examine the potentialities of power among those who own and control the capital wealth of the nation.

THE VARIABLES AS A SYSTEM

The use of these six variables—prestige, occupation, possessions, inter-action, class consciousness, and value orientations—adds precision to our discussion of stratification phenomena. For instance, we can say that Marx was a man who was primarily interested in the effects of ownership of possessions. He claimed that common possessions led to common occupations, which led to common interactions, which created common values and a shared class consciousness. Stringing out his compressed statements into such a chain of implications makes it possible to study each one empirically. Weber, on the other hand, was more interested in the effects of values on the other variables. He showed that interaction in consumption activities produced common values which often overpowered economic interests, and in his historical studies of the effects of the Protestant ethic, he demonstrated the power of religious beliefs over a man's attitudes toward work.

The six variables form a conceptual scheme that describes the social realities of stratification. Each variable can be measured by distinct and separate operations. Each can be used to stratify a given population. And all are mutually dependent, for they influence one another. They have been chosen on pragmatic grounds; they constitute the set of variables that most efficiently organizes the existing empirical data on American class behavior, and they are congruent with the thinking of the major theorists [9].

The history of stratification theory is a history of shifting emphasis on one or another of these six factors. There have been theorists who insisted a priori that some one factor was basic and was the cause of all the others. But different variables have been chosen by different authors as the basic one. Scientific research cannot get very far if the answers to all questions are stated before the research begins. Consequently, in this work we consider all arguments about "first causes" to be misleading. The true function of theory is to clarify the variables involved, to show how to measure each one separately, and then to offer tentative hypotheses about their mutual relations. These hypotheses follow the form, "If you have this much of variable A, then you will have that much of variable B." Or perhaps a better form is, "If variable A changes this much, variable B will change that much," assuming that all the others remain constant (which, in fact, they never do).

When we conceive of our subject matter as made up of a number of mutually dependent variables, we give up the search for original causes and substitute the search for degrees of relationship. We look at a given system—a state of dynamic equilibrium—and say that it can be described in terms of given quantities of each variable. Then we watch it change, expecting that a change in any variable will produce changes in all the others. Sometimes the change occurs because one of the variables is linked to some factor outside the system itself and that factor undergoes change. Sometimes the internal dynamics of the system itself cause "immanent" change, and no outside link need be considered. Modern scientific theory is based on the model of systems of interdependent variables, not on simple cause and effect.

Once theory gives us good hypotheses, which are important questions that have straightforward empirical answers, then research can seek to find the truth. The main body of this book consists of an examination of each variable in turn, with a mustering of the available evidence which shows how it is related to the others in contemporary American society. Let us confess at the outset that we have better questions than answers. Systematic research on stratification in the United States is barely thirty years old, and only the beginnings of reliable knowledge are at hand. Much of that research was going on at the same time that theory was painfully defining the most important variables to be studied, and while techniques of gathering data were being developed and standardized. As a result, the research is disorganized, even chaotic. Different authors use different words for the same phenomenon. Polemic argument and verified fact are intermingled; heat and light appear on the same page. The best we can hope for is to put the available evidence into a first approximation of order, try to distinguish between fact and speculation, and try to keep always in mind the procedures by which speculation can be turned into fact. We can sum up what we think we know, show why we believe it to be true, and point to places where more work is needed.

## WHAT ARE SOCIAL CLASSES?

A *stratified* society is one marked by inequality, by differences among people that are evaluated by them as being "higher" or "lower." The simplest form of inequality is based on the division of labor which always appears according to age and sex. Young children are everywhere subordinate to their elders; old people may have a high or a low position, depending upon cultural values; women are often ranked below men.

But there is another form of inequality that always appears in every society (other, perhaps, than the very smallest and most primitive ones) which ranks families rather than individuals. A family shares many characteristics among its members that greatly affect their relationships with outsiders: the same house, the same income, the same values. If a large group of families are approximately equal to each other and clearly differentiated from other families, we call them a *social class.**

Logically, it is possible for a society to be stratified without having distinct classes, for there could be a continuous gradation from high to

* Here, obviously, we depart from the terminology of Weber in favor of ordinary English.

low without any sharp lines of division, but in reality this is most unlikely. The sources of a family's position are shared by many other
similar families: there are only a limited number of types of occupations
or of possible positions in the property system. One either works the
soil, or uses his hands to manufacture things, or trades, or performs some
function of intellectual, military, or political leadership that allows him
to live from the productive labor of others. There is a tendency for
the persons of each type to become similar to their fellows and distinct
from the members of other types. In other words, the various stratification variables tend to converge; they form a pattern, and it is this pattern that creates social classes. The pattern they form in fact is further
emphasized by the way people think about social matters, for popular
thought creates stereotypes out of abstractions. Thus bankers are conceived of as a homogeneous group, and distinctions between big bankers
and little ones are ignored. Similarly, poor people tend to lump together all bosses, and rich people overlook the many distinctions that
exist among those who labor for an hourly wage.

It would not be true to go so far as to say that every family has
an equal score on all six variables. At least in our society, the stratification
system is too vague and too fluid for that to occur with high regularity.
But in the long run social life is such that a family tends to equalize
its position on all of the variables. The forces toward convergence, toward the crystallization of the pattern, will be emphasized in this book
despite the fact that many disturbing influences, mostly results of rapid
social change, keep the patterns from becoming as clear-cut in reality
as in theory.

The classes that we talk about are *ideal-type* constructs. They are
intellectual inventions based on observation of reality that describe how
the classes would look if the system were freed of extraneous influences.
Ideal types are complex hypotheses about the interrelations among variables; they are guides to research and frameworks for synthesizing the
results of research. They seldom are phrased as specific propositions
that can be completely proved or disproved [10]. Consequently, it is not
surprising that different authors use different sets of class divisions.

Comparing one society to another, we see that stratification systems
differ in two ways: the distinctness of their strata, and the amount of
mobility that occurs between strata. These two characteristics are closely
related, but not identical. The type of stratification system that is most
rigid on both characteristics is called a caste system. In caste systems
each stratum is markedly different from the others; its members have
a special occupation which is hereditary, they are endogamous (marry
within the caste), and they have many special cultural characteristics,
often including religious rites, that are unique to themselves. In law

as well as fact caste membership determines life. A caste system is composed of a number of quite separate social communities that live side by side in economic interdependence. The pure form of caste system is approached only in India, but many other societies, including preliterate ones, have had castelike characteristics. Slaves are often a separate caste, but a caste system need not be an outgrowth of slavery.

At the other extreme of both characteristics is a modern, "open" class system. Here there are no legal recognitions of group inequality, and there are minimum differences between the total ways of life of the classes. Furthermore, there is much movement from one class to another, both in the lifetime of a man and from one generation to another. There are many societies with such open class systems, and they may vary in terms of the degree of differences between classes or in the amount of mobility that occurs among them, or both.

INEVITABILITY OF STRATIFICATION

Every complex society known to scholarship has been stratified. This fact has led many scholars to assert that it is a functional imperative for them to be stratified. A functional proposition of this particular type is one which states that a given social practice exists because it performs a necessary function for society, that group life could not exist without it. The function most often mentioned for stratification systems is the need to motivate men to do the different kinds of work that have to be done in society. A good statement of this case is made by Kingsley Davis [11]:

Any society must distribute its individuals in the positions of its social structure and induce them to perform the duties of these positions. It must therefore solve the problem of motivation at two levels: to instill in the proper individuals the desire to occupy certain positions and, once in these positions, the desire to perform the duties attached to them. [The duties of these positions are not all equally difficult or equally pleasant.] Inevitably, then, a society must have some kind of rewards that it can use as inducements and some way of distributing these rewards differently according to positions. . . . In a sense the rewards are "built into" the position. They consist in the "rights" associated with the position, plus what may be called its accompaniments or perquisites. . . . If the rights and perquisites of different positions in a society must be unequal, then the society must be stratified, because that is precisely what stratification means. Social inequality is thus an unconsciously evolved device by which societies insure that the most important positions are conscientiously filled by the most qualified persons. Hence every society, no matter how simple or complex, must differentiate persons in terms of both prestige and esteem and must therefore possess a certain amount of institutionalized inequality. . . . In general those positions convey the best reward and hence have the highest rank which (a) have the greatest importance for the society and (b) require the greatest training or talent. The first factor concerns the relative functional contribution of the position as compared to others; the second concerns the relative scarcity of personnel for filling the position.

Davis's statement makes sense, but is on a high level of abstraction—a level which may be useful for general theories of comparative social structure, but one which does not help us go into the field for research with the tools we now have. He does not tell us much about how "societies" go about "unconsciously evolving devices" to meet their needs. A more dynamic version of this type of functionalist approach is given by W. Lloyd Warner [12]:

. . . when a society is complex, when there are large numbers of individuals in it pursuing diverse and complex activities and functioning in a multiplicity of ways, individual positions and behaviors are evaluated and ranked. This happens primarily because, to maintain itself, the society must co-ordinate the efforts of all its members into common enterprises necessary for the preservation of the group, and it must solidify and integrate all these enterprises into a working whole. In other words, as the division of labor increases and the social units become more numerous and diverse, the need for co-ordination and integration also increases and, when satisfied, enables the larger group to survive and develop.

Those who occupy co-ordinating positions acquire power and prestige. They do so because their actions partly control the behavior of the individuals who look to them for direction. Within this simple control there is simple power. Those who exercise such power either acquire prestige directly from it or have gained prestige from other sources sufficiently to be raised to a co-ordinating position.

When Warner begins to specify the details of how different positions are coordinated, he starts making simple propositions about the relationships between prestige and power. These propositions can be phrased as testable hypotheses and checked against data. Once they are so phrased, the more abstract functional statement is no longer necessary. It is probably more useful to ask "What aspects of social process always produce institutionalized inequality?"—instead of "Which functional needs require a stratification system?" The first question will be answered in every chapter that follows.

Having defined the variables, we can now consider each one in turn. It will be necessary to keep making references to all six, even though we are attempting to discuss them one at a time; such is a functional necessity of exposition about complex systems. The method will be to concentrate in each chapter on a few authors who have emphasized the particular variable which is the subject of the chapter. We will highlight that part of their work which is of central relevance to the one variable under discussion, and minimize the rest. This method delays a balanced picture of stratification until Chapter VII, where the pieces, first analytically separated and discussed in detail, are put together into a portrait of the whole [13].

### REFERENCES

[1] Quoted in *The Age of Jackson* by Arthur Schlesinger, Jr. (Boston: Little, Brown, 1945), p. 10.

[2] Karl Marx and Friedrich Engels, *Manifesto of the Communist Party* (New York: International Publishers, 1932), p. 9.

[3] One of the best Marxist attempts to work out the details can be found in the work of a man later purged by Moscow: Nikolai Bukharin, *Historical Materialism* (New York: International Publishers, 1932). For a concise analysis that is more objective, see Reinhard Bendix and Seymour M. Lipset, "Karl Marx' Theory of Social Classes," in their *Class, Status and Power* (Glencoe, Ill.: The Free Press, 1953), which is a useful collection of diverse materials on stratification. For a more elaborate analysis of Marx, see G. D. H. Cole, *What Is Meant by Marxism* (London: Gollancz, 1948).

[4] Max Weber, "Class, Status, Party," in *From Max Weber: Essays in Sociology*, translated and edited by H. H. Gerth and C. Wright Mills (New York: Oxford University Press, 1946), pp. 186–93. Published in German in 1925.

[5] *Ibid.*, p. 194.

[6] For a theoretical system which is, in part, built on Weber, see Talcott Parsons, *The Structure of Social Action* (Glencoe, Ill.: The Free Press, 1949; first published, 1937). Applied to stratification, see Talcott Parsons, "An Analytical Approach to the Theory of Social Stratification," *American Journal of Sociology*, XLV (May, 1940), 841–62, which is reprinted in his *Essays in Sociological Theory* (Glencoe, Ill.: The Free Press, 1949). This essay, which has had a very wide influence, has been expanded and put into the framework of Parsons' more recent general theory: "A Revised Analytical Approach to the Theory of Social Stratification," in Bendix and Lipset, *Class, Status and Power*. The reader who is not a sophisticate in the thought of Parsons will do better with the earlier version.

[7] Recent American work in stratification has mainly consisted of empirical research; our intellectual forefathers, however, were more interested in theoretical discussion. See Charles H. Page, *Class and American Sociology* (New York: Dial, 1940), a discussion of such early sociologists as Ward, Small, and Sumner. Of course, our early political leaders were much concerned with class, as evidenced by such disputations as *The Federalist Papers;* it is interesting to note that only in more recent

years has it been considered un-American and divisive to introduce class into political debate. There is one book that combines European theoretical scope with American attention to empirical detail, although it is now out of date: Pitirim Sorokin, *Social Mobility* (New York: Harper, 1927).

[8] A good discussion of power as a concept is Robert Bierstedt, "An Analysis of Social Power," *American Sociological Review*, XV (December, 1950), 730–38.

[9] These six variables do not form a closed system, all on the same level of abstraction, in the strict sense of scientific theory. They have been chosen after much experimentation as the best available set of categories for synthesizing the existing research data. Thus they are an inductive system—a first approximation to a conceptual scheme—which is useful to think about in the manner of closed systems.

I have been much influenced in evolving this set of categories by George C. Homans, *The Human Group* (New York: Harcourt, Brace, 1950). His discussion of scientific systems (based on the thinking of such men as Vilfredo Pareto and L. J. Henderson) is forceful, and his own empirical categories parallel four of mine (activity, which here becomes occupation; sentiment, which here becomes personal prestige; interaction; and norms or values). The natural emergence of ranking in groups is a prototype of social stratification, and small-group behavior is elegantly described by Homans.

Regarding terminology, the most common word for what I will call "prestige" is "status," but this word has so many other meanings in contemporary sociology (such as Linton's status-role) that it seems better to use a less ambiguous term. "Class" is often used in Weber's sense as the economic component in stratification, but this usage is especially confusing to the layman, who knows very well that a social class is a group of people who are similar to each other in all of the stratification dimensions. Furthermore, the Marx-Weber usage does not differentiate adequately between occupation and possessions. The other terms in my scheme follow conventional usage in social science.

Two recent authors have used conceptual schemes not very different from mine, the first in a theoretical statement, the second in a useful short description of American stratification: Milton Gordon, "A System of Social Class Analysis," *Drew University Studies*, Number 2 (August, 1951); and Kurt B. Mayer, *Class and Society* (Garden City, N.Y.: Doubleday Short Studies in Sociology, 1955).

[10] For a classic use of an ideal-type construct, see Robert Redfield, "The Folk Society," *American Journal of Sociology*, LII (January, 1947), 293–308.

[11] Kingsley Davis, *Human Society* (New York: Macmillan, 1949), pp. 366–68. Davis's position, as given in an earlier article with Wilbert E. Moore, has recently been attacked by Melvin M. Tumin, "Some Principles of Stratification: A Critical Analysis," *American Sociological*

*Review*, XVIII (August, 1953), 387–94; Davis, "Reply," *ASR*, XVIII (August, 1953), 394–97; Tumin, "Reply to Kingsley Davis," *ASR*, XVIII (December, 1953), 672–73; Tumin, "Rewards and Task Orientations," *ASR*, XX (August, 1955), 419–23.

[12] W. Lloyd Warner *et al.*, *Social Class in America* (Chicago: Science Research Associates, 1949), p. 8.

[13] For general bibliographies the reader may consult: D. G. MacRae, "Social Stratification: A Trend Report and Bibliography," *Current Sociology*, II (1953–1954) No. 1; Harold W. Pfautz, "The Current Literature on Social Stratification: Critique and Bibliography," *American Journal of Sociology*, LVIII (January, 1953), 391–418. Since these bibliographies are excellent and readily available, my own references will be highly selective, designed either to document my statements or to indicate the most pointed additional reading for the interested student.

There are two additional bibliographies that are available only in scarce mimeographed copies: Social Science Research Council, Inter-University Seminar, 1951, *Bibliography on Status and Stratification*. Erik Rinde and Stein Rokkan, eds., *First International Working Conference on Social Stratification and Social Mobility: Preliminary Papers and Proposals* (Oslo: International Sociological Association, 1951). The latter papers led to an international meeting with additional discussions of the state of research in many countries; see *Transactions of the Second World Congress of Sociology*, Vol. II (London: International Sociological Association, 1954).

# II

# Position and Prestige

FAME DID NOT BRING THE SOCIAL ADVANCEMENT WHICH THE
BABBITTS DESERVED. THEY WERE NOT ASKED TO JOIN THE TONA-
WANDA COUNTRY CLUB NOR INVITED TO THE DANCES AT THE
UNION. HIMSELF, BABBITT FRETTED, HE "DIDN'T CARE A FAT HOOT
FOR ALL THESE HIGHROLLERS, BUT THE WIFE WOULD KIND OF
LIKE TO BE AMONG THOSE PRESENT." HE NERVOUSLY AWAITED
HIS UNIVERSITY CLASS-DINNER AND AN EVENING OF FURIOUS IN-
TIMACY WITH SUCH SOCIAL LEADERS AS CHARLES MCKELVEY
THE MILLIONAIRE CONTRACTOR, MAX KRUGER THE BANKER,
IRVING TATE THE TOOL-MANUFACTURER, AND ADELBERT DOBSON
THE FASHIONABLE INTERIOR DECORATOR. THEORETICALLY HE WAS
THEIR FRIEND, AS HE HAD BEEN IN COLLEGE, AND WHEN HE EN-
COUNTERED THEM THEY STILL CALLED HIM "GEORGIE," BUT HE
DIDN'T SEEM TO ENCOUNTER THEM OFTEN. . . .

*Sinclair Lewis* [1]

IN THE SMALL GROUP, in the local community, in the society as a whole,
we notice that some people are looked up to, respected, considered
people of consequence, and others are thought of as ordinary, unimportant, even lowly. Everywhere we see nabobs and nobodies.

Prestige is a sentiment in the minds of men that is expressed in interpersonal interaction: deference behavior is demanded by one party and
granted by another. Obviously, it can occur only when there are values
shared by both parties that define the criteria of superiority; deference
at pistol point is not the result of prestige. But this does not necessarily
mean that both parties agree about all aspects of the situation. For instance, the subordinate person may feel that the superordinate person
*should* not have the right to deference and may try to foment a revolution to take it away from him; but so long as the subordinate recognizes that the superordinate *does* have the right to claim deference and
feels constrained by group norms to grant it, then a prestige difference
exists. The degree of consensus can range from a situation in which
deference is given joyously as a recognition of moral worthiness that
reflects the will of God, to one in which deference is given grudgingly,
against part of one's own will which cries out against these claims to

special privilege. However, in stable situations both parties usually come to approve as well as accept the prestige inequality, for it symbolizes important cultural values.

The facts of inequality that are recognized in deference behavior usually include inequality in possessions and authority. Values are reinforced by sanctions, and the person of low prestige grants deference partly because he knows that in the long run it is to his advantage to do so. Through symbolic submission to his superiors he gains favor in the eyes of those who are in a position to grant rewards—goods and services, promotion, protection, salvation, or perhaps just good will and a reassuring smile. The distinction between deference at pistol point and from prestige is the distinction between usurpation of power by naked force and authority gained through control of morally legitimated institutions. In neither case is the will completely free.

The most direct way to study prestige is to go into a local community where everyone knows everyone else and observe how they treat each other. Part of that observation would include questions such as "What do you think of Jones as compared to Smith?" If there were complete consensus among all the citizens, the observer could in a short time draw up a list of the inhabitants and rank them from top to bottom. If the community had more than half a dozen members, then it is likely that several persons would share equal ranks, and that there would be more people clustered in the lower than in the higher ranks. It is also likely, again assuming complete consensus, that this rank order would hold good in all situations: that whether one depended on direct verbal testimony of the inhabitants, or watched them at work, at play, or at worship, the rank order would be the same [2].

Such a conceptual model assumes complete consensus among persons acting in a fully integrated social structure, and it is never exactly matched by reality. In the first place, prestige grows out of specific evaluated activities, and each person engages in many different activities. A man who gains high prestige as a banker may get low prestige as a golfer. In the second place, people may not agree on the relative worth of the different activities; granted that a man is a good banker and a bad golfer, which is more important? And in the third place, there are likely to be disagreements as to the relative merits of persons within the same activity: it is not always easy to get four bankers to agree on the town's best financial expert.

The first two problems involve the different social roles that we play; the last involves the question of performance within a role. In their more precise moods sociologists say that the behavior of a man in a given role leads to *esteem* in the eyes of others, but the importance of the role itself is the source of his *prestige*. Thus a good ditch digger gets high esteem and low prestige, whereas a bad banker gets high prestige and low esteem. However, in ranking their friends, informants usually combine esteem and prestige into a single judgment of over-all merit. When many people occupy roles of approximately equal prestige, we call them a *stratum*, such as the combination of bankers, accountants, and sales managers into the stratum of business executives [3].

In spite of the diversity of roles people play, and the differences in evaluation thereof made by different observers in the community, there is usually a trend toward consistency, for an individual carries with him some of his habits and reputation as he moves from one role to another. Insofar as his roles are public and watched by the community at large, they tend to blend into an over-all prestige reputation. For example, a man who is a successful banker gains the general respect of the community, but to keep it he should be a good family man, maintain the appearance of his house, and not curse too loudly when he muffs a shot on the golf course. Since his skill as a cook is not considered important, it neither adds to nor detracts from his general prestige reputation, though this would not be true for his wife.

The prestige hierarchy of a local community represents the synthesis of all the other stratification variables. It is the result of the evaluation by the people of the totality of the class structure. But people can only evaluate others who are known to them personally; thus a prestige hierarchy is limited to a local community, though it may be based on facts and values that are national in scope. An understanding of such a local prestige structure is an excellent beginning for a study of the dynamics of stratification, for if we can picture in detail the hierarchy of prestige, we can then look behind it for the factors that created it, both in terms of local circumstances and national conditions.

In a new field of science where methods are not standardized, it is necessary to ask two questions of each research man whose work is of relevance: what are his results, and how did he obtain them? The answer to the second question determines the validity of the reply to the first one.

## W. LLOYD WARNER

The most extensive studies of prestige of individuals and families in the United States have been the work of Professor W. Lloyd Warner and his students and colleagues. Their research began in the early 1930's through the collaboration of Warner and Professor Elton Mayo of the Harvard Graduate School of Business Administration. Warner had completed a three-year study of Australian aborigines and wanted to employ the techniques of social anthropology—the study of the "whole man" in the complete context of his sociocultural life—to a modern American community. Mayo, a clinical psychologist, had for several years been directing pioneering research into the human factors in industrial production. His work at the Western Electric factory in Chicago had demonstrated the importance of the "non-logical social code which regulates the relations between persons and their attitudes to one another" in determining the psychological state of the worker in industry [4]. Having observed the development of social codes within the factory walls, Mayo wanted to enlarge his view to study the influence of community life.

The two men joined forces. Although they realized that in many ways the metropolis was the typical social environment of modern industry, they felt that the study of the great city "as a whole" from the viewpoint of social anthropology was too vast an undertaking for their techniques and resources. Furthermore, they believed that the city was in many ways disorganized and did not represent a community life that was functionally integrated. "If we were to compare easily the other societies of the world with one of our own civilization, and if we were readily to accommodate our techniques, developed by the study of primitive society, to modern groups, it seemed wise to choose a community with a social organization which had developed over a long period of time under the domination of a single group with a coherent tradition. In the United States only two large sections, New England and the deep South, we believed, were likely to possess such a community [5]." Their first study was of the New England town of 17,000 persons called "Yankee City," and their second of the Southern town of 10,000 called "Old City" and described in the book *Deep South* [6]. Since then the Warner group have studied "Jonesville," a town of about 6,000 in the Middle West, as well as the Negro district of Chicago [7]. After the initial stages of the research the influence of Mayo declined, and the main responsibility for the work rests with Warner.

The decision to concentrate on small and homogeneous communities with a "coherent tradition" may have been practical for research purposes when using the techniques of social anthropology, but it was dangerous from a theoretical standpoint. These communities are not typical of all of America, in spite of the fact that a substantial part of our population lives in places of less than 25,000 inhabitants. In many ways the dominant forces in our society are found in the big cities and their suburbs, where many people with a diversity of cultural backgrounds live side by side. Some critics have said that instead of taking the techniques of anthropology as fundamental and searching for a community simple enough to use them, Warner should have started with the fact of urban heterogeneity and sought procedures that would help him to master its complexity [8].

But there is little point in wishing Warner had done otherwise than he did. If we recognize its proper sphere, we can accept his work as a great contribution to our understanding of prestige stratification in small communities and the methods that can be used to study it. And we can take his findings concerning stratification processes and use them as hypotheses to guide our research in the metropolis. Finally, we can remember that many of those who are now engaged in the study of stratification with methods somewhat more rigorous than Warner's (and it is now one of the most popular fields in sociology, as shown by the numerous articles in the current journals) might well be ploughing other fields if he had not excited their curiosity and stimulated their thought. Before his work, this subject was relatively neglected in American research.

## YANKEE CITY

After Warner found a community that was small and relatively homogeneous (but had some ethnic groups), that was not a suburb or satellite of a metropolis—and incidentally, was not too far for convenient commuting from Harvard—he wanted to make the acquaintance of some citizens who could help him: ". . . we were ready to begin an intensive interviewing program. To do this, it seemed highly advisable to secure the consent and co-operation of the more important men in the community lest we later find it impossible to obtain certain vital information. We finally selected one prominent and, it later developed, much-trusted individual who, we knew, was important in the town . . . he agreed to help us in any way he could. We then asked him to introduce us to some of his friends who were leaders in the city's activities. This he did, and from his friends we received other introductions which shortly spread our sources of information from the top to the bottom of the city" [9]. This procedure shows something of Warner's past training as an anthropologist. He has told in lectures a similar story of his introduction to certain Australian tribal villages, where he would squat on the edge of the settlement while one or two men would come out and talk with his interpreter; once they had established the proper kinship connections, the procedure was broadened to include Warner on an adopted basis. Only after such placement in social space was it safe for him to enter the settlement. In Yankee City, instead of being the adopted third cousin twice removed of the chief, he was a representative of the Harvard Graduate School of Business Administration. And note that he assumed the existence of a prestige hierarchy before he went in, for he began by seeking the acquaintance of "important men."

The town he selected had 17,000 inhabitants and once was a famous seaport. It had had a long history in New England commerce, having been a center of trade, of fishing, and more recently of manufacturing, especially shoes and silverware. It had families who had been there for three hundred years. Half its citizens were born in Yankee City, but a quarter came from other parts of New England and the United States, and a quarter from French Canada, Ireland, Italy, and eastern Europe. In many ways its glory was in the past, when many such towns shared equal fame as thriving ports. In recent years it had become merely a small city not too far from Boston, and many of its young people left for the more exciting life to be found in Boston and New York. One such man was Charles Gray, hero of John P. Marquand's novel, *Point of No Return*, for Clyde and Yankee City are the same place (and Malcolm Bryant and W. Lloyd Warner are the same man, though many people find it difficult to explain the portrait by the sitter).

When Warner began the research, he made explicit to his staff the hypothesis that [10]

. . . the fundamental structure of our society, that which ultimately controls and dominates the thinking and actions of our people, is economic, and that the most vital and far-reaching value systems which motivate Americans are to be ultimately traced to an economic order. Our first interviews tended to sustain this hypothesis. They were filled with references to "the big people with money" and to "the little people who are poor." They assigned people high status by referring to them as bankers, large property owners, people of high salary, and professional men, or they placed people in a low status by calling them laborers, ditchdiggers, and low-wage earners. Other similar economic terms were used, all designating superior and inferior positions.

However, after the research team had been in Yankee City for a while, they began to doubt their original assumptions of economic determinism, for they found that some people were placed higher or lower in the prestige scale than their incomes would warrant. Furthermore [11]:

Other evidences began to accumulate which made it difficult to accept a simple economic hypothesis. Several men were doctors; and while some of them enjoyed the highest social status in the community and were so evaluated in the interviews, others were ranked beneath them although some of the latter were often admitted to be better physicians. Such ranking was frequently unconsciously done and for this reason was often more reliable than a conscious estimate of a man's status. . . .

We finally developed a class hypothesis which withstood the later test of a vast collection of data and of subsequent rigorous analysis. By class is meant two or more orders of people who are believed to be, and are accordingly ranked by the members of the community, in socially superior and inferior positions. Members of a class tend to marry within their own order, but the values of the society permit marriage up and down. A class system also provides that children are born into the same status as their parents. A class society distributes rights and privileges, duties and obligations, unequally among its inferior and superior grades. A system of classes, unlike a system of castes, provides by its own values for movement up and down the social ladder. In common parlance, this is social climbing, or in technical terms, social mobility. The social system of Yankee City, we found, was dominated by a class order.

In these interviews certain facts became clear which might be summarized by saying a person needed specific characteristics associated with his "station in life" and he needed to go with the "right kind" of people for the informants to be certain of his ranking. If a man's education, occupation, wealth, income, family, intimate friends, clubs and fraternities, as well as his manners, speech, and general outward behavior were known, it was not difficult for his fellow citizens to give a fairly exact estimate of his status. . . .

We noticed that certain geographical terms were used not only to locate people in the city's geographical space but also to evaluate their comparative place in the rank order. The first generalization of this kind which we noticed people using in interviews was the identification of a small percentage of the population as "Hill Streeters" or people who "live up on Hill Street," these expressions often being used as equivalent of "Brahmin," the rarer "aristocrat," or the less elegant "high mucky-muck," or "swell," or "snoot."

Warner found from his interviews and observations, in other words, that personal prestige rank was a result of a combination of several variables that included possessions, interaction patterns, occupational activities, and value orientations (with their outward manifestations of manners and style of general behavior). One of the most important of the interaction patterns was determined by kinship: not only did children get assigned the status of their parents, but certain families had a status position that was not entirely explainable by their current possessions or value orientations, and seemed to flow from their ancestry.

When an individual had an equivalent rank on all the variables, his townsmen had no difficulty in deciding how much prestige to give him. But when he had somewhat different scores on the several variables, there was difficulty in knowing exactly how to place him. This usually meant that the person was mobile and was changing his position on one variable at a time; eventually he would be likely to get them all into line. Consequently, time was an important factor in stratification placement. For example, if a man who started as the son of a laborer became successful in business, he would be likely to move to a "better" neighborhood, join clubs of other business and professional men, and send his children to college. But if he himself did not have a college education and polished manners, he would never be fully accepted as a social equal by the businessmen who had Harvard degrees. His son, however, might well gain the full acceptance denied the father. In Warner's words: "Money must be translated into socially approved behavior and possessions, and they in turn must be translated into intimate participation with, and acceptance by, members of a superior class [12]."

After several years of study by more than a dozen researchers, during which time 99 per cent of the families in town were classified, Warner declared that there were six groupings sharp enough to be called classes [13]:

1. Upper-upper, 1.4 per cent of the total population. This group was the old-family elite, based on sufficient wealth to maintain a large house in the best neighborhood, but the wealth had to have been in the family for more than one generation. This generational continuity permitted proper training in basic value orientations, and established people as belonging to a lineage.

2. Lower-upper, 1.6 per cent. This group was, on the average, slightly richer than the upper-uppers, but their money was newer, their manners thus not quite so polished, their sense of lineage and security less pronounced.

3. Upper-middle, 10.2 per cent. The moderately successful business and professional men and their families, but less affluent than the lower-uppers. Some education and polish were necessary for membership, but lineage was unimportant.

4. Lower-middle, 28.1 per cent. The petty businessmen, the school-teachers, the foremen in industry. This group tended to have morals that were close to puritan fundamentalism; they were churchgoers, lodge joiners, and flag wavers.

5. Upper-lower, 32.6 per cent. The solid, respectable laboring people, who kept their houses clean and stayed out of trouble.

6. Lower-lower, 25.2 per cent. The "lulus" or disrespectable and often slovenly people who dug for clams and waited for public relief.

This proportionate distribution among the classes represents not only a long New England history, but also the special conditions of the great depression.

Once the general system became clear to him, Warner says he used a man's clique and association memberships as a shorthand index of prestige position. Thus there were certain small social clubs that were open only to upper-uppers, while the Rotary was primarily upper-middle in membership, the fraternal lodges lower-middle, the craft unions upper-lower. In cases of doubt it seems that intimate clique interactions were the crucial test: a repeated invitation home to dinner appears to be for Warner the best sign of prestige equality between persons.

## PRESTIGE CLASS AS A CONCEPT

Warner maintains that the breaks between all these prestige classes were quite clear-cut, except for that between the lower-middle and the upper-lower. At that level there was a blurring of distinctions that made placement of borderline families quite difficult. Of course, the placement of mobile families at all levels was difficult.

When he says that the distinctions between the classes were clear-cut, he means in the minds of the people of Yankee City. He sees his job of scientific observer as mainly one of staying around long enough to find out what the people "really" think. But here he runs into difficulties. Since there are certain value traditions which maintain that social inequality is un-American, some people deny that it exists while at the same time behaving as though it does. "In the bright glow and warm presence of the American Dream all men are born free and equal. Everyone in the American Dream has the right, and often the duty, to try to succeed and to do his best to reach the top. Its two fundamental themes and propositions, that all of us are equal and that each of us has the right to the chance of reaching the top, are mutually contradictory, for if all men are equal there can be no top level to aim for, no bottom one to get away from . . . [14]." It is because he recognizes this value conflict that Warner said in the passage quoted above that "ranking was frequently unconsciously done and . . . was often more reliable than a conscious estimate of a man's status. . . ."

The conceptual dilemma that Warner faced, and that has plagued his readers, is shown by the contrast between these two statements of his:

These social levels [classes] are not categories invented by social scientists to help explain what they have to say; they are groups recognized by the people of the community as being higher or lower in the life of the city. The social scientist, when he hears that certain groups are superior or inferior, records what he hears and observes and tries to understand what it means. The designations of social levels are distinctions made by the people themselves in referring to each other [15].

Naturally there were many borderline cases. . . . In order to make a complete study, it was necessary to locate all of them in one of the six classes, and this we did to the best of our ability on the basis of the entire range of phenomena covered by our data. . . . It must not be thought that all the people in Yankee City are aware of all the minute distinctions made in this book. The terms used to refer to such definitions as are made vary according to the class of the individual and his period of residence [16].

In one breath Warner says that the class distinctions he makes are simply descriptions of the distinctions that exist in the minds of his subjects, but in the next they become decisions made by him "on the basis of the entire range of phenomena covered by our data," and the subjects may not be fully aware of them. Are they descriptive summaries, or abstract scientific constructs? Do they exist in the minds of the people, or in the mind of Warner?

The answer can only be both. The analyst has to create scientifically neat concepts or variables that approximate, as closely as possible, aspects of the real behavior of his subjects when they evaluate each other. Then he has to formulate standard rules that show him how to add up scores on each separate variable to arrive at the totality which will best predict the over-all prestige judgment concerning a man that is made by his fellows in the community. If he wants to be systematic and approach the goal of variables that make good statistics, the scientist is going to perform mental operations that are not identical to the automatic, half-conscious, and often contradictory thinking of his subjects. His aim is to predict, with reasonable accuracy, what most subjects will do in most circumstances. Furthermore, he must use variables that have theoretical meaning to him in other contexts, for only thus can he learn to explain as well as predict.

Every variable in the mind of the analyst approximates a variable in the minds of his subjects. But each subject will not perceive that variable in exactly the same way as the other subjects; one man may think that the possession of a Buick is a clear mark of top wealth, while another may settle for nothing less than a Cadillac. Furthermore, the different subjects will not all add up the variables in the same way to arrive at the identical total prestige judgment: some will emphasize wealth, others income, and still others family background. Consequently, one cannot claim that the analyst's mental operations are exact reflections of the ratiocinations of his subjects—if the community does not reach complete consensus, how can the analyst always know what to do?

In fact, concepts *always* are "categories invented by social scientists to help explain what they have to say," but they are not invented out of pure imagination. They are based on careful observation, plus scientific reasons for abstracting from those observations a few simple factors that are worth studying in detail. In his more cautious moods, Warner admits the degree of scientific abstraction that lies behind his six classes [17]: "Structural and status analysts construct scientific representations (or 'maps') which represent their knowledge of the structure and status interrelations which compose the community's social system." And a bit farther on, he offers these comments about the degree to which classes are categories that exist in the conscious minds of his subjects [18]:

[Some] informants . . . are explicitly class-conscious, and their presence in a society clearly demonstrates the existence of a class system; but class consciousness, as a critical concept for determining the presence or absence of social class, is largely unsatisfactory. More often than not, its use causes confusion and error. The term has more than one reference; the latter half of it, consciousness, may mean that an individual is explicitly conscious of class, that his behavior indicates the consciousness of class differences, and, consequently, that he makes such distinctions in his daily life in categorizing people. On the other hand, it may mean that the individual is not explicitly conscious of class differences but is implicitly aware of them and acts accordingly. Such a person sometimes actually denies the existence of class. Is such a person "conscious of class" or not, and, if he isn't, must we thereby deny the existence of class in his society even if others like him should agree verbally with him? Obviously, it would be nonsense and poor science to do so.

We can conclude that Warner's classes are ideal-type constructs which help him organize a vast amount of data on attitudes and behavior; they are not mere descriptions of the mental categories used by the inhabitants of Yankee City and Jonesville. As such they stand as hypotheses, and other observers have a right to test them against the data. The only sense in which these classes can be called "real" is to claim that they organize the data more usefully than any alternative set of hypotheses.

ARE THERE SIX CLASSES?

How can Warner's scheme be tested? How can we find out whether his six classes make a better fit to reality than five, or seven, or six that are cut differently from his? Much of the rest of this book will deal with this question, for the full answer involves behavior in terms of value orientations, interactions, class consciousness, and so on. Here we can give only a quick preview, emphasizing direct perception of prestige by local informants who rank people they know and live with.

In *Deep South* there appears an interesting chart showing the "social perspectives of the social classes," or the way the people at each level perceive the people at other levels; it is reproduced below as Figure 1. The chart suggests that the people at each level do not recognize six classes in Old City, but either four or five, though the scientists say that six classes exist in the white population. As a matter of fact, the people make finer distinctions between persons close to themselves than between those who are far away. However, all the distinctions coincide in spite of the fact that they may have different names. Thus the lower-lowers make a distinction between "society" and the "way-high-ups but not society." They do not subdivide society. According to Davis and the Gardners, the line between society and the way-high-ups but not society is precisely the same as the line drawn by upper-uppers between "nice, respectable people" and "good people but nobody" (upper-middle and lower-middle). That is, when names of specific families are mentioned, both lower-lowers and upper-uppers place them in the same one of these two groups. However, the upper-uppers make further sub-divisions not recognized by the lower-lowers into "old aristocracy," "new aristocracy," and "nice, respectable people."

Davis and the Gardners write in *Deep South* that [19]:

> While members of all class groups recognize classes above and below them, or both, the greater the social distance from the other classes the less clearly are fine distinctions made. Although an individual recognizes most clearly the existence of groups immediately above and below his own, he is usually not aware of the social distance actually maintained between his own and these adjacent groups. Thus, in all cases except that of members of the upper-lower class the individual sees only a minimum of social distance between his class and the adjacent classes. This is illustrated by the dotted lines in Figure [1]. Almost all other class divisions, however, are visualized as definite lines of cleavage in the society with a large amount of social distance between them.
>
> In general, too, individuals visualize class groups above them less clearly than those below them; they tend to minimize the social differentiations between themselves and those above. . . . In view of this situation it is not surprising that individuals in the two upper strata make the finest gradations in the stratification of the whole society and that class distinctions are made with decreasing precision as social position becomes lower.
>
> Not only does the perspective on social stratification vary for different class levels, but the bases of class distinction in the society are variously interpreted by the different groups. People tend to agree as to where people are but not upon why they are there. Upper-class individuals, especially upper-uppers, think of class divisions largely in terms of time—one has a particular social position because his family has "always had" that position. Members of the middle class interpret their position in terms of wealth and time and tend to make moral evaluations of what "should be. . . ." Lower-class people, on the other hand, view the whole stratification of the society as a hierarchy of wealth. . . .
>
> The identity of a social class does not depend on uniformity in any one or two, or a dozen, specific kinds of behavior but on a complex pattern or network of interrelated characteristics and attitudes. Among the members of

| UPPER-UPPER CLASS | | LOWER-UPPER CLASS |
|---|---|---|
| "Old aristocracy" | UU | "Old aristocracy" |
| "Aristocracy," but not "old" | LU | "Aristocracy," but not "old" |
| "Nice, respectable people" | UM | "Nice, respectable people" |
| "Good people, but 'nobody' " | LM | "Good people, but 'nobody' " |
| | UL | — |
| — "Po' whites" — | LL | "Po' whites" |

| UPPER-MIDDLE CLASS | | LOWER-MIDDLE CLASS |
|---|---|---|
| "Society" { "Old families" | UU | — |
| "Society" but not "old families" | LU | "Old aristocracy" (older) : "Broken-down aristocracy" (younger) |
| "People who should be upper class" | UM | "People who think they are somebody" |
| "People who don't have much money" | LM | "We poor folk" |
| | UL | "People poorer than us" |
| — "No 'count lot" — | LL | "No 'count lot" |

| UPPER-LOWER CLASS | | LOWER-LOWER CLASS |
|---|---|---|
| — | UU | — |
| — | LU | — |
| "Society" or the "folks with money" | UM | "Society" or the "folks with money" |
| "People who are up because they have a little money" | LM | "Way-high-ups," but not "Society" |
| "Poor but honest folk" | UL | "Snobs trying to push up" |
| "Shiftless people" | LL | "People just as good as anybody" |

*Figure 1.  The Social Perspectives of the Social Classes* [20]

any one class, there is no strict uniformity in any specific type of behavior but rather a range and a "modal average." One finds a range in income, occupation, educational level, and types of social participation. The "ideal type" may be defined, however, for any given class—the class configuration—from which any given individual may vary in one or more particulars.

How does the investigator discover these "modal averages" of behavior; how does he find the classes? He first observes differing patterns of general behavior or style of life—the high-society crowd who hang around the country club versus the little shopkeepers who belong to the Elks. Then he pays particular attention to the names of specific families who belong to each group. If different informants use labels with varying shades of moral evaluation to describe the different groups, the analyst can equate the labels by interpretation: the high-society crowd of one informant and the old aristocracy of another turn out to be identical, because *both* the behavior described and the individuals who are said to belong are the same.

The fact that all people do not recognize six levels is not so important, so long as the breaks that they do make all fit together in a consistent way. Naturally, people make the finest distinctions regarding those whom they know best, and tend to merge others into broader categories. The analyst can take this into consideration, and if he wishes can subdivide a group according to the views of those in and immediately adjacent to it. The problem is like that of accommodating for perspective when making a map from aerial photographs. (These differences in perspective are not mere disturbances to be ironed out by appropriate techniques—they are social facts well worth studying in themselves. If we knew more about them, we would know more about the dynamics of social perception which underlie all prestige judgments.)

It is crucial to demonstrate that the distinctions between ranks are all made at the same level or height. This in turn becomes two questions: Do all observers put Mr. Smith above Mr. Jones in the hierarchy, and if they distinguish between their ranks at all, do they all divide Mr. Smith's group from that of Mr. Jones at the same place? These are the questions of *ranking consistency* and of *cutting consistency*. To answer them we must look in detail at Warner's techniques for status placement.

### EVALUATED PARTICIPATION

In the four volumes so far published about Yankee City, no more detailed information has been given about the procedures for prestige placement than was quoted above [21]. The entire system has been presented as a *fait accompli*, an empirical induction from a multitude of data. No reader without additional training from an initiate could possibly have gone to Yankee City or any other town, repeated the operations in the same way, and seen if the results were the same.

In 1949 Warner published *Social Class in America: A Manual of Procedure for the Measurement of Social Status*, which is supposed to be a rule book with sufficient detail to allow any reader to study a town by the Warner method. It tells of two procedures: Evaluated Participation (EP), a technique for the qualitative analysis of interview material, and Index of Status Characteristics (ISC), a shorthand, quantitative index designed to predict the results of EP with a minimum of effort. It is never made clear whether exactly these procedures were the ones used in Yankee City. Apparently they were in an early and tentative form, but were standardized during the Jonesville study, which came several years later.

Warner writes of Evaluated Participation that it is a method comprising several rating techniques which is [22]

. . . posed on the proposition that those who interact in the social system of a community evaluate the participation of those around them, that the place where an individual participates is evaluated, and that the members of the community are explicitly or implicitly aware of the ranking and translate their evaluations of such social participation into social-class ratings that can be communicated to the investigator. It is, therefore, the duty of the field man to use his interviewing skill to elicit the necessary information and to analyze his data with the requisite techniques for determining social class, thereby enabling the status analyst to determine the levels of stratification present and to rank any member of the community.

There are six components to the EP:

1. *Rating by Matched Agreements.* Free or nondirective interviews are obtained from several informants at supposedly different prestige levels [23]. These are then compared. It is hoped that the informants will talk about the class system in terms of a number of strata each of which will have a label with local meaning. The analyst examines these "social-class configurations" to see how similar they are. To find out whether the informants mean the same thing by the same label (or similar ones which appear to be equated), the analyst must get the names of particular persons at each level. "When the correspondence between the ranking of classes by different informants is complete or very high, and when the count of matched agreements of informants on the class positions of a large number of people is also high, the analyst is assured

that the class system he is studying has a given number of classes, is strong, and pervades the whole community . . . [24]."

2. *Rating by Symbolic Placement.* An individual is placed in a class because an informant specifically puts him there in verbal terms; e.g., "Smith is in the aristocracy." Insofar as the symbols have to be translated, this procedure is only an extension of the first.

3. *Rating by Status Reputation.* "An individual (or his family) is assigned to a given class by the analyst because (informants say) he has a reputation for engaging in activities and possessing certain traits that are considered to be superior or inferior [25]."

4. *Rating by Comparison.* "The subject (or his family) is rated by the analyst as being in a particular class because informants assert he is equal, superior, or inferior to others whose social-class position has been previously determined [26]."

5. *Rating by Simple Assignment to a Class.* "The subject (or his family) is rated by the analyst as being in a particular class because one or more qualified informants assigned the individual to that particular class category; only one class is mentioned, and there is no explicit reference to the other classes which compose the whole system [27]." It is difficult to detect any difference between this procedure and Symbolic Placement, unless here the informant says "Smith is an upper-upper" instead of merely "in the aristocracy" or "a blue-blood." But this could be done only by an informant who has read Warner's books.

6. *Rating by Institutional Membership.* "The subject is assigned to a particular status by the analyst because in the interviews of informants he is said to be a member of certain institutions which are ranked as superior or inferior. The institutions used for such a rating are families, cliques, associations, and churches [28]." This procedure is sometimes called by the dreadful label of "Real Interconnectedness." It is not a direct measure of prestige, but a prediction of prestige from interaction.

The procedure of EP must stand or fall on the adequacy of rating by matched agreements. If the townspeople cannot tell the observer about a system of categories that they use to classify people, then he might as well pack up and go home. All the other techniques are but minor modifications used to place additional persons once the basic structure has been discovered.

Warner quotes at length from a number of interviews with ten key informants, then partly summarizes them in a table which represents his comparison of the social-class configurations that they used. The table looks very much like Figure 1, above, from *Deep South;* although some informants thought in terms of only four levels, most used five, and apparently the five all cut the population at about the same places.

But some informants used six or seven levels, and Warner says that he began the research with a classification of ten levels, gradually combining them until he arrived at five as the proper number. (As compared to Yankee City, there is no distinction between upper-uppers and lower-uppers in Jonesville. Thus there are five instead of six classes; the others are supposed to be exactly comparable in form to Yankee City, though the proportionate distribution of the population among them is slightly different.)

But how did Warner decide that five is the right number of levels? There is no criterion presented that leads to this conclusion. He does not tell us the number of informants who used five levels as compared to four or six. We simply have to accept on faith his statement that most people think in terms of five levels, that they mean the same thing by different labels, and that for those who use a smaller number than five the analyst can properly subdivide into five by the "perspective" approach discussed above.

Let us assume for a moment that five levels is the correct number, and that when any informant talks in terms of levels, Warner can adequately translate his conversation into the basic five. Then it is possible to count the number of times informants agree on the placement of persons in those levels, which is a form of check on the whole procedure. This Warner does for his ten informants, and he reports that of 426 pairs of mentions of an individual, 405 were in agreement, and 21 in disagreement (an agreement of 95 per cent) [29]. This is a very satisfactory degree of agreement. However, it would be much more significant if we had some additional information: (1) Who were the ten informants whose agreements and disagreements were counted? Were they especially class-conscious? All Warner tells us about them is their occupations, and seven are professionals or businessmen. Would seven laborers agree with them? (2) Is it possible that the persons the informants spontaneously mentioned were not typical of the community, but were prominent in some ways that made their class placement artificially easy? (3) Were the persons mentioned spread evenly and representatively throughout the status hierarchy? People at the top and bottom are much more easy to place than those in the middle. (4) How many of the informants spontaneously mentioned five classes, and exactly how did Warner translate into five levels the statements of informants who did not spontaneously use them? If these questions were answered, we would be in a much better position to judge the meaning of "95 per cent agreement."

Before considering Warner's Index of Status Characteristics, it will be worth taking a detour to follow the work of a man who answered some of the questions just raised.

AUGUST B. HOLLINGSHEAD

In 1941, Professor August B. Hollingshead, then at Indiana University and now at Yale, went to Jonesville to study adolescent behavior. He cooperated with the Warner team, which was there at the same time, and much research material was pooled. Later the two men drifted apart, and Hollingshead symbolized this fact—incidentally adding to our confusion—by inventing a different name for the same town; he called it "Elmtown."

Hollingshead wanted to organize his description of the life of the youth of the town in terms of differences between the social classes. Obviously, he first needed a way to place the family of each of his adolescents into its correct niche in the class hierarchy. He worked out a simple and effective rating procedure which is probably the best technique we now have for studying the prestige stratification of a small community. First he developed a small list of families spread throughout the system and learned their prestige rank. Then he asked informants to compare the rank of the families who had children in his sample to those on the list. In this way the master or control list became his measuring rod. The procedure is similar to Warner's Rating by Matched Agreements plus Rating by Comparison, but Hollingshead is more systematic in his operations, and, equally important, he is more careful to describe adequately every step of those operations. Here is what he did:

He examined fifty interviews and took out the names of thirty families who were frequently mentioned. These families were spread throughout the prestige range, and there seemed to be considerable agreement about their positions. The criteria used by the informants to assign prestige could be grouped in five categories [30]: "(1) the way a family lived—this included place of residence, type of dwelling, and furnishings; (2) income and material possessions; (3) participation in community affairs, politics, religion . . . (4) family background, including ancestry, kin, and national origin; (5) reputation or prestige." Hollingshead put the names of the husbands and wives on small cards, and went back to twenty-five of the people who had been interviewed previously. They were asked to place these people in the different "stations" or "classes" where they belonged. No further instructions were given.

The cards were divided up by the raters into stacks of equivalent rank. There was considerable consistency in the number of stacks used: nineteen informants used five groups, three used three groups, two used four groups, and one used two groups. Furthermore, 77 per cent of the placements of specific families were in agreement. It was noted that most of this agreement centered on twenty of the thirty families; the others were mobile, or there was some discrepancy between the standing of the husband and the wife. Consequently, these families were eliminated from the control list.

The shortened list of twenty families was then taken to a completely new sample of twelve informants who had not rated them before. They were long-time residents of the town, and were specifically asked to judge the names on the list according to the criteria given above for prestige placement (excluding family background). Ten of these new raters used five groups, one used four, and one used three. The ratings of those who used five groups were correlated with the ratings of those earlier informants who had also used five groups. The coefficient of correlation was .88. Hollingshead resolved the few disagreements by using his own "clinical judgment." He admits that the high correlation is somewhat spurious, for the names of those families about whom there was most disagreement had been eliminated, and the raters who did not use five classes were also eliminated. However, he concluded that the agreement was adequate to sustain the judgment that the community had five classes and that residents could place their fellows fairly well into one or another of them. The descriptions of the classes are the same as those given by Warner. But note that Hollingshead himself did not decide on how many classes to use, or how to cut them; he did not abstract them from interview data; he let his informants sort the cards into classes according to their own conception of social reality in the town.

After he had his control list of twenty well-known families, he was ready to place the families of his large sample of adolescents. He got thirty-one new informants, all adults who had a stable position themselves and who knew the community well. They were scattered throughout the prestige range. They were interviewed in detail about each of the 535 families of the sample Hollingshead intended to study (which included the families of all adolescents in town of high-school age). Each informant talked about all the families he knew among the 535, and during the course of the conversation was asked to name the family on the control list which came closest in general standing to the family being discussed. The average informant was able to place about seventy-five families, although one woman rated 261 of them (what a busybody!).

Hollingshead then gave a simple score to each family in the large sample in terms of the class position of the family on the control list with which it was equated. Families who were judged by respondents to be equal to those in the top group of the control list (approximately equivalent to Warner's upper class) were scored 1; those in the next group (upper-middle class) were scored 2; and so on to those in the bottom group (lower-lower class) who were scored 5. An average was struck of the ratings given to each family by the several raters who knew it, and this average or mean score became the final class score for that family. The average deviation around those means became a measure of agreement among raters. Hollingshead found that there was most agreement regarding families at the top and the bottom, and least concerning those in the middle of the prestige range. Table 1 summarizes his results.*

*Table 1.  Hollingshead's Class Ratings* [31]

| CLASS | NUMBER OF FAMILIES | NUMBER OF RATERS | MEAN NO. RATERS PER FAMILY | MEAN RATING | AVERAGE DEVIATION |
|-------|------|------|------|------|------|
| I | 4 | 21 | 21.0 | 1.04 | 0.04 |
| II | 29 | 23 | 14.3 | 1.93 | 0.16 |
| III | 129 | 20 | 13.4 | 2.91 | 0.25 |
| IV | 235 | 26 | 12.1 | 4.17 | 0.47 |
| V | 138 | 22 | 10.5 | 4.71 | 0.39 |

Hollingshead emphasizes the difference of 1.26 class intervals between the mean ratings of Class III (lower-middle), Class IV (upper-lower), which is the biggest numerical jump between any two levels. He says that this figure is "indicative of the prestige gulf that exists between the two largest socioeconomic groupings in Elmtown, namely, the 'business and professional classes' and the 'working class.' This difference appeared so persistently that we are convinced that it is symbolic of a fundamental prestige differential between these broad groups [32]." This statement is in direct contradiction to Warner's belief that this break is the hardest of all to distinguish—so much so that in much of his more recent writing he refers to the lower-middle and the upper-lower as a combined "level of the Common Man."

The fact that the average deviation was large for the upper-lowers means that raters frequently disagreed in attempting to place them. It appears that the disagreement was whether they should be placed in the upper-lower or the lower-lower. There were very few raters who wanted to put them in the lower-middle, thus supporting Hollingshead's assertion that the greatest gulf was between the middle and the working classes.

Hollingshead offers these general remarks about agreements among raters [33]:

* Some of the interesting substantive findings of Hollingshead on the class-related behavior of adolescents will be reported below in Chapter V; here we are concerned only with his method of delineating the classes.

Generally speaking, placement of families tended to be uniform from rater to rater when the rater and the rated belonged to the same class, were well known to each other, and when the family being rated was stable in its position. Differential placement was encountered when the rater and the rated came from different classes, especially when the rater was uncertain about the position of a mobile family. When raters belonged to a class below the family rated, there was more uncertainty over a family's position than when raters and rated were in the same class. When the rater was two classes below the family rated, there was greater disagreement than in the case of a single class difference. When three or more classes intervened between the rater and the rated, greater agreement was experienced in the ratings than when there were only two intervals between them. This apparently anomalous situation might be accounted for by a general tendency for persons of low prestige to accord high prestige to persons who are markedly different from themselves; also extreme cases are always clearer as to type than intervening ones.

Fortunately, Warner rated by EP 134 of the families from Hollingshead's sample. The agreement between the two methods was as follows (the upper class in this group contained only two families):

|  |  |
|---|---|
| Class   I (upper class) | 100% agreement |
| II (upper-middle) | 89 |
| III (lower-middle) | 83 |
| IV (upper-lower) | 72 |
| V (lower-lower) | 77 |

It appears, then, that a town like Jonesville-Elmtown can be stratified by various local informants into prestige classes, and that whether one follows the procedures of Warner or Hollingshead, he comes out with substantially the same results, with about 80 per cent agreement among the informants. The remaining 20 per cent represent three kinds of disagreements: (1) differences among the informants as to the number of class levels they perceive and about the precise places to divide them (rater cutting inconsistency); (2) differences of opinion regarding the relative placement of persons growing out of differences in the vantage points (classes) of the informants, or the personal values of the informants (rater ranking inconsistency); (3) differences of opinion regarding the relative placement of persons growing out of ambiguities in the social behavior of those persons—especially their mobility (ratee inconsistency). Much work remains to be done before we can apportion the error among these types of disagreement.

Hollingshead's technique is elegantly simple and appropriate, whereas some readers feel that Warner has oversystematized what is essentially an intuitive procedure based on trained, clinical judgment. But the fact remains that their results are similar. Many people who live in towns like Yankee City and Jonesville agree that Warner has correctly grasped basic patterns of behavior that are very important to the inhabitants. Warner was the first social scientist to describe in detail these patterns in America, and most of the research men who have followed him have simply modified his approach in detail but not in substance.

## OTHER PRESTIGE STUDIES

Several other studies have been made using rating procedures; two of them are worth mentioning at this point.

Gerhard E. Lenski prepared a doctoral dissertation for Yale by replicating the Hollingshead method in Danielson, Connecticut, a town of 6000 persons (the same size as Elmtown) [34]. He asked twenty-four raters to make judgments about a representative sample of their fellow townsmen. The raters were told to divide the names into strata of equivalent prestige. They did not agree: one informant used three strata, four used four strata, seven used five strata, eight used six strata, and four used seven strata. Furthermore, even when several raters used the same number of strata, they did not put equivalent proportions of the population into them. Lenski concluded that although there was agreement about a general prestige continuum in the community, there was no consensus about divisions into strata. The fact that the town was split into major ethnic groups might have influenced his results (48 per cent of the people were French Canadians and only 32 per cent were Yankees).

About the same time that Hollingshead was in Elmtown, Harold F. Kaufman was developing similar methods in a small village in New York [35]. It had 1500 inhabitants, two fifths of whom lived in the village and the rest on the surrounding farms. Kaufman used fourteen raters, and asked them to rate every family in the township that they knew, and told them to use *as many* strata as possible. Two of the raters used four classes, two used five classes, six used six classes, two used seven classes, one used nine classes, and one used ten classes. Kaufman himself was able to distinguish eleven classes.

He compared the ratings of different judges by using his own eleven strata as a skeleton and fitting into it the strata used by each informant. Thus, an informant's middle stratum was given the score of Kaufman's middle group, and the other strata used by the informant were given those scores on the eleven-step scale that seemed to make most sense in terms of the descriptions used by the informant. This procedure depends, of course, on the good judgment of the investigator, but it did allow Kaufman to use all the ratings rather than only those of judges who used six strata, the most popular number, as Hollingshead would have done. Kaufman found that eleven of the raters agreed with the composite ratings with a correlation of .74 or better. Only three were seriously deviant, and two of these were high-school students. The deviant judges appeared to use personal standards of like and dislike instead of attempting to interpret community evaluation.

Kaufman made elaborate analyses of biases among judges, but unfortunately his sample of judges was so small that the results were inconclusive. In general, however, it appeared that those whose own positions were low were less accurate than those who came from the upper classes. There was also a tendency for judges of high status to degrade persons of low status, and for persons of low status to raise their colleagues a bit. Kaufman concluded that judges from the middle of the range were probably the best. The average deviation of only .59 class intervals, plus the high correlation of most judges with the composite ranking, indicated a considerable amount of agreement in the community about prestige placement, although the number of strata used in making judgments seemed to be an arbitrary matter subject to slight changes of instructions from the researcher. Incidentally, Kaufman himself, after a few months of residence, became as good a judge as any of the natives.

The work of Lenski and Kaufman should make us cautious in generalizing from the results of Hollingshead and Warner. We are justified in concluding that most American small towns have a prestige ranking that can be described with reasonable agreement by the ratings of local informants, but we must remain suspicious concerning claims that the informants will agree about divisions into clear-cut strata.

## THE INDEX OF STATUS CHARACTERISTICS

Procedures for placing individuals from interviews are laborious and expensive, and depend upon the efforts of highly skilled interviewers. Furthermore, they cannot be used in large cities where people do not know many of their townsmen by name, and they are difficult to use for comparative studies which draw their subjects from several different towns, for it is hard to decide when the strata of one town are equal to those of another. To meet these difficulties, several attempts have been made to construct short indexes which are supposed to correlate with, and thus predict, prestige placement, but only Warner's has been validated against an independent measure of prestige from qualitative interviews.

Warner devised an Index of Status Characteristics which was constructed to give the best possible prediction of the results of Evaluated Participation as it was used in Jonesville. What he did was to choose four simple characteristics that his data showed were highly correlated with prestige position, and worked out the most efficient weight for each (via regression equations on EP). The four factors that he finally decided on were these (income and education can be used as additions or substitutions under some circumstances):

| Occupation | Weight 4 | House type | Weight 3 |
| Source of income | Weight 3 | Dwelling area | Weight 2 |

Each element was rated on a seven-point scale (with 1 the highest); the rating was then multiplied by the appropriate weight; and finally a sum was computed. This sum was the ISC score for a family and predicted its approximate place among the prestige classes.

The ISC is not completely automatic or "objective." The analyst must first learn something about the town he is studying, and divide the residential areas into seven types according to their general prestige value in the eyes of the local residents (these types could be approximated by statistics on tax or rental values, although Warner does not discuss such a step). Then the analyst must look at the outside of the house of each subject, form an estimate of its prestige value, and rate it on a seven-point scale (again, tax or rent figures might be substituted). Then he must place his subject into one of the following occupational categories:

1. Professionals and proprietors of large businesses
2. Semiprofessionals and smaller officials of large businesses
3. Clerks and kindred workers
4. Skilled workers
5. Proprietors of small businesses
6. Semiskilled workers
7. Unskilled workers

Finally, the analyst must rate the subject according to his primary source of income:

1. Inherited wealth
2. Earned wealth
3. Profits and fees
4. Salary and sales commissions
5. Wages
6. Private relief
7. Public relief and nonrespectable income

Warner standardized the ISC on a sample of 303 families in Jonesville "for whom the E.P. was determinable with a relatively high degree of certainty" [36]. Thus, the sample was a "blue-ribbon" group and did not include mobile persons or others who were difficult to place. This procedure artificially raised all correlations between EP and ISC. Furthermore, the sample was heavily overweighted with persons of the upper and upper-middle classes—who are the easiest to place because most conspicuous (see Hollingshead's average deviations, Table 1, above). There were ninety-three families of noticeable ethnic background, and 210 "old Americans." The basic work was done with the old Americans, and then compared to the ethnics. A preliminary table of equivalents was drawn up, showing the predicted EP placement for various ISC scores; these predictions were then checked against the already determined EP positions.

Warner gives a number of comparisons between the results of his two techniques. For instance, he tells us that the correlation between EP and ISC was .97, and that correlations between EP and single components of the ISC ranged from .78 for education to .91 for occupation. The details are given in Table 2. Although occupation alone could be used as a fairly good predictor of EP placement, its standard error of estimate was considerably higher than for the ISC as a whole; therefore accuracy was noticeably increased by using the composite index. (The standard error of 1.1 for the ISC indicates that in two predictions out of three, the ISC was not off more than 1.1 of the fifteen steps in the "expanded" EP [37].)

*Table 2. Correlations between ISC Components and EP* [38]

| STATUS CHARACTERISTIC | CORRELATION WITH EP | STANDARD ERROR OF ESTIMATE |
|---|---|---|
| Occupation | .91 | 1.8 |
| Amount of income | .89 | 2.0 |
| Source of income | 85 | 2.3 |
| House type | .85 | 2.3 |
| Dwelling area | .82 | 2.5 |
| Education | .78 | 2.7 |
| ISC (ORIGINAL) | .97 | 1.1 |

After the ISC was revised and the weights were added, these results were obtained: 84 per cent of the predictions put an old American family in the correct class (half of them were placed in the correct grade within the class). The greatest amount of error was for persons who were predicted to be in the upper-lower class. It was found that many of the families incorrectly placed were mobile. Among ethnic families, 72 per cent were placed within the correct class. The ISC tended to overestimate the position of ethnic families who were near the top of the hierarchy, and underestimate that of those near the bottom; the former tendency was stronger.

After all the experimentation was done, Warner drew up a final conversion table for predicting EP from ISC for both old Americans and ethnics. It differentiated between sure predictions, those which were only probable, and those which were indeterminate. For the first group of sure predictions (which included two thirds of the subjects), Warner was right ninety-six times out of one hundred. Here are the equivalents for old Americans [39]:

| ISC | EP |
|---|---|
| 12–17 | Upper class |
| 18–22 | Upper class probably |
| 23–24 | Indeterminate |
| 25–33 | Upper-middle class |
| 34–37 | Indeterminate |
| 38–50 | Lower-middle class |
| 51–53 | Indeterminate |
| 54–62 | Upper-lower class |
| 63–66 | Indeterminate |
| 67–69 | Lower-lower class probably |
| 70–84 | Lower-lower class |

The only repeat study that has been reported was done in Rockford, Illinois, a city of 90,000, by two of Warner's associates, Kenneth Eells and Charles Warriner [40]. They obtained a sample of 359 families, and first placed them in EP classes through interpretation of interview materials. The distribution was as follows:

| | |
|---|---|
| Upper-middle or above | 121 |
| Intermediate | 1 |
| Lower-middle | 55 |
| Intermediate | 29 |
| Upper-lower | 35 |
| Intermediate | 13 |
| Lower-lower | 105 |
| Total | 359 |

Again, we have a strange sort of sample. It contains forty-three families called "intermediate" or unclassifiable according to EP procedures. And it has a very low proportion of upper-lowers, yet they are usually the largest single group in town. Thus the distribution is too heavily weighted at the extremes, which artificially increases the correlation with ISC scores. Eliminating the forty-three intermediates, and then cutting the ISC scores into those categories which maximized the prediction of EP, the investigators found that the ISC placed twenty families too high and forty-three too low—thus misplacing 18 per cent of the cases. Add to that the intermediates, and the error was markedly increased.

An investigator who goes to a new city and uses the ISC must work out a table of equivalents between it and EP that fits the local scene. In so doing, it appears that he should expect some 10 per cent of the families to be unplaceable on the EP and another 10 per cent to be doubtful because of disagreements among informants. Then, assuming that he uses a random sample of residents in the city, he should be satisfied to get a maximum of 80 per cent accuracy in predicting the EP of the remaining families from the ISC. In other words, since the EP procedure is at best an approximation, the ISC is but an approximation of an approximation. Yet it has proved useful to many researchers.

There is one study that uses an index very similar to the ISC; it was done by Hollingshead in New Haven, Connecticut. He did not validate his results against an independent measure of EP, but he did find his index to be highly correlated with varieties of psychiatric disorders that are known to be related to social class behavior. Hollingshead's index was based on occupation (weight 8), education (weight 6), and area of residence (weight 5). Using this index, he divided the community into five levels, and the proportions in them are reproduced here as they are the only estimates we have of the prestige class distribution of an urban community (population 250,000) [41]:

|          |     |
|----------|-----|
| Class I   | 3%  |
| Class II  | 8   |
| Class III | 22  |
| Class IV  | 46  |
| Class V   | 18  |

## OTHER INDEXES

There have been many indexes proposed as predictors of prestige placement, usually called measures of "socioeconomic status," but only the ISC has been validated against interview data of the EP type. Consequently, we are not sure just what the other indexes actually measure. One of them in particular has been widely used, that constructed by Professor F. Stuart Chapin of the University of Minnesota in 1933 [42]. It is a scale for estimating the prestige value of living-room furnishings, based on the reasonable assumption that people symbolize their own class values by the way they furnish their living rooms, and that their friends in turn judge them by the symbols they observe. The scale is made up of a number of items like pianos and bookcases which are checked "present" or "absent," plus an estimate by the interviewer of the general upkeep and taste of the room. Chapin did not validate his scale by testing it against an outside criterion, other than to show that it discriminated well between broad occupational groupings, such as professionals and laborers. He did not prove that it does more than would a classification of the occupations themselves. In some versions of his instrument Chapin included items of participation in community activities—or interaction. These items probably help to predict prestige rank, but they make the instrument less definite as a measure of consumption patterns.

The Chapin scale and others like it seem to be fairly efficient measures of consumption behavior—that is, income plus values about expenditure. They are probably better predictors of prestige rank than income alone. But the Chapin scale is now out of date, and should be modernized and reweighted before being used in the contemporary urban scene. Furthermore, there is some evidence that a simpler guide serves equally well: the A, B, C, D rating scheme of the market researchers. Their interviewers simply check their impression of the family's style of life, based on observation of the interior of the house: "wealthy," "average-plus," "average," or "poor." These ratings are reasonably reliable, and they have proved to be useful predictors of political ideology, voting behavior, and purchasing tastes. They correlate highly with occupation [43].

In 1953 James A. Davis and I did a study of Cambridge, Massachusetts, in which we used a somewhat different approach to the problem of measurement indexes. We took all of the variables commonly thought to be central to social class, and abstracted the two statistical factors that best accounted for their variation, using the technique of factor analysis. The first factor consisted of those items closely associated with occupation, such as the occupations of the best friends of the subject; the subject's education, source of income, and self-identification; and the interviewer's direct rating of the subject. The second factor consisted of those items most closely related to the house and residential area of the subject and to the level of his origin as measured by the occupation and education of his father. The two factors were correlated, though distinguishable from each other. A scale of occupations was the best means of measuring the first factor, and a rating on the house or area the best for the second. Income was not a good measure of either. If one desired a measure of the over-all complex of class behavior underlying all the variables, a scale of occupations was clearly the most efficient instrument to use [44].

## CONCLUSIONS

We started with a query about individuals and families in American small towns: could they be placed in a rank order which reflected the prestige given them by their townsmen—and if so, what criteria were used for granting prestige?

The evidence is clear that in a rough way such a rank order exists. People do judge their neighbors according to a mental scale of prestige. There seems to be a general consensus among the townspeople: they tend to agree as to who should be placed high and who low. Furthermore, they tend to group people in clusters—in ordinary situations it is difficult to make minute comparisons that give every person a precise and unique rank; people are thus lumped together into categories of equivalent position: "the high-ups," "the in-betweens," and "the low-downs." But there seems to be less consensus regarding the way these clusters are formed than about the relative ranking of persons.

In making ratings there are both group and individual variations that reflect differences in sensitivity of perception toward various stratification behaviors and differences regarding the relative importance of those behaviors. All of these variations among informants create a problem for the investigator in synthesizing their reports: he must summarize them in a scheme that is simple enough to be useful but not so much so that it violates reality. *The scheme he uses will reflect not only his own values and purposes but the technical procedures he uses to get his data.*

What criteria do people use to rate each other in the context of the local community? The most accurate answer is a vague one: the way people live. Everyone recognizes that some people live in crowded slums, are lucky to get menial jobs from week to week in which they do what they are told, and have values that stress the enjoyment of the moment, whereas other people live in large houses surrounded by manicured lawns, own or manage businesses that provide steady incomes and the opportunity to tell other people what to do, and have values stressing long-run planning. Various elements are combined to make up a life pattern, though in reality the elements fit together into a functioning whole; it is therefore not surprising that informants intermix them when the investigator stands at the door demanding an answer.

The most conspicuous aspect of class behavior is consumption pattern; thus people most readily judge their neighbors by the way they spend their money. Consumption behavior, in turn, depends on income, but not on that alone, for personal values influence the spending of money: two people with pay checks of the same size may use them for different pleasures, one for bourbon, the other for books. These differences in consumption values are significant clues to stratification dynamics. A self-made man who has ambitions to climb higher will often spend more than he earns in order "to make a name" for himself in the community. But one who inherited a fortune and received an education among others like himself is often more modest in his expenditures, for he feels that display is unnecessary and vulgar, and furthermore, that the fortune should be conserved and passed on to coming generations in order to maintain family continuity.

Style of life is not a matter of personal decision alone. People share their lives with their friends, and model their behavior after that of the people they hope to have as friends. Consequently, an important aspect of style of life is group membership: the high-ups are people who both live in big houses and spend their time with each other. The closer an observer is to a group, the more he can notice differences between people who really belong and those on the fringe who think their bank balance entitles them to belong but who do not act quite properly enough for full acceptance. In any group, active leaders get more prestige than passive followers.

Now, the observer has a choice. He can try to construct his summarizing scheme for describing prestige groups by reflecting as closely as possible a composite picture of the groups recognized by his informants, à la Warner, or he can try to describe those conditions which determine, in the long run, the basic elements of different styles of life, à la Marx and Weber. We can expect the field worker to lean in the first direction, the armchair thinker in the second. But these are complementary approaches. One gives us a description of the situation of the moment, the other tells us how it got that way and imagines how it will look in the future.

Succeeding chapters will examine the evidence from both points of view: we will describe differences in the styles of life of the different classes, and the factors by which they are determined and changed. The procedures described in this chapter for ranking persons (or groups) according to prestige are but the beginning of our task, for a knowledge of the prestige hierarchy of a community is not an end in itself. Such knowledge is valuable because it helps us to predict behavior in a wide variety of contexts which may, at first glance, seem unrelated, but which are in fact functionally integrated into a few basic styles of life. Prestige is a token of recognition by people in a community that styles of life are different in ways that have important consequences—and the consequences often outrun their recognition [45].

REFERENCES

[1] Sinclair Lewis, *Babbitt* (New York: Harcourt, Brace, 1922), p. 190.

[2] This model is often compared to the peck order among chickens and other animals: see Warder C. Allee, *Cooperation among Animals* (New York: Schuman, 1951).

[3] There is an excellent discussion of these concepts in Kingsley Davis, *Human Society* (New York: Macmillan, 1949), Chap. IV.

[4] Elton Mayo, *The Human Problems of an Industrial Civilization* (New York: Macmillan, 1933), p. 120.

[5] W. Lloyd Warner and Paul S. Lunt, *The Social Life of a Modern Community* (New Haven: Yale University Press, 1941), p. 5.

[6] Allison Davis, Burleigh B. Gardner, and Mary R. Gardner, *Deep South: A Social-Anthropological Study of Caste and Class* (Chicago: University of Chicago Press, 1941).

[7] W. Lloyd Warner et al., *Democracy in Jonesville* (New York: Harper, 1949). St. Clair Drake and Horace R. Cayton, *Black Metropolis* (New York: Harcourt, Brace, 1945). There have been several subsidiary studies, all reported in the methodological volume, *Social Class in America*, cited below. The reader who wants a short sample is advised to read *Democracy in Jonesville* or Warner's recent series of lectures, *American Life: Dream and Reality* (Chicago: University of Chicago Press, 1953).

[8] See these criticisms of Warner's approach: C. Wright Mills, "Review of *The Social Life of a Modern Community*," *American Sociological Review*, VII (April, 1942), 263–71. Robert Bierstedt, "The Limitations of Anthropological Methods in Sociology," *American Journal of Sociology*, LIV (July, 1948), 22–30. Harold W. Pfautz and Otis D. Duncan, "A Critical Evaluation of Warner's Work in Community Stratification," *American Sociological Review*, XV (April, 1950), 205–15.

[9] Warner, *Social Life of a Modern Community*, pp. 41–42.

[10] *Ibid.*, p. 81.

[11] *Ibid.*, pp. 82–84.

[12] W. Lloyd Warner et al., *Social Class in America* (Chicago: Science Research Associates, 1949), p. 21.

[13] Warner, *Social Life of a Modern Community*, p. 88. The descriptions of the classes are my condensations of much Warner material.

[14] Warner, *Social Class in America*, p. 3.

[15] Warner, *Democracy in Jonesville*, pp. xiii–xiv.

[16] Warner, *Social Life of a Modern Community*, pp. 90–91.

[17] Warner, *Social Class in America*, p. 34.

[18] *Ibid.*, p. 69.

[19] Davis, *Deep South*, pp. 71–73.

[20] This chart is also reproduced, though with a printer's error, in Warner, *Social Class in America*, p. 19. And the problem of differing perspectives is well discussed in another community study: James West, *Plainville, USA* (New York: Columbia University Press, 1945).

[21] The "Yankee City Series" is supposed to consist eventually of six volumes; two are as yet unpublished (a volume on values, and a data book). Those already published, all by the Yale University Press, New Haven, are: Vol. I, W. Lloyd Warner and Paul S. Lunt, *The Social Life of a Modern Community*, 1941. Vol. II, W. Lloyd Warner and Paul S. Lunt, *The Status System of a Modern Community*, 1942. Vol. III, W. Lloyd Warner and Leo Srole, *The Social Systems of American Ethnic Groups*, 1945. Vol. IV, W. Lloyd Warner and J. O. Low, *The Social System of the Modern Factory*, 1947.

[22] Warner, *Social Class in America*, p. 35.

[23] For a description of the interviewing technique, see Warner, *Social Life of a Modern Community*, pp. 45–53.

[24] Warner, *Social Class in America*, p. 37.

[25] *Ibid.*

[26] *Ibid*

[27] *Ibid.*, p. 38.

[28] *Ibid.*

[29] *Ibid.*, p. 65.

[30] August B. Hollingshead, *Elmtown's Youth* (New York: Wiley, 1949), p. 29.

[31] *Ibid.*, p. 37.

[32] *Ibid.*, p. 38.

[33] *Ibid.*, pp. 39–40.

[34] Gerhard E. Lenski, "American Social Classes: Statistical Strata or Social Groups?" *American Journal of Sociology*, LVIII (September, 1952), 139–44. See also Chaps. 5 and 7, John F. Cuber and William F. Kenkel, *Social Stratification in the United States* (New York: Appleton-Century-Crofts, 1954).

[35] Harold F. Kaufman, *Prestige Classes in a New York Rural Community* (Ithaca, New York: Cornell University Agricultural Experiment Station Memoir 260, March, 1944). Harold F. Kaufman, "Defining Prestige in a Rural Community," *Sociometry*, VIII (1945), No. 2, and IX (1946), No. 1—reprinted as "Sociometry Monograph No. 10" (New York: Beacon House, 1946).

Kaufman's exact procedure did not seem clear to me from his published reports. When I asked him about it, he replied in a letter on

November 16, 1953: "In the New York rural community study the prestige judges were told to rank community members in as many groupings as possible. The maximum number was nine and the minimum number was four. As the report states they usually set up a 'top' and 'bottom' pile of cards and one or more intermediate piles. There was an attempt to equate the values of the groupings of the various judges with the values of the eleven classifications made by the investigator [numbered 1, 1.5, 2 . . . 6]. Thus, a grouping that a judge said was exactly in the middle would be assigned to the 3.5 class. If this judge had two groupings above the median class and one below this grouping they might be assigned to class values of 1.5, 2.5, and 4.5, respectively."

[36] Warner, *Democracy in Jonesville*, p. 164.

[37] When comparing ISC and EP ratings, Warner subdivided the latter into fifteen categories by classifying each family into one of three grades within its class: "strong," "solid," or "weak." In computing standard errors of estimate, each of the fifteen categories was considered as one unit of class interval. The comparisons given are between this expanded EP and the "original" ISC which lacked weights, although Warner states that almost the same results were obtained when they used the five-level EP and the revised ISC.

[38] Warner, *Democracy in Jonesville*, p. 168.

[39] *Ibid.*, p. 127.

[40] Kenneth W. Eells, *Social-Status Factors in Intelligence Test Items* (unpublished Ph.D. thesis, University of Chicago, 1949).

[41] August B. Hollingshead and Frederick C. Redlich, "Social Stratification and Psychiatric Disorders," *American Sociological Review*, XVIII (April, 1953), 161–69.

[42] F. Stuart Chapin, *Contemporary American Institutions* (New York: Harper, 1935), pp. 373–97. See also the similar scales of William H. Sewell, *The Construction and Standardization of a Scale for the Measurement of the Socio-Economic Status of Oklahoma Farm Families* (Oklahoma Agricultural Experiment Station Bulletin 9, 1940); and Buford H. Junker, *Room Compositions and Life Styles* (unpublished Ph.D. thesis, University of Chicago, 1954).

[43] See Genevieve Knupfer, *Indices of Socio-Economic Status: A Study of Some Problems of Measurement* (New York: published by the author, 1946; Ph.D. thesis, Columbia University).

[44] Joseph A. Kahl and James A. Davis, "A Comparison of Indexes of Socio-Economic Status," *American Sociological Review*, XX (June, 1955), 317–25. The article contains a bibliography of other comparative studies of indexes. See also Richard Scudder and C. Arnold Anderson, "The Relation of Being Known to Status Rating," *Sociology and Social Research*, XXXVIII (March–April, 1954), 239–41. Arthur J. Vidich and Gilbert Shapiro, "A Comparison of Participant Observation and Survey

Data," *American Sociological Review,* XX (February, 1955), 28–32.
Otis D. Duncan and Beverly Duncan, "Residential Distribution and
Occupational Stratification," *American Journal of Sociology,* LX
(March, 1955), 493–503.

[45] The most vivid descriptions of differences in styles of life and prestige
in small communities are those by skillful novelists. Among them are
Sinclair Lewis, *Main Street* (1921) and *Babbitt* (1922); Theodore
Dreiser, *An American Tragedy* (1926); John P. Marquand, *Point of No
Return* (1949); Carl Jonas, *Jefferson Sellek* (1951), which brings Babbitt
up to date.

# III

# Occupational Prestige
# and Social Change

IN ANY GIVEN SOCIETY, THE MORE OCCUPATIONAL WORK CON-
SISTS IN THE PERFORMANCE OF THE FUNCTIONS OF SOCIAL OR-
GANIZATION AND CONTROL, AND THE HIGHER THE DEGREE OF
INTELLIGENCE NECESSARY FOR ITS SUCCESSFUL PERFORMANCE,
THE MORE PRIVILEGED IS THAT GROUP AND THE HIGHER RANK
DOES IT OCCUPY.                              *Pitirim Sorokin* [1]

IN THE RESEARCH reported in the last chapter, Warner found that a man's occupation was the variable which correlated most highly with the prestige rank granted his family by the local community. There are several reasons why occupation and prestige are so highly related. In the first place, a man's occupation is the source of his income, which in turn provides the style of life that serves as one of the major clues used by his neighbors in making their evaluations. But occupation stands for more than merely a certain level of income. It indicates a man's education; it suggests the type of associates he comes in contact with on the job; it tells something of the contribution he makes to community welfare; it hints at the degree of his authority over other people.

Occupation is a convenient variable to work with. Unlike personal prestige, it is not tied to the particular circumstances of a local community, for it has meaning that is about the same throughout the country, and this meaning has remained relatively stable for a long period of time. Therefore it is possible to compare the occupational hierarchies of different communities and different historical epochs.

## MIDDLETOWN

There is one sociological community study which emphasizes the occupational changes that have occurred in the recent past, the research on "Middletown." It began when Robert S. Lynd and his wife Helen Merrell Lynd (he is now at Columbia University, she at Sarah Lawrence College) went to Indiana to describe a "typical" American

53

community as it existed in 1924. At that time Middletown (a pseudonym) had 35,000 inhabitants. In order to have a base line for contrast, the Lynds reconstructed life in 1890 when the town had only 11,000 people and was going through the first stages of industrialization. Mr. Lynd eventually returned to the city, and he and his wife wrote a second book about it, telling of its growth to 47,000 by 1935, and its reactions to the days of boom and bust which followed the first research [2]. Thus we have three points of time to contrast: 1890, 1924, and 1935.

The method they followed was to live in the town for over a year, meeting and talking to as many people as possible. They interviewed all the "important" people and many of the unimportant ones; they read newspapers, diaries, local histories; they went to various ritual gatherings in churches, luncheon clubs, and civic centers. Occasionally they passed out a questionnaire to get standardized information about such matters as budget behavior or attitudes of students in the high school, but the emphasis was more on qualitative than quantitative data.

In their first book, *Middletown,* the Lynds said this about life in 1924 [3]:

. . . as the study progressed it became more and more apparent that the money medium of exchange and the cluster of activities associated with its acquisition drastically condition the other activities of the people. Rivers begins his study of the Todas with an account of the ritual of the buffalo dairy, because "the ideas borrowed from the ritual of the dairy so pervade the whole of Toda ceremonial." A similar situation leads to the treatment of the activities of Middletown concerned with getting a living first among the six groups of activities to be described. . . .*

At first glance it is difficult to see any semblance of pattern in the workaday life of a community exhibiting a crazy-quilt array of nearly four hundred ways of getting its living. . . . On closer scrutiny, however, this welter may be resolved into two kinds of activities. The people who engage in them will be referred to throughout this report as the Working Class and the Business Class. Members of the first group, by and large, address their activities in getting their living primarily to *things,* utilizing material tools in the making of things and the performance of services, while the members of the second group address their activities predominantly to *people* in the selling or promotion of things, services, and ideas. . . . There are two and one-half times as many in the working class as in the business class—seventy-one in each 100 as against twenty-nine. . . .†

While an effort will be made to make clear at certain points variant behavior within these two groups, it is after all this division into working class

* The others are: making a home, training the young, using leisure, engaging in religious practices, engaging in community activities [JAK].

† It may be that Marxist theory had an influence on the Lynds' perception of the two-class system of Middletown [JAK].

and business class that constitutes the outstanding cleavage in Middletown. The mere fact of being born upon one or the other side of the watershed roughly formed by these two groups is the most significant single cultural factor tending to influence what one does all day long throughout one's life; whom one marries; when one gets up in the morning; whether one belongs to the Holy Roller or Presbyterian church; or drives a Ford or a Buick; whether or not one's daughter makes the desirable high school Violet Club; or one's wife meets with the Sew We Do Club or with the Art Students' League; whether one belongs to the Odd Fellows or to the Masonic Shrine; whether one sits about evenings with one's necktie off; and so on indefinitely throughout the daily comings and goings of a Middletown man, woman, or child.

One of the central themes of the first Middletown volume was that from 1890 to 1924 there were basic changes in the work pattern of both the business and working classes—changes, incidentally, that resulted in a wider gap between them. These changes flowed from three basic causes: larger population, more machinery, increasing emphasis on money. The Lynds described in vivid detail a case study of the great transformation of modern life—industrialization.

Middletown in 1890 was a market town that was just beginning to turn to manufacturing. The work habits and values of its people were extensions of the traditions of their farmer fathers. Those farmers were people who had conquered a wilderness: there had been land for all who would work it, and from such plenty there emerged a society that lacked gradations of rank and privilege, a society that stressed individual initiative and progress, family solidarity, simplicity of manners and style of life, equality among men. As trading and handicraft manufacturing succeeded farming as the base of livelihood, the old traditions could easily continue. A man earned whatever his own efforts deserved. True, there developed a gradation in income that extended from unskilled through skilled laborers to bosses (who were often ex-craftsmen) and a few professional men. But the gradation was not sharply divided into levels; a man often moved through several steps in a few years, and it was understood that the system was open to everybody in fair and equal competition. People started at the bottom of some line of endeavor and worked their way up. Income and prestige were direct outcomes of competence at work, and everybody could understand and agree that as competence increased with age and experience, it brought the right and necessity of teaching and directing the work of less skillful men, and thereby it earned a higher income. But the machine began to change all this [4]:

"When tradition is a matter of the spoken word, the advantage is all on the side of age. The elder is in the saddle" (Goldenweiser). Much the same condition holds when tradition is a matter of learned skills of hand and eye.

But machine production is shifting traditional skills from the spoken word and the fingers of the master craftsman of the Middletown of the nineties to the cams and levers of the increasingly versatile machine. And in modern machine production it is speed and endurance that are at a premium. A boy of nineteen may, after a few weeks of experience on a machine, turn out an amount of work greater than that of his father of forty-five. . . .

The demands of the iron man for swiftness and endurance rather than training and skill have led to the gradual abandonment of the apprentice-master craftsman system; one of the chief characteristics of Middletown life in the nineties, this system is now virtually a thing of the past. . . . With the passing of apprenticeship the line between skilled and unskilled workers has become so blurred as to be in some shops almost non-existent.

There were basic changes among the business class as well. The old businessman was a small merchant or manufacturer, whose capital consisted mostly of his personal savings. He had started as a worker and through hard work had become a businessman. His relations with both employees and customers were personal, even intimate. But the new businessman operated in terms of bank credit, had too many employees and customers to know them personally, and had ties with other businessmen all over the country. True, the petty grocer and his kind still existed in 1924, but the major part of production and exchange in Middletown was passing into the hands of the new businessman (who was sometimes a branch manager of a national corporation).

Money had become the significant link between people. In the old days each family was more self-sufficient; they processed most of their own food and clothing (from purchased raw materials, of course); they entertained themselves at home and with the neighbors; when they did buy things, they paid cash. By 1924 "credit was coming rapidly to pervade and underlie more and more of the whole institutional structure within which Middletown earned its living [5]." Businessmen were much more dependent upon the banks, and individuals upon the credit agencies and merchants who allowed them to buy on time. More articles of use were bought and fewer were homemade; more activities had changed from family and neighborhood affairs to commercial propositions. All of this was well symbolized by the automobile, and the Lynds devote some brilliant pages to the changes in life that centered around the family car. They sum up the transition to a money-centered life in these words [6]:

For both working and business class no other accompaniment of getting a living approaches in importance the money received for their work. It is more this future, instrumental aspect of work, rather than the intrinsic satisfactions involved, that keeps Middletown working so hard as more and more of the activities of living are coming to be strained through the bars of the dollar sign. Among the business group, such things as one's circle of friends, the kind of car one drives, playing golf, joining Rotary, the church to which one belongs, one's political principles, the social position of one's wife, apparently tend to be scrutinized somewhat more than formerly in Middletown for their instrumental bearing upon the main business of getting a living while, conversely, one's status in these various other activities tends to be much influenced by one's financial position. As vicinage has decreased in its influence upon the ordinary social contacts of this group, there appears to be a constantly closer relation between the solitary factor of financial status and one's social status. A leading citizen presented this matter in a nutshell to a member of the research staff in discussing the almost universal local custom of "placing" newcomers in terms of where they live, how they live, the kind of car they drive, and similar externals: "It's perfectly natural. You see, they know money, and they don't know you."

By 1924 Middletown was becoming too large and its productive system too complex and mechanized for community prestige to flow automatically from skill at work. People did not understand just what the activities of others were; a grocer knew little about glass blowing or automobile-parts manufacturing, and a glass blower knew little about financing a grocery store on credit. Concurrently, the money nexus was becoming increasingly important as more spheres of life became parts of the commercial market. The result was that people began to use money as a sign of accomplishment, a common denominator for prestige. The question "How much does he earn?" was heard more frequently than "How much skill does he have?"

The Lynds did not find it necessary to divide the population any further than Business Class and Working Class when they wrote about Middletown in 1924. True, they recognized some gradation within each group, but said that the working class was becoming more homogeneous through time as machines degraded skill, and the business class remained a small and basically undifferentiated group. They felt that no distinctions in Middletown were so important as this one.

The system could not work unless people believed that in a general way authority and income on the job and style of life and prestige off the job were automatic results of relatively free individualistic competition. This belief was brought to Middletown from the farms and villages; it was the American heritage of the frontier. Although some people were beginning to question this belief in 1924, the vast majority of both workers and businessmen clung to it. Indeed, faith in the justice of competition was the essential moral belief that made the wheels go around. Without such faith, prestige would be withdrawn from those who were economically successful, and either ambition would die and the motive force behind free enterprise decay, or revolution would ensue. The Middletown of 1924 believed in itself and its system. Free enterprise was not a mere theoretical discussion by economists of the workings of the market; it was a quasi-religious belief of the people.


## MIDDLETOWN REVISITED

In 1935 Mr. Lynd returned for a restudy. Both he and Middletown had changed. He had gone somewhat to the left in his political credo; as he wrote in the second book, *Middletown in Transition:* "Middletown believes that *laissez-faire* individualism is the best road to 'progress.' The present investigator holds the view, on the other hand, that our modern institutional world has become too big and too interdependent to rely indiscriminately upon the accidents of *laissez faire* . . . [7]." Middletown had grown larger, reaching 47,000 people; its industrial plant was more mechanized, more centralized into larger units, more subservient to national corporations; it had gone through the boom of the late 1920's and the devastating crash of the early 1930's. Yet the interplay between Lynd's assumptions and the reality of Middletown produced a report the dominant note of which is continuity in spite of change. The reader is surprised at how Middletown was able to take so much in its stride, to face such deep threats to its social structure, and yet come out with so many of the same beliefs—somewhat more tense and strained and defensive in their expression, but basically unaltered. "The city's prevailing mood of optimism makes it view prosperity as normal, while each recurrent setback tends to come as a surprise which local sentiment views as 'merely temporary' [8]." In terms of this philosophy, Middletown never really admitted that it had a depression until it was all over.

The trend toward mechanization that was dominant from 1890 to 1924 continued on through 1935. It could be easily measured through occupational statistics. These showed that the city's increase in population went mostly into the service industries, for the machines were getting so efficient that a productive labor force only slightly increased could produce vastly more goods.

The details were these: Using the census figures for 1920 and 1930, Lynd reports that the proportional increase of workers in the production industries was 26 per cent, whereas the increase in the service industries was 66 per cent. These service workers were becoming more professionalized through time; there were more schoolteachers, more social workers, more dental hygienists. The new efficiency of the productive machinery could support more services of a "luxury" type.

Within the factories there were changes in the composition of the work force. The trend toward semiskilled machine tenders continued—

proportionally more men were in that category, fewer either unskilled or highly skilled. But a lot of half-trained men working on a complex production line needed a few very well-trained men to invent the machines and to direct and coordinate their work. These men were more usually trained for supervision in school and college, rather than being promoted from the ranks. For an increase of only 10 per cent in production workers who labored for an hourly wage, there was an increase of 31 per cent in managers and officials, of 128 per cent for technical engineers, and 900 per cent for chemists, assayers, and metallurgists. At the same time the number of independent owner-manufacturers dropped 11 per cent [9]. Thus we see the march of technology: a larger mass of machine tenders gathered into fewer but bigger factories directed by a tiny group of specialized technicians and promoters. The gap between worker and manager had widened. And the manager had changed: he was not so often a self-made owner-businessman; he was more likely to be a member of "the new middle class" of technicians and administrators, trained in college, who worked for a salary. No longer could the complex system of Middletown be adequately described by the simple division into business class and working class.

## MIDDLETOWN'S NEW CLASSES

As a result of the changes he observed in Middletown, Lynd described the class structure in 1935 as follows [10]:

1. A very small top group of the "old" middle class is becoming an upper class, consisting of wealthy local manufacturers, bankers, the local head managers of one or two of the national corporations with units in Middletown, and a few well-to-do dependents of all the above, including one or two outstanding lawyers. . . .

2. Below this first group is to be found a larger but still relatively small group, consisting of established smaller manufacturers, merchants and professional folk . . . and also most of the better-paid salaried dependents of the city's big-business interests. . . . These two elements in Group 2 constitute socially a unity but, in their economic interests, often represent somewhat divergent elements. . . .

3. . . . Middletown's own middle class in purely locally relative terms: the minor employed professionals, the very small retailers and entrepreneurs, clerks, clerical workers, small salesmen, civil servants—the people who will never quite manage to be social peers of Group 2 and who lack the constant easy contact with Group 1 which characterizes Group 2.

4. Close to Group 3 might be discerned an aristocracy of local labor: trusted foremen, building trades craftsmen of long standing, and the pick of the city's experienced highly skilled machinists of the sort who send their children to the local college as a matter of course.

5. On a fifth level would stand the numerically overwhelmingly dominant group of the working class; these are the semiskilled or unskilled workers, including machine operatives, truckmen, laborers, the mass of wage earners.

6. Below Group 5 one should indicate the ragged bottom margin, comprising some "poor whites" from the Kentucky, Tennessee, and West Virginia mountains, and in general the type of white worker who lives in the ramshackle, unpainted cottages on the outlying unpaved streets. These are the unskilled workers who cannot even boast of that last prop to the job status of the unskilled: regular employment when a given plant is operating. [Most of the city's few Negroes would also fit here.]

Lynd adds some general comments to the schematic outline just given [11]:

Psychologically, Groups 1, 2, and 3 cling together as businessfolk, over against Groups 4, 5, and 6. . . . If the nascent "class" system of "Magic Middletown" appears to follow somewhat the above lines, Middletown itself will turn away from any such picture of the fissures and gullies across the surface of its social life. It is far more congenial to the mood of the city, proud of its traditions of democratic equality, to think of the lines of cleavage within its social system as based not upon class differences but rather upon the entirely spontaneous and completely individual and personal predilections of the 12,500 families who compose its population.

Lynd offers us a scheme based on "nascent" tendencies growing out of the occupational system. It is an observer's view, his simplification of life in terms of the factors which he thinks underlie the more observable facts of style of life, social and political attitudes, interaction networks, community prestige. He does not claim that the scheme is a reflection of the categories used in daily life by the people in Middletown; indeed, he says the people tend to deny such groupings as he uses. Instead, he claims that whether a man in the system recognizes it or not, in the long run his life will inevitably be shaped by his position in the occupational system more than by any other factor.

Interestingly enough, this scheme based on occupational niches is almost the same as the Warner scheme based on prestige, consumption style, and interaction networks. Lynd's Group 1 is Warner's Upper Class; Lynd's Group 2 is Warner's Upper-Middle Class; Lynd's Groups 3 and 4 are Warner's Lower-Middle Class; Lynd's Group 5 is Warner's Upper-Lower Class; Lynd's Group 6 is Warner's Lower-Lower Class.

The processes by which occupation and income are transformed into style-of-life symbols, interaction networks, and personal prestige are sharply illustrated by the story of the emergence into prominence of the "X family." They were the leading group of businessmen in Middletown. They had founded their fortune before the turn of the century by starting a small glass manufacturing plant on a capital of $7000.

There were five brothers, four who developed the business, and one who practiced medicine. The legends of Middletown contain many tales of the simplicity and humbleness of these early business pioneers who took advantage of the natural gas that was the base for the city's early industrialization [12]: "One of the city's veteran clothing dealers is fond of telling how one of the brothers borrowed a light-weight overcoat for a week-end party of young people in 1889. 'He didn't feel he could afford a new coat that year, as he was just starting in business.' " Then there is the newspaper editorial that appeared in 1925 when one of the brothers died: "He always worked on a level with his employees. He never asked a man to do something he would not do himself [13]."

These men built up a great production machine that became world-famous. They grew rich; they contributed vast sums to local charities and development projects; they became active community leaders. "In their conscientious and utterly unhypocritical combination of high profits, great philanthropy, and a low wage scale, they embody the hard-headed *ethos* of Protestant capitalism with its identification of Christianity with the doctrine of the goodness to all concerned of unrestricted business enterprise. In their modesty and personal rectitude, combined with their rise from comparative poverty to great wealth, they fit perfectly the American success dream [14]."

The brothers and their sons could not avoid becoming embroiled in all aspects of Middletown life. They became active in politics. They put up the money that kept the banks from collapsing in the depression, thereby gaining control. They were leaders in the fight against unionization. They took over the biggest department store in town when it failed in the early thirties. They opened a new residential subdivision for themselves, and soon were surrounded by all the ambitious families in town who could afford to move. They contributed money to the local college (part of the state system) and one of them was elected president of the state university board of trustees. They bought a substantial interest in the local newspaper. They did not completely run the town, because there were other industries present, including manufacturing plants that were part of the General Motors empire. And the mass of the people still voted. But "the business class in Middletown runs the city. The nucleus of business-class control is the X family [15]."

It was not until the second generation that the X family gained complete prestige priority in consumption affairs [16]:

. . . around the families of the four now grown-up sons and two sons-in-law of the X clan, with their model farms, fine houses, riding clubs, and airplanes, has developed a younger set that is somewhat more coherent, exclusive, and self-consciously upper-class. The physical aggregation of so many of these families in the new X subdivisions in one part of town has helped to pinch off psychologically this upper economic sliver of the population from the mass of business folk. And the pattern of their leisure, symbolized by their riding clubs and annual horse show, tends to augment their difference. . . . Particularly as regards the male members of the older generation, there has always been a continuous preoccupation with business; and they did few of the things associated with a wealthy leisured class. It is the new note of a more self-conscious leisure built upon endowed wealth, and obviously expensive, that the younger generation is bringing to Middletown. They, too, work hard, but they play expensively and at their own sports, with somewhat more definitely their own social set.

Great wealth has to be used. Whether it is ploughed back into business, exchanged for elegance in leisure, used to patronize health, the arts, and education, or devoted to the training of a new generation who will be taught how to spend it gracefully, it enhances the power and prestige of those who own it. The second generation of owners is bound to be different: they cannot have the motives of ambitious men born in poverty. They will have the capital wealth that brings power, the income that brings luxury, and the values of those who have been reared to expect both. They will be slightly different from first-generation businessmen of the same age—a difference that will be less important during the day at business than during the evening at play. They will be bound to seek the company of others like themselves. They will, in other words, create and become an upper class.

### OCCUPATIONAL AND SOCIAL CHANGE

The Lynds' case study indicates that the basic shifts in the prestige system from 1890 to 1935 began with alterations in the occupational system (prodded by technological innovation as accepted and put to use in an existing socioeconomic system). *As occupations changed, so did the distribution of power and income in the market place, skill and authority in the factory, and style of life at home. Prestige readjusted to all of these changes.* Insofar as the variables evolved at roughly similar rates, the total system remained in dynamic equilibrium, and the community had no great problem in assigning prestige to persons.

It is clear that the occupational role was at the center of this equilibrium. Any industrial society will have to evolve a prestige system closely tied to occupation, for an industrial economy takes so much energy and attention and has such control over subordinate aspects of life that it pushes work activity to the forefront of thought and value. That is not to say that technology automatically determines everything, for much depends on the way a given social system shapes technological knowledge into organized social roles—and there is room for variation. But comparisons of industrialized nations (which will be given below) indicate that the variation operates within marked limits, for the prestige systems of them all are strikingly similar.*

The story of Middletown supports the historical materialism of Karl Marx but not his views on the workings of capitalism. Industrial technology did indeed revolutionize society, but did not reduce it to two antagonistic classes based on ownership or nonownership of capital; it divided the society into more grades than ever existed before, and put them into such complex relationships that clear lines of class self-identification and conflict did not appear.

It is true, however, that the Lynds believed that the social system was under more strain in 1935 than in 1924. For more of the workers their past in the farm country was becoming so distant as to be less influential on their current beliefs. They had lived through a very damaging depression, and were beginning to question whether the system would always provide the jobs, the opportunities for advancement up the ladder, and the continuously rising standard of living which were its major inducements to faith and effort. The business class was also worried: they had learned that individual effort was not always enough, that Middletown was in fact affected and even controlled by a national and international market, and that the individual businessman, regardless of wit and energy, could be bankrupted by forces far beyond his control. Furthermore, the divisions within the business class were becoming more pronounced: the little shopkeeper no longer sat at lunch beside the big banker. The little man began to wonder whether the big man was always on his side. Yet the worker expressed his anxieties by cursing individual businessmen or "foreigners" and did not become solidary with his fellows and demand basic change, for he still believed in the system in spite of certain squeaks in the machinery. And the businessman blamed the New Deal in Washington and labor agitators for his troubles, and confidently hoped for an eventual return to Republican sanity. The system was strained but still working.

The key to the functioning of the system in spite of strain was the continuing faith in free enterprise and its hero, the businessman [17]:

* Of course, we have an economy that is both industrial and capitalistic. Yet the changes in Middletown were mostly the result of an increasingly complex technology and the division of labor which it produced, and even if that technology were organized into a socialistic system, the various types of jobs would still be necessary. The extreme radical view that a different form of social organization and a different ideology could eliminate grades of prestige and income but at the same time maintain diversified division of labor seems to be a utopian myth. Recent experience in the Soviet Union, plus the weight of the comparative studies of cultures, indicates that differences in prestige and income must follow those in skill and authority in the activities that are important to the society.

As, therefore, the chief contributor to the community's welfare, the successful businessman in Middletown elicits from his fellow citizens wholehearted praise, as well as envy and emulation. Since Middletown's values are regarded as leading to "success," it follows easily that those who are successful must obviously have these values to have become successful. So, by this subtle and largely unconscious process, Middletown imputes to the successful businessman the possession—again "of course"—of the qualities of being "hard-working," "practical," "sound," "honest," "kindly," "efficient," "enterprising," "thrifty," and so on through the city's other values. . . .

Middletown's working class . . . has in the main followed the same symbols, trying intermittently, as work allows, to affirm them as loudly as does the business class, and to narrow the gap between symbol and reality. It, like the business class, is busy living, manipulating the poker chips at its command, and trying to get more. Its drives are largely those of the business class: both are caught up in the tradition of a rising standard of living and lured by the enticements of salesmanship. . . .

### NATIONAL OCCUPATIONAL SYSTEM

The changes in the occupational system which the Lynds found so basic to the dynamics of stratification in Middletown were typical of what was happening all over the country. And fortunately we have a way of studying at least the skeleton of those changes without multiplying community studies throughout the land: we can use the data of the decennial census.

The United States Bureau of the Census began to ask questions about the occupations of our citizens in 1820, although systematic and comparable series of statistics did not begin until 1870, and for some series, 1910. This material was frequently used to show how new industries arose and old ones decayed, but it was not until the great depression of the 1930's that the data were organized for the purpose of studying social stratification. Before then the Federal government was merely the bookkeeper for our society; the New Deal changed it to the board of directors, and information about social trends became vital to the making of intelligent policy decisions. The man who did the job was an official of the Bureau of the Census, Dr. Alba M. Edwards. He delved into the dusty archives and reorganized the material on occupations into categories representing levels of "social-economic status," and produced a set of comparable data for every tenth year from 1910 to 1940 [18].

Edwards had to find a way of classifying thousands of occupations into a few niches of equal "social-economic status." He did not use a single definition of status; he lumped together factors such as the nature of the work, the skill and training involved in it, the income it brought, and common opinion about its prestige. He probably could have done little else, since his job was to reorganize existing historical data and not do original research; yet it is unfortunate that his rule-of-thumb classifications have been so widely adopted by research men as measures of occupational prestige.

Edwards started with the usual break between business class and working class, or white-collar and blue-collar workers (we shall use those terms interchangeably in later pages), and then subdivided each group into three parts. Then he made certain further divisions (especially, the separate classification of farmers) and the result was the now classic scheme:

> Professional persons
> Proprietors, managers, and officials:
> > Farmers (owners and tenants)
> > Wholesale and retail dealers
> > Other proprietors, managers, and officials
> Clerks and kindred workers
> Skilled workers and foremen
> Semiskilled workers
> Unskilled workers:
> > Farm laborers
> > Laborers, except farm
> > Servant classes

Edwards maintained that these categories were the most practical means for making a rough scale of occupations that would increase in prestige, education, and income as one ascended step by step. He had no way to validate his claim about prestige, but showed that with one or two exceptions, average figures for each group for education and income did follow a cumulative scale.

For the 1950 census the government has modified the Edwards scheme, primarily at the level of blue-collar workers, and given it the new name of "major occupation groups." A new category of "service workers" has been introduced, composed about one quarter of people formerly classified as "semiskilled" and three quarters of people formerly classified as "unskilled." As is the usual practice, the Bureau of the Census gives us a retabulation of 1940 data according to the new scheme so that we can study changes in the last decade, but since they do not give us a tabulation of 1950 data according to the old scheme, it is difficult to understand the latest findings in the light of the entire history of our century. However, some rough estimates can be made that will serve as adequate approximations [19].

Using the new scheme, we can study the degree to which occupational groups currently form a scale on the easily measurable traits of education and income. The data for men are given in Table 1. If we exclude farmers, the urban occupations do form a rough scale on both traits. It would be a better scale if salesmen were listed ahead of clerks, and private household workers put below service workers. But even then some inconsistencies would still be present. Salesmen average slightly more education, though less income, than proprietors and officials. On the other hand, craftsmen make more money with less education than either salesmen or clerks. And the new category of service workers has as much education as semiskilled workers (operatives), but much less income [20].

*Table 1.  Major Occupation Groups: Education and Income*
MEN, 1949 [21]

| MAJOR OCCUPATIONAL GROUP | MEDIAN YEARS OF SCHOOL | MEDIAN INCOME |
|---|---|---|
| Professional, technical, and kindred workers | 16.0 years | $3958 |
| Farmers & farm managers | 8.3 | 1455 |
| Managers, officials, & proprietors, except farm | 12.2 | 3944 |
| Clerical & kindred workers | 12.2 | 3010 |
| Sales workers | 12.3 | 3028 |
| Craftsmen, foremen, & kindred workers | 9.3 | 3125 |
| Operatives & kindred workers | 8.7 | 2607 |
| Private household workers | 8.1 | 1176 |
| Service workers, except private household | 8.7 | 2195 |
| Farm laborers & foremen | 7.1 | 863 |
| Laborers, except farm & mine | 8.0 | 1961 |
| ALL WORKERS | 9.5 years | $2668 |

The category of managers, proprietors, and officials is probably the least satisfactory one for stratification analysis. Obviously the farmers are very different from the urban businessmen, and we must always keep them separate. But the latter category is a hodgepodge, including everybody from pushcart peddlers to bank presidents. Most occupational classifications based directly on community observation rather than on official government statistics make an attempt to subdivide the business group according to the size and importance of the company, and according to the level in the executive hierarchy. Warner did exactly that in Jonesville, and in the Cambridge study described in the preceding chapter his classification proved to be a more direct correlate of the other stratification variables than was the scheme of the Bureau of the Census.

Although the Edwards scheme cannot be justified as a completely valid method of grouping occupations according to prestige, it is useful for its original purpose of making comparisons of different historical periods to study broad changes in the occupational system. Table 2 and Figure 1 show the alterations that have occurred since 1870.

As a result of a more complex technology, the demand for highly trained people has grown to the point that we now have almost three

*Table 2.   Social-Economic Distribution of the Labor Force*
MEN AND WOMEN: 1870, 1910, AND 1950 [22]

| | PER CENT OF THE LABOR FORCE | | |
|---|---|---|---|
| SOCIAL-ECONOMIC GROUP | *1870* | *1910* | *1950* |
| Professional persons | 3% | 4.4% | 8.5% |
| Proprietors, managers, & officials: | | | |
|     Farmers | 24 | 16.5 | 7.3 |
|     Others | 6 | 6.5 | 8.6 |
| Clerks, salespeople, & kindred | 4 | 10.2 | 18.9 |
| Skilled workers & foremen | 9 | 11.7 | 13.8 |
| Semiskilled workers | 10 | 14.7 | 21.7 |
| Unskilled workers: | | | |
|     Farm laborers | 29 | 14.5 | 4.3 |
|     Laborers, except farm | 9 | 14.7 | 8.3 |
|     Servant classes | 6 | 6.8 | 6.3 |
| Not reported | | | 2.3 |
| TOTAL | 100% | 100.0% | 100.0% |
| Number in labor force | 12,924,000 | 37,271,000 | 56,239,000 |
| Per cent of labor force, female | 15% | 21% | 30% |
| Total population | 39,818,000 | 91,972,000 | 150,697,000 |

times the proportion of people working at the professional level as we did in 1870. And we have a great new group who shuffle the papers that keep track of the goods produced by the machines and sell them to the public: clerical and sales workers have grown from 4 to almost 19 per cent of the work force. Since prestige is a scarce and competitive commodity, it is unlikely that these two groups of white-collar workers can claim as much prestige, relative to blue-collar workers, as their grandfathers did in 1870; there are too many of them.

The professional and clerical and sales groups have expanded much more than the urban proprietors, managers, and officials. The latter group has hardly expanded at all, although it has changed character. The table does not show it, but the managers and officials working for salaries have increased at the expense of the independent proprietors. Within the factory there has been a small increase in the proportion

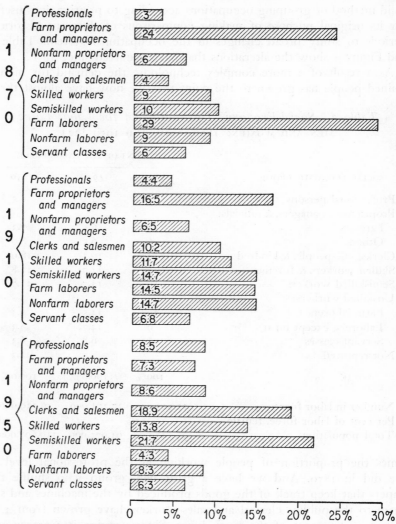

Figure 1. *Social-Economic Distribution of the Labor Force (Source: Table 2)*

of skilled workers and foremen, but a large expansion of the semi-skilled workers, or operatives, who run the machines designed and built by men with much more training than themselves. The essence of mass production is machine production that breaks each operation down to a simple task. And the more machinery, the less need there is for men of no skill to do heavy tasks of digging, hoisting, or moving; thus the unskilled workers declined as a group.

Naturally, these changes in the urban work force occurred at the same time that there was a vast movement from farm to city. In 1870 half the labor force had to work in the fields in order to feed themselves and the people in the cities. By 1950 enough food was produced by 12 per cent of the labor force to feed everybody and then fill the storage bins with so much excess that the government faced the constant worry of getting rid of it.

Furthermore, the labor force changed its age and sex composition. Child labor was abolished and adolescent labor greatly reduced as boys and girls stayed in school longer. Old people were able to retire at an earlier age. But these tendencies, which had the effect of decreasing the proportion of all men who were in the active labor force, were more than offset by the increasing percentage of women who worked. They made up 15 per cent of the labor force in 1870 and 30 per cent in 1950. They were heavily represented in the semiprofessional and clerical groups; therefore a comparison of men's jobs in 1870 and 1950 would not show quite so much shift in types of jobs as the alteration in the total labor force of men and women given in Table 2.*

All of these changes can be summarized in a sentence: The farmers moved to the city, and the city workers were upgraded from dirty work of low skill to cleaner work of higher skill, and the concomitant of both shifts was that fewer people worked for themselves and more worked for wages and salaries paid by big corporations. Each column of figures in Table 2 is a simple profile of the way of life of a certain stage of industrialization.

## PRESTIGE OF OCCUPATIONS

The historical figures of the census merely give a skeleton; they show how the various grades of occupations have expanded and contracted through time. They raise a question which they themselves cannot answer: Does the public think of occupations according to a single dimension of prestige? The public-opinion poll is the appropriate instrument for answering this question.

Before looking at the results of the polls, it is necessary to explore a theoretical issue: What is the source of occupational prestige? So far we have suggested two alternative processes: (1) Occupation is the basis of the income that gets transformed into consumption behavior or style of life, which in turn is the observable criterion that people use to rate each other; (2) occupation is the activity that Americans consider most important, and they confer prestige on men as a direct recogni-

* See Chapter IX.

tion of skill at work.* To the degree that the income from a job and its inherent prestige character are similar, it would be difficult to separate the two processes, but if we could find instances where the income from a job does not directly match its prestige character, then we could study the independent variation.

Unfortunately, the available data do not permit a neat solution to the problem. But some aspects of it can be understood. The key to the solution is the fact that in most instances the inherent prestige quality of a job and the income it brings *are* closely matched, and even more important, the American value system insists that they *should* be. The philosophy of the justice of competition which underlies our faith in free enterprise is so important that we assume the two factors will be closely matched, and when they are not, we tend to shut our eyes to the divergence. Another fact that should be remembered is that prestige and activity are intimately linked, and insofar as people participate in several activity spheres, their prestige may vary somewhat as they change from one role to another. The degree of similarity of prestige among the different roles of the same person is a measure of cultural integration, and the money nexus of our society tends to produce such integration, though it is far from perfect.

Generally speaking, most Americans believe that income is a fair measure of occupational success—both of the importance of the occupation to the society and of a man's individual skill at the job (prestige and esteem). *They are more likely to assume this, the less they know about the work under discussion.* As the Lynds indicated, when the occupational system grows, differentiates, and becomes complex, direct knowledge about the other fellow's work becomes difficult. It is convenient to substitute income as an index and to assume that it measures accurately the prestige and esteem qualities of the actual work. Two neighboring farmers can use subtle standards for evaluating each other, including accidental differences in the quality of their land, the help obtained from able sons, and so on. They know enough to recognize that income is not always an accurate measure of skill as a farmer. But when judging doctors in town, they do not have the requisite knowledge, so are apt to assume that the one who lives in the biggest house and drives the biggest car is the best doctor.

The same perceptual simplification operates when we center our attention on consumption activities. People who know each other directly use all sorts of subtle clues to evaluate each other: skill at conversation, interest in similar recreational spheres, success at disciplining children, and so on. A man may enjoy as friends and equals people

---

* Theorists such as Weber, Veblen, and Warner stress the first alternative; those such as Parsons and Davis stress the second.

whose incomes diverge from his so long as their tastes are not too dissimilar. But if he goes to a new town and seeks new friends, he is likely to assume that *on the average* people whose incomes are roughly similar to his are the ones who are most likely to have the same tastes. And if he is evaluating all the people in his town (familiar with them or not) from one end of the prestige scale to the other, the expenditure of income is most likely to be his index of the quality of their style of life, and by extension, of their quality as people.

Insofar as both the facts of life (again, on the average) and the dictates of our value system indicate that income is a reasonably accurate reflection of skill at work, and that style of life is the observable symbol of income, all of these factors become intermingled in our thinking. Quality as a person is therefore judged by occupation, by income, and by style of life. Difficulty arises when they are not evenly matched, and that occurs oftenest because of inherited income. We feel uncomfortable in the presence of second-generation wealth; we envy the gracious way of life that it often brings, but feel that a man should not take advantage of it to the point of not working. He either should continue to expand the family business (as did the sons of the original X brothers in Middletown), or should find some way of spending his time and money for the benefit of the community, for example as a research scholar or a philanthropist. But if he simply enjoys his wealth, we sneer at him as belonging to the idle rich. We energetically ignore the logical contradiction in the belief that it is wrong to enjoy the wealth for which we worked in the first place; we are still Puritans at heart. We encourage an individual to work for his own gain not merely because he has a right to the fruits of his labor, but also because this motivation energizes the whole system and brings benefits to all the people. If a man has gathered sufficient fruit to want to sit back and enjoy it, we tell him to keep working anyway. If everybody does not continue to run toward ever-expanding goals, we fear that the whole system will slow down and petrify. Therefore, we glory in the wonderful legend of "shirtsleeves to shirtsleeves in three generations"—it stimulates us to work for the benefit of our children, but warns us that our grandchildren might get "soft" and dissipate the family fortune.

Because we vaguely recognize that income is used merely as an index of occupational importance and success, we are able occasionally to bestow prestige on an occupation out of proportion to its income. In the empirical studies that will be discussed below it will be noticed that certain occupations either involving great skill or carrying great legitimate authority over the lives of many men are looked up to with high respect, in spite of their relatively low income. An example of the first would be nuclear physicist, of the second, justice of the Supreme Court of the United States. But let us turn to the data.

## THE NORC STUDY

There have been many small-scale studies of occupational prestige going back some thirty years, but they were mostly based on the opinions of those favorite subjects for research, college students [23]. They are interesting, and show remarkable stability of ratings at different periods of time. However, there is one recent study which dwarfs all the rest, that done by the National Opinion Research Center (NORC), under the stimulus of Professor Cecil C. North and the late Professor Paul K. Hatt, then of Ohio State University. This study was based on the opinions of 2920 persons in March, 1947, a representative sample of the entire adult population of the United States. Here we move out of the local community and look at a study that covers the nation. Urban anonymity may prevent a respondent from rating his neighbors, but he can rank an abstract occupation.

The interviewing procedure was straightforward; the respondent was handed a card printed as follows:

---

For each job mentioned, please pick out the statement that best gives *your own personal opinion* of the *general standing* that such a job has.
  1. *Excellent* standing
  2. *Good* standing
  3. *Average* standing
  4. *Somewhat below average* standing
  5. *Poor* standing
  X. I don't know where to place that one.

---

Then a list of 90 occupations was read off, and the respondent was asked to give his opinion about each one. The technique seemed to bring forth real and stable opinions, somewhat better than is usual for polling operations of this type. Only seven occupations (the esoteric scientific ones, like "nuclear physicist") brought as many as 10 per cent "don't know" answers. And for a check, in two instances two different titles were given to the same occupation, and the answers were almost identical ("public schoolteacher" and "instructor in the public schools"; "garage mechanic" and "automobile repairman").

The ratings were manipulated so as to arrange the occupations in a rank order of "general standing" or prestige [24]. Table 3 illustrates the findings with a sample of representative occupations.

*Table 3.  National Opinion on Prestige of Occupations* [25]

| OCCUPATION | RANK |
|---|---|
| U.S. Supreme Court justice | 1 |
| Physician | 2 |
| Mayor of a large city | 6 |
| College professor | 7 |
| Banker | 10 |
| Minister | 12 |
| Lawyer | 15 |
| Member of board of directors, large corporation | 15 |
| Nuclear physicist | 15 |
| Civil engineer | 23 |
| Owner of factory, 100 employees | 26 |
| Accountant for a large business | 28 |
| Musician in symphony orchestra | 28 |
| Building contractor | 33 |
| Public schoolteacher | 36 |
| Railroad engineer | 37 |
| Farm owner & operator | 39 |
| Official of an international labor union | 40 |
| Newspaper columnist | 42 |
| Electrician | 44 |
| Bookkeeper | 50 |
| Policeman | 54 |
| Carpenter | 58 |
| Automobile repairman | 59 |
| Owner-operator of a lunch stand | 61 |
| Machine operator in a factory | 64 |
| Barber | 66 |
| Clerk in a store | 67 |
| Truck driver | 70 |
| Singer in a night club | 74 |
| Farm hand | 76 |
| Restaurant waiter | 79 |
| Dock worker | 81 |
| Night watchman | 81 |
| Janitor | 85 |
| Shoe shiner | 90 |

The results clearly showed that the public did have a prestige scale in mind and could place various occupations on that scale with considerable consensus. Although respondents often did not agree on whether to call an occupation "good" or "average," the gradation of response from "excellent" through "poor" showed that they did have an understanding of the *relative* position of each occupation despite the particular label they may have put on it. And this agreement held for different groups: men and women, young and old, people with both high and low occupations, people from the East and those from the West. Seldom did people in these various groups disagree on the rank of a given occupation by more than five places in the rank order of ninety occupations. What consistent differences there were can be summed up in two principles: (1) people agreed with each other more concerning occupations that they knew more about, and (2) people tended to raise in rank their own and closely related occupations. Thus uneducated people did not know how to place "nuclear physicist," and people in metropolitan centers rated "sophisticated" occupations with more consensus and with higher scores than did people living on farms.

Hatt explored the data somewhat further to measure the degree of consistency which existed among the respondents [26]. He applied a rigorous criterion, that of "scalability" in the sense worked out by Louis Guttman. A crude idea of the meaning of the criterion is given by this illustration: Noting that garbage collector, street sweeper, and shoe shiner are ranked 88, 89, and 90, respectively, one still might ask what proportion of the respondents put them in that order. It might well be that although most people put those occupations at or near the bottom, they did not all place them in exactly the same order. The Guttman technique provides a measurement of consistency in rank ordering.

Hatt found that for the list of ninety occupations as a whole the consistency in rank ordering was not very high, in spite of general agreement about the approximate place held by each occupation. He then divided the occupations into groups that seemed to be related, on the assumption that people would be more consistent when dealing with occupations within a single group. For example, it would be reasonable to expect more consistency in the relative ranking of private, corporal, sergeant, and lieutenant than in that of corporal, bookkeeper, farm tenant, and sociologist. Hatt discovered eight groups, or "situses," which showed reasonable consistency within themselves:

| | |
|---|---|
| Political | Agriculture |
| Professional | Manual work |
| Business | Military |
| Recreation and aesthetics | Service |

Furthermore, when he subdivided the situses into "families" of occupations, the consistency of judgments went up even more. For example, he got good results for the following families within the business situs:

big business, small business, labor organization, lower white-collar employees [27].

Immediately after rating the occupations, each respondent in the NORC study was asked this question: "When you say that certain jobs have 'excellent standing,' what do you think is the one main thing about such jobs that gives this standing?" The answers were [28]:

| | |
|---|---|
| The jobs pay so well | 18% |
| The service to humanity; they are essential jobs | 16 |
| Preparation requires much education, hard work, money | 14 |
| The jobs carry great social prestige | 14 |
| They require high moral standards, honesty, responsibility | 9 |
| The jobs require intelligence, ability | 9 |
| All other answers | 20 |
| | 100% |

These answers confirm our analysis of the Lynds' material on Middletown: in our industrial culture, skill (ability plus education and training), authority, income, and prestige are a single meaningful complex. People who used different criteria ranked occupations in the same way. There is no point in wasting a lot of ingenuity trying to figure out which is most important: *the significant fact is that the public sees them as fitting together.*


INTERNATIONAL COMPARISONS

It was stressed above that occupation is a good index to use because its meaning transcends local communities. The consensus throughout the country found by the NORC confirms that statement. But the intriguing question arises that perhaps the meaning of occupation transcends national boundaries as well. It appears to be a good premise that because industrial production is relatively similar in its demands wherever it may develop, it may shape the occupational system and the prestige values concerning occupation into a single, world-wide pattern.

Recent data confirm that hypothesis. Alex Inkeles and Peter H. Rossi compared prestige studies of the NORC type that were conducted in the United States, Great Britain, the Soviet Union, Japan, New Zealand, and Germany. They found the same occupations on many of the lists used, ranging from seven comparable occupations in Britain and Russia, to thirty in Britain and New Zealand. They intercorrelated the findings as shown in Table 4. The agreement ranged from a correlation of .74 between the opinions expressed in Russia and Japan, to a startling .97 between New Zealand and either the United States or Great Britain. Careful inspection indicated that the divergent occupations were the ones that were most tied to national cultures and least involved in industrial life. The authors concluded that the material [29]:

. . . reveals an extremely high level of agreement, going far beyond chance expectancy, as to the relative prestige of a wide range of specific occupations, despite the variety of sociocultural settings in which they are found. This strongly suggests that there is a relatively invariable hierarchy of prestige associated with the industrial system, even when it is placed in the context of larger social systems which are otherwise differentiated in important respects.

*Table 4. Correlations between Occupational Prestige Scores in Six Countries* [30]

|  | U.S.S.R. | JAPAN | GREAT BRITAIN | NEW ZEALAND | U.S. | GERMANY |
|---|---|---|---|---|---|---|
| U.S.S.R. |  | .74 | .83 | .83 | .90 | .90 |
| Japan |  |  | .92 | .91 | .93 | .93 |
| Great Britain |  |  |  | .97 | .94 | .97 |
| New Zealand |  |  |  |  | .97 | .96 |
| United States |  |  |  |  |  | .96 |
| AVER. CORRELATION | .84 | .89 | .93 | .93 | .94 | .94 |

OCCUPATIONAL GROUPS

Thus far in analyzing these survey results, we have been exploring the consensus that exists among the public concerning the relative prestige ranking of different occupations. But there remains the problem of grouping: Does the public separate these occupations into distinct types or classes that do not overlap, or do they see a single, uncut continuum? The problem, obviously, is similar to the question of the last chapter concerning the grouping of families into specific prestige classes. The technique used by the NORC automatically produced a continuum of arithmetic scores which could be converted into a rank order, and gave no statistical information about groupings. But inspection of the ranks suggests that the public had in mind certain broad occupational categories when they rated specific titles. Table 3 has been printed in a manner which indicates these categories.

The top occupations are professional and administrative: persons whose decisions influence many men either because they have specialized technical knowledge of a high order or because they wield administrative authority in business or government. All the occupations listed in the first twenty-three ranks fit this description, from Supreme Court justice to civil engineer. Incidentally, government, professional, and business occupations are intermingled—Americans may not worship the businessman with such purity of heart as some writers have assumed.

The next group includes semiprofessional and medium-level administrative positions. They are held by people who have a great deal of special training, sometimes postgraduate, but are not full-fledged professionals; those who are in the next-to-the-top grade of men who run big organizations; and those who own or run medium-sized organizations. The line between these top two classifications is obviously not clean-cut, and only educated people who are familiar with large organizations are likely to draw it with consistency.

Starting with railroad engineer (rank 37), we get a number of occupations that all fall under one of these general rubrics: highly skilled manual workers; owners of small businesses (five or ten employees), and higher level white-collar employees (but not those with great administrative responsibility), like bookkeepers.

Moving further down from the occupations that began with owner-operator of a lunch stand (rank 61), we get a series that includes semiskilled manual workers, owner-operators of petty businesses (one or two employees), and the routine white-collar workers.

The lowest group is that of unskilled laborers, starting with restaurant waiter (rank 79), and descending to the unfortunate man on the bottom, the shoe shiner.

These cutting points are, of course, arbitrary. But they do show a patterning which allows us to compare highly disparate occupations and think of them as approximately equal in prestige, such as newspaper columnist, electrician, and bookkeeper. It is important to notice that the public thinks in terms of *degrees* of professional or technical skill, and *degrees* of administrative responsibility. They do not put all owners above all workers, and they certainly do not put all white-collar above all blue-collar workers. Arbitrary as the cutting points may be that have been suggested here, they seem to correspond to public opinion more closely than the divisions in the Edwards classification (though in the aforementioned Cambridge research they were less efficient than either the Warner or Edwards classifications). For instance, if we arrange occupations according to the census scheme, we get these unhappy results: professional and semiprofessional workers range in rank from physician (rank 2) through singer in a night club (rank 74); proprietors range from banker (rank 10) through owner-operator of a lunch stand (rank 61).

There are two studies which give us additional information on the way the public categorizes occupations. The first is a research done at Harvard in 1952 by John D. Campbell in a fashion that follows Hollingshead. He took seventy of the best known occupations from the

NORC list, wrote the name of each one on a card, and asked some 250 men in Boston to perform the following task [31]:

Here are some cards I'd like you to sort into groups for me. Almost everybody who does this generally likes it. Each card describes a man by his job alone. What I'd like you to do is to sort these into the smallest number of groups of men who seem to be pretty much alike—are interested in about the same things, lead about the same kind of life.

After the respondent had sorted the cards into *groups*, Campbell then asked him to arrange the groups into *levels* according to which ones were higher than others. He permitted the respondent to put two or more groups at the same level.

Campbell first ordered the occupations into a rank order by assigning them scores according to the level in which the respondents placed them. The rank order was almost the same as that found by the NORC. He then studied differences in ranking by respondents of different types. He divided his samples into subgroups according to age, occupation, and degree of satisfaction with present way of life, of expectation for the future, and of aspiration for the future. He found these small but consistent differences:

1. People agreed more about occupations at the extremes of the rank order than about those in the middle.

2. People tended to raise in standing occupations close to their own.

3. People tended to enlarge their own level.

4. People of higher rank showed more consensus than people of lower rank.

5. People of low rank gave higher ratings to government positions.

Campbell did not find that people with different scores on his (Guttman) scales of satisfaction, expectation, and aspiration gave consistently different ratings to various occupations.

The average number of groups used by the respondents was 6.9 (standard deviation, 3.1). These groups were placed into an average of 5.4 levels (standard deviation, 2). *These standard deviations are high and show lack of consensus.* The level of the respondent's own occupation did not affect his judgment about the number of groups or levels to use. But it did make a difference in the relative size of his groups, for most respondents put more occupations in their own than in other levels. Indeed, they averaged 20.7 occupations in their own level as against an average of 13 occupations for all levels. Furthermore, when they put more than one group of occupations in a level, that level was most likely to be their own.

In general, the upper levels tended to be more subdivided into groups —probably reflecting the greater technical variation in the content of those occupations. And respondents from the upper levels tended to use more groups at their own level but put fewer occupations in each group than did respondents from lower levels.

When asked to put labels on the groups they had chosen, respondents used the following terms or their close synonyms (some people used more than one type of label, thus the percentages add up to more than one hundred):

| | |
|---|---|
| Professional | 50% of respondents |
| Laboring | 33 |
| Working | 25 |
| Business | 22 |
| Middle-class | 11 |
| White-collar | 8 |
| Lower-class | 4 |
| Upper-class | 3 |

Campbell also asked his respondents (via an open-ended question) to tell him what criteria they used in putting a number of occupations into the same group or level. His answers show a different distribution from those of the NORC, reported above, indicating that small differences in the wording and context of a question used on a survey—to say nothing of the coding procedures used to add up the answers—can produce large variations in the results:

| | |
|---|---|
| Skill, education, specialization | 72% of respondents |
| Occupational duties | 35 |
| Wages & income | 30 |
| Prestige | 26 |
| Intelligence, talent | 20 |
| Contribution to society | 18 |
| Common interests, style of life | 17 |
| Responsibility & leadership | 8 |
| Ownership vs. nonownership | 6 |
| Miscellaneous | 24 |

Before interpreting Campbell's results, let us look at those obtained by Professor Richard Centers. The small tidbit from his work which is presented here is but an hors d'oeuvre; we shall present his material in fuller detail in Chapter VI.

As part of an elaborate study of class consciousness, Centers used the facilities of the National Opinion Research Center to ask a representative national sample of adults to identify themselves with one of these categories: "upper class," "middle class," "working class," and "lower class." Then he asked them to place a number of occupations from a list that was handed them into one of the four classes. Here his procedure differed radically from that of Campbell, for Centers told his respondents in advance the number of levels to use and provided the labels for them. His results are shown in Table 5. They indicate that the public can, when forced by the interviewer, conceive of an upper class, and when they do so they think primarily of big-business owners and executives, and secondarily of doctors, lawyers, and bankers. They think of a middle class consisting of small businessmen and semiprofessionals,

Table 5. *Class Assignations of Various Occupations* [32]

| OCCUPATIONAL CATEGORY | ASSIGNATION (PER CENT) | | | | | |
|---|---|---|---|---|---|---|
| | Upper Class | Middle Class | Working Class | Lower Class | Not Stated | Total |
| Big-business owners and executives | 82 | 11 | 3 | — | 4 | 100 |
| Doctors and lawyers | 57 | 33 | 7 | — | 3 | 100 |
| Bankers | 49 | 38 | 9 | — | 4 | 100 |
| College professors | 38 | 48 | 9 | 1 | 4 | 100 |
| Department-store and factory managers | 17 | 59 | 20 | 1 | 3 | 100 |
| Schoolteachers | 13 | 53 | 31 | 1 | 2 | 100 |
| Insurance and real-estate salesmen | 6 | 59 | 29 | 2 | 4 | 100 |
| Farm owners | 9 | 53 | 34 | 1 | 3 | 100 |
| Small-business owners and managers | 4 | 65 | 26 | 3 | 2 | 100 |
| Foremen | 3 | 41 | 51 | 2 | 3 | 100 |
| Office workers | 2 | 40 | 54 | 2 | 2 | 100 |
| Barbers | 2 | 27 | 64 | 4 | 3 | 100 |
| Salesclerks | 1 | 29 | 63 | 5 | 2 | 100 |
| Carpenters | 2 | 20 | 74 | 2 | 2 | 100 |
| Tenant farmers | 1 | 19 | 62 | 14 | 4 | 100 |
| Semiskilled factory workers | 1 | 15 | 69 | 12 | 3 | 100 |
| Truck drivers | 1 | 9 | 79 | 9 | 2 | 100 |
| Waiters | 1 | 6 | 76 | 15 | 2 | 100 |
| Coal miners | 1 | 8 | 73 | 16 | 2 | 100 |
| Farm hands | 1 | 6 | 68 | 23 | 2 | 100 |
| Sharecroppers | — | 11 | 47 | 37 | 5 | 100 |
| Janitors | — | 5 | 59 | 34 | 2 | 100 |
| Servants | — | 5 | 55 | 38 | 2 | 100 |
| Unskilled workers | 1 | 3 | 49 | 45 | 2 | 100 |

| | UPPER CLASS | MIDDLE CLASS | WORKING CLASS | LOWER CLASS |
|---|---|---|---|---|
| Big businessmen | 82% | 11% | 3% | |
| Doctors and lawyers | 57% | 33% | 7% | |
| Schoolteachers | 13% | 53% | 31% | 1% |
| Small businessmen | 4% | 65% | 26% | 3% |
| Foremen | 3% | 41% | 51% | 2% |
| Office workers | 2% | 40% | 54% | 2% |
| Salesclerks | 1% | 29% | 63% | 5% |
| Carpenters | 2% | 20% | 74% | 2% |
| Factory workers | 1% | 15% | 69% | 12% |
| Janitors | 0 | 5% | 59% | 34% |

*Figure 2. The Public Classifies Occupations (Source: Table 5)*

and a working class ranging from foremen and office workers down through unskilled laborers. But these classes are somewhat amorphous, for some occupations are voted into two classes with almost equal frequency (college professors, foremen, office workers, unskilled laborers).

Centers then reworked his data to find if there were any systematic differences in grouping of occupations between people who put themselves in different social classes. By now the reader can predict the answer: people enlarged their own level by including more occupations in it. The office workers provide an example. About 63 per cent of the working-class informants claimed them as workers, whereas almost 55 per cent of the middle class included them as members of their category.

Furthermore, the majority of middle-class persons put unskilled laborers and sharecroppers into the lower class, but the majority of the working class claimed them as colleagues. Both middle and working classes agreed on their definition of the upper class [33].

## THE PERCEPTION OF RANK AND STRATA

We now must come back to the general theory of the way people form categories of equivalent positions on a prestige scale—the problem of strata versus continuum. The psychological processes are similar, whether persons or occupations are being considered. It is difficult to construct a neat theory, because the variations in judgment among respondents are partly due to the stimulus and partly to the perceivers. The psychologists tell us that a clear and sharp stimulus is perceived in practically the same way by all normal viewers: for example, a photograph of President Eisenhower. But a completely ambiguous stimulus is perceived according to the psychic needs and processes of the viewer, who shapes the stimulus as he wishes. Thus, an ink blot looks like Eisenhower to some, like a crab to others, and like an automobile to still others. A partly structured stimulus allows the viewer to project his wishes into it to a limited degree: a drawing labeled "President of the United States" but with indistinct features might be called Eisenhower by Republicans and Roosevelt by Democrats.

When a sociologist presents a subject with either a list of the families who are his neighbors in a small town or a list of occupations, and requests that the subject arrange them in categories of equivalent prestige, he is presenting a stimulus that is partly structured and partly ambiguous. Out of his total life experience, the subject has run into a number of situations that indicate prestige differences, but these situations have not been so clear and so consistent that they completely determine his perceptions. The very nature of our society is such that the worker in overalls dons a blue serge suit when he goes to church on Sunday. As he changes from one social role to another, his behavior changes somewhat—but not completely, for if he meets his boss on Sunday he is deferential toward him, even if they both are wearing the same kind of suit. Consequently, the respondent in the survey will have a general idea of a prestige hierarchy, but not a perfectly sharp one with fixed labels for each level, plus standard status symbols to indicate who belonged where. The degree of existing ambiguity allows him to project some of his own personality into the data and shape them slightly to his own desires and values. Therefore, people at different levels give different answers for *two* reasons: their outer experience has been different, and their inner values are different. Stimulus *and* perceiver vary from one respondent to another.

There is no such thing as the objective status structure which can be viewed by the completely neutral observer; prestige is an attitude about relationships between persons, and varies according to the perspective from which persons are viewed. The neutral observer has to find a way of summarizing the agreements and disagreements, but should not fool himself that he is somehow arriving at a reality that is more "real" than the subjective perceptions (and the behavior they determine) of his respondents.

From the many studies we have reviewed three conclusions stand out and are confirmed by every one of them: (1) in American society today there is a prestige hierarchy of both persons and occupations; (2) this hierarchy is not sharply divided in the minds of the citizens into discrete levels or strata; (3) there is more agreement about ranking than about the criteria used in making ranking decisions.

The consensus about the ranking of persons or occupations is not complete, and it does not produce the absolute consistency of relative judgments that would fit the model of a cumulative scale of the Guttman type, but it is marked enough to show without further qualification that Americans are not all equal in the eyes of their fellows, and that they generally agree concerning the nature of the inequality. And the degree of consensus allows us to arrange a rank order firm enough to permit further operations to seek the variables that correlate with it, and to begin to study the causes of that covariation. We then find that the covariation between occupational prestige and personal prestige (at least for small cities) is higher than for most pairs of variables that sociologists are interested in. Either occupational prestige largely causes personal prestige, or else they both flow from the same underlying causes.

The stimulus situation is clear enough to limit to a slight degree the range of idiosyncratic distortions of perception by different persons when they are asked to make a rank order. But that is not the case when they are requested to cut the rank order of persons or occupations into discrete levels. That stimulus situation is vague; personal factors in the experience and values of the respondent shape his perceptions decidedly. It may well be that a small number of categories (seven or less?) are natural to the human mind, so that persons rating types of character, quality of apples, or social classes will always end up with this small number if left to their own choosing. Surely it is easier to think in terms of a small number of groups than of a continuum with a vast number of points; it is easier to classify our friends into short ones, medium ones, and tall ones than to remember their height in feet and inches.

There are some tentative principles that seem to explain some of the differences in perceptions of both ranking and grouping, and these appear in a number of the different studies, though all the data are not completely consistent. These principles should be studied carefully and systematically through experimental design; here is a fine field for a half-dozen Ph.D. theses. The principles can be summarized as follows; they interact with and sometimes offset the effects of one another:

1. People perceive a rank order.

2. People tend to enhance their own position:
   a. By raising their own position relative to others.
   b. By varying the size of their own group. Here the evidence is not consistent: apparently there is a tendency to narrow the group when thinking of individual persons about whom invidious distinctions can be made (especially those lower on the scale), and enlarge it when thinking of general categories of persons who are closely similar to each other.
   c. By perceiving separate but equal groups, thus accepting difference but denying hierarchy.

3. People agree more about the extremes than about the middle of the prestige range. This is probably a result both of clarity of stimulus and of aspects of perceptual organization. There are more people in the middle, and they are less publicized. Also errors at the extremes can go in only one direction.

4. People agree more about the top of the range than the bottom, and make more distinctions about the top than about the bottom. This probably reflects stimulus reality, for those at the top are more conspicuous and also more differentiated.

5. People lump together into larger groups those who are furthest from them.

6. The better persons and occupations are known, the more agreement concerning them.

7. People have more consensus about the relative rank of persons or occupations that are closely related to each other in some functional way.

8. People at the top are more articulate regarding prestige differences, are more consistent with one another, and make more divisions into groups than those on the bottom.

CONCLUSIONS

In the previous chapter it was said that personal prestige in small cities seems to be determined primarily by consumption behavior. In this chapter it has been emphasized that occupation is at the root of prestige. The quotation given above from the Lynds supplies the link: "A leading citizen said . . . in discussing the almost universal local custom of 'placing' newcomers in terms of where they live, how they live, the kind of car they drive, and similar externals: 'It's perfectly natural. You see, they know money, and they don't know you.' "

Summing up the data in an abstract way, we can arrive at this synthesis: In small groups the prestige of an individual is determined by his behavior in living up to the common standards of the group. The activity that is most important to Americans is occupation. A man is successful and earns honor from his fellows to the extent that he does a good job at work (esteem) and that his work is significant (prestige). The significance of work is best measured by those who understand it: a man's colleagues on the job. They use such criteria as the skill the job demands, the talent and training necessary to produce the skill, the responsibility and authority over other men that the job entails, the pay it brings, and the nature of the product. The pay has a double function: it is granted as recognition of skill, responsibility, and authority, but it soon becomes an index of them and assumes symbolic value in its own right. The product is judged in terms of the general values of the community: it is more important to save life than to beautify it; thus the man behind the prescription counter in the drugstore has higher prestige than the man behind the cosmetics counter. Similarly, administrative positions of high influence over the entire society are viewed with high respect.

In a small community it is quite likely that some of these occupational positions will grant universal prestige that spreads to all spheres of life. The doctor and the factory owner become the leading citizens and may run the church and the town hall. People generalize from their one role and assume that they are worthy men in all roles. It is thought just and proper that those who occupy the most significant occupational niches become the richest and most powerful men in town.

But this direct judgment of occupational qualifications becomes more difficult as the division of labor becomes more complicated. People do not know much about the activities in spheres beyond their own immediate bailiwick. They seize upon money income as the common denominator of occupational success, and begin to judge a man by it [34]. The assumption becomes a part of the culture that a rich man is rich because he occupies an important position. But of course money has another aspect: it is not only a symbol; it buys things. A man's style of life becomes largely a function of his income. And people of similar style of life tend to become an organized community of people who interact with each other more comfortably than with outsiders. If you own a yacht, you cannot have much fun with a townsman who owns a rowboat. Eventually the common style of life and common interaction produce common values or ways of looking at the world.

People therefore judge a man more by his occupational competence if he is in an occupation they know something about, and more by his income and his style of life if he is in one that is strange to them. Furthermore, if you go to a respondent in the evening and ask about the neighbors, he will immediately think of style of life, for that is what he knows and sees, but if you go to him during the daytime at his job and ask about the men around him, he will immediately think of technical competence and authority. Warner did the former, and North and Hatt (in effect) the latter—ergo, Warner came up with a consumption-prestige rank, North and Hatt an occupational-prestige rank. But inasmuch as occupational income and the values associated with occupation (mostly through the medium of common education) largely determine consumption style, the two rank orders are similar, and that is what the Lynds emphasize.*

Indeed, the similarity of the two is the key to vitality in our materialistic and competitive culture. As long as our people believe that occupational success determines income, and that the competition for occupational success follows fair rules of the game, they will continue to work hard and, if necessary, fight hard. But if the two diverge too far, then disbelief and disillusionment will follow. During the great depression, exactly that occurred. Men who wanted to work could not find work. Men of property who did not have to work lived in luxury while others starved. Radical measures were taken, and revolution was avoided.

The sources of strain lie in the rules of property and the institution of the family. Sometimes a man can amass a fortune by manipulations in the exchange market that his fellow citizens do not regard as representing significant contributions to the general welfare. In such a case his claims to prestige in the consumption sphere are challenged by the public, and his situation becomes ambiguous. John D. Rockefeller and Samuel Insull are examples. Both tried to legitimize their position by huge gifts to public causes, such as charity, a university, or the opera.

Even more important is the effect of the family. Men like the original

* Occupational indexes correlate more highly with prestige and its concomitants than do money indexes. This is probably due to the fact that occupation is a measure of both education and income.

X brothers in Middletown build up a great industry and are admired and respected for it. Their sons inherit that industry, and may do nothing but live off the profits. Given our values, such a life is wasted and degenerate. In time people suspect that the sons have no right to all that money. Such a group is resented, and can maintain public respect only if the sons either expand and develop the industry (or become occupationally useful in another sphere), or if they devote their lives to the beneficial use of their money for public good (like John D. Rockefeller, Jr.). Often the wives in public charitable activities attempt to spend a little money while their husbands earn some more.

Perhaps the main reason why our free-enterprise society has maintained much of its vitality is that it was founded at just the right time and in just the right place. We started with no landed aristocracy; the continual opening of Western lands prevented its emergence except in the old South. As we industrialized, a triumphant technology and a growing population created an important new industry every few years. The owners of the old ones never became fully entrenched. Indeed, as the sons of so many families who were founded by New England shippers and merchants discovered, if they did not continually reinvest their money in new industries, their fortunes would evaporate. This constant movement west, this constant evolution of basic industry, this constant growth in size—these have made it difficult for the founders of fortunes to pass them on intact for several generations and thereby create an aristocracy that ruled but did not work. Now we have a new type of leader emerging to challenge the owner: the corporation manager. The relations between them will occupy our attention in many of the pages that follow.

### REFERENCES

[1] Pitirim Sorokin, *Social Mobility* (New York: Harper, 1927), p. 101.

[2] Robert S. Lynd and Helen Merrell Lynd, *Middletown* (New York: Harcourt, Brace, 1929), and *Middletown in Transition* (New York: Harcourt, Brace, 1937).

[3] Lynd, *Middletown*, pp. 21-24.

[4] *Ibid.*, pp. 31-32, 73-74.

[5] *Ibid.*, p. 45.

[6] *Ibid.*, pp. 80-81.

[7] Lynd, *Middletown in Transition*, p. xvii.

[8] *Ibid.*, p. 13.

[9] *Ibid.*, p. 68.

[10] *Ibid.*, pp. 458–60. The phrases "old" and "new" middle class were borrowed by the Lynds from Lewis Corey, *The Crisis of the Middle Class* (New York: Covici-Friede, 1935).

[11] Lynd, *Middletown in Transition*, pp. 460–61.

[12] *Ibid.*, p. 75.

[13] *Ibid.*

[14] *Ibid.*, pp. 75–76.

[15] *Ibid.*, p. 77.

[16] *Ibid.*, p. 96.

[17] *Ibid.*, pp. 421–22, 447.

[18] Alba M. Edwards, *U.S. Census of Population, 1940: Comparative Occupation Statistics, 1870–1940* (Washington: Government Printing Office, 1943). Two excellent texts analyzing this type of material are: John D. Durand, *The Labor Force in the United States, 1890–1960* (New York: Social Science Research Council, 1948). A. J. Jaffe and Charles D. Stewart, *Manpower Resources and Utilization: Principles of Working Force Analysis* (New York: Wiley, 1951).

[19] The reader who uses government statistics should watch carefully the changing definitions of the labor force and its components. "The labor force as now commonly defined in surveys utilizing the population approach includes persons 14 years old and over who had a job or were seeking one during a specified week. . . . Population censuses earlier than 1940 used instead a concept of 'gainful workers.' This differed from the labor force concept in that it included all persons 10 years old and over who reported a gainful occupation, regardless of whether or not they were working or seeking work at the time of the census, and excluded in general new job seekers without previous experience in a gainful occupation." U.S. Bureau of the Census, *Statistical Abstract of the United States: 1950* (Washington: Government Printing Office, 1950), p. 170. Many census tables report on the "Experienced Civilian Labor Force" (omitting the armed services and those seeking work without previous experience), or on "Gainfully Employed" (omitting those seeking work). For classification details, see U.S. Bureau of the Census, *1950 Census of Population: Classified Index of Occupations and Industries* (Washington: Government Printing Office, 1950).

[20] For a microscopic study of the way income and prestige become matched on the job, see George C. Homans, "Status among Clerical Workers," *Human Organization*, XII (Spring, 1953), 5–10. For a general discussion of the problems of scaling occupations, see Theodore Caplow, *The Sociology of Work* (Minneapolis: University of Minnesota Press, 1954), Chap. II. He tends to overemphasize discrepancies and underemphasize consensus, however. He finds "behavior control" or authority over subordinates and/or the public to be the best single dimension accounting

for prestige differences among occupations, and he gives useful material on intelligence distributions among occupations.

[21] Sources: Education: U.S. Bureau of the Census, *U.S. Census of Population, 1950*, Vol. IV, *Special Reports* (PE No. 5B), Part 5, Chap. B, Education (Washington: Government Printing Office, 1953), Table 11; the figures are based on a 3⅓ per cent sample of men twenty-five and over. Income: U.S. Bureau of the Census, *U.S. Census of Population, 1950*, Vol. II, *Characteristics of the Population*, Part I, U.S. Summary, Table 129, covering "Experienced Civilian Labor Force," based on 20 per cent sample.

[22] Sources: For 1870, rough estimate from Edwards, *Comparative Occupation Statistics*, p. 101, plus C. Wright Mills, *White Collar* (New York: Oxford University Press, 1951), pp. 63–65. For 1910, Edwards, *op. cit.*, p. 187. For 1950, *U.S. Census of Population, 1950*, Vol. II, Part I, Table 53, with "service" occupations allocated half to "servant classes," one fourth to "semiskilled," and one fourth to "laborers." This latter distribution covers the "Experienced Civilian Labor Force."

[23] For a review, see A. F. Davies, "Prestige of Occupations," *British Journal of Sociology*, III (June, 1952), 134–47.

[24] National Opinion Research Center, "Jobs and Occupations: A Popular Evaluation," *Opinion News*, IX (September 1, 1947), 3–13. Reprinted in *Class, Status and Power*, Reinhard Bendix and Seymour M. Lipset, eds. (Glencoe, Ill.: The Free Press, 1953).

[25] *Ibid.*, pp. 412–14.

[26] Paul K. Hatt, "Occupation and Social Stratification," *American Journal of Sociology*, LV (May, 1950), 533–43.

[27] The occupations within a situs scaled with a "reproducibility" of about 80; those within a family, about 85 to 90.

Some people have wondered whether Hatt's situses indicate that the best model for a prestige hierarchy might be one of overlapping pyramids rather than a single pyramid. According to this model, the public could be expected to rank-order only those occupations (or persons) that fit together into a single functional pyramid. The evidence so far appears to me to indicate that such separation of pyramids is very slight, and does not compare in importance to the general agreement about over-all rank. It should be remembered that the Guttman criterion of scalability is very strict. Furthermore, equalities of income among different occupations, and the mutual interaction to which they lead, create a single rather than a multiple prestige structure (except, perhaps, for racial or ethnic groups who live apart from the rest of the community).

[28] NORC, "Jobs and Occupations," p. 418 of *Class, Status and Power*.

[29] Alex Inkeles and Peter H. Rossi, "National Comparisons of Occupational Prestige," *American Journal of Sociology*, LXI (January, 1956), 339.

[30] *Ibid.*, p. 332.

[31] John D. Campbell, *Subjective Aspects of Occupational Status* (unpublished Ph.D. thesis, Harvard University, 1952), p. 62.

[32] Richard Centers, "Social Class, Occupation, and Imputed Belief," *American Journal of Sociology*, LVIII (May, 1953), 546.

[33] Some useful comparative data (which show the same principles as the American material) can be found in Chapters II and III of D. V. Glass, ed., *Social Mobility in Britain* (London: Routledge and Kegan Paul, 1954).

[34] The classic account of this process is Thorstein Veblen, *The Theory of the Leisure Class* (New York: The Modern Library, 1934; first published in 1899).

# IV

# Income, Wealth, and Style of Life

DURING THE REIGN OF SOME OF THE PHARAOHS [OF EGYPT] AL-
MOST THE TOTAL SURPLUS OF THE PEOPLE WAS CONCENTRATED
IN THE ERECTING AND FURNISHING OF THE PYRAMID WHICH
WAS TO HONOR THE RULER UPON HIS DEATH. . . . THE CHEOPS
PYRAMID, TOGETHER WITH ITS FURNISHINGS, ABSORBED ALL THE
SURPLUS ENERGY [BEYOND SIMPLE SUBSISTENCE] PRODUCED
DURING THE LIFETIME OF ABOUT 3 MILLION PEOPLE. DURING
A 20-YEAR PERIOD 100,000 SLAVES ARE SAID TO HAVE WORKED
TO PRODUCE THE TOMB. THIS WAS ABOUT 1/25 OF THE TOTAL
POPULATION. *Fred Cottrell* [1]

WEALTH, LIKE SUFFRAGE, MUST BE CONSIDERABLY DISTRIBUTED
TO SUSTAIN A DEMOCRATIC REPUBLIC; AND HENCE, WHATEVER
DRAWS A CONSIDERABLE PROPORTION OF EITHER INTO A FEW
HANDS, WILL DESTROY IT. AS POWER FOLLOWS WEALTH, THE
MAJORITY MUST HAVE WEALTH OR LOSE POWER.
*John Taylor* [2]

THERE IS AN American adage, "Them as has, gits." It summarizes neatly
the connections between prestige rank and material possessions. High
prestige is based in part on an expensive style of life; to be looked up to,
one has to live well. But a high position in the prestige-consumption
hierarchy leads to opportunities to make more money. Such a position
provides a good education, it imbues a man with values that make him
work hard to earn more, it offers contacts with people of substance
who can be helpful as prospective employers, customers, or clients, it
supplies training in the manners that permit easy communication with
those people of substance, and it provides monetary capital and credit
for starting new businesses or professional practices. The relationships
between prestige and possessions are circular.

Possessions are of many kinds, depending on the definitions of a given
culture which indicate the things in the world that are important to

own and control [3]. Primitive tribes grant property rights in ritual songs and magical practices; the "ownership" of the family name of Rockefeller opens many doors in New York; possession of marvelous voices has brought fame and fortune to Marian Anderson, Yma Sumac, and Bing Crosby; the ownership of a farm under which oil is discovered is the most elegant way to get rich in Texas, but south of the border the owner of the farm does not possess the oil, for Mexicans consider minerals to be the property of all the people and they are controlled by the government.

One of the distinctive features of modern society is the fact that most forms of property can be transformed into money; we will therefore follow the standard procedure in economic thought and consider *money income* and *capital wealth*. We will make a further distinction between income and pattern of consumption or *style of life*, for the sociological variable of values intervenes between them. People with similar pay checks spend them for different things according to their personal values (and these depend in large measure upon the standards of the groups to which they belong).

An outstanding long-term trend has been the decreasing importance of personal wealth as the source of a man's income. In the capitalistic agricultural society of our early republic, the majority of the people owned productive property and earned most of their income from it— the tools of the artisan, the land of the farmer, the stock of the trades-man. The way to rise in the stratification ladder was the way eulogized by ideologists such as Franklin: start working for another man, save every possible penny, become one's own employer, and get rich. One made the grade by accumulating property and skill as he went along. But now more than 80 per cent of the people are employees; they own neither their land, their tools, nor their businesses.

It is still true that the way to make a great fortune is to be an en-trepreneur; but it is erroneous to maintain that the best way to earn a comfortable living is to start at the bottom in some trade, save a little money, and start one's own business. Most independent businesses are marginal affairs; corner grocery stores, tiny machine shops, lunch counters. Every year 10 per cent of existing business firms fail; most of these employ fewer than four people. Lipset and Bendix estimate that about a quarter of the urban work force have been in independent business at one time or another in their careers, and that over half have dreamed of so doing, although only about 5 per cent are proprietors at any given time [4]. These authors are no doubt correct in their state-ment that the dream of independent business is now mainly a working-class hope of escape from factory routine; but entrepreneurship is no longer the basis of middle-class life, so the dream is mostly an illusion.*

The basis of a comfortable income in our bureaucratized society is a specialized occupation based on a good education. The best advice for an ambitious young man who seeks a comfortable life but does not want to gamble on getting rich is to aim at a professional, technical, or managerial job. Education is more important for such a job than capital wealth. If one should demand a single oversimplified distinction underlying class differences in contemporary America to replace the outworn one of Marx, the answer would be this: the possession of a college degree.

First let us take a look at the facts concerning income: its distribution, the reasons why some people get more than others, and recent changes in distribution patterns. Then we will trace a few of the connections between income and wealth, and between wealth and power. Finally, we will turn to consumption and see how the various social classes spend their money.

INCOME DISTRIBUTION

One of the most useful recent discussions of income (and expenditure) was prepared by the editors of *Fortune* magazine and published as a series of articles and finally as a book called *The Changing American Market* [5]. They analyzed the 1953 cash income after taxes of *family units* (families living together, plus unrelated individuals), for the income of the family unit is usually pooled and spent for everybody's joint benefit. We will follow these writers, but will occasionally use some other figures as well, especially those of the 1950 census, as analyzed in detail by Herman P. Miller of the Bureau of the Census [6]. Incidentally, it is interesting to note that income was long considered too private a matter for census inquiry; only the censuses of 1940 and 1950 contained questions about it. In the latter year, a random sample of 20 per cent of all families were asked to report on their cash income received the prior year.

There were 51,200,000 family or consumption units in 1953, and their median cash income was just under $4000. The average size of the units was slightly more than three persons. The percentage distribution of families among the different income levels was as follows [7]:

* Independent farmers are still an important part of American life, despite the fact that they made up only 7 per cent of the total labor force in 1950 and are decreasing in percentage every year. It should also be noted that the proportion of farmers who are owners rather than tenants has been increasing in recent years.

| | |
|---|---|
| $10,000 and over | 4.4% of families |
| $7500–9999 | 5.6 |
| $5000–7499 | 15.4 |
| $4000–4999 | 19.5 |
| $3000–3999 | 17.4 |
| $2000–2999 | 14.8 |
| $1000–1999 | 13.3 |
| Under $1000 | 9.6 |
| TOTAL | 100.0% |

The top 10 per cent of families, those earning over $7500, received 30 per cent of the total cash that was distributed to all families. On the other hand, the families in the bottom 10 per cent who earned less than $1000 received only 1.1 per cent of the disposable income. With respect to the very top, about 1 per cent of the family units reported incomes over $15,000, and they took in about 8 per cent of the available cash [8].

The graduated Federal income tax somewhat lessened the inequality of income distribution, but not so much as might be supposed around April 15 when one hears so much discussion of high taxes. The average income in 1950 for the richest 20 per cent of families was reduced by Federal income taxes from $10,941 to $8880; for the top 5 per cent of families, the reduction was from $19,545 to $14,740 [9]. Income taxes take a sizable bite out of the receipts of only the families at the very top of the hierarchy, and they are so small a group that redistribution of their money makes only a minor change in the lives of the bulk of the population. Of course, total state and Federal taxes, including those on land, buildings, corporate profits, and inheritances, take a larger portion of the incomes of the well-to-do than income taxes alone, and spread this income in the form of national defense, roads, schools, hospitals, and other benefits that are enjoyed by poor as well as rich families.

Irregularity of employment is an important factor in annual income, especially for blue-collar workers. For instance, mail carriers, who work steadily, make more on an annual basis than carpenters or painters, who earn much more per hour, for the latter seldom have work fifty-two weeks out of the year.

When studying family income, attention must be paid to the number of people in the family who work. About one quarter of the married women work at least part time, and it is traditional in many families (particularly at the blue-collar level) for older children still living at home to work and contribute part of their earnings to the family purse. Of course, the work habits of such people being much less regular than those of heads of families, they average less income.

About 40 per cent of the recipients of incomes under $2000 were single individuals—young people just starting to work, divorced women, widows and widowers, and casual laborers who led a disorganized social life. A substantial portion of the remainder were unemployed, disabled, or retired couples. As a recent study of income distribution expressed it: "Low income is thus not so much a matter of rates of pay for work as it is the system of support of those unable to work and the amount of income provided by social-security programs [10]."

Throughout careers there is a difference in the pattern of income that has important implications for family life. A factory worker doing a routine semiskilled task can earn almost as much the first month on the job as after twenty years of experience. The typical career pattern for such a worker is to shift from one routine job to another throughout his lifetime, and after he reaches fifty years of age he begins to slow down a bit and gets less desirable jobs. A young fellow from such a family background is tempted to leave school early and go to work, for he can immediately command almost as much pay as his father, and a year or two more in school will not make any difference. He becomes independent of parental control, is likely to marry early, and then settles down to a succession of semiskilled jobs for the rest of his life. In other words, his income curve throughout his work career is almost flat.

By contrast, a white-collar worker often earns progressively more as the years go by, and he either builds up his own business or profession or advances up the bureaucratic hierarchy. He knows while still in school that his education is vital to his career, and that he would not earn much (relative to his eventual expectations) if he cut his schooling short and started to work early. Thus, he stays in school much longer, marries later, and remains dependent on his parents for a greater period —indeed, may even receive some help from them (if they too are business people) for a time after his marriage, for their income is high relative to his, and they will want to help him get a good start without having to sink to a low level of consumption [11]. As his career develops, his income may increase steadily until the day he retires. Consequently, his whole family life is often based on expectations of a rising curve of income instead of a flat one.

## FACTORS INFLUENCING INCOME

Of the total income flowing to individuals, about two thirds is received from wages and salaries. About 9 per cent is farm income. Business profits and professional fees account for 11 per cent. Dividends, rent, and interest each account for a little less than 4 per cent. Another 6 per cent represents transfer payments [12]. Wages and salaries constitute the major source of income for the bulk of the urban workers in the middle of the income distribution. Only at the extremes are other sources important: those with incomes under $2000 get almost half of their money (on the average) from public aid, whereas in the case of those receiving over $25,000, more than three quarters of their income is from business profits, professional fees, and return on invested property [13].

The size of the wage or salary earned in an occupation is thus the factor that accounts for the size of the income of most of our people. The median nonfarm family income,* according to the occupation of the head of the family, was estimated as follows for 1950 [15]:

| | |
|---|---|
| Professional, technical and kindred workers | $5029 |
|     Self-employed | 7429 |
|     Salaried | 4724 |
| Managers and officials | 5157 |
| Proprietors | 4003 |
| Clerical and kindred workers | 3833 |
| Sales workers | 4149 |
| Craftsmen, foremen, and kindred workers | 3925 |
| Operatives and kindred workers | 3407 |
| Private household workers | 1170 |
| Service workers, except private household | 2976 |
| Laborers, except farm and mine | 2524 |

Considering only full-time workers who are employed fairly regularly (most of whom are heads of families), it is clear that no factor accounts for differences in income so much as occupation. However, holding occupation constant, there are certain other factors that do make a difference: region of the country, size of the town of residence, race, and education [16].

The South lags behind the rest of the country in income. The median income for men in 1949 was under $1800 in the South compared to over $2700 for the other regions (which did not differ much among themselves). The difference was even greater for Negroes, for they averaged about half as much income in the South as in other regions. Much of the disadvantage of the South can be explained by a different occupational structure, for the region is more rural, and the industry less skilled, than the rest of the country. But even when these factors are held constant, some difference still remains, for white workers in the large Southern cities earn about 10 per cent less than their Northern

* The figures for family income are several hundred dollars higher than those for the income of men given above in Chapter III, Table 1, showing the effect of working wives and children. *Within* most occupational categories, the distribution of income for employed men does not depart a great deal from normality [14].

colleagues in the same occupation, and those in the smaller Southern cities earn about 15 per cent less. The higher the occupation, the less the difference.

It has long been known that people earn more money in big cities than in small towns and villages. These differences are in large part the result of a different distribution of occupations, for the larger the city, the more professional, managerial, and white-collar workers in the labor force. But again, holding occupation constant, a small differential remains.

Negroes (or to be technical, what the Bureau of the Census calls "nonwhites," of whom 96.2 per cent are Negroes) earn much less than whites; in 1949 the median income of Negro men in the North was about $2000, compared to $2700 for white men. In the South, Negro men earned about $1000, compared to twice that amount for white men. Again, occupation accounts for much (but not all) of this differential, for race discrimination in American industry keeps Negroes in the lower paying jobs. Only in recent years in the North has the Negro been allowed to become a semiskilled factory operative; even now he is seldom permitted to become a foreman. In the South he still has difficulty entering many factories at all. Race discrimination has a particularly harsh effect on educated Negroes, for they have little chance to get full benefit from their training. A Negro professional man, for instance, usually serves only Negro clients, who cannot afford to pay much for his services. And it is practically impossible for an educated Negro to climb into the upper levels of the corporate bureaucracy. Thus in the North, whites who have finished college average 60 per cent more income than their colored colleagues, whereas those who have only finished grammar school have an advantage of but 30 per cent. In the South the comparable figures are 85 per cent and 48 per cent.*

Education and occupation are very highly related, as illustrated in Table 1, Chapter III. Another way to state the case is to say that middle-aged men who have completed high school earn 76 per cent more than those who stopped with a grammar-school education; men who finished college earn 150 per cent more than the grammar-school group [17]. It usually takes a good education to get a good job. But even within any given occupation, the men with more education make a little more money.

We have been ignoring farmers in most of our discussion so far. It is very difficult to compare their incomes to those of city workers, for they eat home-grown products that cannot easily be added into income figures, and furthermore, a third of the farmers get the majority of

---

* Race differences are explored more fully in Chapter VIII, below.

their cash income from wage work off the farm. Recent estimates suggest that despite large reported differences in income, the average level of consumption of farm families is about the same as for city workers within any given region of the country [18].

## TRENDS IN INCOME DISTRIBUTION

On March 5, 1952, *The New York Times* ran a story on the front page headlined as follows:

SHIFT IN INCOME DISTRIBUTION IS RE-
DUCING POVERTY IN U.S.

Rise in National Output Benefits "Forgotten Man"—Vast "Leveling Up"
Held Proof of Our Vitality—No Similar Soviet Record

The article began with the sentence: "The United States has undergone a social revolution in the last four decades, and particularly since the late Thirties."

On May 4, 1953, the *Times* had another article which was headlined this way [19]:

TOP INCOMES FOUND IN SHARP DECLINE

Study Shows Effect of Shift in Distribution on Savings and Purchasing
Power

And in 1953 and 1954 *Fortune* magazine ran its series on *The Changing American Market,* beginning with a sentence in typical style: "All history can show no more portentous economic phenomenon than today's American market." Through these articles the American public was told about the work of research scholars whose tomes of statistics usually enter the world with less fanfare, men like Simon Kuznets and Herman P. Miller, who utilize the facilities of the National Bureau of Economic Research and the Bureau of the Census.

The new findings which so excited the editors of the *Times* and of *Fortune* can be easily summarized:

1. The average real income (after adjustments for inflation) of the American people has been going up a great deal, approximately doubling in the first half of the century. The rise was not steady, however, for the rate of increase was fastest in the boom periods of the 1920's and the years since the end of the Second World War.

2. At the same time that per capita income increased on the average, income was being redistributed. The very rich actually lost ground

during this period; the middle-income people gained, but the major gains were scored by the people at the bottom.

3. The poorest section of the country, the South, and the poorest group in the country, the Negroes, made the greatest gains of all.

In short, real income was going up for almost everybody, and inequalities in income among different groups were being markedly reduced, for the least affluent people were gaining ground much faster than the more affluent ones.

Why these changes? Partly full employment and general prosperity, which always benefit the poor and the marginal people more than others; partly a steady increase in the efficiency of industry, which led to an average increase in output per man of between 2 and 3 per cent a year; partly the increasing share of income in wages and salaries and the decreasing share in profits and return on investments; partly the effects of new tax policies; partly the results of greater union strength, which brought higher and more equal wages.

Let us take a few examples. The South increased its per capita income in the twenty years preceding 1949 (in current dollars unadjusted for price changes) by 133 per cent, while the other parts of the country moved up by only 72 per cent [20]. This improvement came from industrialization, with its movement of poor workers from depressed rural areas to expanding cities in the South, and out of the region to Northern industrial areas. And Negro men had an increase in wage and salary income of half again as much as white men in the decade preceding 1949. So the poorest region and poorest racial group have had the greatest benefit from economic growth.

Particular occupations showed these increases in income from 1939 to 1950, again using current rather than standard dollars: service and unskilled workers, 176 per cent; operatives, 172 per cent; clerks, 111 per cent; proprietors and managers, 95 per cent; professional and technical workers, 114 per cent [21]. Again, the lowest paid group scored the greatest gains.

As time passed, the *very* rich were getting a smaller slice of the income pie. The share of the top 5 per cent of families in total income fell from about 30 per cent in 1929 to about 20 per cent in 1950, and that was before income taxes [22]. Although there were more than twice as many persons who reported incomes over $15,000 (up to a half million), there were only half as many who reported incomes over $250,000 (down to 1523) [23].

Considering the other end of the scale, three out of four nonfarm families had incomes of less than $2000 in 1939, but only one out of five was in that situation by 1949. The preceding figures somewhat exaggerate the change, for they do not make an adjustment for the fact that 1939 dollars were worth much more than 1949 dollars. Adjusting to standard dollars and switching our comparison a bit, we find that the average (mean) real income of the bottom 20 per cent of families increased by about three quarters at the same time that the average income for all families increased by about a half [24].

*Fortune* dramatized the changes by concentrating on the middle-income group, which was defined as family units receiving from $4000 to $7500 after taxes (and getting dollars of standard purchasing power, as of 1953 prices). In 1929 this group consisted of only 15 per cent of the American family units, and they received only one quarter of the total cash income. By 1953 the group had expanded to 35 per cent of the family units, and their share of the national income had gone up to 42 per cent. If noncash income of farm families were included, more than 40 per cent of the family units would be in this middle-income category. The greatest growth took place in the few years between 1947 and 1953 [25].

One of the striking facts about this expanded middle-income group is that it contained so many families who did not fit the pattern of the bourgeoisie of traditional analysis (professional and business men); indeed, less than half fit this description. Considering only the nonfarm families, the middle-income group was made up in this way [26]:

| | |
|---|---|
| Professionals, proprietors, and managers | 26% |
| Clerical and sales workers | 16 |
| Skilled workers | 26 |
| Semiskilled workers | 23 |
| Service and unskilled workers | 9 |
| TOTAL | 100% |

Once again, we meet the working wife, for two fifths of all of the above listed families had somebody working besides the family head. However, 70 per cent of the service and unskilled families earning middle incomes had an extra worker, as did almost half of the families headed by semiskilled workers or clerical and sales people [27]. Consequently, we had a situation in which many family units were able to consume as if they belonged to the middle-income group despite the fact that the normal earnings of the principal wage earner did not bring in that much money. It is to be expected that such families will spend their money rather differently from those who earn it from father's regular salary, because they will not expect the extra earnings to be so stable—if a depression comes, or a baby is born, or an older child gets married, family income will take a sharp drop.

One of the basic Marxist predictions about capitalist industrialization has failed to come true: the bourgeoisie has not usurped an ever greater proportion of the income while driving the workers into deeper and deeper misery. Instead, everybody is getting richer, with the depressed groups gaining the fastest. This appears to be true for every advanced industrial nation. The greatest inequalities in income are found in agricultural and backward nations where the unequal distribution of wealth (especially land) is more directly reflected in income differences

Comparisons of average incomes in different countries are difficult to make. Translating currencies by standard exchange rates often ignores vast differences in costs of living. In some societies many services are performed free by extended family groups or by community organizations, and the average worker needs less income in money. Comparisons of industrial and agricultural countries exaggerate those distortions already noted in contrasts of farm and city areas in the United States. With all these difficulties in mind, it still might be interesting to compare figures on average per capita income in various parts of the world; here is one set of figures for 1949 expressed in U.S. dollars [28]:

| United States | $1450 |
|---|---|
| Canada | 870 |
| Argentina | 350 |
| Chile | 40 |
| Switzerland | 850 |
| United Kingdom | 770 |
| Italy | 230 |
| Israel | 390 |
| Syria | 100 |
| Korea | 35 |
| Communist China | 30 |
| Union of South Africa | 260 |
| Egypt | 100 |
| Ethiopia | 40 |

## WEALTH AND LAND

It has been emphasized above that in an advanced industrial society the income of most citizens comes from wages and salaries, which in turn depend on occupations which in turn depend primarily on education. As long as incomes are unequal, a stratification order will exist; styles of life will differ radically between occupational levels. But to the degree that education is free and available to all, the society will approach the maximum possible fluidity within its stratification order. Each generation will sort itself according to talent and ambition, and the effect of inheritance of position will be minimized.

This model of complete fluidity only partially fits the facts of life in America today. Differences in income and style of life affect the values, ambitions, and educations of each succeeding generation. And the effect of capital wealth, though perhaps less important today than ever before in its consequences on the stratification order, is still of great significance, especially because wealth gives power.

Some notion of the relative importance of wealth can be achieved by comparisons with other types of societies. In a simple agricultural society it is obvious that the system of land ownership is of supreme importance for all other aspects of life. The kinship system, the property system, the rules of inheritance, the stratification system—all are united in a single bundle.

In areas of more advanced agricultural techniques, larger populations can be supported in a given territory, and the surplus gathers in cities. A division of labor emerges, which often produces a basic split between the traders and artisans living in the cities and the farmers who work the soil. The traders tend to be a fluid group; a small amount of capital and a great deal of skill often bring success, and new men constantly rise to positions of wealth and power [29]. The farmers tend to remain more conservative; the land is handed down through the generations within a family according to the local rules of inheritance, and change is resisted as a threat to the basic values of family life. But there is a constant flow of excess population from farm to city; if one son inherits all the family farm, the others usually seek work in the city.

If such an agricultural society permits individuals to own land without working it, then the emergence of an aristocracy is likely. Sometimes successful farmers slowly buy up more land; sometimes traders who have become rich transform their wealth into land; sometimes kings grant land to soldiers and statesmen as a reward for services. Regardless of their origins, a group of men who come to own vast amounts of land develop certain characteristics: a disdain for manual work (for that is the mark of the peasants or serfs beneath them); a great emphasis on family continuity and pride in family name; often a high cultivation of art and science made possible by their leisure; a concern for politics, for they must be constantly on guard to protect their property interests from the landless who look covetously upon their privileges. Such a group is correctly labeled a "ruling class," for acting as an organized group, it makes all the important decisions. In order to keep the great estates intact, they are generally passed on to only one son, usually through primogeniture. In highly developed aristocratic traditions, the land may even be entailed, that is, the law may prevent its being sold outside the family.

Thomas Jefferson understood that the rules of property were basic to such a social order, and because he felt that such an order was antithetical to the republican principles of America, he led a successful campaign to change the laws. During the Revolutionary War he resigned from the Continental Congress, took up a seat in the Virginia legislature, and proposed to reform society. He wrote in his autobiography [30]:

I obtained leave to bring in a bill declaring tenants in tail to hold their lands in fee simple. In the earlier times of the colony, when lands were to be obtained for little or nothing, some provident individuals procured large grants; and desirous of founding great families for themselves, settled them on their descendants in fee tail. The transmission of this property from generation to generation, in the same name, raised up a distinct set of families, who, being privileged by law in the perpetuation of their wealth, were thus formed into a Patrician order, distinguishable by the splendor and luxury of their establishments. From this order, too, the king habitually selected his counsellors of State; the hope of which distinction devoted the whole corps to the interests and will of the crown. To annul this privilege, and instead of an aristocracy of wealth, of more harm and danger, than benefit, to society, to make an opening for the aristocracy of virtue and talent, which nature has wisely provided for the direction of the interests of society, and scattered with equal hand through all its conditions, was deemed essential to a well-ordered republic. To effect it, no violence was necessary, no deprivation of natural right, but rather an enlargement of it by a repeal of the law. For this would authorize the present holder to divide the property among his children equally, as his affections were divided; and would place them, by natural generation, on the level of their fellow citizens.

Jefferson believed that four bills he helped pass in Virginia formed "a system by which every fibre would be eradicated of ancient or future aristocracy; and a foundation laid for a government truly republican [31]." These four acts were the abolition of entail, of primogeniture, of the established church, and the creation of the public-school system. His activities illustrate the reciprocal influence between property and cultural norms: because a system of property created a social stratum with norms he did not like, he used an appeal to democratic ideology to change the property laws which in turn changed the social structure and its norms.

Land has never created a closed aristocracy in America for the simple reason that there was always free land available; the underprivileged, instead of working for a landlord, could move west. The one section of the country that came close to aristocratic conditions was the South, for the slaves were not free to move. But the Southern landlords never regained their glory after the Civil War.

Before that war, a merchant class rose to wealth and power in New England and the Middle Atlantic states. Many early merchant princes succeeded in establishing family lines still prominent, particularly in New England: Cabot, Perkins, and Forbes are names to reckon with in

Boston [32]. But family wealth was usually divided among many sons and daughters; it was spent in various parts of the country as the descendants moved about; it had to compete constantly with new fortunes made through rising industries. Those sons who wished to preserve inherited fortunes had to become active financiers, reinvesting in new industries as the old ones declined. The early New England fortunes were founded, at least in retrospective tales, from whaling and the China trade. But Standard Oil replaced whale oil, and trade with China became subversive. No stable aristocracy emerged, despite the pretensions of some of the plutocrats [33].

What is the situation today? In the great farm areas of the Middle West land is still supreme, but it is mostly owned by the families who work it. In the South, land is owned partly by working farmers, partly by landlords—but not in great holdings that create aristocratic conditions. There is much turnover in farm holdings as families get old and retire, as land rises and falls in market value. Similarly, ownership of urban real estate is the basis of income for many families, but again, turnover is high.

### CORPORATE WEALTH

Despite the fact that only 3.3 per cent of personal income is handed out in the form of corporate dividends, the most important property in our industrial age is the productive machinery of the great corporations. Here there is great concentration of wealth, but it is in the hands of companies rather than individuals [34]. Just before the Second World War, there were about 2,000,000 business firms in the United States; of these, 500,000 were corporations, and they accounted for 90 per cent of the total business of the country in manufacturing and distribution. *About 1 per cent of the biggest (nonfinancial) corporations employed half the workers and controlled almost three quarters of the productive assets of the country* [35]. In 1947 a new study showed that a mere 139 corporations held 45 per cent of our manufacturing assets, and the 200 biggest companies employed almost 17 per cent of the nonagricultural work force [36]. The evidence on the long-term trend is scanty, but suggests that the degree of concentration has not changed much since the turn of the century.

The biggest manufacturing company in the world is the General Motors Corporation. It produces 3 per cent of the gross national product of the United States (the total goods and services turned out in a year). It earns over 1 billion dollars a year in net profits. It employs over half a million people, has 17,000 independent retail dealers who in turn have a vast payroll, and deals with 21,000 independent suppliers who, under subcontract, make things that go into the cars and trucks and airplane engines and refrigerators that are sold under the GM label. About half the cars that are sold in the country are made by the company, and its over-all effect on the economy is so great that many people credited its well-publicized expansion program in 1955 with heading off a business slump [37].

Who owns the corporations? In 1951 about 6,500,000 people representing slightly less than 10 per cent of American families, owned some corporate stock. They were families with high incomes, for less than 3 per cent of families with incomes under $3000 owned any shares, but about half the families with incomes over $10,000 held some stock [38]. About one third of the outstanding shares owned by individuals were held by the one tenth of one per cent of families who had incomes above $50,000; *approximately 65 per cent of the shares were held by the one per cent of families with incomes above $15,000* [39].

However, almost one third of the outstanding shares were not owned by individuals but by organizations of various kinds: banks, insurance companies, foundations, pension funds, universities. Peter F. Drucker estimates that these "fiduciary investors" have "effective working control" of three quarters of the companies listed on the New York Stock Exchange, a phenomenon that has occurred principally in the last ten years. "The shift of the center of security buying since then represents an unprecedented 'democratization' of business ownership, for the real owners of these holdings are 'small people,' the middle class and the workers. It also represents an unprecedented concentration of legal ownership, for the number of 'fiduciary institutions' is fairly small [40]." Drucker adds that the institutional investors rarely make any attempt to influence the operation of their companies, which greatly increases the actual power of management.

A major study of the great fortunes of the United States was that of Ferdinand Lundberg, *America's Sixty Families*, published in 1937 [41]. He used income-tax returns for 1924; they were made public then, as they are not now. He estimated that sixty families controlled a substantial portion of our productive wealth. Indeed, according to his figures, seven extended families *each* owned over 100 million dollars' worth of assets. Lundberg claimed that the sixty families formed the "*de facto* government" of the United States, a claim which certainly went beyond his data. But he showed how those families interlocked through marriage; he indicated that a few great financial houses served as their agents, multiplying their power through concentration; he examined their influence over newspapers, charitable foundations, universities, politics. Most of his evidence looked backward toward the turn of the century, when the plutocracy was smaller and more powerful than now. As the giant corporations matured, their stock became more widely distributed. When one looks at more recent data, it is hard to find out who does control the great corporations that are the focus of contemporary wealth. In most big companies no single individual owns as much as 10 per cent of the stock.

For instance, 155 of the largest corporations were studied in 1935, and it was found that the officers, directors, and largest stockholders *as a group* controlled half the voting stock in only 15 companies. The conclusion was "that for most of the largest corporations ownership and control have become largely separated. This condition appears to be particularly characteristic of the corporations that have traveled furthest along the road of corporate development, such as the railroads and others of the older corporations [42]." We have created a strange new social institution: a mammoth organization of immense wealth and power and productive skill, that has the legal status of a personal businessman, but is self-perpetuating and is "owned" by thousands of people across the nation.

If the owners of the corporations seldom control them, who does? The answer is management, plus a small group of active stockholders who own blocks of stock which may represent only a small minority interest, yet add up to a bigger voting unit than any other group can muster. This collection of managers and active owners is not large. When the 200 largest nonfinancial and 50 largest financial corporations in 1935 were treated as a group, it was found that there were 3544 positions on the boards of directors. They were held by 2725 individuals, for many men held several positions. Indeed, the 400 most active men held nearly a third of the directorships, and 1000 men held over half of them [43]. *If there is any single group that can be held to dominate American wealth, it is those 1000 men.*

But 1000 men do not necessarily constitute a homogeneous group. It is one thing to isolate them in a statistical table, quite another to find out how they operate, to what degree they constitute an organized "inner circle." There may be many conflicts of interest among them; they may be constantly competing with the little fellows whose small businesses are individually meaningless but collectively important. There is evidence that in local communities, perhaps even in subregions of the country, the active owners and managers of the big corporations do form a small coterie who know each other well and feel a community of interest—we will examine some of that evidence in the chapter on "Interaction." But data on the national scene are scarce. The National Resources Committee estimated that there were eight major-interest groups that represented functioning clusters of industrial concentration, headed by the financial empire of the J. P. Morgan-First National Bank of New York, which controlled 30 billion dollars of assets in 1935, including the United States Steel Corporation, 37 per cent of the electric generating capacity of the country, and 26 per cent of the first-class railroad mileage [44]. However, details on how that control is used are hard to get; secrecy is vital to the operation of such power.

David E. Lilienthal, once head of TVA, believes that new forces in society effectively check the power of the large corporations and that we need no longer worry about industrial concentration [45]:

> In short, as a result of the new comprehensive role of government in economic affairs, the new power and influence of organized labor, the rise of the New Competition (largely based upon research), a change in the power of large *buyers*—Sears, Roebuck, General Motors, etc.—and most of all a change as to the social responsibility of Big Business (in the public mind and that of its management as well), corporate control, far from being a virtual absolute in the majority of directors or stockholders, is now divided and *diffused*.

This theme has become a common one in recent years as postwar prosperity creates a mood of optimism that we have the best of all possible systems. Another influential observer, David Riesman, who is usually a short jump ahead of current moods, writes that the search for a single "ruling class" is the search for a phantom [46]:

> The lobby in the old days actually ministered to the clear leadership, privilege, and imperative of the business ruling class. Today we have substituted for the leadership a series of groups, each of which has struggled for and finally attained a power to stop things conceivably inimical to its interests and, within far narrower limits, to start things. . . .
> Nevertheless, people go on acting as if there still were a decisive ruling class in contemporary America. Recent investigations show that businessmen think labor leaders and politicians run the country. Labor and the left think that "Wall Street" runs it, or the "sixty families." Wall Street, confused perhaps by its dethronement as a telling barometer of capital-formation weather, may think that the mid-western industrial barons, cushioned on plant expansion money in the form of heavy depreciation reserves and undivided profits, run the country. . . . But these barons of Pittsburgh, Weirton, Akron, and Detroit, though certainly a tougher crowd than the Wall Streeters, are . . . coming more and more to think of themselves as trustees whose moves are largely dictated by the expectations, only marginally manipulated, of their beneficiaries.

Current industrial wealth is spread throughout the nation, and competes for political power with organized small business, organized labor, organized farmers, organized consumers. There are many competing groups, with a concentration of power in the hands of their leaders. They work out a functioning equilibrium under the watchful refereeing of the government. Great wealth always influences, sometimes dominates, but it does not rule. The interesting problem in the study of power thus shifts from the concentration of wealth to the *de facto* relationships between the leaders of various interest groups, and the actual study of their behavior as contrasted to polemics about it is a difficult research operation that has only begun [47].

This contemporary situation is vastly different from that in an underdeveloped country where the ownership of wealth usually means direct power, and it is modified in many areas of our country where local power is more closely related to local wealth. Where a few landlords control all the good farm land, or a few employers dominate the only factories, they are likely to control the police and the schools as well. Their sons inherit the wealth and the power. And the power becomes visible to those who are told what to do, often building up fear and resentment and some measure of countercontrol through the mores of *noblesse oblige* and the politics of the organization of the little fellows [48]. Power on our national scene is diffuse, indirect, and invisible, and those subject to power are not likely to be aware of what is going on behind the scenes. Resentment arises only through visibility: it is the policeman or first sergeant or local banker who arrogantly orders one around who stirs up hatred. Propagandists of class antagonism have a notably hard time convincing the American worker that he is being ruled by an abstraction called capitalists. Yet residents of small towns can readily understand that a clique of "big shots" make the important decisions behind the closed door of the bank's conference room.

## STYLES OF LIFE

Prestige tends to be bestowed through consumption behavior rather than income, for only that which can be seen can be judged. Consumption patterns and interaction networks are intimately linked; people spend their leisure time with others who share their tastes and recreational activities, and they learn new tastes from those with whom they associate.

Consumption is a constant struggle between what people want and what they have, between *standards* of living and *levels* of living. The former is best studied by asking people about their attitudes and values, the latter can be gauged by records of budgets showing their various expenditures. We have an immense amount of information about levels of living, going back a century in time—and from these data a few inferences are possible about value standards [49]. But we have scant knowledge from direct studies of the attitudes that make up the standards or norms of consumption held by various groups in the population; yet this knowledge would be vital to a full understanding of the dynamics of our system: people are ambitious because they seek what they consider an "appropriate" way of life, and *the definition of appropriateness varies enormously from person to person, from group to group.* Perhaps the greatest repository of information on this subject lies uncollected and unpublished in the files of the market-research companies who have been badgering the American housewife for two decades with questions on her tastes and desires.

In societies or groups where the standard of living is fixed and traditional, people simply stop working when they have earned enough to cover their usual expenses; beyond that point, extra work has no meaning. A plantation worker, for instance, knows that he cannot ever save enough to become an owner, nor will the owners permit him to live in the type of house or wear the kind of clothes that are above his station. So he goes on a spree when he has saved a little money; he quits his job, takes a vacation, may perhaps invite his family and friends on an extended drunk. When the spree is over, he goes back to work and resumes his habitual style of life. This lack of ambition on the part of many people who have a fixed notion of the proper way to live is a constant source of bewilderment for managers who come from an outside culture where thrift and ambition to change one's lot are thought to be basic to human nature.

Ordinary observation of American life permits a few rough generalizations about standards of living. We have, probably more than any European country, a standardized mass market for consumption goods. It is promulgated through the newspapers and magazines and movies, which build up a picture of the way of life of the "typical" or "average" American that is supposed to be the gift of God and the constitution to all loyal citizens. This pattern, which we can label "living well," begins with a single-family house of some six or seven rooms on a small but neat plot of suburban land. In it live a mature but perpetually youthful couple with their two (recently, three) small children. They own their home and maintain it by hobby labor with garden tools and paint brushes. There may be a weekly cleaning woman, but no full-time servant. They own a small and new automobile, a refrigerator, a television set, and a clothes washing machine. Many have a dishwasher and a room air conditioner. They dress in stylish ready-made clothes. They take a two-week vacation in the country every year. They watch the TV a couple of hours every evening when not at the movies or visiting neighbors for a game of scrabble. They read a daily newspaper, a weekly news magazine, and a monthly women's magazine, but not many books. They are clean and sanitary beyond the dreams of a Dutch housewife, and eat a wholesome diet that in recent years has become far more interesting as garlic and spices have lost their immigrant, lower-class connotations. The children are brought up according to the latest scientific theories of personality development—which at the moment are swinging away from extreme permissiveness toward a middle position of sympathetic understanding within the framework of firm limits to behavior that give the children "security."

According to mythology almost every American lives this way, and the few who do not expect to as soon as they "get on their feet." But according to statistics, only about four tenths of our families come close to the ideal. This is the way of life of *Fortune's* middle-income group, which makes from $4000 to $7500 after taxes.*

About one family in a hundred lives in "great luxury." They inhabit a mansion instead of a house, own country establishments, employ servants, travel throughout the world, wear expensive, made-to-order clothes. They are the sort of people who appear in the Sunday supplement perched upon horses.

About nine families in a hundred live "opulently," but far from the great luxury of the plutocrats. Earning somewhere between $7500 and $15,000 a year, they can afford a suburban house, a Buick or possibly a Cadillac, clothes copied from Dior rather than made by him, and a trip to Europe once or twice in a lifetime but not periodically. They automatically send their children to college, and in some instances aspire to the Ivy League.

About half of our families live neither luxuriously, opulently, nor even well. About three tenths of the total barely live "adequately." They are likely to have a four- or five-room apartment in the heart of a city (or an old house on a small farm). Their furniture is plain and as old as the marriage, for they cannot afford to keep up with the latest styles. In fact, this may be one of the most useful symbols of the dividing line between them and the next higher group, for they can seldom afford to discard anything usable, be it a chair or a dress or a washing machine, just for the pleasure of a new one. Their food is nourishing but not elegant, and is bought with a shrewd eye for bargain cuts of meat and cheap seasonable vegetables. There is little space for their children to play other than in the streets. Mother worries about contacts with tough kids, but does not resort to the latest word of Dr. Spock before spanking an unruly youngster. In general, their way of life is determined in large measure by the number of children they have. If only one son appears, he might even be encouraged to go to college. If the house is full of children, older ones will be allowed to quit high school to help bring in a little extra cash. These families just manage to

* The proportions indicated here at each level differ somewhat from those given above for "cash income," for I will make adjustments (following *Fortune*) for estimated noncash farm income.

get by; there is usually enough, but never any extra money. This is the way of life of the urban factory worker; the Bureau of Labor Statistics calls it a "modest but adequate" standard, and estimated that for a family of four in 1947 it would cost from $3100 to $3300. At that time the median cash income of urban families with two children under 18 was $3455 [50].

Despite our steady increase in average income, there are still many families in the United States who have a low level of consumption. It is difficult to establish satisfactory criteria for a minimum but adequate level of living inasmuch as judgments about what is necessary are subjective and depend upon the subculture of a given group of people. Consumption experts have been trying for years to agree upon standard criteria, but with little success. Does a retired couple living on old-age assistance need a TV set? How many rooms do they need? Is a telephone necessary?

One criterion of adequate living is a diet that provides the necessary nutrients. Despite the paraphernalia of nutrition science, even this judgment is difficult to make; a diet adequate in calories based on rice costs a small fraction of one based on meat. It has been estimated that a small shift away from meat and tobacco in Britain would completely change the British balance of trade. However, using a diverse standard of calories plus other nutrient factors that make up a minimum acceptable standard *according to American habits,* the Department of Agriculture estimated that in 1948 only 74 per cent of two-person urban families receiving less than $2000 a year had an adequate diet, whereas 92 per cent of those making over $5000 met the standard [51]. Many health authorities believe that our major dietary problem nowadays is overeating and obesity; this is a remarkable shift from the depression days when one third of the nation was pronounced ill-fed. Some authorities estimate that two thirds of the world's population are at present underfed.

As for housing, it was estimated in a study of one city in 1950 that although most families earning over $4000 lived in modernized dwellings that were not dilapidated, only 63 per cent of the renters and 80 per cent of the owners who made less than $2000 lived in dwellings that met minimum standards [51].

It is clear that many people still live in or near poverty—perhaps half of the two tenths of family units who earn less than $2000. But, as was stated above, a substantial portion of these are not ordinary families of parents and children. They are the people who are too old or too sick to work; mothers without husbands; marginal workers on the fringe of organized family life. They are cared for by irregular or part-time work and a confusing variety of pension and assistance schemes. How-

ever, they are not cared for adequately according to the standards that
most Americans take for granted and that our productive economy
could easily meet if we paid more attention to the needs of these people.
For the first time in the history of the world it would be possible to
abolish poverty completely, but we have not yet done so [52].

How satisfied with their level of living are various groups of people?
How many families in tenements seek and expect to escape? How many
families at the modest-but-adequate level feel that it is not satisfactory
and aspire to the middle-income style idealized by the mass media?
How many who are comfortable yearn to live in luxury? We do not
know. It seems probable that the majority of families, at least above the
tenement level, are relatively satisfied with what they have and consider
it to be natural and necessary. In verbal terms, they would admit to
fantasies of a higher level of life, but most of the time they do not think
much about it and do not see that the real world offers much hope of
change. In other words, they have accepted a certain standard of living
as appropriate for their group.

But some people at each level have their eyes one step up, and seek to
emulate the style of life of those immediately above them. They often
furnish their homes on borrowed money in order to make them look
more elegant than current income will permit; they seek to raise their
incomes by having father keep alert for chances of promotion and perhaps by having mother work part time; they encourage their children
to buckle down in school and explain to them that if they want to get
further ahead than father they must get more education. This pattern of
ambition is, according to myth, universal, but the scanty available
evidence indicates that it is followed by only a minority of families.

One interesting study of contentment with style of life was a public-
opinion poll conducted just after the war. It showed the following
proportions of people satisfied with their current weekly incomes [53]:

| | |
|---|---|
| Under $20 | 19% satisfied |
| $20–30 | 21 |
| $30–40 | 23 |
| $40–60 | 39 |
| $60–100 | 53 |
| $100 or more | 77 |

The more they made, the happier they were. That seems obvious
enough, but what about another finding? Among the dissatisfied, the
more they made, the more they thought they would need to make them
happy. Persons receiving $25 would be happy with an additional $16,
but persons receiving $100 wanted another $100. Standards of living
(what people want and think is necessary) are relative to levels of living

(the way they actually live). The people who look up do so by one step.

One research that would be of small significance to the fate of the world but would interest those of us who write textbooks would be a study of the style of life of academic people. They are in the middle-income range, and they want single-family houses and good and expensive educations for their children. But many of the younger among them look down upon some of the more expensive symbols of bourgeois life. They would not want their wives to be seen in minks, they prefer Volkswagens to Cadillacs, and they are not greatly concerned about a good address (just so it be good enough to keep their children from mixing with the uneducated and uncouth). They strive in most expenditures to replace conspicuously expensive styles with conspicuously artistic styles, and with a flair this can be done cheaply. A guess might be in order: they can, through group support of their special tastes, live for 10 to 20 per cent less than young businessmen who must seek respect from other businessmen.

Some observers believe that despite the entry of so many blue-collar workers into the ranks of the middle-income group, there is still an important distinction between their value standards and those of white-collar workers. According to this view, those at the top of the blue-collar hierarchy feel that they have arrived as far as they can go, or as far as a man should desire; they are satisfied, and do not spend their money for conspicuous symbols of display that would raise their prestige in the eyes of the community, such as a "good address." Indeed, they would consider it snobbish to behave that way. By contrast, the clerks and salesmen who earn about the same amount of money are thought to be less satisfied with it, for they compare themselves to the richer men above them in the business world. They are supposed to be at the bottom of their ladder, whereas the successful blue-collar workers are at the top of theirs. Consequently, the white-collar worker is supposed to be relatively less satisfied with his lot in life. He is described as belonging to a "frustrated lower-middle class," and is even feared to be especially susceptible to fascism as an outlet for his dissatisfaction.

Although it is true that on the average white-collar workers spend more for clothing and housing than blue-collar workers who earn the same amount, it is also true that many of the white-collar workers are children of immigrants and feel that their status is a cherished accomplishment rather than a basis for discomfort. I would suggest that the evidence does support the view that some people in the middle-income group (and in the group just below it, for that matter) are indeed dissatisfied with their level of living, and others are quite content. The difference in attitudes makes a great deal of difference to them and to their children. But we simply do not know whether this distinction is based on the color of the collar that is worn to work. It is time to stop generalizing on psychological matters from the European experience of fifty years ago to the United States of today. As is so often the case, all we can say with certainty is that more research is needed [54].

## EXPENDITURE PATTERNS

Perhaps the most ancient observation we have concerning consumption is that people who have recently arrived at a given level tend to exaggerate the established style of life of those who are already there; the flamboyance of the *nouveaux riches* is notorious. It takes time to learn the culture of a new environment, and the more obvious aspects are acquired first. As Warner is so fond of insisting, money is not enough; one must learn how to spend it appropriately before he can blend unobtrusively into the background. Often this takes a full generation; only the sons achieve the social acceptance which was the goal of the fathers (or better, the daughters succeed for the mothers).

What do Americans buy with their money? In 1951 the personal consumption expenditures were divided up this way [55]:

| | |
|---|---|
| Food | 23.9% |
| Alcoholic beverages | 3.3 |
| Clothing | 9.7 |
| Personal care | 1.0 |
| Housing | 8.6 |
| Household operation | 10.8 |
| Medical care and death expenses | 4.0 |
| Personal business | 3.7 |
| Automobile | 7.2 |
| Other transportation | 1.3 |
| Recreation | 4.5 |
| Tobacco | 1.9 |
| Private education | .7 |
| Foreign travel and remittances | .5 |
| Religion and welfare | .8 |
| Total personal expenditures | 81.9 |
| Taxes, personal | 11.4 |
| Savings, personal | 6.7 |
| TOTAL | 100.0% |

These percentages have remained relatively stable for many years. The only important shifts since 1929 were these: food went up about 4 per cent, mainly because there is more processing of food now than before—instead of preparing her own fruit and vegetables before cooking, the contemporary housewife buys them frozen. Relative clothing expense has decreased about 3 per cent, and the cost of housing about 5 per cent (probably a result of wartime price control which has not fully outworn its effects; but housing cost is slowly going up again).

Over the long run, a rough though useful index of the level of living of a nation or a segment of it is the proportion of its consumer budget that goes for food. It may range from more than 60 per cent down to 20 per cent for a total population, and to 5 per cent for a rich group within the population. Industrialization means that a great many commodities other than food are produced, and the more efficient farming that goes with it means that a larger percentage of the population is freed to produce the nonedible goods. The more industrial and prosperous a group is, the smaller is the proportion of its budget spent on food.

Now that we have passed well beyond the level of food subsistence, what specific things do we buy? About half of our families own their homes. In 1940, 79 per cent of our homes were electrified; in 1954, 98 per cent had electricity. In 1954, over 90 per cent of the homes had a refrigerator, 61 per cent a television set (in some cities there were more television sets than bath tubs). Some authorities estimate that in ten more years half of the families will have air conditioning, and perhaps close to that many will own two cars (three quarters of our families now have at least one automobile). The production of gadgets seems to have no bounds [56].

A less obvious aspect of our consumption behavior is the amount of time we have to spend on it. In 1840 the average factory workday was 11.4 hours long, and most factories worked six days a week. Now we work no more than 8 hours a day for 5 days a week, and it will not be long until the 35-hour week becomes standard.

In general, people of the same income divide their expenditures about the same way—variations are important, as emphasized above, but fine-grained by comparison with differences between income levels. These differences between levels have been summarized by Holbrook Working, who used the two largest budget interview surveys ever done in the United States, one based on a sample of 16,000 families, the other on 300,000 families, which were conducted by government agencies in the middle 1930's. Working reports that proportional expenditure for food decreases in arithmetic progression as total expenditure increases in geometric progression. The proportion spent for recreation and transportation increases from 4 per cent up to about 16 per cent and then levels off. The fraction on clothing goes up moderately with the size of total expenditures, whereas that for housing varies considerably from one subgroup to another at the same income level [57].

The proportions just given refer to the division of expenditures among the different categories of goods and services that are bought. They do not show a major change as one goes up the income scale: the proportion of income that is not spent at all, but is saved. People at the lowest levels spend more than they earn; they go into debt. People of very high incomes, on the average, save at least a quarter of what they receive. The cumulative effect of saving a higher proportion of a higher income produces some startling aggregate statistics: about half of the total money saved in a given year is saved by the 10 per cent of families who receive the highest income; the second highest decile saves only 15 per cent of the total [58]. This high rate of savings begins at an income level of about $7500 and accounts, in part, for the concentration of ownership of industrial stocks that was reported above. It produces this odd situation: if small family farms and businesses are not considered, only the very highest incomes (the top 1 per cent or less) flow from the ownership (often inherited) of capital wealth; yet the moderately high incomes in the highest decile (excluding the very top incomes), produced by salaries and professional fees, provide a surplus that allows the slow accumulation of capital wealth [59].

Since capital investment is vital to the growth of our economy, it can be easily understood why the economists are so concerned with the savings and investments of the top decile of income receivers. An interesting facet of the economists' research has been the discovery that although the rate of saving is much higher among people of high than of low incomes, the over-all rate of savings for the country has not gone up through the years as average income increased. For many years it was assumed that there was some level of living so comfortable that once a family reached it, they would save any surplus they earned. If that were true, as a higher and higher proportion of families passed that fixed level, the average rate of savings should have gone up—but despite fluctuations due to war and the business cycle, it has averaged about 6 per cent of disposable personal income. Thus it seems that there is no fixed level that is considered comfortable and adequate, but that *average expectations go up at the same rate as average income.* Apparently people consider that they have passed the level of comfort only by comparing themselves with their neighbors, not with a fixed standard. Thus people in the top 10 per cent always feel sufficiently well off to save a substantial portion of what they earn, whereas those in the bottom 90 per cent do not—and this is true regardless of the absolute levels of income [60].

Those whose incomes take them above the requirements of bare subsistence—food, shelter, clothing—have a range of choice in the expenditure of their funds. How they meet those choices is a reflection of their values concerning what is important, and provides an index to the

ways of preferred life among people at different levels of the stratification hierarchy.

In the Yankee City research Warner and his colleagues collected detailed budgets for a sample of just over 1000 individuals (not families).
It should be remembered that the work was done in 1933, in the depths
of the depression; unemployment was high (over 70 per cent of the
lower-lower class but only 6 per cent of the lower-upper class) and income was low. The dollar was worth about twice as much in purchasing
power as it is now. Average family income for each class was as follows:

| | |
|---|---|
| Upper-upper | $6400 |
| Lower-upper | 6189 |
| Upper-middle | 2887 |
| Lower-middle | 1621 |
| Upper-lower | 1216 |
| Lower-lower | 882 |

Note that the sharpest break was between the two upper classes and the
rest of the population. There was a great deal of variation in the average
for each class; for example, the upper-uppers ranged from a family
receiving $18,000 to one receiving $1485. The lower-lowers ranged from
$2725 to $340. Obviously, although money was an important deter-
minant of class in the Warner sense, it was by no means the only one.

Warner writes [61]:

The desires of all those who spent money for the things they wanted were
basically physical, but the values which dominated the expression of their
wants were social. . . . When a man in the lower-upper class rented a house
he paid for physical shelter for his family, but he also paid for the "right
kind" of house in the "right" neighborhood which would bring the approval
of his friends and his social superiors. In other words, he rented a house which
he believed would correspond with and reflect his family's way of life. . . .
The etiquette and social rules of the higher classes were more rigid and more
restricted; [yet] choice in action was much more than in the lower classes
[because of more money to spend].

Let us note a few examples of the symbolic nature of purchases. Food
expense per person ranged from $75 per year for the lower-lowers to
$311 for the lower-uppers. Food took 45 per cent of the lower-lower
budget, but only 14 per cent of the lower-upper. If we use the approximate $150 spent by the middle classes as an estimate of the cost of
an adequate diet, we can assume that the people at the bottom were eating far below the minimum for health, and those at the top were spending twice as much as necessary in order to obtain the expensive luxuries
of conspicuous digestion. Indeed, the lower-uppers spent $75 per person
more than the upper-uppers, indicating the greater restraint in consumption of the old-family elite.

Another good contrast is that of the two upper classes in their expenditures for automobiles and formal education. The lower-uppers
averaged three times as much as the upper-uppers for automobile expense, but less than one tenth as much for formal education (vagaries of
a small sample may well have exaggerated these differences, especially
for formal education). Expensive New England prep schools are a necessity for old-family children even during a depression, whereas a luxuri-
ous automobile is the mark of American *nouveaux riches*—indeed it is
the perfect symbol, for it is mechanical and is conspicuous beyond
comparison.

The one item that varied least by class was tobacco: all groups spent
over $16 per person, and none over $30.

The total proportion spent for food, shelter, and clothing in each class
gives a good idea of the amount of leeway left for less urgent purchases
—although variations in the expense of those basic purchases has just
been shown to be enormous. The proportions spent for these necessities
were as follows [62]:

| | |
|---|---|
| Upper-upper | 33% |
| Lower-upper | 35 |
| Upper-middle | 51 |
| Lower-middle | 59 |
| Upper-lower | 66 |
| Lower-lower | 75 |

Warner summarizes his results as follows [63]:

In the budget study one sees the upper-upper class a settled, somewhat sober-
minded people spending their money not for automobiles and other items of
conspicuous expenditure but on charity, taxes, and traveling for business purposes. The lower-upper class, with money to express its preferences, goes in
for conspicuous display, as indicated by expenditures on houses, automobiles,
travel for pleasure, and for sports.

The upper-lower class in contrast with the lowest one clearly indicates that
their values accent social mobility as much as their pocketbook will allow. For
example, they outranked all others for the proportion of their budget spent
on informal education and on moving (the lower-upper class was second). Yet
they show the pinch of circumstances by ranking second only to the lower-
lower people for the money they spent on food and shelter. The lower-lower
people ordinarily spent their money on the sheer necessities but the upper-
lower extend themselves to add a few activities to their lives "to improve their
lot."

These small sample results are supported by the analysis of the much
larger studies summarized by Working that were reported above. It will
be remembered, for instance, that he found that the *proportion* of ex-

penditures spent on clothing went up as the total expenditures went up; thus obviously the *absolute amount* went up much faster. As soon as people had money to spare after feeding and housing themselves, they bought fancy clothes for adornment beyond protection. Similarly, for people whose total expenditures were the same, business and professional folk spent a higher proportion for housing than did clerical workers, and clerical workers a higher portion than did blue-collar workers.

CONCLUSIONS

Social stratification exists within a framework of economic stratification. Our present economic system is one of capitalistic enterprise based on private ownership of property and competition for the rewards of the market. There are social limitations on every phase of the economic system, however. Property cannot be used entirely as desired by the owner; the community sets limits as to what he can and cannot do. Property being taxed differentially, large owners pay more than small ones. Inheritances are controlled and taxed by law. The accumulation of individual property into the corporate collectivities that do the big work of production and exchange is controlled by a changing law that adjusts to shifts in the public conception of common welfare. It has always been thus: the value system of a culture defines property and to some degree controls its relative distribution among individuals. Then it permits some freedom of individual action, and the resulting distribution of incomes becomes one of the prime causes of invidious distinctions between individuals. These distinctions of income and prestige produce an unequal distribution of consumption goods, of power, of life chances.

As our industrial economy has matured, the role of individually owned property in the productive system has weakened. Farmers and businessmen continue to exist and thrive, but an increasing portion of work is done within the framework of large corporations that are "private enterprises" only by virtue of semantic liberality. They are a new species of social institution and have changed our way of life. They create a vast pool of semiskilled workers who float from one job to another as corporate production expands and contracts, and an increasing group of educated technicians in engineering and management who direct the labor of the workmen. All are employees, none owners. Their places in the system depend upon the rules of bureaucratic entry and promotion; business is coming more and more to assume the shape of the government civil service. A man chooses the basic level within which he will work by the amount and type of schooling he gets; the rest depends upon bureaucratic competition. Ownership of these mammoth organizations is dispersed among millions; control is concentrated in the hands of a self-perpetuating management, responsible primarily to it-self [64].

Income is determined by functional role in the bureaucracy. There is competition that sets wages by the interplay of supply-and-demand fac-tors; there is also control that sets wages by fiat and tradition. Who can really estimate how much more a company president is worth than a plant superintendent, or a foreman compared to a sweeper?

The trend of income distribution has been toward a reduction in in-equality. Owners have been receiving a smaller share relative to em-ployees; professionals and clerks have been losing some of their ad-vantage over operatives and laborers. But a lessening of inequality does not necessarily presage an eventual equality; there would be a long way to go before even rough equality is reached, and there is no reason to suspect that the trend will move on without eventually stopping at a new equilibrium far short of equality, unless deliberate political action upsets the trend of the market. In fact, *Fortune* says that the redistribu-tion "has been slowing for some time," and that the further burgeoning of the middle-income group depends on an increase in absolute income for everybody [65].

It is possible to classify American styles of life into five types. The exact lines of division between them in monetary terms have to be drawn arbitrarily, but the styles themselves are quite distinct. As of 1955, the picture looked like this:

At the very top are the one per cent of family units who have an in-come of over $15,000, with an important part of it coming from return on invested capital wealth. They live in "great luxury," for they are plutocrats.

Nine per cent of the families fall between $7500 and $15,000 per year in income. They earn most of it from the salary of the father, who is a professional or business man. They usually live in the suburbs in large houses in a style which we can consider "opulent" but far from the great luxury of the plutocrats.

About 40 per cent (if we include in our calculations the noncash in-come of farmers) of the people live "well." They are in the growing middle-income group that receives between $4000 and $7500. They can afford to own their modest homes, buy a small new car, and perhaps send their children to college. Their income comes from wages and salaries, but in almost half the cases there is more than one worker in the family. A little less than half of these families are headed by a man who wears a white collar, slightly more than half by a man with a blue collar. The entry into this group of so many blue-collar workers, mostly within the last decade, is one of the major social changes in recent history.

About 30 per cent of our families, almost all of whom are headed by blue-collar workers, live "adequately" but not well on incomes that range from $2000 to $4000. They can afford an adequate diet and a warm home. Utilizing that great modern invention, the installment plan, they can often manage to get a secondhand car. But they live from month to month, have no savings, and suffer greatly when they are unemployed.

At the bottom of the scale are the 20 per cent of family units that receive less than $2000 a year. Many live in a way that they, and most other Americans, consider a life of poverty. But they do not all suffer so much as their low incomes suggest, for many are retired and their needs are small (and their incomes are supplemented by savings), many others are young persons without families just starting their work careers, and many live on small farms in a style that may be frugal but is not always difficult. We simply do not have enough information to decide what proportion of these people are actually suffering from poverty.

The two subjects covered in this chapter about which we know the least are the relationships between wealth and power, and the way standards of living are organized in group terms.

Our lack of information about power stems from its nature: people who wield it hide it. The important decisions in our society are made by groups of men who work out compromises among the conflicting interests of organized segments of the population. Sometimes this is done in noisy debate in open legislative sessions or on the floors of large conventions. But there always remains the suspicion, at least for the cynical, that a lot is going on behind the scenes or out in the lobbies that determines the outcome of the open voting. Especially when it comes to the question of the true effects of the concentration of corporate wealth, we remain ignorant. We know the concentration exists, but do not know how to measure the weight it carries compared to other concentrations of countervailing power.

Regarding group standards, both general observation and bits of systematic evidence suggest that families do not decide about an appropriate way to live by always wanting just a little more than they have. True, most would like more money, but that does not mean that they are willing to organize their lives (or feel that they have a realistic chance to organize them) in a way that will maximize their chances of substantially improving their incomes. People think in terms of reference groups of "our sort of folks." Probably the majority of young couples starting their matrimonial careers have *one* of the above described styles of life as their realistic expectation and goal. Father seeks the kind of job that will help him reach it. If there are no small children in the house, mother may well work to help out, but once the goal is reached,

she quits her job, and father reduces his striving in favor of the contentment of relaxation.

REFERENCES

[1] Fred Cottrell, *Energy and Society* (New York: McGraw-Hill, 1955),
p. 33.

[2] Quoted in Arthur Schlesinger, Jr., *The Age of Jackson* (Boston: Little,
Brown, 1945), p. 22.

[3] See Talcott Parsons' discussion of "facilities" in *The Social System*
(Glencoe, Ill.: The Free Press, 1951), *passim*. Also Robert H. Lowie,
*Social Organization* (New York: Rinehart, 1948), Chap. VI, "Property."

[4] Seymour M. Lipset and Reinhard Bendix, "Social Mobility and Occupational Career Patterns; II. Social Mobility," in Bendix and Lipset,
eds., *Class, Status and Power* (Glencoe, Ill.: The Free Press, 1953).

[5] The Editors of *Fortune, The Changing American Market* (Garden City,
N.Y.: Hanover House, 1955).

[6] Herman P. Miller, *Income of the American People* (New York: Wiley,
1955). Miller also uses information from the annual samples of 25,000
families reported in *Current Population Reports*. The small inflation
from 1949 to 1953 will be here ignored in making various comparisons;
the reader should remember, however, that it occurred, and that there
was a considerable increase in average earnings in this short period.
Miller, pp. 152–57, estimates that information on income from direct
questioning of respondents understates actual income, on the average,
by 10 to 20 per cent.

[7] The Editors of *Fortune, The Changing American Market*, p. 262.

[8] *Ibid.*, p. 267.

[9] Selma Goldsmith *et al.*, "Size Distribution of Income since the Mid-
Thirties," *Review of Economics and Statistics*, XXXVII (February,
1954), 3–4.

[10] Elizabeth Hoyt *et al.*, *American Income and Its Use* (New York: Harper, 1954), p. 128. This book is an excellent guide to recent income and
consumption data. See also Hazel Kyrk, *The Family in the American
Economy* (Chicago: University of Chicago Press, 1951).

[11] See Marvin B. Sussman, "The Help Pattern in the Middle Class Family,"
*American Sociological Review*, XVIII (February, 1953), 22–28.

[12] Henry W. Spiegal, *Current Economic Problems* (Philadelphia: Blackis-
ton, 1949), p. 250. The figures are for 1947.

[13] The Editors of *Fortune, The Changing American Market*, p. 266.

[14] Miller, *Income of the American People*, Chap. II.

[15] Hoyt, *American Income and Its Use*, p. 349; based on Census Bureau
samples.

[16] All figures in the following paragraphs are from Miller, *Income of the American People*, Chap. 4.

[17] Hoyt, *American Income and Its Use*, p. 103.

[18] *Ibid.*, p. 112, and The Editors of *Fortune*, *The Changing American Market*, pp. 58–59.

[19] *New York Times*, March 5, 1952, p. 1, and May 4, 1953, p. 20. These articles by Will Lissner are excellent summaries of the basic research studies. See the appendix of the *Fortune* book for references to the original sources.

[20] Hoyt, *American Income and Its Use*, p. 96.

[21] *Ibid.*, p. 107.

[22] Estimate of Simon Kuznets; see Goldsmith, "Size Distribution of Income," p. 18. This trend has been in existence since the Civil War; see Rufus Tucker, "The Distribution of Income among Income Taxpayers in the United States, 1863–1935," *Quarterly Journal of Economics*, 52 (August, 1938).

[23] J. Keith Butters *et al.*, *Effects of Taxation: Investments by Individuals* (Boston: Harvard Graduate School of Business Administration, 1953), p. 106.

[24] Miller, *Income of the American People*, pp. 110–11.

[25] The Editors of *Fortune*, *The Changing American Market*, Chap. 1.

[26] *Ibid.*, p. 264.

[27] *Ibid.*, p. 61.

[28] Hoyt, *American Income and Its Use*, p. xii.

[29] See Henri Pirenne, "Stages in the Social History of Capitalism," in Bendix and Lipset, *Class, Status and Power*. For a general synthesis of the social changes accompanying the transition from primitive agriculture to modern industry, see Cottrell, *Energy and Society*.

[30] Thomas Jefferson, *The Life and Selected Writings of Thomas Jefferson*, Adrienne Koch and William Peden, eds. (New York: Modern Library, 1944), p. 38.

[31] *Ibid.*, p. 51.

[32] See Cleveland Amory, *The Proper Bostonians* (New York: Dutton, 1947).

[33] For the story of the plutocrats see Frederick Lewis Allen, *The Lords of Creation* (New York: Harper, 1935).

[34] The classic study of industrial concentration is Adolf A. Berle and Gardiner C. Means, *The Modern Corporation and Private Property* (New York: Macmillan, 1934). It was followed by the vast but rather inconclusive work of the Temporary National Economic Committee, summarized by David Lynch, *The Concentration of Economic Power* (New York: Columbia University Press, 1946), and by the work of the

National Resources Committee, *The Structure of the American Economy* (Washington: Government Printing Office, 1939). A more recent study is M. A. Adelman, "The Measurement of Industrial Concentration," *Review of Economics and Statistics*, XXXIII (November, 1951), 269–96.

[35] Lynch, *The Concentration of Economic Power*, Chaps. V, VI.

[36] Adelman, "The Measurement of Industrial Concentration."

[37] *Time*, January 2, 1956, pp. 40–51.

[38] Lewis H. Kimmel, *Share Ownership in the United States* (Washington: Brookings Institution, 1952). His data were collected in 1951, under sponsorship of the New York Stock Exchange. Considering that sponsorship, perhaps we should not be surprised that he stresses the large number of persons who own a little stock, and ignores the concentration of most of the outstanding shares in the hands of the few big owners.

[39] Butters, *Effects of Taxation: Investments by Individuals*, p. 25. The data refer to 1949–50.

[40] Peter F. Drucker, "The New Tycoons," *Harper's Magazine*, 210 (May, 1955), 39.

[41] Ferdinand Lundberg, *America's 60 Families* (New York: Vanguard, 1937).

[42] National Resources Committee, "The Structure of Controls," in *Class, Status and Power*, Bendix and Lipset, eds., p. 135.

[43] *Ibid.*, p. 136.

[44] *Ibid.*, pp. 141–42.

[45] David E. Lilienthal, *Big Business: A New Era* (New York: Harper, 1953), p. 26.

[46] David Riesman, *The Lonely Crowd* (New Haven: Yale University Press, 1951), as reprinted in *Class, Status and Power*, Bendix and Lipset, eds., pp. 155, 158. See also in that volume Daniel Bell, "America's Un-Marxist Revolution," pp. 163–72.

[47] It is a startling experience to compare the tone of books written about the concentration of wealth before the war with the more recent versions. Robert A. Brady, *Business As a System of Power* (New York: Columbia University Press, 1943) stressed the national trade organizations that influenced the government, and compared trends in the U.S. with the fascist systems in Germany and Italy. A somewhat different view was expressed by James Burnham, *The Managerial Revolution* (New York: Day, 1941). Now even those who cried in alarm in the past have decided that the big corporations have matured, have responsible managements, are held in check by the power of unions, consumers, and the government. The current theme is that large corporations are inevitable, efficient, and controllable, and that they are creating a system that in actual operation is not very different from socialism, despite vast differences in theory. See Peter F. Drucker, *The Concept of the Corporation* (New York:

Day, 1946); John K. Galbraith, *American Capitalism: The Concept of Countervailing Power* (Boston: Houghton Mifflin, 1952); Lilienthal, *Big Business: A New Era;* Adolf A. Berle, Jr., *The 20th Century Capitalist Revolution* (New York: Harcourt, Brace, 1954). For a dissent, see Paul M. Sweezy, *The Present as History* (New York: Monthly Review Press, 1953).

[48] Good examples of community studies showing local power are: Robert S. Lynd and Helen M. Lynd, *Middletown in Transition* (New York: Harcourt, Brace 1937); Allison Davis et al., *Deep South* (Chicago: University of Chicago Press, 1941); Floyd Hunter, *Community Power Structure* (Chapel Hill: University of North Carolina Press, 1953); August B. Hollingshead, *Elmtown's Youth* (New York: Wiley, 1947).

[49] A summary and interpretation of the many budget studies done throughout the world up to the date of its publication is Carle C. Zimmerman, *Consumption and Standards of Living* (New York: Van Nostrand, 1936). It is encyclopedic in its coverage but diffuse in its synthesis. The classic consumption theory is Thorstein Veblen, *The Theory of the Leisure Class* (New York: Modern Library, 1934; first published, 1899).

[50] Hoyt, *American Income and Its Use*, pp. 342–45.

[51] *Ibid.*, Chap. 9.

[52] Some amusing and shrewd observations on aspects of style of life not so closely tied to income are offered by Russell Lynes, "Highbrow, Lowbrow, Middlebrow," *Harpers' Magazine*, February, 1949.

[53] Richard Centers and Hadley Cantril, "Income Satisfaction and Income Aspiration," *Journal of Abnormal and Social Psychology* (January, 1946); reported in Hoyt, *American Income and Its Use*, pp. 170–71. The 12 per cent "don't know" answers are not included in the percentages.

[54] Some scanty evidence will be presented below in Chapter X.

[55] Hoyt, *American Income and Its Use*, p. xvii.

[56] The figures in this paragraph are taken from Arthur Stratton, "Record Boom in the Works," *Boston Herald*, July 18 and 19, 1954.

[57] Holbrook Working, "Statistical Laws of Family Expenditure," *Journal of the American Statistical Association*, XXXVIII (March, 1943), 43–56.

[58] George Katona, *Psychological Analysis of Economic Behavior* (New York: McGraw-Hill, 1951), p. 178. Katona, the University of Michigan's Survey Research Center, and the Federal Reserve System cooperate in making annual sample surveys that provide what appear to be the richest available data on consumer behavior; they ask for both behavior and attitudes. Katona's book summarizes some of the data and develops a theoretical analysis of it that unites psychological and economic viewpoints—but is weak on the sociology of stratification. See also George Katona, *Consumer Attitudes and Demand* (Ann Arbor: Survey Research Center, University of Michigan, 1953), and current issues of the *Federal Reserve Bulletin*.

[59] See Butters, *Effect of Taxation: Investment by Individuals*.

[60] This thesis has been advanced by James S. Duesenberry, *Income, Saving and the Theory of Consumer Behavior* (Cambridge, Mass.: Harvard University Press, 1949).

[61] W. Lloyd Warner and Paul S. Lunt, *The Social Life of a Modern Community*, Yankee City Series, Vol. 1 (New Haven: Yale University Press, 1941), p. 287.

[62] *Ibid.*, p. 298.

[63] *Ibid.*, pp. 299–300.

[64] Two excellent studies of the data on our economic system from a sociological point of view are Theodore Caplow, *The Sociology of Work* (University of Minnesota Press, 1954), and Wilbert E. Moore, *Industrial Relations and the Social Order* (New York: Macmillan, rev. ed., 1951). And a valuable source book is J. Frederick Dewhurst *et al.*, *America's Needs and Resources: A New Study* (New York: Twentieth Century Fund, 1955).

[65] The Editors of *Fortune, The Changing American Market*, p. 20.

# V

# The Web of Interaction

A LAWYER WON HIS CASE FOR A HEAVY INCOME TAX DEDUCTION
BY PROVING THAT HIS COUNTRY-CLUB ACTIVITIES HAD A DIRECT
EFFECT ON HIS INCOME. FURTHERMORE, HE HATED PLAYING
GOLF. . . . THE BEST APPROACH IS THE INDIRECT ONE IN WHICH
THE YOUNG EXECUTIVE NEVER TALKS SHOP, NEVER SEEMS TO BE
SELLING ANYTHING. INSTEAD, HE LETS THINGS TAKE THEIR NAT-
URAL COURSE, PICKS UP A GAME IN THE OCCASIONAL TWOSOME OR
THREESOME, MAKES POLITE CONVERSATION, MAY LATER OFFER
TO BUY A DRINK, PLAY A HAND OF CARDS, SWAP A STORY OR TWO.
MEANWHILE, HIS WIFE IS GETTING TO KNOW THE OTHER WIVES,
HIS CHILDREN ARE BUSY MAKING FRIENDS IN THE CLUB SWIM-
MING POOL. . . . EVENTUALLY, IT PAYS OFF IN DOZENS OF
DIRECT AND INDIRECT WAYS.                    *Time* [1]

PRESTIGE was defined above as a "sentiment in the minds of men that is
expressed in interpersonal interaction." Most of the studies of it have
emphasized the sentiment. But insofar as a knowledge of the sentiment is
primarily useful because it helps predict what the interaction will be like,
a few researchers have attempted to study the interpersonal contacts
themselves, and we shall examine their results in this chapter.

Interaction, or direct contact between persons, has long been close to
the surface of sociological thought. Marx and Weber used it as an
intervening variable which they knew was operating, although they did
not attempt to watch it [2]. For instance, they said that given certain
economic conditions, some people would be brought together with
common financial interests, and that their contact would eventually
produce common values. Only by this process could groups such as the
proletariat or the bourgeoisie become class conscious—their common
interests would become known to them only through their mutual
interaction. Yet sometimes the process went wrong, and the people
retained "false consciousness" based on old traditions rather than current interests. The theorists could not explain why this happened.

The empiricists of American sociology utilize interaction as a key
variable; it suits their desire for objectivity. It has become a major conceptual tool for those who study process in small groups, either in the

laboratory or the community [3]. For those who wish to study behavior *as it occurs*, interaction becomes the central variable around which others are linked in theoretical systems. The easiest procedure is to find out who interacts with whom, how often, for how long. Initiation of each act of interaction also can be observed to determine who is leader and who is follower. Finally, the quality or content of the interaction can be classified: asking questions, giving opinion, expressing solidarity, venting anger, and so on. This last has not been systematically done outside of the experimental laboratory.

For the student of stratification two types of interaction are important: that of the occupational world, and that of the community of residence. Marx was primarily interested in the first, and Warner in the second. We have discussed many aspects of occupational interaction in the two previous chapters, and therefore will start this chapter with what is known about community interaction.

Warner says that persons of similar prestige associate more with one another than with persons of lower or higher prestige, and that out of this interaction emerge the subcultures peculiar to each prestige level. This interaction may be in informal cliques or formal associations. He defines the clique as follows [4]:

> The clique is an intimate nonkin group, membership in which may vary from two to thirty or more people. As such, it is a phenomenon characteristic of our own society. When it approaches the latter figure in size, it ordinarily breaks down into several smaller cliques. The clique is an informal association because it has no explicit rules of entrance, of membership, or of exit. It ordinarily possesses no regular place or time of meeting. . . . (but) it does have very exacting rules of custom which govern the relations of its members. In-group feelings are highly charged, and members speak of others in the community as outsiders. Feelings of unity may even reach such pitch of intensity that a clique member can and does act in ways contrary to the best interests of his own family. A person may belong to several cliques at the same time.

The statement that cliques are "characteristic of our society" would not be true if "characteristic" were taken to mean "unique," but it does point to the fact that as the social functions of the kinship group and local community decline, many of them are assumed by the clique. In primitive societies or very small and isolated rural areas of modern society there are not many people available to interact with, and a sizable proportion of them are relatives. Thus much of one's time at work and play is spent with relatives and with the few people of one's own age and sex who live nearby. There is not much choice to be had.

In larger towns and cities the choices become many. The extended family weakens as a functioning unit, and thus releases the individual and married couple to search for intimate contacts other than kin. The people of one's age with whom one works on the job usually live in a different part of town; thus if one desires to have close friends outside the nuclear family of spouse and children, one has to organize a special group for that purpose. This special group of friends who meet for recreation, usually in the evening and on weekends, is the clique. It sometimes includes relatives or people with whom one works during the day, but that is a matter of personal choice. Because recreational interaction and style of life are so closely intertwined, the studies of prestige-consumption classes and of cliques are complementary.

Our society is one that is dominated, perhaps more than any other, by change rather than tradition. Not only does the basic structure constantly change, but the placement of persons in various parts of that structure is always being altered. The society changes form, and individuals are mobile. Consequently we cannot learn very much about how to act and what to believe from our grandmothers. Instead, we strive to keep up to date about things. When we want to choose a movie, we go to the one "they say is a swell picture." If we want to discipline our children, we are careful to follow the methods "they" consider proper. If we think of politics, it's "they say the President is slipping." This omnipresent "they" is a vague symbolization of vague currents of opinion. When we look carefully for their source, these opinions seem to come most often from our friends. These friends may get their ideas from a book or a newspaper, but the ideas do not become active parts of our ways of thought until they are talked about and become established as current fashion. Some observers believe that Americans are losing much of their vaunted individuality and becoming more and more subservient to what "they say" [5]. Cliques create and mediate much of our contemporary culture.

## ADOLESCENT CLIQUES

There are characteristic clique patterns for each age group. As every mother knows, children form cliques at an early age, and they soon become so important that Johnny's major weapon against his mother is the cry, "But Billy and Tommy do it, why can't I?" The first clique relationship is likely to be with the boy or the girl next door: mother doesn't permit her four- or five-year-old child to play very far from home. At this age children are not too discriminating; they do not ask whether their potential friends share the same interests concerning all aspects of life. The desire for companionship is paramount, and interests emerge from shared activity. But there is a selective factor at work; the ecological patterning of the city usually means that the children next door are roughly of the same socioeconomic level. This is so important a sorting device that it is often the major motivation behind a family's choice of residence: they want to control the influences of peers on their children by living in an "appropriate" neighborhood [6].

The interactions of the children often bring the mothers together as friends (in a relationship that has certain parallels to the friendships that spring up among men at the factory or office). There are common interests (children) to talk about and common problems to solve (Who started the fight?). Occasionally the fathers also become friends, but less often.

When the children start grammar school, they have a much larger group of age mates to play with, yet for the first few years they are more likely to stay with those friends they already know in their immediate neighborhood, partly because mother wants them to come home directly after school and not wander far away. *But as the children grow older, the physical area they are permitted to cover in their play activities grows, and so does the number of people that are available from which to choose intimate friends.* Some new principles of choice must take the place of mere proximity.

By the time of junior high school, several definite patterns of adolescent clique relationships usually emerge. Some boys and girls will remain isolates, but most will have a close buddy or two, and also will belong to a larger circle of friends. Some of these cliques will remain based on neighborhood proximity, especially those boys' gangs that are mainly concerned with sports. But others will have grown out of school contacts and be centered around specialized activities that would not have enough supporters in the local neighborhood, such as music or hunting or hot rods. These cliques are characterized by the activity that most interests the members; adolescents do not just sit and "interact," they do things together. But the cliques do not draw their memberships from everyone in the school interested in the central activity, for they are composed of boys and girls from a similar prestige-class background. In fact, the activities themselves become class-related, partly because the amount of available spending money has a lot of influence on the activity. Thus, upper-class boys will play golf and tennis and squash and go sailing, while those of the lower class will play baseball and football and learn to box—activities that can be pursued on the streets or on vacant lots.

The typical American public high school is a large and comprehensive one which teaches all things to all boys and girls. In a small town there will be only one high school, and there is a common idea that it is completely democratic because "everybody" is mixed together. The facts are quite different.

First, about half of the adolescents will quit school before receiving a diploma, and these will come almost entirely from the lower classes. Once they have withdrawn, they have very little contact with those who stay in. Second, most of the upper and some of the upper-middle-class children will be sent to private schools, and many of the Catholics to parochial institutions. Third, there is separation within the public school according to curriculums (in Massachusetts, for instance, there are four distinct courses of study: college preparatory, commercial, general, and trade). There is a substantial correlation between prestige class and curriculum chosen, and this separation carries over into recreational cliques. Fourth, even within curriculums boys and girls separate into groups according to family background.

It is true that the mere presence of all sorts of adolescents in a school makes it *possible* for a person to make contacts with others who come from a class different from his own—and in fact, most mobile students make a specific effort to do just that. But it is also true that *on the average* students separate themselves into cliques that are relatively homogeneous in their prestige-class composition. This is even truer in large cities with many high schools, for the schools in middle-class neighborhoods are very different from those in lower-class neighborhoods.

A high-school boy whom I interviewed described the groupings in his public school in New England in the following terms [7]:

Q: What about the good students, what kind of people are they?
A: The really good ones are fruits—you wouldn't want to associate with them. But the middle ones, the majority of the good kids, you get along O.K. with them. When you get lower you get in cliques—your marks get lower —they don't seem to know any better. I don't know, if they would stop and figure it out and realize what they are doing in playing around and having a good time.
Q: You think it is mainly the ones with the lower grades that get in gangs?
A: Yes, definitely.
Q: What sort of things do they do?
A: Oh, well they just go around and they stand on street corners and they are always in a crowd and they never can be alone—always their crowd. . . . They don't want to be told anything; they know it all.
Q: How many are there in a class?
A: Well, in the college course I don't think you will find hardly any. They are all good kids there.
Q: They are mostly in the general course then?
A: Definitely.
Q: What about trade school?
A: Yeh, you will find them there. And in the business course—that is the biggest course in the school. You will find a lot of it there. In the general course, I mean, that is so individual—they take their boxing lessons.
Q: No one can get along with them except their own kind?

A: That is right, definitely. They will bump into you and you could get a broken back and they wouldn't care—you are supposed to watch yourself, you know what I mean.

Q: What age do you think those guys begin to get that way? Was it that way in junior high?

A: Yes, it was. About the 9th grade it started.

Q: Not in grammar school, though?

A: No, I don't think so. Of course, you find a little bit of it there, but it doesn't amount to anything. You know there is a gang, but everybody is in the gang.

Q: So then you are describing three groups in the high school. You've got the big middle group of the fellows that are easy to get along with, you've got the fruits at one end, and the gang guys down at the other end.

A: Yes.

The boy went on to say that his own group was composed of "good" kids of the middle type. He was in the college-preparatory course, did fairly well in school (though he was more interested in amusement and horseplay than studies), and planned to go to a liberal-arts college. His three categories were recognized by most other informants, although some could make finer distinctions; for example, a division of the middle group into the active boys and girls who were leaders in various school activities and the quiet ones who were hardly ever noticed. Here is an example of such a four-way breakdown, offered by a boy in the commercial course who was an active school leader:

Well, there was one bunch of wise guys, there always is. They always hang around together. And then there's some that just sit around and don't do anything, you know, "good" boys. And then there's always, I don't know, ones who like to have a good time, and once in a while they may get into some trouble, but generally pretty good. Just like to have some fun. They're just regular school kids. Then there's always the scholar. . . . I don't like these wise guys. . . . They don't get along too well in school. They don't get good marks in school and they bother the other kids. They're the wise guys with the teachers, too. I suppose you'd call it a sort of bullying crowd. . . . They have cars, a lot of 'em have cars and they go someplace. They have girls with 'em all the time.

It is interesting to compare these New England descriptions with the similar ones Hollingshead got in his study of the Middle Western town of Elmtown (Jonesville). In Chapter II, above, we analyzed his procedures in placing the families of the town into five prestige classes. Here we can turn to his substantive findings about adolescent behavior.

Hollingshead found that just under one half of the 735 adolescents of high-school age had withdrawn from the one public high school in Elmtown, and that they had very little contact with those who stayed on. Most of those who quit school were from lower-class families: 89

per cent of the Class V adolescents, 41 per cent of the Class IV, 8 per cent of the Class III, but none of the Class I or Class II boys and girls had left school.

Hollingshead then studied the clique patterns of those who remained in school. He watched them in the hallways, he observed who went home with whom after school, he interviewed and questionnaired the students to find out "who they hung around with." He discovered 106 cliques of about five members each that were mostly based on associations in the school during and after classroom hours. He found 120 recreational cliques that gathered away from the school; they were slightly smaller in size and often had many of the same members as the school cliques. There were thirty-three cliques based on church or other institutional ties.

The students tended to associate with others of the same family-prestige class. Indeed, 63 per cent of interpersonal relationships with cliquemates were with persons of the same prestige class, 33 per cent crossed one class line, and only 4 per cent crossed more than one class line. Most relationships were among students in the same year of school. When asked to name their best friend, over 70 per cent of the students named someone of their own prestige class, and it was always someone that belonged to a common clique. Dating patterns were similar, except that boys tended to date girls a year younger than themselves and occasionally dated one from a prestige class lower than their own (but seldom from a higher one).

The details of the clique memberships of the high-school students are shown in Table 1, which represents 1258 clique ties among some 390

Table 1. *Elmtown High School: Percentage of Clique Relations within and between Prestige Classes* [8]

| | BOYS | | | | |
|---|---|---|---|---|---|
| Class | I & II | III | IV | V | Total |
| I & II | 49 | 38 | 13 | 0 | 100 |
| III | 11 | 61 | 27 | 1 | 100 |
| IV | 5 | 33 | 60 | 2 | 100 |
| V | 0 | 13 | 31 | 56 | 100 |

| | GIRLS | | | | |
|---|---|---|---|---|---|
| Class | I & II | III | IV | V | Total |
| I & II | 56 | 26 | 18 | 0 | 100 |
| III | 7 | 64 | 28 | 1 | 100 |
| IV | 4 | 21 | 70 | 5 | 100 |
| V | 0 | 4 | 36 | 60 | 100 |

adolescents. In every instance each prestige class cliqued more among itself than with outsiders. This is all the more remarkable at the extremes when it is remembered that there were only 35 Class I and Class II students and only 26 Class V students in school, so they had a very restricted choice at their own level. Yet it can be noted, for example, that of all the clique ties maintained by boys of Classes I and II, 49 per cent were with persons of the same class, 38 per cent with Class III students, 13 per cent with Class IV students, and none with Class V students.

Hollingshead picked a few students from different prestige levels and asked them to rate the reputation of their fellow students in a manner similar to the way in which he derived the prestige classes of families. They agreed with each other to the extent of a mean coefficient of correlation of .76, and divided their fellows into three broad groups (with some subdivisions ignored by Hollingshead), which were described as follows [9]:

1. *The Elite.* The elite is composed of leaders in extracurricular student activities, as well as in church work, in the youth groups, and in social affairs. . . .

2. *The "Good Kids."* In adolescent language the "good kids" are "never this or that." They come to school, do their work, but do not distinguish themselves with glory or notoriety. Some two-thirds of the students are in this category.

3. *The "Grubby" Gang.* "Grubbies" are set off from the other students for many reasons—unfortunate family connections, personality traits, lack of cooperation with teachers, living in the wrong part of town. Boys and girls identified as grubbies are "nobody" in the eyes of the non-grubbies. To be rated a grubby is comparable to being blacklisted. According to student beliefs, grubbies have no interest in school affairs; besides, they are trouble makers. . . .

Reputation among high-school peers was a function of family-prestige class; there was a corrected coefficient of contingency of .77 between the two variables. Seventy-seven per cent of the Class I and Class II students were put into the "elite"; 78 per cent of the Class III and 73 per cent of the Class IV students were considered "good kids"; and 85 per cent of the Class V students were rated as "grubbies." *Thus clique relationships, dating patterns, and personal reputation among peers were explained to an extraordinary degree as flowing from family-prestige class membership.* Hollingshead adds that in those cases where an adolescent spent his time with members of a clique whose class standing was higher than his own, he was usually a person of considerable charm and talent who was on the path of upward mobility.

If one adds the few "scholars" in Elmtown to the groupings just described, he will have a system of classification that is exactly parallel to the one found in the New England school discussed above. However, there was an important difference: the latter school had very few upper-middle-class students (Class III), so that the elite (or active members of the vast middle group of "good kids") were energetic and ambitious working-class adolescents, many of them aiming for occupations that would raise their status. This difference made the class groupings in the school less pronounced than those in Elmtown.

The notorious boys' gang that has so captivated the imaginations of magazine writers is usually composed of lower-class boys who have either quit school or are on the verge of so doing. Often these gangs turn from generalized hostility and aggressive forays to genuine lawbreaking. There can be little doubt that their behavior is largely a reflection of their position at the bottom of the class hierarchy: they are reacting to a lack of hope for success within the dominant culture [10].

The adolescent clique is a crucial medium for maintaining the stratification system. It reinforces the attempts of most families to shape their children in their own images. The cultures of the various types of cliques specifically adapt to the activities of teen-agers the general values of the class level of their parents, and thereby teach those values more effectively than the preachments of the parents. A boy who goes around with a group of adolescents who all take the college-preparatory course in high school and expect to go to college absorbs a way of life that keeps up his motivation for the minimum requirements of bookwork in high school and subtly prepares him for the years ahead. He learns to behave in school in a way that does not alienate the teachers; he learns the manners and the poise that will get him into a college fraternity; he learns that dependence on parents for an allowance, although often inhibiting, is a small price to pay for the long-run rewards of an occupation that will bring leadership and community prestige. By contrast, the boy from the other side of the tracks learns to value other behaviors. Athletic prowess is more important than success with books; early sex activity is the mark of masculinity; a constant though subdued war with authority figures—be they parents or teachers—is the mark of a man of self-respect, for the rewards the authorities can offer are not worth the price of subservience. The clash between these values and the ones emphasized by the teachers motivates such boys to quit school, to go to work early, and to end up with low-skilled jobs.

The ambitious boy from the wrong side of the tracks early discovers that if he wants to be a big success with teachers, he has to pull away from his companions and enter, even if only on the fringe, a middle-class clique. The "democracy" of the American high school does not lie in equality; it is based on the fact that there is sufficient flexibility in the system for boys and girls to associate with peers from social levels other than their own if they work at it hard enough. The adolescent clique is thus a conservative device that reinforces the stratification system, but it is also a means for the ascent and descent of individuals within that system.

Out of adolescent life grow marriages. Many studies indicate that marriage choices tend to occur among prestige-class equals. Part of this may be due to the sheer factor of propinquity, for residential areas sort people into class levels, and a man is likely to meet (and perhaps to propose to) a girl in his own neighborhood. But many other factors put class equals in contact, such as adolescent cliques, clubs and associations, college fraternities, and the like. As an example, we can cite a study of Hollingshead in New Haven. He tabulated the thousand marriages that occurred in 1948, and rated the spouses according to the socioeconomic quality of the area in which they lived, dividing the city into six strata. There were no interracial marriages, and very few that crossed the lines between Catholics, Protestants, and Jews. Within religious groups there was considerable mixing of ethnic stocks. Regarding class level, he found that in 58.2 per cent of the cases both partners came from the same stratum. In 82.8 per cent they were from the same or an immediately adjacent stratum. In cases where there was a crossing of class lines, the man married down more often than he married up. (Are women more class-conscious than men?) [11].

### ADULT CLIQUES: MEMBERSHIP

What about the clique patterns of adults? Let us first examine quantitative data on the amount and range of participation. The Warner material on Yankee City is summarized in Table 2, which represents 22,063 clique memberships; the table is the result of detailed observation and interviewing over a period of several years. Each clique that a person belonged to was classified according to whether it contained members from only the same class as himself, the same class plus the one above it, the same class plus the one below it, the same class plus the ones immediately above it and immediately below it, and all others. We cannot make a direct statistical comparison between the figures for Yankee City and those for Elmtown, for Warner gives us membership in "pure" and "impure" cliques, while Hollingshead classifies individual clique relationships (pairs of persons). For instance, a Yankee City man in the upper-lower class who belonged to a clique with members from both the upper-upper and the lower-upper class has ties with persons of both classes, but we do not know in what proportion.

Although precise comparisons between Elmtown and Yankee City are impossible, given the form in which the data are presented, it can be seen that in both instances the lower-middle class interacts down more than up, while in the case of the upper-lower the tendency is up more than down—indicating the blurred line between those two groups and

## Table 2. *Yankee City: Percentage of Clique Memberships within and between Prestige Classes* [12]

| CLASS | PER CENT OF MEMBERSHIPS IN CLIQUES THAT INCLUDE PERSONS FROM: | | | | | |
|---|---|---|---|---|---|---|
| | Same Class Only | Same, Plus One Class Above | Same, Plus One Class Below | Same, Plus One Class Above & One Below | All Others | Total |
| Upper-upper | 37 | .. | 39 | .. | 24 | 100 |
| Lower-upper | 21 | 35 | 18 | 12 | 14 | 100 |
| Upper-middle | 20 | 8 | 30 | 3 | 39 | 100 |
| Lower-middle | 14 | 13 | 28 | 15 | 30 | 100 |
| Upper-lower | 16 | 28 | 15 | 19 | 22 | 100 |
| Lower-lower | 24 | 32 | .. | .. | 44 | 100 |

their relative isolation from the upper-middle and the lower-lower groups. And it looks as if the adolescents may have a tighter system than the adults, for the number of class-mixed cliques in Yankee City is extensive (perhaps reflecting certain adult activities, such as politics, that draw from all levels). There is enough variation around the trend of cliquing within a class level to make it dangerous to define a prestige class as those people who associate exclusively with one another, as Warner occasionally does (see Chapter II, above).

Warner tried to accumulate data on every family in Yankee City. Such thoroughness is impossible in a big city, but sampling methods can be used. For instance, in our study of Cambridge, Massachusetts (part of the Boston metropolitan area) in 1953, Davis and I asked 199 men between the ages of thirty and forty-nine to tell us the occupations of their three best friends (whom they met, incidentally, about equally through residential propinquity, work, and school). The occupations of the respondents and their friends were coded according to prestige level. The code, which represents slices out of the continuum published by North and Hatt (see Chapter III), was as follows:

| North-Hatt Ranks | Description | Code |
|---|---|---|
| 1–23 | Professional, top business, or government | 0 |
| 24–36 | Semiprofessional, medium business, or government | 1 |
| 37–60 | Skilled worker, small business, upper white collar | 2 |
| 61–77 | Semiskilled worker, petty business, lower white collar | 3 |
| 78–90 | Unskilled worker | 4 |

After coding, the scores for the three (or fewer) best friends of each respondent were averaged, and the distribution is shown in Table 3. Once again, the relationship is clear: people tend to associate with persons of similar socioeconomic status. The tetrachoric coefficient of correlation is .70. And once again, the top level is the most exclusive in its behavior [13].

Table 3.  Cambridge: Percentage Distribution
of Status of Best Friends

| STATUS OF RESPONDENT | N | AVERAGE STATUS OF THREE BEST FRIENDS: | | | | | |
|---|---|---|---|---|---|---|---|
| | | 0-0.9 | 1-1.9 | 2-2.9 | 3+ | Has none | Total |
| 0 | 19 | 74 | 16 | .. | .. | 10 | 100 |
| 1 | 34 | 32 | 38 | 15 | 3 | 12 | 100 |
| 2 | 82 | 10 | 15 | 50 | 12 | 13 | 100 |
| 3 | 47 | .. | 9 | 38 | 30 | 23 | 100 |
| 4 | 17 | .. | .. | 35 | 35 | 30 | 100 |
| TOTAL | 199 | | | | | | |

It is interesting to note that the proportion of isolates who live without close friends goes up as one descends the status scale (which has been found in several other studies as well—for example, by Rossi in Philadelphia [14]). Indeed, the Cambridge data give a tetrachoric coefficient of correlation of .21 between occupational level and number of friends (defined as those with whom one exchanges house visits once a month or more).

The quantitative data from these studies are representative of several others that come to the same conclusion: although recreational participation is not completely limited to a given prestige level, in general people associate "with their own kind." Furthermore, people at lower levels have less interaction than those at higher levels, at least in terms of exchange of visits in their homes. We need more comparative studies in different communities using a refined and standardized index of amount and range of clique interaction, for such an index is probably the simplest and the most objective measure of "tightness" in a prestige order. Such studies would permit us to make precise comparisons, for instance, between an old New England community and a new and presumably more equalitarian community in the Pacific Northwest, or between the various ethnic groups and the white Protestant majority [15].

## ADULT CLIQUES: STYLE

The qualitative data we have on differences in activities among cliques at different prestige levels are not adequate. They are hard to get, for the only fully satisfactory technique is participant observation—sharing the lives of one's subjects. Furthermore, the content and style of clique behavior, as compared to its amount, probably varies more as one moves from one region of the country to another, or from small town to big city. Yet we have some information. Novels are one good source of material, and the Middletown studies have many suggestive descriptions, as do the "profiles" in the first Yankee City volume. But the most systematic analysis appears to be the chapters on both white and Negro cliques in *Deep South* [16]. Allison Davis and Burleigh B. and Mary R. Gardner describe clique life among the white people in this way [17]:

. . . these persons conceived of themselves as being members of a small, very intimate group—"our little crowd" (the clique) to which, for certain types of affairs they were willing to add a few more couples to form "our large crowd" (the *extended clique*). Beyond these there was a somewhat wider circle of persons with whom they were willing to participate, who could not be ignored, and whose opinion mattered, but with whom they did not associate intimately. Any very large affair should include the entire extended clique, and to omit a member suggested discrimination. Members of the wider participation circle, however, might be deliberately excluded and there would be no ill-feeling, while beyond this latter group there were types of people who, under no conceivable conditions, could be invited to a social affair.

By observation, interviewing, and a study of the social columns of the local newspaper (which reported upper- and middle-class affairs, but not lower-class ones), they identified more than sixty cliques of some seven hundred people. They illustrated upper-class behavior by describing one typical group which included a few upper-middles but was dominated by the elite. This group met at least once a week, usually in the home of a member. But the gatherings were not planned. "Just drive around past our houses any night about nine o'clock and see where the most cars are and then come in."

Behavior at their gatherings was described as "carefree" [18]:

Each man brings his own whiskey which he deposits in the kitchen and from which he mixes drinks for himself and for the woman. The host supplies glasses, ice, sugar, and water, and occasionally Coca Cola, the favorite mixer. Both men and women drink heartily, and all prefer to mix their own drinks. Early in the evening the group may sit in one room discussing personalities, group activities, and community affairs or making plans for future group participation. As the evening wears on, the conversation begins to pall; couples dance; the group spreads out into other rooms and the garden, and flirtatious activities begin. . . . These affairs are recognized by the group and are expected of members, but are usually conducted surreptitiously and privately, in dark corners, in the garden, or in parked cars. For the most part, however, these flirtations are confined to group gatherings, and men do not generally have private or secret appointments with other men's wives.

The activities of this clique, then, and the behavior which members expect of each other center about three things: drinking, talking, and flirting. . . . Members must be able to participate in the conversations of the group spontaneously and without intellectual effort—conversations which deal principally with the "crowd" and its activities. The bulk of this conversation is apparently related to drinking and is a significant element in the clique behavior. In most of it there is little attempt to convey information or to discuss ideas. The clique members are not communicating but communing.

Davis and the Gardners point out that the clique members often met during the day in separate groups: the women for lunch and shopping, the men in their offices or at lunch. They generalize that upper-class cliques rarely had systematic organization in the form of clubs, although they did sometimes give formal parties with an invitation list.

A typical middle-class clique is described this way [19]:

The behavior of this group is much more formal and restrained than that of the groups already described. They meet about once a week to play bridge at some member's home; and they participate together, periodically, in other activities, such as week-end parties and picnics. Neither the men nor the women have much other activity in common. . . .

At the weekly bridge parties, although the hostess serves refreshments, alcoholic drinks and flirtations are absent. The mother of one of the women called the clique members "nice, quiet young people" who "get together and play bridge and just have a good time without all the drinking" . . .

Middle-class cliques in general are much more frequently characterized by formal organization into card clubs, by more restrained behavior, and by more definitely limited activity than among the upper class. In the middle class, mixed groups are not the rule, as they are among the upper-class people; men have their groups and women have theirs. . . .

Often in their clique or club gatherings the women concern themselves with elaborate decorations and refreshments, vie with one another for the most unique appointments or the most unusual delicacies. This behavior is especially characteristic of the upper-middle class, where such embellishments are economically possible and where display of wealth has the greatest significance. This kind of preoccupation is almost entirely lacking in upper-class groups, where little effort is made to decorate the house as a setting for a gathering, where food refreshments are considered of only minor importance, and where a large quantity of corn whiskey is often the primary criterion for the "good party."

In Old City, lower-class people do not participate in cliques of the type just described. Women gossip in neighborhood clusters "over the back fence"; men may meet in a tavern, but "lower-class husbands and wives have little social participation together outside of the home. They do not often visit or entertain as a family group, except occasionally for kinspeople [20]." But this does not necessarily mean that they have no friends, for the neighborhood women and men on the job may feel close without forming cliques.

A careful analysis revealed that the more active (mainly female) cliques whose meetings were reported in the paper overlapped in membership, with some women belonging to two or more. But the linkages were systematic, and divided the whole group of four hundred persons into two sections, with very few people belonging to cliques in both. One section included most of the upper and some younger upper-middle-class people, and only a few others. The other section included some older upper-middles and the active lower-middles. The younger and more mobile people associated with others slightly above them; older people hardly ever did. In general, the younger the average age of a group, the more limited was its range of ages and the more extensive the range of class levels included in it.

*Deep South* also gives an excellent description of Negro cliques. They show the same general patterns, adapted to the different economic circumstances of the Negro community.

The authors conclude that the clique "cements the individual to his class and also provides an opportunity for the mobile person to rise a notch in the social scale through his acceptance by those who are already slightly 'above' him [21]." This type of grouping offers solidarity with persons beyond the family that promotes emotional stability, a sense of well-being and belongingness, a belief in personal worth. Clique mates are helpers in time of trouble, celebrants in time of joy. Consequently, they are the locus of social norms or values originally learned from family and from adolescent friends. One seeks companions in adult life who share one's central beliefs; norms are subtly changed as fashion changes in the group; one radically shifts values by joining a new group; one passes his group's standards on to his children.

## THE CONTRAST BETWEEN MIDDLE AND WORKING CLASS

Let us explore a little further the contrast suggested in *Deep South* between the socially active upper-middle class and the inactive working class. Many middle-class people combine clique activity and business life. In a crude sense we may say that they use social opportunities to make contacts that have a business or professional function in that they provide new customers or clients. But in a broader sense it is better to say that these people simply merge the two spheres and do not see them as separate compartments of living. The husband meets people through his business life, entertains them, and they become friends; or his wife meets people in the community who become business contacts. It is a basic part of the job of most businessmen to be at ease in their contacts with new people; they come to value sociability as an end in itself, and it cannot be expected that they will suddenly reverse themselves at 5 P.M.

Business people live in neighborhoods filled with others like themselves, who share the values of sociability. Their homes are not overcrowded, and they can entertain without strain. They tend to be stable residents who stay long enough in one house to become acquainted with their neighbors. They become activists in club work, and are likely to run into the same townsmen at the parent-teacher association, the Rotary Club, or the country club. Particularly in small towns, the number of such active business families is small enough for them all to become acquainted. Even their children form a single, extensive web of contacts.

In the past, business connections were primarily based on buying and selling: the insurance man, the doctor, the owners of the retail stores and the small factories all were tied together in a mutual exchange of goods and services. Sinclair Lewis wrote of their relationships in *Main Street* and *Babbitt*. But the more recent tendency is for these men to turn into executives in large corporations, for the local stores and factories have often become branches of national chains. This change means that the executives are less permanent members of their local communities, for their companies shift them around from one part of the domain to another. And it means that the relationships among them have changed flavor somewhat, for instead of independent entrepreneurs who both cooperate and compete with each other in the open market, they have become incumbents within hierarchies who are more likely to seek personal esteem and advancement than a sale. Their social life has found a new spokesman in John P. Marquand.

William H. Whyte, Jr., of *Fortune* magazine, wrote a penetrating account of the clique behavior of the new type of executive in *Is Anybody Listening?* He got most of his information from their wives, but also interviewed many junior executives as well as some of their bosses. The senior men told him, "with a remarkable uniformity of phrasing," that the social activities of junior executives and their wives were extremely important for business success, and that the good wife is [22] "(1) . . . highly adaptable, (2) highly gregarious, (3) realizes her husband belongs to the corporation." Here are a few examples of descriptions of the ideal wife [23]:

EXECUTIVE: She should do enough reading to be a good conversationalist. . . .
Even if she doesn't like opera she should know something about it, so if the
conversation goes that way she can hold her own. . . .

EXECUTIVE: The hallmark of the good wife is the ability to put people at their
ease.

WIFE: The most important thing for an executive's wife is to know everybody's
name and something about their family so you can talk to them—also, you've
got to be able to put people at their ease.

There are patterns of behavior that are appropriate for each level
of the hierarchy, and no ambitious junior executive dares to get far out
of line. He cannot drive a Cadillac before he has passed through the
Buick stage or he will be thought "pushy." On the other hand, he must
not drive an old Ford or he will look like a failure. One wife, speaking
of this pattern, told Whyte [24]:

It makes me laugh. If we were the kind to follow The Pattern, I'll tell you
just what we would do. First, in a couple of years, we'd move out of Ferncrest
Village (it's really pretty tacky there, you know). We wouldn't go straight
to Eastmere Hills—that would look pushy at this stage of the game; we'd go to
the hilly section of Scrubbs Mill Pike. About that time, we'd start going to the
Fortnightly's—it would be a different group entirely. Then about ten years
later, we'd finally build in Eastmere Hills.

Whyte emphasized that the rule is to keep up with the Joneses but
never to get far ahead of them. The timing of each shift must be carefully calculated. Similarly, one must not have odd personal tastes that
make him too "different." An "intellectual" or "aesthete" is mistrusted
because he is different, and different people cannot be understood, thus
their actions cannot be anticipated. It is because competition within
corporate hierarchies depends so much on the interpersonal relations
among executives (equals and immediate superiors) that their total way
of life, which includes their wives and children, becomes important.
If you deal with a man in a market situation, you deal primarily with
the quality of his goods or services. But if you have to work with him
every day, his total personality is relevant. Therefore, corporations
think of themselves as "one big happy family," and most families are
intolerant of too much "difference" among members which might
threaten the smooth operation of joint living.

The most difficult problem for a wife is to keep adjusting her friendships as her husband moves up the hierarchy. At first she may well
protest, for she has probably been brought up to believe that friends
are friends and need not be dropped if their husbands fail to move up
the ladder. But soon she learns of the difficulties. A promotion for her
husband means more money and a more opulent way of life which

embarrasses her old friends if they cannot match it. And most important of all, promotion means power [25]:

I love people and I've made many intimate friends in the company, but since Charlie got his new job it's just been hell on us. He has so much control over their lives, and it's gotten so complicated.

All of this means that a wife's growth in social skill must match her husband's growth in business skill; as Everett Hughes puts it, marriage is a mutual mobility bet. And sometimes the betters lose [26]:

I've seen it happen so many times. . . . He marries the kid sweetheart, the girl next door, or a girl from the jerkwater college he went to. They start off with a lot in common—but then he starts going up. Fifteen years later he is a different guy entirely; he dresses differently, talks differently, thinks differently. But she's stayed home—literally and figuratively.

In order to avoid problems with wives who cannot adjust, many corporations now interview the spouse of a man they propose to hire. If she does not seem capable of growth, if she is not willing and eager to subordinate herself to the corporation, her husband does not get the job.

These examples have been stressing the clique life of executives working for the same company, but of course in most communities the executives from many companies mix together. There is rather rigid age grading, for the promising young men interact in their own set where they feel comfortable; only rarely are they invited to the homes of the older and more senior men. Such occasions require "company manners" and the younger men must always be on guard, for they are being watched and evaluated by their boss or his friends.

Junior executives gain many advantages from clique ties with young men from other companies. Such contacts give them a chance for a social circle in which it is possible to relax, in which the competition among men in the same company can be avoided. But this interaction also provides useful contacts, for it is much easier to do business with another company through people who are friends. And sometimes the contacts turn into opportunities; junior executives are relatively interchangeable, and often move from one company to another when there is a good opening and a chance for promotion. To take advantage of such an opening, a man has to know about it.

There is a sharp contrast between this merged recreational and business life and the separated work and family spheres of the average factory worker. He seldom brings his work mates home; he never entertains the foreman, and the foreman certainly gives no thought to a worker's wife before promoting him.

A study that illuminates this difference was done by Floyd Dotson in

New Haven, Connecticut, in 1948 [27]. He interviewed fifty working-class couples in their homes. They no longer lived in the ethnic districts of their parents, and were typical of the "new" working class who were reared in American cities and not on farms or in Europe. Most of the husbands held semiskilled jobs in the factories. Most of the wives stayed home and did not work for pay.

Dotson found that in some respects the way of life of these people approximated middle-class norms: they emphasized the importance of the nuclear (as compared to the extended) family, and preferred not to live with relatives nor to depend upon them much for exchange of such services as baby sitting. The notions of "companionship" in husband-wife relations, and of "permissiveness" in child rearing, were widespread. It appeared to Dotson that as these young couples had learned American ways different from those of their parents, they had learned family patterns that were not far divergent from middle-class standards.

However, there were two striking differences: (1) these working-class people had very few intimate friends other than kinfolk; (2) they interacted frequently with siblings. It must be remembered that because they came from working-class homes, they tended to come from large families and had many brothers and sisters available. Furthermore, a sizable proportion of their siblings lived in or near New Haven, as working-class people tend to stay put if employment opportunities are available. Dotson says [28]:

According to our data, a high percentage of the intimate social contacts of working-class people are confined to siblings and siblings-in-law. . . . In at least 15 of the 50 families, social activities were dominated by the spouses' sibling groups. In another 28 families, regular contacts of varying strength were maintained. Two families had no living siblings and in only five cases was there a clear-cut absence of important contacts between siblings.

Considerable interaction with siblings and parents (more often than not the wife's family) was accompanied by lack of nonkin clique ties. About two fifths of the families had no intimate friends other than kin; an almost equal number belonged to loose friendship groups that included husbands and wives, but exchange of visits was not frequent. In only two instances (out of fifty!) did the husband and wife participate in a tight clique of the middle-class style. In six instances the wife continued to interact with a group growing out of her school contacts, and in five the husband continued to spend much time with his boyhood friends (usually via an athletic club). Rarely did a man interact in evening hours with friends from work.

Why did these people not participate in much clique activity? The sheer availability of siblings was one reason, for they offered all the companionship many of the couples desired. Furthermore, they were easy to interact with—they all understood one another, lived in the same way, did the same things. It was simple to bundle up the kids, take them to sister Jane's house, put them to sleep on any available bed, and then play cards and talk and drink beer. In those few instances where the respondents had a sibling who had climbed into the middle class, visits were rare. Several couples reported receiving invitations to Christmas dinner from successful siblings which they declined because they would not feel natural and relaxed in the more opulent homes.

Similarly, a few of the respondents found it easy to maintain contact with some old school chums. But as the number of small children in the house multiplied, interaction rates went down. Money was one reason: it was expensive to hire a baby sitter, and they felt less free in taking infants on visits with nonrelatives. Furthermore, the emphasis on family life led many people to prefer the company of their children [29]: "Sure, kids are a hell of a lot of expense and trouble, but what would a home be without them? If you want the honest-to-God lowdown on me, you can say that my real life is right here with my family. We're family people; we find most of our fun in life right here at home."

Through the years these factors (plus movement from one part of town to another) broke up most of the adolescent cliques that these people once had. Dotson expected new friendships formed from the immediate neighborhood or from work to replace them, and was surprised to find so little interaction. Although the informants verbalized about the ideal of neighborliness, mostly they meant only that it was proper to smile and say hello. One man said [30]: "I've found out you can't really be friends with most people because pretty soon they'll do you dirt."

Dotson explained the fear of intimacy on four grounds: (1) the antisocial aspects of crowded and flimsy apartment houses which made privacy a rare pleasure; (2) the fear of lack of control over intimacy—people might come in when they were not wanted, or stay too long; (3) a concern that too much borrowing of food and other items might ensue; (4) dislike of gossip. Despite these fears, some women did have one or two close friends among immediate neighbors (about two fifths of the respondents). And interestingly enough, most of the couples remembered with pleasant nostalgia the more intimate atmosphere that existed in the ethnic neighborhoods of their youth, and regretted that their current area was "colder." Yet they made it cold by their own behavior.

Dotson reported that the men did make friends with work mates, but seldom tried to extend those friendships to include the families of both parties. Often the work mates were of a different ethnic group, and the men did not believe that their wives would get along well together. Often they lived in a different part of town. And because the pattern of sociability off the job was lacking, an individual who might want to extend an invitation was hesitant and feared it might be rebuffed.

The Lynds remarked about Middletown that working-class people were taught to use their hands, and middle-class people their personalities—that the one group sold physical labor, the other social skill. It may well be that social skill is a trait of personality that, on the average, gets people into middle-class occupations. Or it may be that the cultural traditions of urban working-class life do not teach people how to make friends easily, or to trust them too fully. At any rate, the evidence indicates a marked quantitative and qualitative difference in clique behavior between the two strata [31].

FORMAL ASSOCIATIONS

Every study of formal associations—large groups with explicit purposes and rules of membership—shows the same trend: people of higher prestige status belong to more voluntary formal associations than people of lower status—this despite the fact that many associations are especially designed for lower status people.

For instance, Warner and Meeker report that in Jonesville the distribution of memberships per family in formal organizations is as follows: [32]

| Prestige Class | Per Cent Belonging to One or More Associations | Average Memberships per Family |
|---|---|---|
| Upper | 100 | 3.6 |
| Upper-middle | 100 | 3.5 |
| Lower-middle | 55 | 1.1 |
| Upper-lower | 50 | 0.9 |
| Lower-lower | 30 | 0.7 |
| All families | | 1.3 |

The figures from Yankee City, those from Komarovsky's study of New York City, and Reissman's more recent study of Evanston, Illinois, all show the same tendency: middle- and upper-class people are *much* more active in formal organizations than members of the working and lower classes [33]. Furthermore, when an organization contains persons of mixed prestige background, the higher status persons are much more likely to be the leaders—with the exception of some instances where upper-class persons stay in the background and use upper-middle-class representatives as their agents.

Warner and Meeker say that in Jonesville most associations draw their membership from only one or two strata, and the prestige of the association matches that of its members. Furthermore, each stratum favors different types of organization.

The small upper class patronizes the country club, three exclusive women's clubs, and certain professional and business groups. The women's groups are partly social, partly charitable in function. Actually these organizations have as many upper-middle as upper-class members, but the latter dominate them and set the tone. This tone is well described for the women's clubs [34]:

> The members of the upper class profess an interest in travel, a knowledge of foreign lands; they value objects associated with tradition and antiquity; they are preoccupied with leisure-time pursuits, with activities which have dubious economic value, but which are considered worthy, noble, and honorable. The upper-class woman who has both sufficient money and sufficient leisure time (with servants to take care of her home) is expected to become a patron of the arts.
>
> Through these associations, the members of the upper class not only express their common interests, but also perform activities of high value to the total society. They preserve relics and other symbols of prestige which are valued by the community. They patronize and sponsor the arts, through lectures and discussions of books, music, and the theater. They perform charitable activities by contributing to needy individuals and institutions.

Many upper-middle-class people belong to the upper-class organizations, but stand somewhat aside in deference to their superiors (the small size of the upper class in Jonesville forces them to mix with those of slightly lower rank). The upper-middle class also belong to many groups that reach far below them in status, such as lodges. But their major energy and leadership aspirations go into civic clubs—the Rotary, the women's clubs, educational and health groups. Instead of emphasizing graceful leisure pursuits, the civic clubs are busy promoting community improvement. Most characteristic, probably, are the male luncheon clubs, which feature conviviality and ritual expressions of community solidarity, guest speakers with messages of uplift, and committees that promote betterment projects of various sorts. The fact that leadership in such a club contributes to a man's business and professional success is one of those happy accidents that blends public and private good.

There is, in general, a sharp break between the upper-middle and lower-middle classes with respect to the kind and amount of participation in associations. While the members of the upper and upper-middle classes participate together, there is little participation between the upper-middle and the lower-middle classes. . . . While the differences between the upper-middle and the lower-middle classes are quite clear, it is difficult to distinguish between associational behavior of the lower-middle class and that of the upper-lower [35].

This gap in participation above the lower-middle group, and the continuity between that group and the upper-lower, parallel their behavior in informal cliques, as discussed above. But Warner and Meeker report that this vast "common-man" group displays two different types of activity: the fifth who are white-collar workers tend to participate either in the civic clubs already mentioned, or in others that are modeled after them but cater to the "little fellows." Thus they are either quiet members of Rotary, or more active members of Lions. They also belong to the more ritualized lodges like the Masons and the Eastern Star. Their wives participate in the ladies' auxiliaries of the lodges, emphasizing a more rigid sex separation than is the case with higher status families. These white-collar families are usually very active church members (probably more so than any other group), and participate extensively in the clubs sponsored by their churches.

The four fifths of the common-man group that are foremen and skilled workers and steady semiskilled operatives are much less active in formal organizations. They may belong to a church or a lodge or a labor union, but in general they prefer to stay at home.

The organizations of the common man stress inclusiveness—they say they are friendly folk, and anybody can belong. Thus their clubs have a wider spread of rank within them than do the exclusive groups of the top people in town. Warner and Meeker add [36]:

The ideologies of the lower-middle and the upper-lower associations express the ideologies of the people—patriotism, brotherhood, democracy, equality—and the symbols are those which provoke common interest on the part of the "common man." This preoccupation with equality gives satisfaction to individuals of low status, for it minimizes, or overlooks, status distinctions and gives them a sense of similarity with other individuals regardless of their position in the community. It reflects the attitudes of those people who are reluctant to accept an inferior status and declare, "We haven't any classes here, we're all equal."

The lower-lower class, feeling hostile and suspicious toward the "snotty" folk above them, seldom join anything, and attempt to reduce interaction with people outside their own level to an absolute minimum. They withdraw to escape being snubbed.

Even churches—institutions supposedly rejoicing in the common brotherhood of a common Father—are class typed. In most American towns the people of higher status belong to those Protestant denominations that feature services of quiet dignity and restrained emotion, such as the Episcopal or Unitarian groups. The common men are more often seen at the Methodist and Baptist churches, where the services are more vigorous, or in Catholic churches (reflecting their origins as part of the "new" immigration from southern and eastern Europe). Those lower-class individuals who go to church at all are most likely to join revivalistic and fundamentalist sects. Some authors believe that the higher status groups are expressing in ritual and dogma attitudes of conformity and support for the good life within the current social system, whereas the religions of the lower status people are offering a palliative for failure in this life through salvation in the next [37].

Warner points out that formal associations perform several functions. Some of them are vehicles of exclusion: restricted groups for the pursuit of certain activities that represent the interests of a limited number of persons, often of similar prestige class. Thus there are upper-class social clubs that do not admit anyone without an approved pedigree. There are labor unions that are organized as conflict groups to obtain through struggle a greater share of economic benefits for the working class. There are trade associations, churches, ethnic societies, professional associations. Every interest in modern society is represented by a cluster of special organizations.

But formal associations also serve as unifying forces that cut across special interests. There are community and patriotic organizations that appeal to all status levels and emphasize the common interests of all citizens. They tend to hold together a social fabric that might otherwise be torn apart by factional interests. Yet even in these groups prestige status is not forgotten: they are usually led by active upper-middle-class businessmen for whom "community service" and personal advancement go hand in hand. These men are motivated to lead, and they have the necessary social skill. Ordinary workmen usually stand modestly aside.

Formal associations and informal cliques are mutually dependent structures. Many formal associations grow out of friendship groups that decide to regularize by a written constitution procedures that started over cups of coffee. And membership in formal groups introduces people to each other and often leads to clique activity. This is particularly true among leaders, who interact regularly to conduct association business and end up as personal friends.

## INTERACTION AND POWER

Formal associations are one of the key structures that are utilized to exercise power in a community. True, the ultimate in power rests with government, which monopolizes the use of force. But governmental agencies do not live in a world unto themselves, initiating their decisions according to their whims. They are mediating agencies that compromise the interests of various groups in the community. Those groups attempt to influence government through their formal associations.

In the chapter on occupational activities, we discussed some aspects of power on the national scene. It was pointed out that the crucial point at which to study the exercise of power is in actual decision making. However, that turns out to be a very difficult task, for secrecy is usually thrown around the decision-making process in order to protect it from too much outside pressure. It is a little easier, however, to study this process in the local community.

For a private citizen to have more influence than his vote automatically gives him, he must have contacts with the men who control important affairs. Thus the study of interaction networks is one way of analyzing the actual exercise of power. There is a network of interlocking cliques and associations that activates the latent power in a community. Our best study of this system is Floyd Hunter's *Community Power Structure* [38], an analysis of a Southern city of half a million persons.

Hunter was interested in the process by which the community made decisions about major projects, such as the Community Fund or the expansion of the city limits. He assumed that there were hierarchies of power in government, business, labor, "high society," and the Negro community that somehow got together on such matters. He first assembled a rather large list of all people who appeared active in community projects by inquiring at the Chamber of Commerce, the Community Council, the League of Women Voters, and similar organizations. Then he asked fourteen judges (who were themselves active persons) to pick the names of the fifty most important people on the list. He found fairly good agreement among the judges; for instance, one leader received votes from eleven of the fourteen judges; one received ten votes; one received eight; four received six, and so on. He finally narrowed the list to forty leaders, and was able to interview twenty-seven of them. He asked about their backgrounds and particularly about their interaction with the other leaders.

He discovered that twenty-three of these persons were important men in business (finance, commerce, manufacturing). Four of the leaders were officials in government, two were labor-union officials, six were professional men (five lawyers and a dentist), and five were leaders in the leisure pursuits of the society crowd. Although many were members of the upper class in prestige terms, this was not true of all of them, and certainly many of those in the city who had top prestige were not among the power elite. The power and the prestige hierarchies were related, but were not identical.

In general, the businessmen dominated the councils of the decision makers. They were presidents or board chairmen of the important firms in the region. Their offices in those firms, and often (but not always) their private wealth and family prestige, were the sources of their power. But holding office was not enough: *a man had to be active through long periods of time before he became important in influencing major decisions.* Young men served a sort of apprenticeship, and worked their way up by committees and board memberships in community organizations. Older men often pulled back from those memberships and exercised power through their younger agents.

Interviews with the leaders (and with the many persons in the community who dealt with them on big issues) showed that they operated as one extended clique—they all knew each other, and understood how to organize the latent power of the group for specific projects. Each was influential in some special sphere of city life, and their informal contact with one another thus was the route whereby the strength of the various spheres (each represented by one or more formal organizations) was mobilized. But the real initiation of action came from the few leaders; not, ordinarily, through the regular activities of the larger associations.

Furthermore, it became clear that about a dozen of these persons had the greatest power. When the whole group of leaders was asked to designate the top few men in town, or to pick the one they would consider most important in starting some new project, the same dozen names were always chosen. In turn, these top men reported that their dozen colleagues were the ones they knew best, interacted with most often, considered most powerful. Most of them were in fact the leaders of one or another subclique growing out of some functional grouping— thus one would be at the head of the banking crowd, another represented the utility interests, and so on.

Of the twenty-seven leaders interviewed, all except the two labor leaders and one merchant were college graduates. Sixteen were natives of the state (twelve of the city). Of the top forty leaders fifteen inherited their fathers' businesses and three others inherited a name and a fortune sufficient to make them potential men of influence. The remaining twenty-two were "self-made" men; that is, they were able to climb from middle-class backgrounds and educations to positions of top influence (and substantial wealth) through success in corporate bureaucracies and their legal satellites.

The Negro community was essentially a separate universe. It had a leadership structure of its own that was only dimly understood by the white men of prominence. Indeed, the few Negroes who were occasionally consulted by the white leaders exaggerated their position and power—their influence was partly due to the mere fact that the whites did consult them.

About half a dozen of the leaders specialized in liaison work with state and national power figures. They worked in the shadows of the lobbies where so much legislative and administrative work gets done. Hunter told me that he is now studying the interactions among the leaders who link local power groups into national networks. He believes that some three to four hundred men are the active and influential persons that make up the core of the national power structure. But as was pointed out in the preceding chapter (and as Hunter himself wrote), it would be a mistake to assume that there is a single power pyramid in each community, and a single power pyramid in the country as a whole. There are shifting groups that organize and dissolve around specific issues. Yet it does seem that the same faces appear very often in one group after another. Certainly the smaller the community, the more likely it is that the same persons will dominate all of the more important activities. Their interaction network, which often combines recreation and business, is the place where the many interests in the community represented by large formal organizations come together for compromise and adjustment. In Hunter's study it was obvious that the major active interests were business interests. Although there were two labor leaders, a couple of politicians, and some Negro leaders who presumably spoke for mass interests and had some connections with the top group, the interests of the ordinary folk were represented mainly through the feelings of *noblesse oblige* of the business leaders.

CONCLUSIONS

Feelings of superiority and inferiority are acted out when men and women meet to work and play. Thus direct observations of interaction and interpretations of verbal prestige rankings are different means of studying the same basic phenomena.

The evidence is clear: persons of similar prestige are likely to associate with one another in those recreational situations where free choice is available. The differential costs of the activities engaged in at different status levels, and the different educations, habits, and values that characterize people at the separate prestige levels make people more comfortable when interacting with their own kind. Furthermore, the ecological patterning of cities puts people of similar buying power together as neighbors.

In those more structured situations that produce formal organizations, the same forces are at work, but in even greater strength. The different economic and social interests of the various strata lead them to organize separate organizations that seek to advance their special goals.

The direct observations of frequencies and qualities of interaction in local communities and national networks are just beginning. The techniques of study are more advanced in social-psychological studies in controlled laboratories than in field studies of actual communities. But many investigators are trying to apply the more rigorous techniques to the field situation. As their procedures improve, we shall be able to systematize knowledge that now has to be discussed in more vague terms such as "influence," "power," "cliquishness," "standoffishness," "community solidarity," and "gossip channels."

REFERENCES

[1] *Time*, August 8, 1955.

[2] And Weber's contemporary and friend, Georg Simmel, made interaction his key concept; see Kurt H. Wolff, trans. and ed., *The Sociology of Georg Simmel* (Glencoe, Ill.: The Free Press, 1950). It is interesting to note that the adroit Marxist sociology of Nikolai Bukharin, *Historical Materialism* (New York: International Publishers, 1932) draws heavily on Simmel but not on Weber.

[3] For a brief overview, see Chris Argyris, *An Introduction to Field Theory and Interaction Theory* (New Haven: Yale Labor and Management Center, 1952), and Henry W. Riecken, Jr., and George C. Homans, "Psychological Aspects of Social Structure," in Gardner Lindzey, ed., *Handbook of Social Psychology*, Vol. II (Cambridge, Mass.: Addison-Wesley, 1954).

[4] W. Lloyd Warner and Paul S. Lunt, *The Social Life of a Modern Community*, Yankee City Series, Vol. I (New Haven: Yale University Press, 1941), pp. 110–11.

[5] David Riesman *et al.*, *The Lonely Crowd* (New Haven: Yale University Press, 1950).

[6] The generalizations in this and succeeding paragraphs about childhood and adolescent cliques are based on unpublished interview materials of mine gathered with the cooperation of "The Mobility Project" at Harvard's Laboratory of Social Relations in 1951. See also Celia Burns Stendler, *Children of Brasstown* (Urbana: College of Education, University of Illinois, 1949); Bernice L. Neugarten, "Social Class and Friendship among School Children," *American Journal of Sociology*, LI (January, 1946), 305–13; and W. Lloyd Warner *et al.*, *Who Shall Be Educated?* (New York: Harper, 1944).

[7] A recorded interview from "The Mobility Project"—see the preceding footnote.

[8] August B. Hollingshead, *Elmtown's Youth* (New York: Wiley, 1947), p. 214. Hollingshead gives a brief summary of his book in W. Lloyd Warner *et al.*, *Democracy in Jonesville* (New York: Harper, 1949), Chap. 12.

[9] Hollingshead, *Elmtown's Youth*, p. 221.

[10] See Frederick Thrasher, *The Gang* (Chicago: University of Chicago Press, 1927).

[11] August B. Hollingshead, "Cultural Factors in the Selection of Marriage Mates," *American Sociological Review*, XV (October, 1950), 619–27. He gives a useful bibliography of other studies.

[12] Warner, *Social Life of a Modern Community*, p. 354. I have reordered and condensed the original data.

[13] Joseph A. Kahl and James A. Davis, "A Comparison of Indexes of Socio-Economic Status," *American Sociological Review*, XX (June, 1955), 317–25. The table in the text was not published in the article.

[14] Peter H. Rossi, *Why Families Move* (Glencoe, Ill.: The Free Press, 1955).

[15] For studies of interaction networks in rural communities and villages see Otis D. Duncan and J. W. Artis, *Social Stratification in a Pennsylvania Rural Community* (State College, Pennsylvania: Pennsylvania State College Agricultural Experiment Station Bulletin 543, 1951). Also James West, *Plainville, U.S.A.* (New York: Columbia University Press, 1945).

[16] Allison Davis, Burleigh B. Gardner, and Mary R. Gardner, *Deep South: A Social-Anthropological Study of Caste and Class* (Chicago: University of Chicago Press, 1941), Chaps. VII, IX.

[17] *Ibid.*, p. 138.

[18] *Ibid.*, p. 139.

[19] *Ibid.*, pp. 144–45.

[20] *Ibid.*, p. 147.

[21] *Ibid.*, p. 170.

[22] William H. Whyte, Jr., *Is Anybody Listening?* (New York: Simon and Schuster, 1952), p. 146. See also his description of life in a suburban community occupied by young couples: "The Transients," *Fortune*, May through August, 1953.

[23] Whyte, *Is Anybody Listening?*, pp. 152–54.

[24] *Ibid.*, pp. 154–55.

[25] *Ibid.*, p. 160.

[26] *Ibid.*, p. 174.

[27] Floyd Dotson, *The Associations of Urban Workers* (unpublished Ph.D.

thesis, Yale University, 1950). See also his "Patterns of Voluntary Association among Urban Working Class Families," *American Sociological Review*, XVI (1951), 687–93.

[28] Dotson, *The Associations of Urban Workers*, p. 139.

[29] *Ibid.*, p. 122.

[30] *Ibid.*, p. 161.

[31] For further discussion of the relations between family, class, and clique, see Talcott Parsons, "Age and Sex in the Social Structure of the United States"; "The Kinship System of the Contemporary United States"; and "An Analytical Approach to the Theory of Social Stratification," all in his *Essays in Sociological Theory, Pure and Applied* (Glencoe, Ill.: The Free Press, 1949). Allison Davis, "The Motivation of the Underprivileged Worker," in William F. Whyte, ed., *Industry and Society* (New York: McGraw-Hill, 1946). Marvin B. Sussman, "The Help Pattern in the Middle Class Family," *American Sociological Review*, XVIII (February, 1953), 22–28. E. Franklin Frazier, *The Negro Family in the United States* (Chicago: University of Chicago Press, 1939).

[32] Warner *et al.*, *Democracy in Jonesville*, Chap. IX. This chapter was written by Marcia Meeker.

[33] Warner, *Social Life of a Modern Community*, Chap. XVI; Mirra Komarovsky, "The Voluntary Associations of Urban Dwellers," *American Sociological Review*, XI (December, 1946), 689–98. Leonard Reissman, "Class, Leisure and Social Participation," *Ibid.*, XIX (February, 1954), 76–84; Reissman cities additional studies. See also Genevieve Knupfer's excellent synthesis of many studies, "Portrait of the Underdog," *Public Opinion Quarterly*, Spring, 1947, pp. 103–14. John M. Foskett, "Social Structure and Social Participation," *American Sociological Review*, XX (August, 1955), 431–38.

[34] Warner, *Democracy in Jonesville*, p. 133.

[35] *Ibid.*, p. 138.

[36] *Ibid.*, p. 142.

[37] For example, see the essay by Max Weber, "The Social Psychology of the World Religions," in *From Max Weber: Essays in Sociology*, H. H. Gerth and C. W. Mills, eds. (New York: Oxford University Press, 1946). See also Chapters 9 and 10 of Warner, *Democracy in Jonesville*.

[38] Floyd Hunter, *Community Power Structure* (Chapel Hill: University of North Carolina Press, 1953). Other relevant community studies were cited above in the previous chapter.

# VI

# Class Consciousness and Political Ideology

IN PITTSBURGH 73 YEARS AGO, THE MEN WHO BEGAN THE AMER-
ICAN FEDERATION OF LABOR . . . WROTE IN THE PREAMBLE TO
ITS CONSTITUTION: "A STRUGGLE IS GOING ON IN ALL THE NATIONS
OF THE CIVILIZED WORLD BETWEEN THE OPPRESSORS AND THE OP-
PRESSED OF ALL COUNTRIES, A STRUGGLE BETWEEN THE CAPITAL-
IST AND THE LABORER, WHICH GROWS IN INTENSITY FROM YEAR
TO YEAR."

IN WASHINGTON LAST WEEK, 20 A.F.L. AND C.I.O. LEADERS, WHO
PLAN TO MERGE FORCES AT A JOINT CONVENTION NEXT DECEM-
BER, AGREED ON A NEW CONSTITUTION. . . . INSTEAD OF ECHO-
ING THE MARXIST MANIFESTO, THE NEW PREAMBLE PROCLAIMS
ALLEGIANCE TO "OUR WAY OF LIFE AND THE FUNDAMENTAL
FREEDOMS WHICH ARE THE BASIS OF OUR DEMOCRATIC SOCIETY."
THE WORDS "STRUGGLE," "OPPRESSED," "CAPITALIST" AND "LA-
BORER" ARE NOT EVEN MENTIONED IN THE DOCUMENT.

*Time* [1]

WHEN PARENTS SAY to their children, "Our type of people don't behave that way," whom do they mean? When they say, "Don't play with children like that," to whom do they refer? How do Americans categorize themselves vis-a-vis others, and what do these categories imply about shared ideas and joint action?

If you ask a man who he is, he will probably reply by using one or two labels [2]. If you persist, and ask for all the labels that properly apply to him, you might get a list something like this:

| | |
|---|---|
| John O'Connel | Catholic |
| American | Irishman |
| Lawyer | Chicagoan |

He is unlikely to add: upper-middle class. In that sense Americans are not class-conscious.

But suppose you continue the conversation. You ask him what it means to be a lawyer. He might tell you that he became a lawyer

157

through hard struggle, for his parents were immigrants who had a hard life. They encouraged him to "make something of himself" so that life would be easier. They gave him a little money, and he earned some more himself, thus managing to pay his way through college. He had a particularly difficult time starting his law practice, for the people he knew in his neighborhood could not afford lawyers. However, through some friends he met in college he managed to get a job in a big law firm. He married, soon moved to a suburb, and joined several clubs. Eventually he was even accepted into a club which seldom admitted Irish Catholics. He made many contacts with the right people. He reared his children to be "Americans, not micks," though they continued to be good Catholics. Although he still loved his parents, he felt a little awkward when he visited them and their elderly friends came in to talk, for the grammar used was poor and the manners displayed were crude. Similarly, he suspected that his parents were a little uncomfortable in his house if his "fancy" friends happened to be there at the same time; his father had once asked him, "How can you have anything in common with those people?"

To the degree that both the lawyer and his parents recognize, even without having clear labels to use, that they now live in different social worlds, Americans are class-conscious.

Prestige ranking and class consciousness are opposite sides of the coin. When people in a community rate each other as "higher" and "lower," it is likely that they have some notions about where they themselves fit. But it would be a mistake to assume that everyone sees himself just as others see him. Before we have a complete picture, we must ask our respondents both to talk about other people and to tell us about themselves. Then we can put the various descriptions together. Up to this point we have been primarily interested in the way respondents evaluate other people; here we ask them to look in the mirror and tell us what they see. Furthermore, we explore the current evidence pertaining to the Marxist hypothesis that people who consider themselves alike will have similar beliefs about economics and politics and will tend to act in concert to promote their special interests.

Research men like Warner arrive at their conclusions about class consciousness in the same way as they decide about prestige rankings: by living with their subjects, watching their behavior, listening to them talk, and abstracting generalizations that appear to them to organize and simplify their observations. So much of their material has already been presented in this book that we need add no more here. But there is a more direct approach: go to the door and ask. As a representative of that method, we can take Professor Richard Centers, now of the Uni-

versity of California at Los Angeles. He was motivated to ring doorbells because he was interested in a theory.

Centers observed that much of the theoretical argument concerning
the importance of social classes in our society arose from a basic premise,
namely, that membership in class groupings gave people certain interests—that is, it was to their advantage *over that of some other group*
if decisions were made in certain ways. For instance, the rich people
would gain by a sales tax that would take a bigger proportional bite out
of the incomes of poor people than of the rich, whereas the poor would
gain if tax monies were raised through a graduated income tax that had
higher rates for higher incomes. But before "interests" could be translated into organized group action, people had to recognize what their
interests were, and had to get together with other people who had
similar interests so that they could multiply their effectiveness in the
political arena. According to the theory, when any category of persons
who had certain realistic or "objective" interests in common became
aware of that fact, they would likely begin to think of themselves as the
same sort of people and would begin to act in concert. This is what is
known as the "interest-group" theory of social class behavior. Note that
it involves several steps: objective interests in common, recognition of
that common bond, an evolving group or class consciousness, and
finally, organization to promote the common advantage. Centers put
the theory this way [3]:

. . . a person's status and role with respect to the economic processes of society imposes upon him certain attitudes, values and interests relating to his role
and status in the political and economic sphere . . . furthermore, the status
and role of the individual in relation to the means of production and exchange
of goods and services gives rise in him to a consciousness of membership in
some social class which shares those attitudes, values and interests.

Obviously, this theory is similar to that of Marx, who believed that
most social attitudes were rationalizations of the interests created by
one's economic position. Furthermore, Marx believed that in modern
capitalist society there were basically only two sets of interests—those
of the bourgeoisie and those of the proletariat, and that they were so
fundamentally opposed that open warfare and revolution would be
bound to occur as soon as the proletariat were fully conscious of the
objective facts. Such full consciousness would arise at a certain stage in
capitalistic development when the proletariat would be herded together
into great factories, would interact under circumstances of misery, and
would begin to pay heed to the small group of agitators and propagandists who would point out the facts to them. Marx seems to have

meant that class consciousness was a necessary prerequisite for the common political ideology.

The Marxist interpretation of class consciousness leads to predictions diametrically opposite from the Warner approach. To oversimplify, Warner would say something like this: Every community is stratified into prestige levels. Most individuals would like to have as much prestige as possible. So long as they believe that prestige differences are inevitable and even just, individuals will not attempt to overthrow the system but will simply try to climb within it. If the country-club set were abolished, how could anyone have the fun of maneuvering to get accepted as a member? *Warner says that Americans try to climb as individuals; Marx predicted that the proletariat would, once we reached full capitalism (and we certainly have done that), attempt to get ahead as a group.* Feeling that individual advancement was impossible, the group would have to get together and change the system, which seemed to be designed solely for the benefit of the bourgeoisie.

It is clear that we have not had a class revolution. It is also clear that the communist revolutions in the world so far have occurred in backward countries long before they reached full capitalism. We cannot here examine the sweep of modern history in order to learn what was wrong with the Marxist theory or attempt to construct a better one, but we can look at one crucial aspect of the problem and analyze the empirical data on class consciousness in our country. Let us follow Professor Centers as he approached the doorbells of the nation.

THE RESEARCH OF CENTERS

Centers began by noting that in previous public-opinion surveys (such as the famous one conducted by *Fortune* magazine in 1940) about 80 per cent of Americans consistently called themselves "middle class." Some popular writers seized upon these figures to proclaim that America was almost completely a middle-class country—that if we had any class consciousness at all, it simply meant that we mostly thought of ourselves as belonging to the same big group. But Centers noticed that the figure quoted came from the following question, which offered only three alternatives:

"What social class do you consider that you belong to?

      1. Upper class
      2. Middle class
      3. Lower class"

He also noticed that when respondents were asked the question in open-ended form (without a specific list of answers from which to choose), many would call themselves "working class." Centers made a reputation for himself by changing the wording of the fixed answers through the addition of "working class" as one of the possible replies. When he asked a nationally representative cross section of 1097 adult white men in 1945 which class they belonged to, offering them the four alternative answers, he got the following replies:

| | |
|---|---|
| Upper class | 3% |
| Middle class | 43 |
| Working class | 51 |
| Lower class | 1 |
| Don't know | 1 |
| "Don't believe in classes" | 1 |
| | 100% |

In subsequent samples he got almost the same distribution. He rightly concluded that Americans do not like the term "lower" class, and that this dislike was the main conclusion to be drawn from the *Fortune* survey, not that they actually thought of themselves as overwhelmingly middle class. But his conclusions went a bit further, and leaped beyond his data; he pointed to the low number of "don't knows" and to the consistency from one sample to another, and said [4]: "The authenticity of these class identifications seems unquestionable." But Centers did not try any other lists of answers. Actually, the search for the basic labels of self-identification used by the public should be pursued by systematic open-ended interviewing without fixed alternative answers (which Centers did not attempt); once established, the labels can then be used in closed questions in order to discover other attitudes with which they may correlate.

However, let us accept Centers' position for the moment and look at the rest of his data. What types of persons called themselves upper class, or middle class, or working class? Using occupation as the method of sorting the respondents, Centers found that each occupational group gave themselves class labels as shown in Table 1. Obviously, professional, business, and white-collar people considered themselves predominantly middle class, and manual workers considered themselves predominantly working class. But we must not overlook the lack of complete consensus: about one third of the white-collar men thought of themselves as working class, and about one fifth of the manual workers considered themselves middle class. Thus, there was a clear-cut average tendency, but there was also considerable overlap among groups.

Both the agreement and the disagreement were also shown in another study by Centers which was reported in Chapter III, above. In that study he asked a national sample to tell him which specific occupations they thought belonged to the upper class, middle class, working class, or lower class. It will be remembered that the majority of respondents put big businessmen, doctors, and lawyers into the upper class; other professional persons and small businessmen into the middle class; and artisans and factory workers into the working class. But there was systematic disagreement; people enlarged the composition of the particular class they identified with themselves. Thus, the majority of both those who called themselves middle class and working class claimed white-collar people as colleagues.

*Table 1. Class Identification of Various Occupational Groups* [5]

| | | PER CENT WHO CALLED THEMSELVES: | | | | | |
|---|---|---|---|---|---|---|---|
| OCCUPATIONAL GROUP | N | *Upper Class* | *Middle Class* | *Working Class* | *Lower Class* | *No Answer* | *Total* |
| Large business | 54 | 13 | 78 | 7 | .. | 2.0 | 100 |
| Professional | 73 | 4 | 81 | 10 | .. | 5.0 | 100 |
| Small business | 131 | 3 | 70 | 24 | .. | 3.0 | 100 |
| White collar | 172 | 2 | 61 | 34 | 0.6 | 2.4 | 100 |
| Skilled manual | 163 | 2 | 26 | 71 | 1.0 | .. | 100 |
| Semiskilled | 174 | 1 | 14 | 83 | 1.0 | 1.0 | 100 |
| Unskilled | 77 | .. | 18 | 75 | 7.0 | .. | 100 |
| Farm owners & managers | 153 | 3 | 42 | 51 | 1.0 | 3.0 | 100 |
| Farm tenants & laborers | 69 | 2 | 16 | 73 | 2.0 | 7.0 | 100 |
| ALL GROUPS | 1066 | 3 | 43 | 51 | 1.0 | 2.0 | 100 |

After concluding that occupation was the major criterion of class membership, Centers asked his respondents to choose from a closed list the most important secondary criteria. They picked the items in the following order, with almost half the respondents choosing the first one: beliefs and attitudes, education, family, money. There were some minor variations in votes according to the class of the respondent, and Centers was gratified to find that most of the people who were identified with a given class tended to define it similarly.

Incidentally, Centers has compared the answers to his identification question given by various groups of people classified according to the Warner system. He used a sample of five hundred "old Americans" in Los Angeles in 1949, and found that the correspondence between the two systems was rather good. In particular, the break between the middle and working (or in Warner terms, upper-lower) classes came at the same point on both scales. Specifically, a score on the Index of Status Characteristics of 51 to 53 is the indeterminate point for Warner; people with that score might be either lower-middle or upper-lower class. Above that score Warner predicts that they will almost surely be lower-middle or higher; below that point they will be upper-lower or below. And Centers found that it was the people with I.S.C. scores of 51 to 53 who identified themselves as either middle or working class in equal proportions. Above that score they went middle class in about 70 per cent of the cases; below it they went working class in almost equal percentages [6].

Once he had defined his classes according to the criteria of self-identification and had shown that identification was closely linked to occupation, Centers went on to explore ideological differences. He constructed a "conservatism-radicalism battery" from six questions:

1. Do you agree or disagree that America is truly a land of opportunity and that people get pretty much what's coming to them in this country?

2. Would you agree that everybody would be happier, more secure and more prosperous if the working people were given more power and influence in government, or would you say that we would all be better off if the working people had no more power than they have now?

3. As you know, during this war many private businesses and industries have been taken over by the government. Do you think wages and salaries would be fairer, jobs more steady, and that we would have fewer people out of work if the government took over and ran our mines, factories and industries in the future, or do you think things would be better under private ownership?

4. Which one of these statements do you most agree with? (1) The most important job for the government is to make it certain that there are good opportunities for each person to get ahead on his own. (2) The most important job for the government is to guarantee every person a decent and steady job and standard of living.

5. In strikes and disputes between working people and employers do you usually side with the workers or with the employers?

6. Do you think working people are usually fairly and squarely treated by their employers, or that employers sometimes take advantage of them?

He then scored each question according to whether the answer favored the working people and government intervention (radical), or employers and individual initiative (conservative). Each question was weighted equally, and an additive score was computed for every respondent showing whether his answers were predominantly in one direction or the other. Centers ended up with five categories of persons: ultraconservative, conservative, indeterminate, radical, ultraradical.

The questions in Centers' battery do not form a scale in the rigorous sense of Guttman (as described above in Chapter III); for example, two persons giving conservative answers to four out of the six questions will not necessarily answer the same four questions conservatively [7]. The criterion of scalability that Centers applied was much less rigorous; he intercorrelated the answers to the specific questions and found that they tended to hang together. It seems permissible to use the battery as a first approximation toward politico-economic attitudes, but future research could well do with a more refined instrument. After all, why should we assume that conservatism-radicalism is a single dimension? If the literal meaning of those words is followed, a conservative is a man who wants to leave things about as they are, and a radical is one who wants to change them. But some radicals will want to change things to improve the lot of the manual laborer, some the farmer, some the white-collar worker, some the Negro, some the Southerner, and so on. It takes adroit political maneuvering to get all these radicals working together to make up a single platform of change through government action; for a brief period the Democrats managed to do that, as discussed below. Under more ordinary circumstances the various radicals may tend to work together more harmoniously than they will cooperate with conservatives, but they are not a homogenous lot. Consequently, we need several conservative-radical scales covering different types of issues.

The problem of validity flows from the questions of reliability and scalability just discussed. The test of validity that Centers used was voting behavior. He found that, in general, the conservatives voted for Dewey in 1944 and the radicals for Roosevelt, but the correlation was far from perfect. Five per cent of the ultraradicals voted for Dewey, compared to 55 per cent of the ultraconservatives. But that left 45 per cent of the ultraconservatives voting Democratic, which makes predictions of voting from ideological attitudes rather weak. (Because of the way the questions were worded, most people tended toward "conservative" answers, even many Roosevelt voters.)

The Centers battery is probably a better measure of ideology than the correlations with voting would suggest. There is only a general tendency for Republican candidates to be more conservative than Democrats; divisions within the parties are deep. Furthermore, in national elections, and even more in local contests, other issues are involved besides economic reform. Voting behavior is not a good test of the validity of an ideological scale.

How do conservatism and radicalism relate to class identification? *Perhaps the main finding of Centers was that answers to the identifica-*

*tion question were predictive of answers to the ideological battery.* Let us contrast the percentages of self-labeled middle-class and working-class persons who fell into the various ideological categories [8]:

|  | Middle Class | Working Class |
|---|---|---|
| Ultraconservative | 35% | 12% |
| Conservative | 33 | 23 |
| Indeterminate | 21 | 33 |
| Radical | 7 | 19 |
| Ultraradical | 4 | 13 |
|  | 100% | 100% |

The conservative persons were more likely to come from the middle class, the radicals from the working class (all five differences within rows were statistically significant). The over-all tetrachoric correlation between class identification and ideology was .49 (it was slightly higher for urban than for rural persons). Note, however, that the differences were due entirely to the middle-class persons, who were conservative and consistently avoided radical answers. But the working class gave as many conservative as radical answers (and a great many working-class persons were "indeterminate," which means they gave inconsistent answers).

Centers further discovered that if he held occupation constant and varied class identification, he got substantial variations in ideology. Thus business, professional, and white-collar people were generally conservative, but those who called themselves middle class were much more so than the minority who called themselves working class. Similarly, the minority of manual workers who called themselves middle class were more conservative than the rest of the manual workers who called themselves working class (though this difference was less marked than the preceding one). The details are shown in Table 2. Comparisons such as these led Centers to say that his data supported the "interest-group" theory of social class behavior, for it seemed that appropriately class-conscious members of a stratum had attitudes more typical of that stratum than did the minority whose objective occupational status and subjective identification were at variance.

We might add, "Almost, but not quite." Careful inspection of Table 2 discloses that one gets slightly better prediction of ideology by varying occupation than by varying class identification. This is neatly summarized by Centers' tetrachoric correlation coefficients: The correlation between identification and ideology is .49, whereas that between occupation and ideology is .56 [9]. True, the difference is small, but if class consciousness were an intervening variable between occupation and ideology, the difference should go in the opposite direction. That is,

Table 2.  *Occupational Stratum, Class Identification,*
*and Conservatism-Radicalism* [10]

PER CENT WHO WERE:

| STRATUM AND CLASS | N | Conservative | Indeterminate | Radical | Total |
|---|---|---|---|---|---|
| *Urban business,* *Professional &* *White-collar:* | | | | | |
| Middle class | 298 | 74 | 20 | 6 | 100 |
| Working class | 100 | 47 | 30 | 23 | 100 |
| *Urban manual* *workers:* | | | | | |
| Middle class | 83 | 37 | 30 | 33 | 100 |
| Working class | 318 | 25 | 34 | 41 | 100 |

if occupation produces class consciousness, which in turn produces ideology, then people who have "false consciousness" should have false beliefs—i.e., manual workers who consider themselves middle class should have middle-class beliefs. The data show that their beliefs are in between, but closer to other workers than to business people. A cautious interpretation of the data would suggest that both class consciousness and ideology tend to be consequents of occupational position, but the sequence of causation between class consciousness and ideology is not clear. Furthermore, there is much causation left entirely unexplained after occupation has been accounted for, inasmuch as the correlations between occupation and the other variables, though significant, are not high.

Centers found some small but interesting differences between the classes on attitudes other than conservatism-radicalism. In general, the middle class (compared to the working class) were more satisfied with their jobs and their incomes, less envious of the high incomes of such persons as doctors and lawyers, less concerned about the low incomes of factory workers and laborers, more convinced that individual success was based on ability rather than luck or "pull," more liberal in feeling that it was proper for women to take jobs outside of the home, more convinced that they have an adequate chance to enjoy life, and more optimistic about the chances of their children to succeed in the world. In comparing the desirable aspects of a job, the middle class were more interested in a chance for self-expression, the working class in security [11].

As a final test of the validity of his notion that occupational status was at the root of class consciousness and ideology, Centers correlated those variables with several other possible determinants. The only one that seemed to have any relationship independently of occupation was education. The more educated a man was, the more likely was he to consider himself middle class—regardless of occupation. And in general, the more educated he was, the more likely was he to be conservative, except for those who had postgraduate degrees (professional people were about as conservative as high-school graduates, thus slightly less so than college graduates, who were mostly businessmen) [12].

Arthur Kornhauser summarized the results of Centers' work and that of other investigators up to the beginning of 1950 [13]:

The opinion surveys and political and social studies as a whole indicate that class differences are greatest in regard to issues that obviously and directly affect the interests of people at upper, middle, and lower levels differently. Rather consistently the lower income groups are more in favor of government control of business and extending government welfare activities, sacrificing certain institutional property rights and unlimited opportunities for individual achievement in the interests of increasing security, overcoming the concentration of influence in the hands of the wealthy. There is also evidence that the poorer groups have more extreme nationalistic attitudes, greater religious traditionalism, and generally a more restricted outlook on the world, associated presumably with limited education.

It is tempting to catch up the main differences in a simple generalization that upper classes are more conservative, lower classes more radical; that the former rest content with things as they have been, while the have-nots desire reform. . . . If one accepts a definition of radical and conservative opinion that is limited to question responses pertaining to distribution of income, regulation of economic affairs in the interests of the common man, and similar economic-political reforms, there can be little doubt that pronounced differences are found in relation to socioeconomic status. Questions on other issues, however (religious doctrine, international questions, race relations, for example), fail to support the conception of a neat general pattern of radicalism-conservatism in which social classes manifest consistent contrasts. The differences, in general, are in directions to be expected if people's opinions coincide with their own self-interest as they perceive it and the means to advance it. Be it noted, however, that there are great numbers of exceptions—substantial minorities who do not go along with their fellows who are similarly situated.

OTHER STUDIES OF IDENTIFICATION

Since Centers' work, several other studies have been made which add to our understanding of the subtleties of class identification.

In our Cambridge, Massachusetts, research in 1953, Davis and I asked 219 white men to tell us about themselves [14]. With the exception of a slight excess of professionals, the sample approximated the occupational distribution of the Boston metropolitan area. The specific questions about class membership came after a whole series of items about the respondent's occupation and education, thus to some extent we had hinted to him what we meant by "social class." We began our questioning about identification with this open-ended item:

There has been a lot of talk recently about social classes in the United States. I wonder what you think about this. What social classes do you think there are in this part of the country?

That item was followed by a series designed as standardized probes to get additional information:

Which social class do you think you are in?
What puts you in that class?
Which class is next below yours in social standing?
In what ways are people in that class different from people in your class?
Which class is next above yours in social standing?

Finally, the Centers question was asked, along with an additional probe he did not use:

If you were asked to use one of these four names for your social class, which would you say you belonged in: the middle class, the lower class, the working class, or the upper class?
*If middle:* Would you say you were in the upper-middle or the lower-middle?

When the schedules were coded, the whole series of open-ended questions (thus excluding the Centers question) was treated as a single unit and the answers were combined. We found that 12 per cent of our respondents had no conception of a class order; 6 per cent understood the questions well enough to deny explicitly that a class order existed in the United States; 5 per cent recognized a class order, but either disapproved of it so strongly that they did not want to describe it, or said it was too complex to describe. The remaining 77 per cent of the respondents were able to give a fairly coherent description of their own and other strata of society; 10 per cent said the system contained two strata; 42 per cent claimed it consisted of three strata; 20 per cent recognized four strata; and 5 per cent detected five or more strata.

Of those who described a system with a given number of strata, 61 per cent used as the *main criterion* that separated one level from another income and/or the style of life it bought (e.g., "rich people," "those who live comfortably"). Eight per cent mentioned a specific occupational level as the main criterion (e.g., "professionals," or "people who work with their hands"). Fifteen per cent of the answers were scattered among a variety of categories such as family background, education and training, and innate ability. And 16 per cent of the respondents insisted that there was no single criterion, and said that a man's place in society was determined by a combination of many factors. Ethnic membership was seldom mentioned. The category of morals was most popular as the secondary criterion for class membership.

When asked the open question, "What social class do you think you are in?", 68 per cent of our respondents spontaneously used a label that was either exactly like one on the Centers list or was an obvious synonym for one of them. The other favorite type of category was the occupational one (especially "professional"). The distribution was as follows:

| | |
|---|---|
| Upper class | 1% |
| Upper-middle class | 4 |
| Middle class | 44 |
| Lower-middle class | 3 |
| Working class | 14 |
| Lower class | 2 |
| Subtotal | 68 |
| Occupational category | 7 |
| Other category | 7 |
| Denied class, or no conception, or "don't know" | 18 |
| TOTAL | 100% |

When we asked the closed question with fixed answers, we got results almost exactly like those of Centers:

| | | |
|---|---|---|
| Upper class | | 5% |
| Middle class | | 43 |
| Upper-middle | 19 | |
| Undifferentiated | 12 | |
| Lower-middle | 12 | |
| Working class | | 47 |
| Lower class | | 3 |
| Don't know | | 2 |
| | | 100% |

Look at the difference in the answers to the open and the closed questions! In what sense can we consider the Centers labels as "authentic"? In one case we get 44 per cent middle class and 14 per cent working class, and in the other case 43 per cent middle class and 47 per cent working class. Notice that the middle-class total remains constant, but the working class jumps from 14 per cent up to 47 per cent. Who are the people who shift?

Cross-classification of the answers to the two forms of the question showed some interesting patterns. The similarity of the totals answering middle class on both questions was spurious; it did not represent all the same persons. Slightly more than one third of the people who answered middle on the open question shifted to working on the closed question. Most of them were skilled or semiskilled workers. The men who called themselves middle on both the open and closed questions tended to be professional men, businessmen, salesmen, or clerks. The men who called themselves working on both questions tended to be skilled workers.

Those who answered the open question by calling themselves "professional" or "intellectual" mostly switched to upper-middle on the closed question. And those who used some other category or denied class or had no conception of it, switched in two thirds of the instances to working on the closed question.

Therefore it appears that we have a hard core of the business and professional plus some of the white-collar persons who call themselves middle class, no matter how you ask the question. And we have a hard core of manual workers who are working class, regardless of the form of the question. But we may have two intermediate groups who are not sure of themselves. One consists of some low-level white-collar people and some manual workers; they sometimes see themselves as middle, sometimes as working class. The form of the question determines the answer. The other intermediate group consists of the people who are the least class-conscious; they say there is no class system—but on second thought, if they have to choose, they will tend toward working class.

The Centers question forces people to classify themselves, even those who would prefer not to. And it appears that according to occupational criteria, the forced answers may be more realistic than the indecision which some people would prefer. From this point of view, we can accept the Centers question as useful (and indeed, it is predictive of ideological attitudes, as we have seen). But it is not fully authentic, for it is an authentic fact of American life that a great many people *do not* spontaneously think of themselves with the same label that they use in answer to the list of forced alternatives. This very ambiguity is so significant it should be studied directly instead of considered simply as an annoying source of error.

The connections between a workingman's perception of the stratification system and his political conclusions about it were explored in a study by Jerome G. Manis and Bernard N. Meltzer. They interviewed ninety-five men who were stable textile-mill workers in Paterson, New Jersey. They were union members, and strongly in favor of unionism. They lived in a city of almost 140,000, in one of the most highly industrialized parts of the nation. Thus they were workers in an advanced stage of capitalism; not villagers who might be reflecting the conservative notions of an outworn rural ideology.

The interviews were "open-ended." They showed that class identification was not a paramount aspect of their thinking, but that most of the men recognized and could use the term when it was introduced. They, like Centers' informants and the Cambridge respondents, saw a two- or three-class system based primarily on money and occupation, secondarily on beliefs and attitudes. Although a few saw relationships between the classes in terms of enmity, an equal number talked of partnership. Actually, the predominant opinion was that the relationship was one of paternalism, or the necessary combination of leaders and followers. As one worker expressed it [15]:

If the bosses would treat the working people right, they would get along all the time. It's like a dog with a bone. If you give him food, he will be all right. Just treat us right and we'll follow right along.

Another man said:

The people who have money own businesses and the rest of the people work for them. If there were no rich people, who would the poor people work for?

Most of the workers agreed that this system was inevitable and desirable. Although one third of the men thought it was getting more rigid, one half held the contrary view, which was particularly expressed in terms of increasing educational opportunities for children that allowed them to rise in the hierarchy. The opinions of the latter stressed the individualism that is so basic to our ideology:

It's better this way. Everyone will push and try to get up a little higher than he is now. Otherwise, people wouldn't have ambition, wouldn't work.

## SAMUEL LUBELL

The direct public-opinion studies summarized by Kornhauser indicated that on economic issues there was a tendency for political opinions to be based on class position, but not on most other issues. However, there is one other basic issue in the United States that is also class-related, namely, the treatment of ethnic groups. This is not to say that the various class levels among the white Protestant majority have markedly different attitudes toward minorities, but rather that the minority groups are predominantly in the working class and therefore combine their minority and class interests into a single ideology.

The effect of the merger of ethnic and class interests seems to have been greatest during one period of American politics, from 1928 to 1948. This period is described by Samuel Lubell in his *The Future of American Politics* (which might better have been labeled "The Recent Past of American Politics"). Lubell painstakingly analyzed election statistics and added adroit interpretation based on many years of experience as a political journalist.

According to Lubell, there was a pattern that explained the trends in voting, and it might be called the emergence of the urban, ethnic working class. The generation preceding 1925 witnessed the greatest mass immigration that this country had ever experienced, and most of the newcomers went to work in the factories of the big cities (as we shall see in more detail in Chapter VIII). Simultaneously, the farmers were streaming into the cities where they could make more money in the new industries; during and after the First World War, this internal migration included hundreds of thousands of Negroes. By the twenties these people and their children were becoming voters in great numbers, and for the first time the urban workers approached dominance in national politics, for it was not until then that more people lived in cities than on farms. And these urban workers were primarily Democrats; by 1928 the Democrats outvoted the Republicans in most of the big cities. It is Lubell's central thesis that although economic issues have always been important in our politics, in earlier years they were more closely connected with regional interests, but by 1928 the parties had taken on the color of class parties, with the Republicans representing business (and successful farmers) and the Democrats representing workers (and unsuccessful farmers). This one split tended to override regional differences and divisions based on noneconomic issues, though of course they were still significant [16]:

. . . Never having known anything but city life, this new generation was bound to develop a different attitude toward the role of government from that of Americans born on farms or in small towns. To Herbert Hoover "rugged individualism" evoked nostalgic memories of a rural self-sufficiency in which a thrifty, toiling farmer had to look to the marketplace for only the last fifth of his needs. The Iowa homestead on which Hoover grew up produced all of its own vegetables, its own soap, its own bread. . . .

In the city, though, the issue has always been man against man. What bowed the back of the factory worker prematurely were not hardships inflicted by Mother Nature but by human nature. He was completely dependent on a money wage. . . . A philosophy that called for "leaving things alone" to work themselves out seemed either unreal or hypocritical in the cities, where nearly every condition of living groaned for reform. . . . If only God could make a tree, only the government could make a park.

Al Smith made his appeals directly to the urban masses, particularly the ethnic groups who felt especially underprivileged. Roosevelt did not do so until after his first election; but his reforms in 1935 were designed as much to produce social justice as to end the depression, and in 1936 he swept every state except Maine and Vermont.

By the end of the Second World War, the situation was changing again. The ethnic groups were disappearing, for no major immigration occurred after 1925. Furthermore, the prosperity of the war and post-war years, plus the reforms of the New Deal, plus the seizure of local government in most the big cities, gave the ethnic groups a chance for a full civic life and an opportunity to utilize the schools and business as routes into the middle class. As they felt less ethnic, and as so many climbed into the middle class, and as the remaining members of the working class enjoyed improvement in family income, the causes of a politically oriented ethnic and class consciousness declined. Lubell interprets Truman's victory in 1948 more as a conservative than a radical vote, for so many people seemed to be saying, "Let us preserve the gains of the New Deal and not take a chance on another depression." They were not asking for further reform. Eisenhower's sweep in 1952, and the acceptance by the Republican party of most of the New Deal reforms, simply accentuated that trend.

The evidence indicates that as people climb into the middle class they usually turn Republican, though perhaps not to the degree of old members of that stratum. But the new Republican party under Eisenhower is a party that has accepted urban life and attempts to meet its challenges. Similarly, the new Democrats like Stevenson are more conservative than their predecessors, for they recognize the increased size of the middle-income group and are attempting to keep them from turning Republican. Both parties, in other words, are appealing to what is now the dominant majority in the country: relatively contented urban workers, both blue collar and white collar. Neither party is able to muster a substantial and durable majority of the country like the one the Democrats had for twenty years; even Eisenhower's popularity failed to bring him a Republican Congress in 1954. We have approached a stalemate, and politics has lost the strong ethnic and class flavor it had for the space of one generation. As long as prosperity continues, then other issues are likely to predominate. Only one ethnic group, the Negroes, still feel underprivileged and actively use politics as a weapon for reform.*

* It so happens that I am reading galley proofs on this chapter on the day following Eisenhower's landslide re-election in November, 1956. The paragraphs in the text were written several months earlier. The election campaign seemed to bear out the trends discussed in the text. The lack of class feeling was reflected in the lack of interest in economic issues in the campaign and the emphasis on the personality of Eisenhower. The one big issue on which Stevenson based the final weeks of the campaign, foreign policy and especially the control of the H-bomb, was unrelated to social class. Harry Truman's speeches in the campaign attempted to stress the middle-class bias of the Republican party, but nobody seemed much interested, and union labor voted in the majority for Eisenhower. Even the Negro vote, which had

AMERICAN EQUALITARIANISM

Most observers who are acquainted with both sides of the Atlantic feel that Americans are less class-conscious than Europeans, although systematic evidence is lacking [17]. Similarly, they feel that we pay less attention to prestige differences. From De Tocqueville on, travelers in the United States have reported on our "equalitarianism," and Americans who have gone abroad were disturbed by European class distinctions. For instance, Thomas Jefferson advised against European education, for he said that the student who goes to the old country [18]:

. . . acquires a fondness for European luxury and dissipation, and a contempt for the simplicity of his own country; he is fascinated with the privileges of the European aristocrats, and sees, with abhorrence, the lovely equality which the poor enjoy with the rich, in his own country; . . . he recollects the voluptuary dress and arts of the European women, and pities and despises the chaste affections and simplicity of his own country.

Notice that Jefferson did not deny that differences in wealth existed in America, but insisted that the poor and the rich enjoyed a "lovely equality" here. And he lived in the South, where aristocratic pretensions were most marked.

Colonial countries that are settled by people who themselves work the land produce equality of circumstance compared to noncolonial countries; only by dominating a native population can the colonials maintain great economic and social superiority (as occurred in most of Latin America). The United States was settled predominantly by workers and peasants, and throughout most of our history we had a labor shortage and a land surplus. Except for control over Negro slaves, no man could gain permanent advantage over another and, to use the Marxist term, continually appropriate the surplus products of his labor. These facts of economic life were combined with an ideological tradition (stemming from revolution) that was against aristocratic pretensions. The joint effect of facts plus ideology minimized economic differences among men and taught them to pay as little attention as possible to what differences did exist.

But when we industrialized after the Civil War, it appeared for a

---

been solidly Democratic for years as a result of both race feeling and class feeling, finally began to shift and divide rather evenly between the parties. That the President won re-election on his personality rather than on the economic principles of the Republican party was conclusively shown by the fact that his enormous popularity was not sufficient to bring him a Republican Congress. It is clear that at the moment the overwhelming majority of Americans favor the middle of the road in politics, and the old debates based on the interests of ethnic groups and social classes are much weakened.

while as though the situation would completely change. Plutocrats of trade and manufacturing collected wealth that no landed proprietor ever approached. Vast masses of uneducated and unskilled laborers gathered in the big cities. Some people pointed to the warnings of Jefferson and said that his fears were being realized, for he had written that urban life was incompatible with the American social philosophy. Certainly the way of life of the cities in the first part of the current century showed a gap between rich and poor, in both economic and social terms, that appeared un-American.

The strains were present for a long time, but the crisis appears to have come with the great depression. In 1932 the Socialist party received almost one million votes, and its leader, Norman Thomas, has ever since maintained that the New Deal adopted his platform and saved the country. Certainly the New Deal reforms were important, for they represented a greater deliberate attempt on the part of government to alter society than we had ever before experienced. But they were part of a long-term trend that has recently come to fruition in Europe as well. Once it passes through certain earlier stages, industrialization itself creates forces for equality. Large-scale industry widely distributes ownership, and it creates management that is based primarily on demonstrated competence. As long as entry into management competition is open to all ranks of society—and we achieved that stage earlier than Europe because we were the first great nation to create an adequate public-school system—there is great movement up and down the social ladder, and movement itself tends to blur the lines of distinction. Furthermore, as education becomes more widespread, and as incomes become more equalized, stratum differences become narrower.

Seymour M. Lipset and Reinhard Bendix recently reported to an international congress of sociologists on our ideological equalitarianism. They admitted that our belief in our special equalitarianism was somewhat stronger than the facts warranted, but pointed out that the belief itself had an influence on the facts. And they noted that recent evidence seems to indicate that there is now about as much mobility in Europe as in America (though, through lack of data, they could not say how long that similarity has existed). Consequently, the continuation of the belief became a problem which they wished to explain. In summary, they proposed six factors of explanation [19]:

(1) the absence of a feudal past, whose legacies could have been perpetuated under capitalism to strengthen the claim to legitimacy of the new class of capitalists; (2) the continued high rate of social mobility in American society which has tended to support the traditional belief in the value of an "open class" society; (3) the increase in educational opportunities which has been

especially important in sustaining the belief in the continuous expansion of opportunities; (4) the patterns of business careers at the bottom and at the top, which seem to reflect and support the same belief; (5) the presence of immigrants and racial minorities on whose shoulders the children of previous generations of immigrants or of more or less segregated ethnic groups could rise; and (6) the combination of relative wealth and mass-production of consumer's goods which has had the effect of minimizing the differences between the standard of living in working-class and middle-class occupations.

Some of these factors we have already discussed at length; ensuing chapters will examine the roles of immigration and social mobility.

### FRAMES OF REFERENCE

The various sets of data concerning self-identification or class consciousness in America, and the connections between identification and ideology, do not automatically fit together because the researchers used different techniques. However, if we borrow some general ideas from social psychology, and also attempt to apply to American data some interpretations that were first suggested by British researchers exploring very similar data which they gathered, we can arrive at a tentative synthesis [20]. This synthesis extends the discussion of the psychology of classification behavior introduced in Chapter III, where we considered the way people categorize occupations; here we pay more attention to the respondent's conception of himself, and we include other criteria than occupation.

Elizabeth Bott has pointed out that "people do not experience their objective class position as a single clearly defined status." We might add that such clear definitions are the result of calculated decisions on the part of academic researchers; *they* are the ones who create concepts like "upper-middle class" or "bourgeoisie" and through hard thinking attach some specific empirical criteria for membership (granted, they may start with words in popular usage, but by the time they have finished their ratiocinations, the original words have taken on new meanings). Naturally, they endow their concepts with connotations that derive from the researchers' own general philosophy; thus Warner thinks of strata of prestige, and the Marxists of actual or latent conflict groups. Then the researchers go into the field and try to discover the degree to which the populace thinks as the concepts suggest they should, and the investigators feel a growing sense of triumph the more closely they can fit the data to the concepts.

But, says Bott [21]:

. . . when an individual talks about class he is trying to say something, in a symbolic form, about his experiences of power and prestige in his actual membership groups both past and present. These membership groups—place of work, friends, neighbours, family, etc.—have little intrinsic connection with one another, especially in a large city, and each of the groups has its own pattern of organization. The psychological situation for the individual, therefore, is one of belonging to a number of segregated, un-connected groups, each with its own system of prestige and power. When he is comparing himself with other people or placing himself in the widest social context, he manufactures a notion of his general social position out of these segregated group memberships. . . . The group memberships are not differentiated and related to one another; they are telescoped and condensed into one general notion.

The man in the street is aided in his conceptualizing by words and theories that have diffused into popular culture from the academic ratiocinations. Thus, especially in Europe, there are many factory workers who have been subjected to long propaganda that stems from Marxist ideology; naturally, they not only use class-conflict terminology, they actually perceive their own position and interpret their everyday experiences in conflict terms. Similarly, the American middle classes have been bombarded with propaganda about our equality and absence of classes. Consequently, they tend to perceive as individual differences experiences that a European would see as common class experiences.

Therefore, any individual's perception of himself in a stratification order is a combination of (1) his actual experiences in a wide variety of contexts in his many membership groups, and (2) his verbal theories about society, which are usually vague and somewhat contradictory common-sense notions that have filtered down from the theorizing of intellectuals and propagandists. Consequently, the social reality of identification that we are studying is complex rather than simple, and when we simplify it (as we must for certain purposes) into categories like middle class or working class, we do violence to the original facts. The simpler and neater the scheme, the further it is from reality.

Let us complicate the picture even more. Bott goes on to point out that [22]:

. . . the individual performs a telescoping procedure on other people as well as on himself. If they are people who have the same, or similar, group memberships as himself, he is likely to feel that they have the same general position and belong to his own class. If they are outsiders, his knowledge of them will be indirect and incomplete so that there is plenty of room for projection and distortion. . . .

The suggestion advanced here is that there are three steps in an individual's creation of a class reference group: first, he internalizes the norms of his primary membership groups—place of work, colleagues, friends, neighbourhood, family—together with some more hazy notions about the wider society; secondly he performs an act of conceptualization in reducing these segregated norms to a common denominator; thirdly, he projects his conceptualization

back on to society at large. . . . The main point is that the individual himself is an active agent. He does not simply internalize the norms of class which
have an independent external existence. He takes in the norms of certain actual
groups, works them over, and constructs class reference groups out of them.

Finally, Bott reminded us that because the conceptualizations were
both hazy and tied to a variety of actual experiences in the life history
of an individual, they could shift in the course of an interview. Sometimes a respondent would think in terms of the people he knew in his
home town as a child; sometimes of his work mates; sometimes of his
dreams for his children. These shifts, plus those of the forms of the
questions he was being asked, would lead him to shift frames of reference, so that in one moment the class system he saw would be based on
lineage and family origins, the next on occupation, then on consumption
patterns, finally on education. All of these were equally real to him. As
he shifted his points of reference or "reference groups," he shifted his
self-identification.

The interviews that Bott conducted in London paralleled those of
Hammond in Australia and also much of the American data in that they
showed at least four different models of the class structure that could
be used by different respondents, or by the same respondent at different
points in an interview:

1. Two-valued power models
2. Three-valued prestige models
3. Many-valued prestige models
4. Mixed power and prestige models

The power model tends to be reduced to a two-level system because
it takes two to make a fight, and the respondent tends to think primarily
of himself (and his colleagues) versus all the rest. Respondents whose
own experiences had been conflicting, whose personalities stress opposition (perhaps those who would have high scores on the currently
popular scale of "authoritarianism"), those who have been exposed to
Marxist ideology—they would be likely to think of a two-level system
of conflict. *But they would almost all be members of the working class.*
A middle-class person, despite a personality predisposition to conflict,
would have certain experiences and interests that would make it difficult for him to accept the Marxist conception. For one thing, most of
his personal conflict would have been with other members of the middle
classes; he competes as an individual with other individuals. Whatever
success he has had he would want to feel was a result of personal
qualities rather than group membership; it makes him feel that the
success was his, rather than automatic and thus undeserved. If he is a
failure, he may begin to blame it on the system and think of the un-

fairness of the higher-ups—but he still must acknowledge that some people (manual workers) are worse off than he; so he resists the notion of basic class conflict between haves and have-nots. He does not want to have to identify with the workers in order to blame the bourgeoisie for his troubles. Given our economic system, it is difficult to construct a three-valued power model, for it is hard to find a cleavage as basic as that between workers and bosses. The nearest approach to this is to see a struggle between workers, independent businessmen, and large corporations, and many frustrated petty businessmen do think in those terms. But the conflict-minded worker lumps all the businessmen together into "they." As soon as he does, he has declared common cause with all other workers, and has given up notions of individual mobility into the upper level.

People who think in terms of prestige, and who recognize the possibility of rising and falling, almost inevitably use a model with at least three levels. Prestige implies someone above you and someone below you. Only the really "down and out" will admit that they are on the bottom; a self-respecting workingman will always look down on bums beneath him and gain psychic satisfaction from his own superiority. Thus, contented workers who do not stress conflict and who feel some personal success will think in terms of at least a three-valued prestige hierarchy with themselves in the middle, bums on the bottom, and business and professional men on top. Middle-class persons also use the three-valued model, but they shift the dividing lines between the levels and lump all workers together as the ones below them, and recognize the upper class as the group on top. You can almost always get a person who uses a three-valued system to make finer distinctions just by pushing the questioning; as you narrow his focus of attention to any part of the system, he begins to think of subtler differentiations between men. *The prestige concept, unlike the power idea, is infinitely divisible.* You have only to polish your glasses and take a closer look to see how any group that appears homogeneous from a distance is in fact minutely subdivided. A businessman will at first lump all academics together; but he also knows something about the divisions between instructors, assistant professors, associate professors, and full professors, and he knows the difference in prestige between Southwest State Teachers' College and Columbia University. If you ask him to think about it, he can come up with these additional distinctions. But most of the time they are not relevant to his thinking; therefore, unlike the author of this book, he pays little attention to them. Thus the form of the questioning is more important when dealing with respondents who are using a prestige model than with those who think in terms of basic class conflict.

Bott suggests that the three-valued prestige model is most common among the people who think of themselves as belonging in the middle. She found that the many-valued model was used by those who placed themselves in the working class but felt some incompatibility in their position. Thus, those who were somewhat better educated than their colleagues or who had pretensions to a more cultured outlook would admit that they were occupationally rather near the bottom but intellectually higher up. They would resolve the difficulty by seeing a society of many layers, with themselves second from the bottom, and more like the level above them on some characteristics than on others.

The mixed prestige-power models were used by intellectuals who tried to reconcile Marxist theories with the more complex facts of contemporary life.

We can now hypothesize that the men in the Cambridge sample who shifted from middle on the open-ended questions to working on the closed probably used the many-valued prestige model in their thinking. They knew they were occupationally in the working class, but when they had the chance to think in other terms (such as education or values) they could see themselves as toward the middle of a complex system. Those who denied class at first but then called themselves workers when forced to make a choice also probably thought of a many-layered system without clear lines of demarcation. Those who stuck to middle class through both forms of the questions were most likely to use the three-layered model. Those who remained with working class through both forms probably came closest to the power model which simplifies and consolidates shades of difference.

## CONCLUSIONS

Self-identification is intertwined with a man's basic interpersonal experiences, the theoretical ideas he has been exposed to, and the traits of his personality that lead him to organize experience and ideas in ways congenial to himself. It is probably true that the most important single experience he has in this complex flows from his occupation. But occupation is only part of the total complex. His ideology is in part a consequence of his occupational experiences, but the way he interprets those experiences is influenced by his ideology, and that in turn is influenced by his education, his family background, and so on. Every man thus sees a slightly different class order, and the words he uses to describe himself depend on the points of reference he has in his own subjective perception of the class order. The best the scientific observer can do is to abstract fundamental similarities in perception among wide groups of people by using a scheme something like Bott's which simplifies but does not deny the differences in modes of perception. Then we can ask each man to tell us at which level he usually places himself in terms of one of these few types of models. Marx and Warner and Centers all insist that there is only one true model, and force the respondents' answers into it. But all the models are partially true, therefore we must go back to the public with more flexible questions which *allow the respondents to choose both the model and their position within it.* When we do, and when we get more adequate measures of the several components of ideology, we will get higher correlations between "objective" attributes of status position, "subjective" perception thereof, and ideological beliefs.

### REFERENCES

[1] *Time*, May 16, 1955.

[2] For an exploratory study that shows the several categories people use to identify with, see Herbert Hyman, "The Psychology of Social Status," *Archives of Psychology*, 1942. The general problem is brilliantly discussed in Robert K. Merton and Alice S. Kitt, "Contributions to the Theory of Reference Group Behavior," in *Continuities in Social Research*, Robert K. Merton and Paul F. Lazarsfeld, eds. (Glencoe, Ill.: The Free Press, 1950).

[3] Richard Centers, *The Psychology of Social Classes* (Princeton: Princeton University Press, 1949), pp. 28–29. Centers gives references to the main empirical studies which preceded his. See also Paul F. Lazarsfeld *et al., The People's Choice* (New York: Columbia University Press, 2nd ed., 1949), which studies the vote of one county in the 1940 elections; Bernard R. Berelson *et al., Voting: A Study of Opinion Formation during a Presidential Campaign* (Chicago: University of Chicago Press, 1955); and Arthur Kornhauser, "Public Opinion and Social Class," *American Journal of Sociology*, LV (January, 1950), 333–45, which is a discussion of the logical and methodological difficulties in research, and a summary of the findings to date. There is a sharp critique of Centers in H. J. Eysenck, "Social Attitude and Social Class," *British Journal of Sociology*, I (March, 1950), 56–66.

[4] Centers, *The Psychology of Social Classes*, p. 78.

[5] *Ibid.*, p. 86.

[6] Richard Centers, "Toward an Articulation of Two Approaches to Social Class Phenomena, Parts I and II," *International Journal of Opinion and Attitude Research*, IV (Winter, 1950–51), 499–514, V (Summer, 1951), 159–78.

[7] Herman M. Case, "Guttman Scaling Applied to Centers' Conservatism-Radicalism Battery," *American Journal of Sociology*, LVIII (May, 1953), 556–63. Davis and I (see below) got similar negative results with simplified versions of the Centers questions in our Cambridge survey

(this part of our data is unpublished). We then constructed another, though similar, set of questions that did scale—but its relationship to voting behavior in 1952 was even less marked than that found by Centers. Had Eisenhower turned electioneering away from economic conservatism-radicalism?

[8] Centers, *The Psychology of Social Classes*, p. 120.

[9] *Ibid.*, p. 114.

[10] *Ibid.*, p. 126.

[11] *Ibid.*, Chap. IX.

[12] *Ibid.*, Chapters X, XI. Another revealing study of economic and political ideology is Alfred W. Jones, *Life, Liberty and Property* (Philadelphia: Lippincott, 1941). Jones constructed a series of vignettes describing actions which reflected varying attitudes toward private property. He then had various persons in Akron, Ohio, tell him what they thought of the behavior of characters in the stories, thus revealing their own attitudes. He was able to demonstrate clearly the relation of occupational level to basic attitudes toward property. See also Dewey Anderson and Percy E. Davidson, *Ballots and the Democratic Class Struggle* (Stanford University: Stanford University Press, 1943).

[13] Kornhauser, "Public Opinion and Social Class," p. 334.

[14] Joseph A. Kahl and James A. Davis, "A Comparison of Indexes of Socio-Economic Status," *American Sociological Review*, XX (June, 1955), 317–25.

[15] Jerome G. Manis and Bernard N. Meltzer, "Attitudes of Textile Workers to Class Structure," *American Journal of Sociology*, LX (July, 1954), 33, 35. For another vivid description of the attitudes of manual workers, see Katherine Archibald, "Status Orientations among Shipyard Workers," in *Class, Status and Power*, Reinhard Bendix and Seymour M. Lipset, eds. (Glencoe, Ill.: The Free Press, 1953).

[16] Samuel Lubell, *The Future of American Politics*, 2d ed. (Garden City, N.Y.: Doubleday Anchor Books, 1956), pp. 33–34.

[17] The only comparative data I know are in Chapter II, "National Patterns in Class Consciousness," of William Buchanan and Hadley Cantril, *How Nations See Each Other: A Study in Public Opinion* (Urbana: The University of Illinois Press, 1953). The material is based on the use of the Centers' question in nine countries, but the problem of the differences in the meaning of the question in different languages and cultures was not solved.

[18] Thomas Jefferson, letter to J. Bannister, Jr., October 15, 1785; quoted in Marcus Cunliffe, *The Literature of the United States* (Harmondsworth, Middlesex: Penguin Books, 1954), p. 57.

[19] Seymour M. Lipset and Reinhard Bendix, "Ideological Equalitarianism and Social Mobility in the United States," in *Transactions of the Second World Congress of Sociology*, Vol. II (London: International Sociologi-

cal Association, 1954), p. 34. See also Daniel Bell, "Marxian Socialism in the U.S.," in *Socialism and American Life*, Donald D. Egbert and Stow Persons, eds., 2 vols. (Princeton: Princeton University Press, 1952).

[20] See F. M. Martin, "Some Subjective Aspects of Social Stratification," in *Social Mobility in Britain*, D. V. Glass, ed. (London: Routledge and Kegan Paul, 1954). Elizabeth Bott, "The Concept of Class as a Reference Group," *Human Relations*, VII (1954), 259–86. S. B. Hammond, "Stratification in an Australian City," in *Readings in Social Psychology*, rev. ed., Guy E. Swanson et al., eds. (New York: Holt, 1952).

[21] Bott, "The Concept of Class as a Reference Group," p. 262.

[22] *Ibid.*, p. 263.

# VII

# Classes as Ideal Types: Emergent Values

THE MOB GIVE VENT TO THEIR IMPULSES, AND WE DEPRIVE OUR-
SELVES. WE DO SO IN ORDER TO MAINTAIN OUR INTEGRITY. WE
ECONOMIZE WITH OUR HEALTH, OUR CAPACITY FOR ENJOYMENT,
OUR FORCES: WE SAVE UP FOR SOMETHING, NOT KNOWING OUR-
SELVES FOR WHAT. AND THIS HABIT OF CONSTANT SUPPRESSION
OF NATURAL INSTINCTS GIVES US THE CHARACTER OF REFINE-
MENT. . . . OUR WHOLE CONDUCT OF LIFE PRESUPPOSES THAT
WE SHALL BE SHELTERED FROM THE DIREST POVERTY, THAT IT IS
ALWAYS OPEN TO US TO FREE OURSELVES INCREASINGLY FROM
THE EVILS OF OUR SOCIAL STRUCTURE. THE POOR, THE COMMON
PEOPLE, COULD NOT EXIST WITHOUT THEIR THICK SKIN AND
THEIR EASYGOING WAYS. WHY SHOULD THEY FEEL THEIR DESIRES
INTENSELY WHEN ALL THE AFFLICTIONS NATURE AND SOCIETY
HAVE IN STORE ARE DIRECTED AGAINST THOSE THEY LOVE; WHY
SHOULD THEY SCORN A MOMENTARY PLEASURE WHEN NO OTHER
AWAITS THEM? THE POOR ARE TOO POWERLESS, TOO EXPOSED, TO
DO AS WE DO. *Sigmund Freud* [1]

OF THE VARIABLES we have dealt with so far, value orientations, which
were discussed in the first chapter, are the most difficult to point to in
the real world. By comparison, money is easy to count, and a man can
readily be classified by occupation as a banker or a baker. Even a
clique can be seen when a bunch of boys hang around together on a
street corner. But who has ever seen a value orientation? Yet we all have
seen the manifestations of values. When a mother disciplines her
daughter for accepting a date with "that no-good fellow" and says
"You *ought* to know better"; when an American businessman goes into
debt in order to buy an expensive house because he and his wife feel
that they are the sort of people who *ought* to live in such a house; when
a Japanese soldier commits suicide because he feels that his behavior has
disgraced his family and he *ought* to make amends—then we observe
the results of deeply felt values. Whenever people behave according to

184

their standards of what ought to be done, whenever they act according to what they believe is right, proper, decent, or moral, then they are expressing their values.

Technically speaking, values are constructs in the mind of the scientific observer that summarize the general principles used by his subjects to guide their behavior. The more abstract these constructs, the more useful they tend to be, for then they explain a whole set of separate actions that otherwise would seem unrelated. Obviously, it would not be very helpful for the scientist to invent a new value as the explanation for each separate act that he observes. Instead, he needs a small number of values that in combination can be used to predict how subjects will behave in any given set of circumstances. For instance, the scientist may describe a businessman as ambitious and ruthless and kindly. Then he can understand why the businessman works very hard, is a tough competitor, and will drive a rival out of business when it is to his advantage to do so; yet at the same time he gives large Christmas bonuses to his workmen. In order to emphasize the abstractness of the key values that lie behind many actions, we use the term "value orientations" [2].

Actually, value orientations usually combine aspects of *ought* (value) and aspects of *is* (existential beliefs about reality). For example, American culture is said to stress individualism. In the Jeffersonian sense this means the belief that the nature of man, as established by God, is such that individual freedom and initiative automatically produce the best society. Thus we believe that man both is and ought to be free and independent.

We study values, as we study prestige, by two basic operations: (1) we observe many specific acts and by a process of induction abstract those values that we believe are the important motivations behind the behavior of the subjects, and (2) we ask our subjects what they believe is right and proper. The trouble with the second procedure is that subjects often find it extremely difficult to articulate their values. People know how to behave; they do not always know how to describe their rules of behavior. As a matter of fact, most scientists use both approaches simultaneously. The more they learn from observation, the more astute they become in phrasing questions that help the subjects talk about their basic values.

One way of thinking about value orientations is to recognize that they represent a long-term response to the total historical situation a group is in. For instance, Eskimos face constant battle with the weather and the meager food supply; it cannot be surprising that they evolve a culture that gives central focus to food and cold. Similarly, a group engaged in constant warfare develops a culture adapted to that fact, a culture which in many values reflects the overwhelming orientation of militarism—young men are likely to have the highest prestige, courage will be the supreme virtue, and a tight system of authority and discipline will be established.

Having reviewed many descriptive studies of specific aspects of class behavior, we can now generalize about the total situation that each class is in, and see what value orientations tend to emerge as a response to that situation. To the extent that the various classes live apart from one another, they develop recognizable subcultures with values that give a special and unique flavor to life. National cultures are sufficiently flexible to incorporate such class variations, and to some extent the class variations are similar as one moves from one country to the next, despite national differences. Thus, Freud's description of the middle class would be recognizable to an American, a Frenchman, and probably a Japanese.

In previous chapters we were concentrating on measurable facts; here we turn to the way people evaluate those facts. Our knowledge of the evaluations is much less satisfactory than our knowledge of the facts, partly because evaluations are difficult to measure. Good observers who have fluent pens can often describe values in a vivid and convincing way, but if (as sometimes is the case) they happen to disagree, the hard-headed scientist finds it difficult to resolve the argument with a precise measuring rod. Consequently, all we can do here is attempt to synthesize in a meaningful way the most convincing of the evaluations [3]. We can try to be suggestive, but cannot be conclusive.

What classes shall we discuss? Surely the various researches that have been examined thus far come to no clear conclusions as to the number of classes in the towns and cities of America, to say nothing of their relative sizes. Each investigator comes out with somewhat different answers according to his predilections and his techniques. Yet the answers are not really contradictory, for the basic outlines are agreed upon, and it is mainly the question of precise divisions between the levels that causes argument. Let us avoid that argument altogether, and admit that we will discuss five classes as a matter of arbitrary decision, based on the criterion of convenience in synthesizing the results of various investigators with a minimum of distortion to each [4].

These five classes are "ideal types." They are not precise descriptions of reality, but scientific constructs which indicate that there are patterned relationships among the stratification variables; they hang together in a meaningful way. Through time there is a tendency for a group of people who have a given occupation and a given income to interact with each other, spend their money in a certain way, be assigned a quantum of prestige by the community, come to think of themselves as a group, and finally, develop a set of values that is a special variant of the national culture. For complete consistency and integration, they would need a long time and an absence of change (both in the total system and movement of individuals in and out of the class). The real world does not give them much time, for change is constant. Consequently, we can hypothesize about the long-run tendency but never catch up to it with our measuring instruments.

A specially important consequence of lack of integration is the fact that many people believe in values that appear, on the average, to be characteristic of some other stratum than the one in which they live. For instance, an ambitious workingman who is going to school in the evenings and hopes eventually to become an engineer may well attempt to organize his family life on a pattern that we recognize as middle class, despite inadequate income to buy the things and interact with the people whom the community considers middle class. In fact, he is trying to integrate his life by following his values in a long-term plan that will eventually turn him into a completely middle-class person. But according to most of our measurements, he fits into the working class.

Therefore, if for convenience in exposition we describe the classes in terms of the objective characteristics of occupation, income, and network of interaction, and then analyze those values that *typically* accompany such characteristics, let it not be supposed that all families at a given objective level cling to those values.

In the chapter on styles of life five classes were described, and with one adjustment they will serve as an adequate skeleton for our present purpose. Let us assume that only half of those families and single individuals who receive less than $2000 actually are adjusted to a life of poverty. It is a fair assumption, because so many are young people just starting to work or old people who have other resources in savings and help from children. Placing these latter people in the next higher level, we arrive at the following distribution for the average American city, using labels that approximate the familiar ones of Warner (though our distribution is rather different):

| | |
|---|---|
| Upper class | 1% |
| Upper-middle class | 9 |
| Lower-middle class | 40 |
| Working class | 40 |
| Lower class | 10 |
| TOTAL | 100% |

## THE UPPER CLASS: GRACEFUL LIVING

In every community there are a number of families who are clearly recognized as superior to all the rest: they are richer, more powerful, more exclusive in their interactions. In large cities there are enough of them to form neighborhoods or even complete suburbs of people who live in mansions. They constitute an upper class.

Income alone will not put a family into this class; they also must be personally accepted by the other upper-class families of the community. A man gains acceptance for himself and his family either by virtue of forebears who belonged to the elite, or by his position in the commercial hierarchy—he must be a man who cannot be ignored, one who must be consulted when the big decisions are made. Thus, although money is a prerequisite, it is not an automatic ticket of admission; it must be respectable money, and it must put its owner into an interaction network of consequence. The upper class in any local community is, relative to other strata, small and cohesive; it is an organized social group, not merely a statistical category of similar people. In this sense it is qualitatively different from the other classes.

The upper class can be subdivided into two categories: the self-made men who have climbed from middle-class origins to the very top positions in business and the professions, and the men who have inherited wealth and position from the efforts of a previous generation. There are subtle distinctions between them in values and manners, for only the rarest newcomer can behave like a gentleman to the manner born. But these distinctions are of importance primarily among themselves; most outsiders neither care about nor even perceive the differences. And the distinctions are temporary; the sons of the newcomers marry the daughters of the established.

Upper-class men are the ones who sit on the boards of directors of businesses and banks and universities and community chests. They are the men who make the most important decisions (at least outside of the formal sphere of government) in our society. Often their wives are active in the functions that make up "society" as reported on the woman's page of the urban newspapers. *The Social Register* lists many of them by name and pedigree; *Who's Who* adds some more who are not of sufficient lineage to deserve mention in the Register [5]. They send their sons to Harvard, Yale, and Princeton and their daughters to Radcliffe, Bryn Mawr, and Vassar. Within their own region of the country they are intertwined in networks of kinship, of common club affiliations, of interlocking memberships on committees and boards. And the regional groups have connections via certain active persons with the upper class of other regions of the country. Upper-class people travel extensively, and many adroitly combine a national and international outlook with roots in the local communities which are the bases of their lineage, property, and position.

What are their values? We shall emphasize the values of the established families, the "old elite," as the newer families tend to absorb them as fast as possible in order to gain acceptance; and by emphasizing the values of the old elite we usefully sharpen the contrast with the ideal type of the upper-middle class. But it should be remembered that many of the self-made men cling to the predominantly middle-class values of their upbringing, and ambivalently ridicule their wives and daughters for playing the society game.

What is the basic distinction that identifies a member of the old elite? It cannot be money alone, for there are people who have as much money who do not belong. It is an attitude toward life.

This attitude is based on membership in a family line that has been established for at least one, and preferably two or three generations as members of the upper class. Only by being born into such a family can one fully learn its manners and mores. Such a family has a sense of permanence and of position; its members are "somebody," have been for a long time, expect to continue to be for a long time. Indeed, the longer the better, and if history is embellished a bit by legend in order to lengthen the family tree, we should not be surprised. Because money is taken for granted, it seems to be of less importance. For the old elite it appears crude and boorish to display one's wealth or even to talk too much about it. The important thing is not the money nor the skill with which it was earned, but the style in which it is spent.

Our creative literature has had many specialists who portrayed the old elite; F. Scott Fitzgerald was one of the best. He stood at the outer fringe; he knew them, but was not of them. He combined intimate acquaintance with outside perspective in just that balance which produces great stories. He wrote about one of his heroes in this way [6]:

Let me tell you about the very rich. They are different from you and me. They possess and enjoy early, and it does something to them, makes them soft where we are hard, and cynical where we are trustful, in a way that, unless you were born rich, it is very difficult to understand. They think, deep in their hearts, that they are better than we are because we had to discover the compensations and refuges of life for ourselves. Even when they enter deep into our world or sink below us, they still think that they are better than we are. They are different. . . .

Anson's first sense of his superiority came to him when he realized the half-grudging American deference that was paid to him in the Connecticut village. The parents of the boys he played with always inquired after his father and mother, and were vaguely excited when their own children were asked to the Hunters' house. He accepted this as the natural state of things, and a sort of impatience with all groups of which he was not the centre—in money, in position, in authority—remained with him for the rest of his life. He disdained to struggle with other boys for precedence—he expected it to be given him freely, and when it wasn't he withdrew into his family. His family was sufficient, for in the East money is still a somewhat feudal thing, a clan-forming thing. In the snobbish West, money separates families to form "sets."

The smaller the city, the more important is the history of the family; it is known by more local inhabitants, it is tied up more obviously with the local past. A family founded by shipowners in Yankee City, the descendants of plantation people in Georgia, the heirs of the early ranchers in Texas—these are the people whose glory lies most in the past. Making a fortune in those days seems now to be romantic and daring and artistic; it appears a bit more dashing than the dealings of the current market place. In the bigger cities life is more contemporaneous, and newer money more acceptable.

A sense of awe toward the giants who founded the family line is combined with the actual power of elders over the fortune to create a feeling of respect and devotion to old people and to old things. The past has much relevance to the present, and is surer than the future. The middle-class man is more likely to want to forget his past; especially if he has risen from among the workers, his parents and grandparents are of little use to him now, and they may be a hindrance. He stands upon his own accomplishments. A man of the old elite may have accomplishments, but they are embellishments upon those of his ancestors. Consequently, the family is solidary through the generations; a grandmother may be a matriarch to whom all pay homage; old people have power and knowledge and connections that are useful to young ones. The family members all realize that their position depends upon the behavior of the whole group, and that they cannot completely go off and lead their own lives. Marriages take on a significance for everybody, for through them the family line gets perpetuated. Children must be properly reared and educated, or all may suffer disgrace.

Upper classes in many societies have been based on land ownership. Land gives great stability in agricultural societies; it is easy to get others to farm it, and the income of the owners can keep coming in through the generations with little attention on their part. Furthermore, land ownership gives direct power over the tenants; usually they have no place else to go, and must do as they are told. This combination of permanence and power creates a landed aristocracy.

Our upper class is not based on land, but on ownership of fluid capital and on the skills of management. The managers are usually mobile individuals who did not start with capital; but their tremendous earnings give them capital to pass on to their children. The capital must be wisely managed if it is to survive through the constant changes in our industrial system; it must be transferred from buggies to automobiles to airplanes as the situation demands. Consequently, the families who maintain a top position for several generations must have some members adroit in finance to keep the fortune intact and help it grow—a complete disdain for the market place would spell doom. Furthermore, this system allows much more movement into and out of the upper class than would occur in a landed aristocracy; the new managers must be absorbed, and the old families who lose their money or do not renew it must be quietly dropped. There are important consequences to this instability: the upper class is always in close touch with the values of the middle class and cannot feel itself to be totally unique; and there is competition among members of the elite which prevents complete joint action to promote class interests. Our upper class is not so permanent, not so solidary, not so homogeneous, as a landed aristocracy.

Many aristocracies have little work to do. They escape boredom by a serious cultivation of the arts or of politics. Our upper class does not have so much free time. Business is often more important than art and learning. What free time they have is likely to be devoted to community leadership, which has business implications. Yet the upper class is always trying to differentiate itself from the middle in other terms than money and power (which seem slightly crass when faced overtly); they use the art of graceful living as the criterion. Only those who are used to money know how to spend it "properly," which means spending it almost as though it were unimportant. This is the art peculiar to the old elite.

Once again, reverence for the past is important. The art of graceful living is traditional, like all arts. One must learn the appropriate skills from elders; he must appreciate the distinction of an old house or an old painting. To be too modern in style is to identify with the newcomers; to be surrounded by antiques suggests that one has a past of note.

The man who has learned well the art of graceful living can be a very pleasant companion. He is versatile, a dilettante in many matters. He can talk of music or politics or business; he knows a smattering of history and literature; he is knowledgeable. He is not compulsive about his business or his learning—he allows neither to dominate his conversation. He has no overwhelming career upon which his entire position is based. He is himself, he is somebody, even if he does nothing. The career man, whether it be a businessman or a professor, often finds the dilettante to be slightly dull because he does not invest all of his energy into a central passion; the dilettante in turn finds the career man to be an obsessive fellow who pays more attention to accomplishment than to people. The elite man's concern with people, and his long training in the responsibilities of high position, lead him to be gracious with subordinates as well as equals. He is usually much less overbearing than is the middle-class man.

There is, however, a price to pay for dilettantism in a country de-

voted to accomplishment. One can end up feeling like a useless orna-
ment. The skeleton in the family closet is usually a bored cousin who
recognized too soon that he need not work hard at anything, and sought
stimulation in chorus girls. If the symbolic middle-class neurosis is obsessive compulsivity, complicated by ulcers, the upper-class illness is
ennui, complicated by alcohol.

The security of elite position allows a man to be an individualist;
by accepting certain traditions without question he becomes free to
experiment with details. He can think a bit differently from his fellows
and not fear rejection. He can be a little odd and not be punished. Indeed, his sense of security and his actual community power allow him to
"get away with things" so long as he does not overdo it. He can get
drunk, and the privacy of his home or his club protects him from
repercussions; he can drive a little too fast, and the sheriff will let him
off with a warning; he can go to New York for a fling, and his wife will
accept him back. He can even be a radical in politics, like Franklin
Roosevelt or Averell Harriman; he may be called a traitor to his class,
but he is unlikely to be expelled from his club.

Although the old elite and the newer men of the upper class who have
reached their positions through their own efforts in business have their
differences, there are many forces that pull them together. At the top
levels of business, ownership and management must work together;
indeed, they merge, for many owners will sit on boards of directors in
order to keep some control over their capital, and most top managers
earn so much more than they can spend that they buy into their company and become owners. Furthermore, community interests are shared;
both segments of the upper class feel an obligation to be active in the
spheres of local decision making; they want to serve their communities
and also protect their interests.

And they share a common sense of exclusiveness; great wealth and
power expose people to so many pressures and demands that they feel
some desire to withdraw among themselves, to share the company of
equals where men can relax and not suspect that a friendly grin is always
the prelude to a request for a favor. In the classic phrase of the rich
girl: "I want to be loved for myself, not my money." The only way she
can be sure is to marry someone who has as much money as she does.
In most parts of the country the upper class is so small that the old elite
cannot afford to reject the newcomers too much, or they might become
too lonely. Those newcomers who are sufficiently flexible and adroit to
learn quickly can gain at least partial acceptance, and their children,
once polished in Ivy League schools, need fear no snubbing.

The upper class, in short, can be described as a group who believe in
tradition, in continuity of behavior with the past; they emphasize

familism and lineage, which is cemented by the family fortune either as something inherited from the past or to be passed along in the future; they favor the skills of graceful living and dilettantism, and tend to value the man more than the accomplishment. They are conservative, both in the sense that they want to preserve the system which put them on top, and because they revere the relics of the past which give them a personal link to those forces and people who legitimate their claim to superiority. Yet they often are also liberal, for their family position guarantees enough security to permit individualistic expression and variation. And although they feel superior, they also vaguely recognize that much of the nation is suspicious of their right to do so; they are defensive, for the American values of equalitarianism and of prestige through accomplishment are at variance with inheritance and dilettantism.

### THE UPPER-MIDDLE CLASS: CAREER

The upper-middle class is close to, but not at the top of the system. Above them are the small group of upper-class families who have greater prestige, power, wealth, and income. Below them are the anonymous, or little people—the vast masses who can be hired interchangeably to do the routine jobs in factory or office. They themselves are the active people who are the leaders of the American work world. They are trained specialists in business or professional pursuits who make the daily decisions that guide the work of the little people. Upper-middle-class people do not have jobs, but occupy positions; they do not work, they pursue careers. The basic split in our society is that which divides the big people from the little people.

There is a conventional distinction in the literature between the "old middle class" and the "new middle class" [7]. The former are the entrepreneurs, the independents in business and the professions. The latter are the salaried men, the bureaucratic officials. It is hard to tell from the way census statistics are organized what the proportions are, but even if the independents make up a substantial portion of the upper-middle class, they are steadily losing ground in influence on value orientations. The rear guard of the old middle class are the retail merchants and the independent physicians; they are more powerful in small cities than in big ones; their pronouncements appear shriller and more defensive every year. But these pronouncements echo values that prevailed but a short while ago and thus are a power still to be reckoned with. However, we shall emphasize here the values of the new middle class, for we are more interested in tomorrow than in yesterday.

Upper-middle-class families live either in respectable apartment houses in the cities or in single-family homes in the suburbs. In a vague way they recognize themselves as a class: they use the terms middle or upper-class in their own conversations, and they think of themselves as educated, successful people who are the active and respected leaders of their local communities. They are almost all white and American born, and those born of immigrant parents tend to minimize their ethnic backgrounds and instead stress their own wide participation among nonethnic Americans. College has rubbed off most of their ethnic characteristics, and business competition has completed the job. They are interested in the latest styles for their homes, their clothes, their cars, and their thoughts. They have a sense of active participation in their communities and in the affairs of the world.

The central value orientation for the upper-middle class is "career." Their whole way of life—their consumption behavior, their sense of accomplishment and respectability, the source of much of their prestige with others—depends upon success in a career. The husband's career becomes the central social fact for all the family.

A career has a beginning. Given our industrial system, it must be learned; even if a sizable advantage in the form of a business is inherited, a man must learn how to run it or he is considered a wastrel and a failure. Consequently, the man must be educated either in a specific profession or in the general arts of salesmanship and business administration. The former are based primarily on technical knowledge, the latter on skills in manipulating people. But both types require an ability to mix easily with semi-strangers, to talk fluently, to be a man of the world. Consequently, there are prerequisites for admission into career competition: a certain minimum of intelligence, a personality that is sufficiently outgoing and flexible, a motivation for success strong enough to lead one to work and plan and often to sacrifice for it, an appropriate education in intellectual and social skills. *Birth into a middle-class family vastly increases the chances of meeting these prerequisites, and most middle-class sons remain in their class of birth.* However, our system of formal education permits many working-class sons to climb into the career competition if they start early enough.

Once a career has begun, it must be nurtured. An understanding and cooperative wife is most helpful. She reinforces her husband's motivation: he wants to succeed "for her," and he knows she will be unhappy if he cannot buy enough goods and enough prestige to make her respectable. She can establish a home that has prestige value, a place her husband can be proud to use as a base for entertaining business friends. She can make contacts in the community which are useful in fostering her husband's career. She can rear children whose needs for expensive educations keep her husband's ambitions high. She can refrain from complaining if he works at night in order to get ahead. She can offer an oasis of emotional repose to balance the strains of occupational competition.

A career does not stop when a man leaves the office. A career is a public thing, and is watched by many people in the local community, and often in the national community of those concerned (fellow professionals; colleagues in an industry). A man must live well, marry well, participate adequately in community affairs. He must be known and trusted *as a man* if he is to get ahead. Consequently, a career man is always concerned about his public behavior and reputation. His network of contacts is important. He cares what others think about him. This concern is especially acute in bureaucratic situations, where at each stage of his career a man is judged and promoted by his immediate superiors. They cannot concentrate only on technical qualifications; they must be concerned with his total personality, his ability to get along with others. To a somewhat greater degree the independent entrepreneur sells ideas and goods and services; the bureaucratic official sells himself.

Here is the way one corporation executive explained to me the system of bureaucratic selection and advancement; he can be considered an expert in this matter, for he started at the bottom and forty years later was a top official in a large company of high prestige [8]:

> Yes, I suppose my rate of advancement was about average. But I would say, as in any type of business, there are more who did not get that far than those who did. The mortality is rather high.

INTERVIEWER: Could you describe the characteristics of the people who succeed, and those who don't succeed, in that line of work?

> No, I don't think I could. You mean are they college men or noncollege men?

INTERVIEWER: That would be one sort of thing; perhaps also certain kinds of personalities are especially suitable for it.

> I don't know what to say about that. I think that at the present time the college graduate aspect of it has much more importance than it did when I was getting along. And just why, I don't know. But men of my own age group, I would say that about fifty-fifty are college or noncollege. The men in the age group starting out now are probably ninety per cent college.

INTERVIEWER: I'm very interested in that. Could you speculate a little as to what has brought about this change?

> It's the attitude of top management; they have felt, or perhaps learned, over the years, that from a dollars and cents standpoint it is an asset to the company, for the college-trained man is a better risk for promotion and advancement. The mortality is not as high. Providing they have a well-rounded and

balanced personality. That's the essential thing, of course. You've got to have a well-balanced man who gets along with people, which is the first essential.

INTERVIEWER: Do you agree with this attitude?

I've never thought much about it; but I think it's probably so. Perhaps it's best reflected by what I said to you the other evening; if I were to do it again, I'd get a general college education. As I look around at these younger men—they've got something, there isn't any doubt at all. Call it culture, facility of expression, broadness of vision, whatever it is I don't know, but they've definitely got something that the person who did not go to college has to get the hard way. I wouldn't be surprised if it might not be summed up as saying that the man who has gone to college has four more years of training in the necessity of getting along with people socially. The personnel department is going out after them nowadays.

INTERVIEWER: Is there any particular point at which the mortality is especially high—where the differences in people showed up?

Well, when I say mortality it isn't so much that people left the company. There are dozens of people doing clerical jobs; they're just put somewhere doing clerical jobs and they're happy and contented; that's just their nature. It's a good thing we have a lot of people like that. There wasn't a good deal of firing; some just left; others went into clerical work. And those that had the urge, who were never satisfied, always wanted to be doing something else, they just kept pushing. . . . Now we have a training program. The personnel department goes out and hires these bright young men from college. Some come in because they have good family connections. But then they all have the same training program; they get moved from department to department and are watched. The thing they're watched for more than anything else is their ability to adjust to their environment, to get along with their associates, their superiors, their contemporaries, their subordinates. That's the most important thing. If they antagonize people, if they don't get along, they're just not for us. No matter what their brilliance is, if they can't get along with people, we don't want them. All you can judge them on is what you see in the office. It isn't like, take a person with a nasty disposition or an arrogant nature or extreme shyness who may be a brilliant chemist or research man, why that's all right; but the basis of our business is human contact.

INTERVIEWER: Do you think this would be true in the management of most large businesses?

Oh, definitely. In pure research, a man goes into the laboratory and works with materials; his personality doesn't concern anybody. But in business, the basic ingredient is to get along, to adjust to your environment. . . .

INTERVIEWER: Does each generation of top management pick its own successors?

I don't think that the management picks its successors; I think that the successors just rise by their own ability and the force of their own personalities. It's perfectly obvious who's coming to the top. . . . Talent is limited. It's a constant search. It's difficult to get men to take responsibility, who are capable. . . .

A career man must have leadership traits that will help him stand out amongst his fellows. These are fostered by active participation in community affairs, and many corporations insist that their executives belong to various clubs and committees in the local community. Leadership training begins at an early stage in a career: a boy is active in high-school extra curricular affairs in order to develop a balanced personality that will make him popular in college; he participates in collegiate activities partly because he knows that professional schools and employment officers evaluate such activities when they are considering his application. Business favors the "well-rounded" man, even at the expense of high excellence in a specialized area.

The career man must be ever alert, ever competing. There is always someone else who also hopes for promotion; the higher one goes in the hierarchy, the fewer are the jobs—some men must fall by the way. And the competition is always over a long span of time. One starts at the bottom of a given level (not at the bottom of the whole system), and must slowly work his way up. He expects to take twenty years or more before reaching his highest position. All during that time he expects a steady increase in income, in reputation, and in power, to match his growth in experience and competence.

Riesman and others have said that our culture is shifting from an emphasis on production to an emphasis on consumption, that our new upper-middle class is less concerned with making a lot of money than was its predecessor and more concerned with the fun of spending a moderate amount of money. The deep drives of an economy of scarcity are shifting to the more relaxed ways of an economy of abundance. I agree. But if our comparison is not with the past but with other classes in the present, then the upper-middle class can still be described as basically oriented to career. However, the meaning of career has broadened, and includes many consumption skills. A career based on the subtleties of bureaucratic competition includes a man's taste in clothes, wives, and wines.

A career is interesting and satisfying. It may be that the contemporary business official feels somewhat less inner compulsion to work than the driving entrepreneur of the Puritan past, but nevertheless he feels that his work is important and challenging. He grows as his career advances and he assumes larger responsibilities; he has a sense of accomplishment and of continuity. He keeps up to date in his field, and he feels progressive, creative, and in control of important affairs. He senses that he is doing the big work of his culture. He is not alienated from work.

The man who has emerged successfully from competition wants to feel that the competitive rules were fair and that he won through superior ability and energy. It would be a devastating blow to his ego to think of the results as pure luck. Consequently, belief in the existence of free competition and the rightness of individualistic effort are essential to the upper-middle class. The only way they can justify to themselves their successful position is to believe that in the long run their success grew out of greater talent and greater devotion. They can no longer cap this credo with the Calvinistic notion that behind their success stands the direct will of God who "elected" them, for most American businessmen lack that supreme gall, but they do and must believe that their success is more than mere accident. Otherwise they would become usurpers in their own eyes.

This rationalization appears in all cultures, no matter what the criteria of success may be. A Comanche warrior did not become a hero by accident; a Chinese scholar did not attain eminence by accident; a medieval priest did not become a bishop by accident. They believed that they were *superior persons* because they lived up to the values of their culture more completely than ordinary people. Superiority of talent at birth and superiority of willful exploitation of talent by following the rules of the game were believed to bring, in the long run, success. Of course, there is always the influence of good and bad luck. But men cannot believe that in the long run all happens by luck; such chaos would remove all motivation. If a culture is to be vital, people must believe that the men who follow the rules get a just share of the rewards. And the way that "functional necessity" of a culture gets established is through the rationalizations of the people who have become successful: they insist that virtue pays.

This belief can maintain itself regardless of considerable statistical deviation from reality. In spite of the many virtuous people who die poor, we can cling to our values so long as there is some connection in reality between talent plus energy and success, and some opportunity for most men to get into the race if they choose. No one knows how far the discrepancy between reality and ideology must widen before the ideology is overthrown, but the gap can be fairly wide and the system can still function.

A crucial test of the ideology of individualism came in America after the Spanish-American War when the large corporations began to dominate the scene. No longer could the old beliefs of competition among individual businessmen be fully accepted even by the businessmen. But a beautiful substitute was invented: equality of opportunity in education, and fair competition within the corporations for people of similar education. In place of the old right of every American to start his own business, we have the new right of every American to educate himself to his fullest possibilities, with the expectation that his rewards will be commensurate with his education. Again, there is some gap between myth and reality, but the two coincide sufficiently for relatively smooth functioning. America's passion for education which makes the high school the most imposing building in town is not an accident.

Despite the fact that most sons of upper-middle-class parents remain in it, the class as a whole contains many newcomers. The absolute size and the relative proportion of the upper-middle class in the total population are both growing. In addition, upper-middle-class people have not, in the past, produced enough sons to replace the fathers, and some upper-middle-class sons slip down. The net result is that an enormous number of individuals climb each generation from the lower-middle and the upper levels of the working class into the upper-middle class. (It should be remembered that because the lower-middle and working classes are so much larger than the upper-middle class, a small proportion of people climbing out of the former makes a large proportion climbing into the latter.) Furthermore, there is constant change and shifting within the upper-middle class—sons of businessmen become professionals, sons of preachers become industrial managers, and so on.

Consequently, the American upper-middle class is an unstable group. People are moving from one occupation and one town to another. Very few can behave appropriately to their current positions by the simple rule of imitating their parents. Thus they must learn by imitating others, and they do so by adopting the external symbols—it takes time to absorb fully the inner attitudes that go with the symbols. They demonstrate their position to themselves and to others by their houses, their furniture, their clothes, their motorcars. Separated from kinsmen and from ancient ties to a local community, they accentuate the new, the flexible, the shifting in life. They ignore their past if the future seems more promising. This lack of tradition leads them to seize upon the formalities of behavior as a substitute for the ease and grace of habit—even if the current formalities stress the studied informality of "California style" living. When so many so quickly adopt the same style, it appears that they read the same magazines. It is this group that epitomizes "conspicuous consumption" and "other orientation."

Carried to extreme, this type of behavior becomes snobbery, and as is usually the case, an understanding of the extreme helps us comprehend the average. Lionel Trilling, a perceptive literary critic, writes [9]:

> Snobbery is pride in status without pride in function. And it is an uneasy pride of status. It always asks, "Do I belong—do I really belong? And does he belong? And if I am observed talking to him, will it make me seem to belong or not to belong?" It is the peculiar vice not of aristocratic societies which have their own appropriate vices, but of bourgeois democratic societies. For

us the legendary strongholds of snobbery are the Hollywood studios, where two thousand dollars a week dare not talk to three hundred dollars a week for fear he be taken for nothing more than fifteen hundred dollars a week. The dominant emotions of snobbery are uneasiness, self-consciousness, self-defensiveness, the sense that one is not quite real but can in some way acquire reality.

Money is the medium that, for good or bad, makes for a fluid society. It does not make for an equal society but for one in which there is a constant shifting of classes, a frequent change in the personnel of the dominant class. In a shifting society great emphasis is put upon appearance—I am using the word now in the common meaning, as when people say that "a good appearance is very important in getting a job." To appear to be established is one of the ways of becoming established. The old notion of the solid merchant who owns far more than he shows increasingly gives way to the ideal of signalizing status by appearance, by showing more than you have: status in a democratic society is presumed to come not with power but with the tokens of power. Hence the development of what Tocqueville saw as a mark of democratic culture, what he called the "hypocrisy of luxury"—instead of the well-made peasant article and the well-made middle class article, we have the effort of all articles to appear as the articles of the very wealthy.

The break between the big people and the little people may be growing more clear-cut at the same time that movement across the line may be getting easier. (At any rate, there appears to be at least as much movement as there ever was.) In those occupations based on complex technology or complex learning of the legal-administrative type, there is a sharp distinction between the man who knows and understands the science and philosophy behind what he does and the one who simply carries out instructions. Such learning must be organized, and must be obtained through formal schooling which begins early in life and lasts a long time. An intelligent man without learning has great difficulty teaching himself. In this sense advancing technology widens the gap between the educated men who manage ideas and people and the working folk who handle objects or papers. No longer is the skill hierarchy modeled on the apprentice-journeyman-master system, under which a man can slowly advance in his lifetime from the bottom to the top of a given trade. No longer is the bulk of manufacturing and trade carried on by entrepreneurs who started on a shoestring and built up their enterprises through aggressive competition [10].

Yet this gap between managers and workers is softened by an educational system that gives unprecedented opportunity for sons of little people to train themselves if they want to. And it is softened, at least in terms of American values, because bureaucratic competition is reasonably fair. It seems to us to be fairer for individuals to compete on the basis of education and performance than for families to compete on terms of inherited wealth. As long as the bureaucratic organizations stick to equal rules for everybody and do not succumb to nepotism, most Americans are satisfied. And it is to the benefit of the corporations to follow such principles of equality, for in that way they are likely to discover and nurture the best managerial talent.

Let us summarize. We have in America today a growing upper-middle class of college-educated, prosperous people who are technicians, professionals, managers, and businessmen. They are going suburban. They tend to interact a great deal in the community, but almost wholly with their own kind. Although there is considerable spread in their incomes, their conception of a proper standard of life is essentially similar; some are able to achieve it to a fuller degree than others.

What do they believe? Primarily, they believe in themselves and in organization. They stress individual initiative combined with smooth group functioning. They have faith that anything can be accomplished by this combination. They say that a man must be smart, must be educated, must be energetic, but at the same time he must be cooperative, must not stand out too much from his crowd of equals, must not be eccentric or "controversial." These are the values of the upper levels of most bureaucratic structures. They are very effective in their proper situation; they may not produce great art or literature or scientific theory, but they certainly produce efficient organizations.

The upper-middle class believe in themselves and in the American way of life, and they are devoted to their careers. They stress planning for the future and not too much regard for the past; they stress activity, accomplishment, practical results; they stress individualistic achievement within the framework of group cooperation and collective responsibility. They are not much interested in tradition, in art, in any sort of theory for its own sake. They always ask of an idea, "What good is it; how can you use it?" They are on the move, "on the make," and they have the zest of winners (though the tensions of racers).

Many of these values are modern adaptations of historic American commitments. There has been a smooth transition from the values of the pioneer who conquered the wilderness through strength and practical sagacity, to the values of the managerial technician who conquered the system through ambition and wit. Tocqueville's description of the middle class of early nineteenth-century America sounds almost contemporaneous, if we ignore details and concentrate on abstract orientations. Because of this, our upper-middle-class people feel (though they are too ignorant of history to know) that they are peculiarly American. They feel that other classes who deviate from these values are not behaving in a fully patriotic way. In this sense, general American values are predominantly upper-middle-class values.

## LOWER-MIDDLE CLASS: RESPECTABILITY

The basic split in our stratification order is between the big people and the little people. As we now turn to the little people, we will find that the differences among them are not sharp, that demarcation lines are hard to draw.

At the turn of the century we might have said that a high-school education was the criterion that separated the lower-middle class from the working class—it was scarce, it brought prestige, it signified American rather than foreign skills, it brought a white-collar job and a higher income. The girl who raised herself by becoming a stenographer, the boy who learned bookkeeping—these were the typical symbols of the lower-middle class. These people worked with papers rather than on materials; they worked in or near the offices of the bosses; they identified with those above them and struggled to live like their superiors. Their incomes may not have been adequate to live opulently, but they could at least buy respectability.

Some of these distinctions persist, but all are weakened. About half our population now graduates from high school, and in some parts of the country the figure approaches three quarters. The proportion of native born is much higher than it was, so this distinction is less important. Much office work has been mechanized, and much factory work has been made clean and easy. The relative superiority in income of white-collar work has declined. Unions have not only raised the wages but have added to the power and the dignity of the wage worker. The general rise in income has made it possible for factory wage workers to live comfortably and respectably.

Yet there remains enough distinction to make it useful for the purpose of studying values to keep the separate labels of "lower-middle class" and "working class." *

Part of the lower-middle class works at occupations that are "semi"—semiprofessional, semimanagerial. Another part are "petty"—petty businessmen, petty farmers. They are at the bottom of the various ladders that lead upward; the working class are not on the ladders at all. The lower-middle-class people who wear white collars work with the big people, and sometimes are trying to become big people, but they live with the little people. Thus they are often not sure where they belong.

But we must not exclude all blue-collar workers from the lower-middle class. The foremen belong; management claims them and workers reject them. Many skilled craftsmen also belong; they make high incomes, and often assert middle-class values. Even a number of operatives should be included.

In previous chapters there has been evidence that these people are,

* Warner often combines them into the stratum of "the common man."

in some ways, similar and belong together. They are in the fast-growing middle-income group. They live in the same parts of town, in small, single-family houses, in two-family dwellings, or in small but fairly modern apartments. Most have had a high-school education, and a great many have had some additional special training: normal school, secretarial college, a technical course in electricity or accounting. The high-school graduates of yesterday are turning into the "part-college" people of tomorrow. They are the people who seldom make basic decisions about their work, yet carry out the instructions of others with intelligence, technical understanding, and considerable initiative. They accept many of the career values of the upper-middle class, and are constantly striving to get ahead; *yet most will never get very far, and after they have outlived the romantic dreams of youth, they know it.*

Furthermore, if asked, most of these people would call themselves middle class (though with some hesitation and ambivalence). They feel superior to routine wage workers who drift from job to job without developing a specialty. Yet, when the interviewing is pushed, they recognize that they are not "in the know" about important decisions; and they recognize that they do not make as much money as they need in order to live in an elegant style. They know that they are not big people.

Lower-middle-class people are thus on the fence; they are more conscious of being in between than are any other group. They cannot cling too strongly to career as the focus of their lives, for their jobs do not lead continuously upward. Instead, they tend to emphasize the respectability of their jobs and their styles of life, for it is respectability that makes them superior to shiftless workers.

Respectability can be expressed in various ways. Education is highly valued; people are proud of their high-school diploma and any training achieved beyond it; they can urge their children to try to get to college, even though it means financial sacrifice that makes college a much more difficult goal for them than for the upper-middle class. In terms of value orientations, a useful clue to identify a lower-middle-class person is the strength of his desire to have his children go to college.

Religion is another mark of respectability. The lower-middle class are probably the most regular churchgoers in our society (although the upper-middle may have a greater proportion who maintain a formal church membership). Religious attitudes toward family morality are typical; divorce is frowned upon, and many lower-middle-class people suspect that those above them and those below them in the hierarchy are prone to loose sexual behavior. Moral and well-behaved children are a central goal for lower-middle-class families; it is more important for them to be "good" than free to "express themselves."

Home ownership is respectable, and is a symbol of stability and of family solidarity. Lower-middle-class people are very proud of their small homes; they seek to buy them, spend twenty or thirty years paying off the mortgage, and put in many hours of personal labor to keep home and grounds in good condition. Home furnishings tend to be more standardized, with suites of matching chairs and sofas, than is the case with other groups (who either feel more freedom to experiment or else do not care).

Respectability has its price. Particularly when the rewards are minimal, when the consumption pleasures and prestige returns are slim by comparison to the upper-middle class, the white-collar man may come to feel that he is bound by a very stiff collar. The successful blue-collar worker enjoys his respectability much more, for he tends to compare himself to the run-of-the-mill workers who stand immediately below him. But the petty white-collar worker looks up; he feels that he is constantly holding his impulses in check in order to be liked by his boss, by his customers, by his neighbors. He has to sell his personality as well as his labor. As C. Wright Mills puts it in his book, *White Collar* [11]:

In the world of the small entrepreneur, men sold goods to one another; in the new society of employees, they first of all sell their services. The employer of manual services buys the workers' labor, energy, and skill; the employer of many white-collar services, especially salesmanship, also buys the employees' social personalities. . . .

One knows the salesclerk not as a person but as a commercial mask, a stereotyped greeting and appreciation for patronage; one need not be kind to the modern laundryman, one need only pay him; he, in turn, needs only to be cheerful and efficient. Kindness and friendliness becomes aspects of personalized service or of public relations of big firms, rationalized to further sale of something. With anonymous insincerity the Successful Person thus makes an instrument of his own appearance and personality. . . .

In the normal course of her work, because her personality becomes the instrument of an alien purpose, the salesgirl becomes self-alienated.

When carried too far, this public sale of one's personality produces tragedy, for eventually even the salesman learns that some aspects of the self are too precious for the market. Willy Loman in Arthur Miller's *Death of a Salesman* is a case in point. Indeed, our recent literature, both scientific and fictional, has tended to emphasize the extremes of lower-middle-class life, perhaps because the values there expressed are so diametrically opposed to those of the intellectuals who write books. The intellectuals portray little people with restricted lives, tight and authoritarian personalities, and a tendency toward fascistic attitudes that support narrow fundamentalism and McCarthyism. I do not doubt that when the lower-middle-class way of life goes to extremes it produces just such reactions. The extreme version of upper-middle-class values is snobbery, that of lower-middle-class respectability, prudery. But must we judge each group by its extremes? For many the lower-middle-class way of life is quietly satisfying; it connotes the accomplishment of moderate education and moderate occupational achievement; it means successful Americanization from not-too-distant ethnic roots; it brings a strong, stable, family-centered life; especially in the smaller towns and cities, it brings a degree of public recognition as solid citizens. This way of life may be dull, but it is not necessarily stultifying.

THE WORKING CLASS: GET BY

The ordinary working-class man is a semiskilled factory operative. He quit high school before graduation. Although he seeks to work steadily, he has no particular specialty, and drifts from job to job as the labor market dictates. He made almost as much on his first job as he does twenty years later. His basic value orientation is simply to "get by." The most typical representative is the automobile worker, and we have three recent researches that tell his story.

The first study is *The Man on the Assembly Line* by Charles R. Walker and Robert H. Guest of the Institute of Human Relations, Yale University. These research workers and their associates interviewed 180 automobile workers in their homes in 1949. All the men were employed in a new and ultramodern assembly plant. Somewhat later, Guest conducted another study based on 202 interviews with automobile workers in a somewhat older plant [12]. The third study is Ely Chinoy's *Automobile Workers and the American Dream* [13]. Chinoy worked in the plant he studied, and then he interviewed 62 workers in their homes. Let us combine the results of these studies, for they all point in the same direction, and talk about "typical" automobile workers.

Automobile workers are at the top of the semiskilled level with respect to hourly earnings, averaging about twenty per cent more than workers in all other manufacturing industries combined. But it is important to note that the spread of pay was very small from job to job in the plants studied; the difference between the lowest and highest paid jobs on the assembly line was only ten or fifteen cents an hour. Twenty years of experience and seniority were worth a pittance. True, skilled workers like machine-tool makers earned considerably more, but they were usually not men who had started "on the line"; they had learned their trades as apprentices when they first got out of school. It was extremely rare for an assembly-line man to become a skilled worker, or to be promoted to a foreman. Here is a basic fact about semiskilled working-class life: it is on a flat level. *There are few differences in pay or responsibility from job to job, from year to year. There is not too much point in working hard to get somewhere, for there is no place to go.*

The tasks these men did were subdivided into small routine operations that were repeated hour after hour. A man could learn his job in a few hours, or at most, a few days. As the automobiles moved along the line, each worker added some small part, or tightened a few bolts, or sprayed on a little paint. He had to work fast, but he need not think much. Some workers fitted into the rhythm of the work without complaint, but most disliked repetitive work. One man said [14]: "The job gets so sickening —day in and day out plugging in ignition wires. I get through with one motor, turn around, and there's another motor staring me in the face. It's sickening."

The men did not like assembly-line work, and they remembered their previous jobs as having been more interesting. Why, then, did they come to the automobile plant? For the high pay it offered and the relative steadiness of its employment. In other words, a working-class job is something that one has to do in order to earn a living, and one accepts unpleasantness in order to bring home a good pay check. One does not expect to enjoy it, to be particularly interested in it, to have it mean anything to him in and of itself. This characteristic attitude, plus the fact of high movement from one job to another, alienates men from work. Such alienation is the exact opposite of a "career" orientation.

There is fairly typical sequence in the development of alienation, just as in the development of a career. A working-class boy who does not have a driving ambition to climb into the middle class approaches work with a casual attitude. For him high school has relatively little meaning; it is not a necessary step toward college, and it has little direct use in training for a factory job. He either quits school before graduating, or just hangs around until the diploma is handed to him. Then he thinks of a job as an opportunity to earn a lot of spending money; he still lives at home with his parents, and even if he contributes toward room and board, there is enough money left over for a car, for girls, for fun. Psychologically, this money is far more important to him than the pay a middle-class career man gets on his first job. The working-class boy needs money more because his parents cannot give him much; the rate of pay on his first factory job is not far from what his father makes, so it seems like a high rate; his values allow him to spend and enjoy his money rather than save it for the future. Often the first job is a romantic escape from the boredom of school.

If the boy has any dreams at all, he thinks of the first factory job as temporary; he expects eventually to climb up the hierarchy in the plant, or to leave it for something better. As the months go by, the first thing the boy learns is that there is not much opportunity within the factory.

One upward route is skilled work, but that means taking a long period of apprenticeship at lower pay, and many young men will not make the sacrifice. The other route is into supervision, but the number of openings there is small; Chinoy estimated that in the plant he studied only ten or twelve workers a year, out of a force of six thousand, were promoted into supervisory levels [15]. And they could not expect to rise above foremanship, for all the higher jobs were held by men who had special technical training, usually in college.

Soon the boy begins to reorganize his aspirations to fit the facts of his environment. Instead of dreaming of foremanship, he learns to seek the easiest job on the assembly line, or to maneuver into one of the jobs off the line, which brings a less hectic and more varied work pace. Or he tries to get placed somewhere under a better boss. Then he settles down and waits for seniority to bring him a few cents an hour more, along with an increased guarantee of steady work (the union contracts specify that when work is slack, workers of lowest seniority must be laid off first).

What of the American values of success, of getting ahead? Many boys from the working class never paid much attention to the success dream. As one high-school boy has expressed it [16]:

I'm not definite what I'd like to do. Any kind of job. Anything as long as I get a little cash. . . . What the hell? I got nothin' to look forward to.

Others who may have flirted with the idols of success soon readjust to the realities of the factory, and learn to seek a slight improvement in the job as their success goal. Others concentrate on the symbols of improvement in their lives *outside* the factory: the new car or TV set, or the payments on the mortgage that bring their homes closer to being their own. And some wage workers actively disparage the success story. They sneer at lower-middle-class folk who strive so hard, who "think they are better than we are," who are "white-collar snobs," who are so respectable and stuffy they "don't know how to have any fun." By being less concerned about his public reputation, about his house or children as symbols of respectability, the factory worker has more psychic freedom.

But some wage workers are not content with their position, and consider the factory as a temporary expedient. The favorite escape goal is independent business: the gas station, the little retail store, the farm [17]:

Interest in the possibility of leaving the factory ran high among the workers interviewed and out-of-the-shop goals were frequently discussed in the day-to-day talk of men in the plant. We have already noted that forty-eight of the sixty-two workers interviewed answered in the affirmative to the question: Have you ever thought of getting out of the shop? . . . This widespread interest in leaving the factory stemmed chiefly from dissatisfaction with work in the plant rather than strong commitments to out-of-the-shop goals. These men saw in business or farming an escape from the disabilities of factory work, not an opportunity to become wealthy.

Most of those who went beyond idle fantasy and actually made plans to escape from the factory were younger men. But it was not easy to escape; once a man got married, the steady wages from the factory were essential for daily living, and little surplus remained to be saved for use as business capital. Returning to Chinoy's sample: seventeen out of the sixty-two men seriously schemed to get out of the factory. Four years later only six had made it. Three young workers had achieved their dreams: one was a student in the local college, one a policeman, one had opened his own tool-and-die shop. Three other workers were not so successful: one had exchanged his automobile job for another one not too dissimilar; one had left the factory for a while and then returned; one older worker had left the plant, but Chinoy could not learn what had happened to him. Other studies confirm these small-sample results: the dream of opening a small business has changed from the standard aspiration of middle-class sons to an escape myth for factory workers, and the chances of succeeding in such a business are low; for relatively few of those who manage to get started can stay in business for very long [18].

As they get older and pass into their forties, most of the men accept the fact that they are going to be factory workers for the rest of their lives. They concentrate on their steady pay and growing seniority; they jockey for the best job in the plant that they can get; and they learn to pay as little attention to work as possible. Their satisfactions in life come from outside the factory. Their families, their homes, their vacations, their hopes for their children—these become important, while work becomes a necessary chore that is easiest to bear the less one's personality is invested in it.

These psychological consequences of semiskilled work, and their effects on basic value orientations, are subtly explored in a study of another industry: meat packing. Fred H. Blum has reported on the attitudes of workers at the Hormel plant in Austin, Minnesota. The study is especially significant because this plant is one of the most progressive in the United States. The workers have had a guaranteed annual wage for twenty years; they share in the profits of the company; they set their own work pace; supervisors and foremen are expediters who keep materials flowing but give few direct orders to workers. The net result is that they turn out over thirty per cent more work than laborers in similar types of plants; they earn over thirty per cent more than other meat-packing employees; they have great respect for the company and the union; they appreciate their jobs.

Yet despite these extraordinary circumstances, Hormel workers show the same apathy and alienation from work as do the automobile workers. They realize that work is better than idleness, and that they would "go nuts" if they just sat around the house all day. But work does not have positive interest beyond its function of "killing time." Blum writes [19]:

Most workers are so busily engaged in pushing the flow of work that they do not *consciously* suffer from the inherent monotony of their work. They are well adjusted, because they have reduced their level of aspirations to the rather low level of the job. They coast along, keeping busy, visiting, talking, making time go by, and getting the work done in order to "get out of there" in order to get home! A worker to whom this passage has been read commented on it as follows: "True worker brings aspirations to level of job. That's why a new man is not so good. The first six months are the toughest. I was at the verge of quitting. After a while, you get used to it."

Blum adds: "In view of this situation, it is not astonishing that the overwhelming majority of the workers derive their greatest satisfaction from the money they earn rather than from the work they do."

The workers told Blum that they seldom talk about their work when they go home; they make as complete a separation as they can between "work" and "life." Some find themselves too tired and apathetic when they get home to build themselves a very satisfying life outside the factory. When they leave the gates others find new energies that are channeled into various activities around the house, allowing them to do "something that comes natural," that expresses their own inner drives toward creativity. Unfortunately, true creativity is rare, for the men carry over into leisure activities the attitudes they have so deeply absorbed on the job, attitudes of passivity that demand something to do to pass the time. A man cannot get full satisfaction from hobby activities when he realizes that work is at the center of one's life and all else is, for Americans, peripheral [20]:

Alienation from work in a culture which gives work a central place in the life of the people means alienation from life, and from the very core of workers' personalities—their real selves. It means unrelatedness to the inner sources of creative living, inability to feel free in the sense of freedom to express oneself.

Alienation from work is but a part of a larger sense of alienation from contemporary life that is shared by many industrial workers. They see that they are not the people in the world who really count; they know that others make decisions, and then they carry them out. In their community living as well as the factory, they have a sense of being little people who are on the outside of things. In Chapter V Floyd Dotson's study of working-class life showed little participation beyond the range of the family. The results of many public-opinion polls are similar: compared to middle-class people, workers are uninterested in public affairs because they feel less sense of participation and control; they read less, understand less, and generally live in a world that is much narrower in psychological space [21].

In summation, semiskilled workers have values that are sharply different from the career orientations of the upper-middle class, and also from the respectability strivings of the lower-middle class. Workers' values are different because their lives are different.

A worker is not greatly concerned about his public reputation. He expects to move from one routine job to another as opportunities expand and contract, and he knows that he will be hired as an anonymous person. He need not sell his personality, his family background, his consumption skills; all he needs is a pair of willing hands. His work has little intrinsic interest; he learns to adjust, to lower his aspirations, to become adroit at working without thinking and without dreaming of future advancement. As he retreats from work as a thing of inner importance, he turns to his family and to consumption pleasures. He cannot live extravagantly, but in our productive economy he can live comfortably and can expect his home slowly to add one gadget to another. He takes pride in this method of "getting ahead." He and his family learn to be amused by the mass media of entertainment—most predominantly, television. In smaller towns like Austin, he devotes an extraordinary amount of time to fishing. He does not participate much in community life nor in active group recreations. He is a spectator in recreation just as he is in work. Once he passes beyond the unrealistic visions of youth, he becomes a man primarily interested in merely getting by from day to day [22].

## THE LOWER CLASS: APATHY

Hollingshead gives us this description of the lower class in Elmtown as seen through the eyes of their superiors [23]:

It is looked upon as the scum of the city by the higher classes. It is believed generally that nothing beyond charity can be done for these people, and only a minimum of that is justified since they show little or no inclination to help themselves. It is the opinion of the upper class that:

They have no respect for the law, or themselves. They enjoy their shacks and huts along the river and across the tracks and love their dirty, smoky, low-class dives and taverns.

Whole families—children, in-laws, mistresses, and all—live in one shack.

This is the crime class that produces the delinquency and sexual promiscuity that fills the paper.

Their interests lie in sex and its perversion. The girls are always pregnant; the families are huge; incestual relations occur frequently.

They are not inspired by education, and only a few are able to make any attainments along this line. . . .

If they work, they work at very menial jobs. . . .

The lower-class persons themselves react to their economic situation and to their degradation in the eyes of respectable people by becoming fatalistic; they feel that they are down and out, and that there is no point in trying to improve, for the odds are all against them. They may have some desires to better their position, but cannot see how it can be done. Hollingshead says [23]: These "persons give the impression of being resigned to a life of frustration and defeat in a community that despises them for their disregard of morals, lack of 'success' goals, and dire poverty."

Now, respectable people exaggerate when they talk about those they consider disrespectable, yet most of the statements Hollingshead lists are half-truths. Let us examine them further.

Every town and city contains a sizable group of people who live in decrepit houses in slum areas, work irregularly at unskilled and semi-skilled jobs, and are usually suffering from poverty. This group contains an undue proportion of Negroes and foreign-born, yet there are also many families with as long a line of Yankee forebears as the local old-family elite. Many studies confirm the same conclusions: although the actual rates will vary according to the business cycle, these people contribute far more than their proportionate share to the relief roles, to crime and delinquency rates, to the list of unmarried mothers, to divorces and desertions. They are the least educated group in the population and the least interested in education.

Why? The lower class lives in the mesh of a vicious circle; it does not matter too much where we begin to examine it, for each aspect of the circle fits into the others.

Although there are some people of good native intelligence among them, the average intelligence level is low. Their health and physical stamina are also low. Environmental conditions contribute to these deficiencies, but inferior biological stock is for many an inescapable handicap. And they are culturally deficient: ordinarily they have no more than a grammar-school education. For the immigrant or the Southern Negro migrant, even that schooling is of poor quality and of little use in the industrial city.

Employers frown upon them, and will hire them for only the most routine jobs. It so happens that routine jobs are also the most unstable; as business expands and contracts, routine workers are the last to be hired and the first to be fired. Given this unsteady employment at low rates, they have no choice but to live in the poorest and cheapest rental housing they can find. They must crowd into small space, so that one or two rooms for a whole family are all that can be obtained.

Hollingshead writes about Elmtown [24]:

The family pattern is unique. The husband-wife relationship is more or less an unstable one, even though the marriage is sanctioned either by law or understandings between the partners. Disagreement leading to quarrels and vicious fights, followed by desertion by either the man or the woman, possibly divorce, is not unusual. The evidence indicates that few compulsive factors, such as neighborhood solidarity, religious teachings, or ethical considerations, operate to maintain a stable marital relationship. On the contrary, the class culture has established a family pattern where serial monogamy is the rule. . . . Doctors, nurses, and public officials who know these families best estimate that from one-fifth to one-fourth of all births are illegitimate. Irrespective of the degree of error in this estimate, 78 per cent of the mothers gave birth to their first child before they were 20 years of age. Another trait that marks the family complex is the large number of children. The mean is 5.6 per mother. . . . Death, desertion, separation, or divorce has broken more than half the families (56 per cent). The burden of child care, as well as support, falls on the mother more often than on the father when the family is broken. The mother-child relation is the strongest and most enduring family tie. . . . Fifty-five per cent of the mothers "work out" part or full time as waitresses, dishwashers, cooks, washwomen, janitresses, cleaning women, and unskilled domestic workers.

The historic pattern in America is for immigrant groups to come to our cities from the rural areas of Europe. They arrive without the skills of language, education, or industrial experience that would fit them readily into the upper parts of the occupational hierarchy. So they are forced into the lower-class way of life. The more intelligent, energetic, ambitious, and lucky among them are able to climb quickly; some alien cultures are more akin than others to the values of ambition, and their members tend to climb more readily than the rest [25]. The immigrants themselves are often able to get good and stable jobs, marry, move to better parts of the city, and become respectable members of the working or middle class within a few years after arrival. And their children can, if they choose, get a good American education and climb even further. Such is the American dream.

In recent years the European migration has been slowed, and its character has changed; many of the refugees from Hitler and Stalin are professional and business people who are able, with some help, to enter our class system at the middle. But we have a newer migration that fulfills the function of the old in supplying the routine but necessary labor at the bottom of the occupational hierarchy: Southern Negroes, who move from the farms to the Northern cities. And in the New York area they are joined by many thousands of Puerto Ricans. They are repeating much of the pattern of the older European immigrants, but have a harder time climbing because they cannot change their skin color as easily as they can drop their accents.

However, many of the migrants, and many of their sons and daughters, find it too difficult to become successful. They settle down and expect that lower class life is theirs forever. They adjust by creating a value system that softens their failure to live up to the demands of American culture. This value system has many compensations; its adherents often think it superior to others. Either because they like the lower-class way of life, or because they feel that they have no opportunity to change, many families remain at the bottom for generation after generation.

The central assumption of the lower-class value system is that the situation is hopeless. Because he has to struggle merely to stay alive, because he knows that respectable people sneer at him as "no good," because he lacks the technical and social skills necessary for success, the lower-class person gives up. The way this apathy is created is described in detail by Allison Davis in "The Motivation of the Underprivileged Worker." His description is based on the study of some four hundred white and Negro families in Chicago by Davis and his colleagues (including Robert J. Havighurst and W. Lloyd Warner). Davis maintains that lower-class culture represents *"normal* responses that the worker has learned from his physical and social environment. His habits constitute a system of behavior and attitudes which are realistic and rational in *that environment* in which the individual of the slums has lived and in which he has been trained [26]."

Davis emphasizes the importance of the large families so common in the lower class [27]:

The actual daily pressure of 5 to 10 hungry stomachs to fill, backs to clothe, and feet to cover forces an [underprivileged] parent to reduce his ambitions to the level of subsistence; to lower his sights as far as long-term planning and studying for better jobs and finer skills are concerned; to narrow, limit, and shorten his goals with regard to the care, nutrition, education and careers of his children.

This terrible pressure for physical survival means that the *child* in the average underprivileged family does not learn the "ambition," the drive for high skills, and for educational achievement that the middle-class child learns in his family. The [underprivileged] individual usually does not learn to respond to these strong incentives and to seek these difficult goals, because they have been submerged in his family life by the daily battle for food, shelter, and for the preservation of the family. In this sense, ambition and the drive to attain the higher skills are a kind of luxury. They require a minimum *physical security;* only when one knows where his next week's or next month's food and shelter will come from, can he and his children afford to go in for the long-term education and training, the endless search for opportunities, and the tedious apple polishing that the attainment of higher skills and occupational status requires.

The response to economic pressure that becomes standardized is not saving and hard work, but helping one another. The large family means that the individual has a source of help and protection. When one person is out of work, another feeds and houses him. There is no shame or loss of respectability in this dependence, for everyone expects to be in the same boat from time to time.

Once accustomed to this way of life, a worker feels that a steady job is not important even when it is available. The worker assumes that he is subject to dismissal at the whim of his boss, and he always knows that he can manage to get by for a while without important loss of prestige in his own community by living with others or by going on relief. Consequently, if he gets mad at his boss, or feels a desire for a short vacation, he quits. He feels little sense of responsibility either to himself or to his employer.

Instead of a sense of responsibility and concern for the future, the underprivileged worker has a desire for those pleasures that are open to him [28]:

The most powerful of all the forces that keep him in his way of life and of work are the pleasures that he actually can attain by following his under-privileged culture. He gets strong biological enjoyment. He spends a great deal of his nights in sexual exploration, since he does not have to go to work the next day. He lives in a social world where visceral, genital, and emotional gratification is far more available than it is in a middle-class world.

These observations of Allison Davis describe the realities of slum life. It is important to emphasize the role of the self-image of a man who knows he is despised by respectable people. He can react in only two basic ways: withdraw, and convince himself that respectable people are not worth worrying about, that they are snobs and stuffed shirts who have false values that emphasize cutthroat competition rather than human cooperation; or fight back. Young people, in particular, are inclined to fight. If the world despises them, why not kick the world? Such youthful aggression is commonly reported in the newspapers as juvenile delinquency. As people get older, they tend to make an adjustment; they often learn that they cannot win by fighting because they are too weak. Instead, they retreat into apathy.

Historically, every large-scale urban society has had a lower class (often they were slaves). The low productivity of the ancient economy and the system of unequal distribution of income created a lower class that appeared inevitable. There have been epochs when the other classes so despaired of doing anything to help that they wrote off the poor as God's will and went about their business without worrying about the starvation, illness, and despair of the derelicts.

But now we face a different situation. Our economy has eliminated the necessity of poverty, and our more equalized distribution system has gone a long way toward ending it. In periods of full employment, all able-bodied persons who want to can find work. As we make progress in social welfare, we are finding ways of eliminating urban slums, of protecting people during periods of illness or temporary unemployment.

Yet, as of the moment, we still have a lower class, though it may well be smaller than in the past. There is still a "hard-core" group of people who live beyond the pale of respectability. Some of them are unable to help themselves; they suffer from long-term illness, from intellectual or physical inferiority, from inadequate education, from prejudices against the weak and the lame and the immigrant and the Negro. But some of them retain a value heritage of retreat or revolt; they don't want to be helped. They have been hurt so often in the past that they prefer to be independent rather than be pushed around by patronizing do-gooders. Prosperity is not enough; such people also need love.

## CONCLUSIONS

Although there is a great deal of controversy over details, and considerable variation from one part of the country to another and from small towns to large cities, many researchers agree that contemporary American urban society can usefully be described as having five social classes. No single variable defines a class; instead, the interaction between several variables creates the total way of life which characterizes a class. Value orientations emerge from, integrate, and symbolize the class way of life. The classes can be labeled as follows:

1. *Upper Class.* Wealthy families who strive for a stable pattern of refined and gracious living. In its ancient form an upper class is based on inherited property and fixed traditions, and the earning of more money takes second place to the spending of income from property. But our upper class is mixed, and contains many newly successful persons who learn the gracious way of life and become accepted by their peers.

2. *Upper-Middle Class.* The successful business and professional men (but not those at the very top), and their families. Income is mostly from current occupation, thus the emphasis is on long-term careers.

These people live in large houses in good suburbs or in the best apartment houses; most are college graduates; they dominate industry and community organizations.

3. *Lower-Middle Class.*   The less successful members of government, business, and the professions, and the more successful manual workers. This is the least clearly defined level, shading imperceptibly into the working class. These people live in small houses or in multiple-family dwellings. Most are high-school graduates, and some have had a little additional training. They are the model for the popular stereotype of America's "common man." They emphasize respectability.

4. *Working Class.*   Factory and similar semiskilled workers. These are the people who work from day to day; they live adequately but on a small margin, have little hope of rising, aim at getting by. They are graduates of grammar schools, with often some high-school training.

5. *Lower Class.*   People who have the lowest paid jobs, work irregularly (especially in bad times), live in slums. They usually have not gone beyond grammar school (and often have not finished it), their family life is unstable, their reputations poor, and their values are based on apathy or aggression, for they have no hope.

These ideal-type classes are helpful abstractions, but cannot be used without practical judgment; they will help us order our thinking about the complexities of social reality, although they may encourage us to assume falsely that a community can be neatly divided with each family tagged and placed in its niche.

Flexibly interpreted, the ideal types imply that the majority of families in most communities can be placed in one of the five categories. These families will have scores on the several key stratification variables that fit into a pattern; their occupations will provide incomes that permit a style of life and a network of associations that bring them prestige, and they have a class identification and a set of values that harmoniously integrate their social lives—they know who they are and their neighbors know who they are, and they have beliefs that are "appropriate" to their position.

But many families would not fit. One or two of the index scores they would receive would be out of phase with the others [29]. Does this mean that the ideal types are useless in understanding these families? On the contrary, the discrepancy of one or two variables from the expected pattern is usually best understood by considering it as a deviation from the typical. Often the discrepancy indicates that the family is mobile. Their values may be typical of the next higher class; in order to live according to their values, they are likely to be ambitious people who are striving to increase their incomes so as to achieve a style of life they consider appropriate to their values, and one that will bring them contact with and approval from the people they consider suitable for friends.

Or they may be people who are slipping down in the hierarchy. They will cling to old values, and will feel squeezed because they no longer can buy the prestige they believe they are entitled to. Such people are often miserably unhappy; they think of themselves as failures, and believe the world to be a hard and vicious one.

Or they may be young people who are at the beginning of their careers. They may have high occupations but low beginning salaries. They need time to get into their appropriate niche.

Or they may be people who take a certain pride in being "different." If there were not some standard in their minds of what is typical, how could they enjoy being different? Many intellectuals and artists are, in this special sense, "outside the class system." (In a more general sense, of course, all creative individuals—from Albert Einstein to Al Capp— are "different" by the very nature of their work.) The point here is that so-called Bohemians, creative or not, stand on the margins, and deliberately flout some of the rules. They are critical of the conformity of the middle classes (on whose margins they usually stand); instead of living in "bourgeois homes" in "deadly" suburbs, they rent apartments in working-class neighborhoods and then furnish them in a creative variation of upper-middle-class style. But they seldom give up all middle-class values; they think they are entitled to professional incomes, they hope to send their children to college, and they find it difficult to find much to talk about with uneducated proletarians. However, people who in this way stand at the margins of the typical modes of behaving still are subject to the usual social laws: they seek friends and prestige and they emulate others. They establish a small circle of their own and exchange prestige with one another. In recent years prosperity has softened their rebellion; they find good jobs in colleges and in advertising agencies and in government. They follow a modern and insipid form of Bohemianism in contrast to their forebears of a generation ago; instead of pulling up stakes and going to Paris to study with Gertrude Stein and Pablo Picasso, they stay at home and give Sunday dinners featuring French casserole dishes and recordings of Bach and Bartók [30].

Of course, there are other types than the Bohemians who stand at the margins of the class system; professional criminals, for instance. But most of our families are content to adjust. Either they spin a web of values that integrates their current lives, or they strive to change aspects of their lives that do not match their values. Although there are people who are always a little out of phase, and standards are always shifting, the observer can better understand both conformity and deviation by recognizing the typical patterns.

REFERENCES

[1] Sigmund Freud in a letter to his fiancée, August 29, 1883 (stimulated by a visit to the opera *Carmen* with its vivid mob scenes); quoted in Ernest Jones, *The Life and Work of Sigmund Freud* (New York: Basic Books, 1953), Vol. I, pp. 190–91.

[2] I draw heavily on the writings of the Kluckhohns. See Clyde Kluckhohn, *et al.*, "Values and Value-Orientations in the Theory of Action," in *Toward a General Theory of Action*, Talcott Parsons and Edward A. Shils, eds. (Cambridge, Mass.: Harvard University Press, 1951); Florence R. Kluckhohn, "Dominant and Substitute Profiles of Cultural Orientations: Their Significance for Social Stratification," *Social Forces*, XXVIII (May, 1950), 376–93; Clyde and Florence R. Kluckhohn, "American Culture: Generalized Orientations and Class Patterns," in *Conflicts of Power in Modern Culture* (New York: Harper, 1946).

My thinking has also been strongly influenced by Talcott Parsons, *The Structure of Social Action* (New York: McGraw-Hill, 1937). For a general description of American values that stems from the same philosophic and scientific roots, see Robin M. Williams, Jr., "Value Orientations in American Society," in *American Society* (New York: Knopf, 1951), Chap. XI.

[3] Much of the material in this chapter represents generalizations from data presented elsewhere in this book; references will not be repeated here.

It is my opinion that the newer techniques of attitude scaling and group projective testing would be helpful in testing generalizations such as these, and that it would now be a more strategic use of research effort to conduct such tests rather than repeat community studies to get more qualitative descriptions of class values.

[4] Much of the current empirical data on American life shows differences related to class level—differences in intelligence, personality, health, physical and mental disease, consumption behavior, tastes in reading, sex, family patterns, and so on. Some are tied to one aspect of stratification, such as education or income; others reflect the total class pattern. For some summaries that will lead the reader beyond data in this book, he may consult: Pitirim Sorokin, *Social Mobility* (New York: Harper, 1927); Kurt B. Mayer, *Class and Society* (Garden City, N.Y.: Doubleday, 1955); "Differential Class Behavior," *Class, Status and Power*, Reinhard Bendix and Seymour M. Lipset, eds. (Glencoe, Ill.: The Free Press, 1953), Part III; Frank Auld, "Influence of Social Class on Personality Test Responses," *Psychological Bulletin*, XLIX (July, 1952), 318–32; A. Anastasi and J. P. Foley, *Differential Psychology* (New York: Macmillan, rev. ed., 1949), Chap. XXIII; August B. Hollingshead and Frederick C. Redlich, "Social Stratification and Psychiatric Disorders," *American Sociological Review*, XVIII (April, 1953), 163–70.

[5] E. Digby Baltzell has made good use of these books to show the connections between the old and the new families in the upper class:

" 'Who's Who in America' and 'The Social Register': Elite and Upper Class Indexes in Metropolitan America," in Bendix and Lipset, *Class, Status and Power.*

[6] F. Scott Fitzgerald, "The Rich Boy," in *Modern American Literature,* Bernard J. Duffey, ed. (New York: Rinehart, 1951), pp. 46–47. First published in *All the Sad Young Men,* copyright 1922, 1926 by Charles Scribner's Sons.

[7] The most comprehensive book on the American middle classes uses this distinction: C. Wright Mills, *White Collar* (New York: Oxford University Press, 1951). The book usefully organizes the available data on the shift from the old to the new middle classes, and gives vivid portraits of some of the new types. But its interpretations suffer from Mills's lack of sympathy for the new white-collar people; he sees them as automatons, with false and empty lives. He writes from the disillusion of the thirties; he fails, in my opinion, to catch the spirit of the fifties. However, it must be admitted that we may now be living in a fool's paradise; if major war or economic collapse should come, the thirties may live again.

A more accurate picture of the values of the upper-middle class can be found in David Riesman *et al., The Lonely Crowd* (New Haven: Yale University Press, 1950). This brilliant book is the sociological best seller of the fifties; its evidence may be unsystematic, but its interpretations ring true.

For a comparative study, see Roy Lewis and Angus Maude, *The English Middle Classes* (New York: Knopf, 1950).

[8] From my interview files.

[9] Lionel Trilling, *The Liberal Imagination* (New York: Viking, 1950), pp. 209–210. Trilling uses social class as a tool in much of his literary analysis.

[10] Many of the same effects of technology on stratification can be observed in Russia; see Alex Inkeles, "Social Stratification and Mobility in the Soviet Union," *American Sociological Review,* XV (August, 1950), 465–80.

[11] Mills, *White Collar,* pp. 182–84.

[12] Robert H. Guest, "Work Careers and Aspirations of Automobile Workers," *American Sociological Review,* XIX (April, 1954), 155–63.

[13] Ely Chinoy, *Automobile Workers and the American Dream* (Garden City, N.Y.: Doubleday, 1955). My only serious reservation about Chinoy's work is the assumption that most working-class boys believe in the dream of success until the facts of adult life destroy their faith; I suspect that many, probably the majority, never accept the dream as relevant to their lives.

[14] Charles R. Walker and Robert H. Guest, *The Man on the Assembly Line* (Cambridge, Mass.: Harvard University Press, 1952), p. 55.

[15] Chinoy, *Automobile Workers and the American Dream,* p. 44.

[16] Joseph A. Kahl, "Educational and Occupational Aspirations of 'Common Man' Boys," *Harvard Educational Review*, XXIII (Summer, 1953), 202.

[17] Chinoy, *Automobile Workers and the American Dream*, p. 82.

[18] For validation on a substantial sample of California workers, see Seymour M. Lipset and Reinhard Bendix, "Social Mobility and Occupational Career Patterns, Parts I and II," *American Journal of Sociology*, LVII (January and March, 1952), 366–74, 494–504.

[19] Fred H. Blum, *Toward a Democratic Work Process* (New York: Harper, 1953), pp. 85, 87.

[20] *Ibid.*, p. 168.

[21] Genevieve Knupfer, "Portrait of the Underdog," *Public Opinion Quarterly*, XI (Spring, 1947), 103–14.

[22] For an excellent descriptive account of the working class in Great Britain, see Ferdynand Zweig, *The British Worker* (Harmondsworth, Middlesex: Penguin Books, 1952).

[23] August B. Hollingshead, *Elmtown's Youth* (New York: Wiley, 1949), pp. 110–11.

[24] *Ibid.*, pp. 116–17, 112. An excellent account of the adjustment of the family pattern to changing lower-class circumstances can be found in E. Franklin Frazier, *The Negro Family in the United States* (Chicago: University of Chicago Press, 1939).

[25] See W. Lloyd Warner and Leo Srole, *The Social System of American Ethnic Groups* (New Haven: Yale University Press, 1945).

[26] Allison Davis, "The Motivation of the Underprivileged Worker," in *Industry and Society*, William F. Whyte, ed. (New York: McGraw-Hill, 1946), p. 86. Davis calls his four hundred families "Working class," but it is clear that the people he writes about are, in our terminology, "lower class."

[27] *Ibid.*, p. 89.

[28] *Ibid.*, p. 103. A subtle analysis of the pleasures and pains of lower-class life can be found in John Dollard, *Caste and Class in a Southern Town* (New York: Harper, 1937 and 1949), especially Chapter XVII, "Gains of the Lower Class Negroes."

[29] The study of the degree to which stratification variables hang together, and the special characteristics of those persons who are out of phase, has usually been confined to mobile persons. A somewhat broader approach is suggested by Gerhard E. Lenski, "Status Crystallization: A Non Vertical Dimension of Social Status," *American Sociological Review*, XIX (August, 1954), 405–13.

[30] See Milton Gordon, "Social Class and American Intellectuals," *Bulletin of the American Association of University Professors*, 40 (Winter, 1954–55), 517–28.

# VIII

# Ethnic and Race Barriers

WITH EVERY PHASE OF THE PRODUCTIVE SYSTEM EXPANDING,
OUTSIDERS WERE CONTINUALLY PUSHING IN. THE NEWCOMERS
HAD ALWAYS THE ATTRACTION OF WILLINGNESS TO WORK AT
MINIMAL WAGES IN ORDER TO GET ESTABLISHED AND THEIR PRES-
SURE WAS DIFFICULT TO RESIST. SO THE IRISH WHO HAD MANNED
THE NEW ENGLAND TEXTILE MILLS INEXORABLY GAVE WAY TO
THE MORE RECENT IMMIGRANTS; ITALIANS, PORTUGUESE, AR-
MENIANS AND FRENCH-CANADIANS EDGED IN AS PICKERS AND
SWEEPERS, AND SOON WERE EVERYWHERE IN THE PLANT. . . .
THE SPREAD OF EDUCATION ENABLED THE SONS OF LABORERS TO
COMPETE FOR SITUATIONS WITH THE SONS OF MEN HIGHER IN
THE OCCUPATIONAL SCALE; THE SCHOOLS DISTRIBUTED THE COM-
MAND OF LANGUAGE, THE PRACTICAL SKILLS, AND THE WISH TO
PUSH UPWARD. ALL THESE FACTORS LESSENED THE IMPORTANCE
OF INHERITED ADVANTAGES. *Oscar Handlin* [1]


IT HAS BEEN EMPHASIZED that men evaluate one another in terms of group
values; individuals are considered worthy of deference if their behavior
exemplifies the ideals of their culture. In ordinary circumstances a man
cannot be a model citizen if he is not thoroughly familiar with the culture, and this is not possible if he has not grown up in it. Most groups
distrust outsiders and even before they have observed them sufficiently,
assume that they will not behave as well as group members. Consequently, outsiders are devalued and granted low prestige.

The outsider has other disadvantages. Not being familiar with all the
intricacies of the local culture, he is less likely to have occupational skills
that will earn him a high income. He will not have friends and relatives
in high places who can assist his career. He will not have a family name
that bestows prestige through the halo effect of noteworthy ancestors.

Each of those disadvantages can be great or small, depending upon
the circumstances. If the outsider is a well-trained physician who comes
to a backward community that desperately needs medical service, he is
likely to be honored. If he is an ambitious farm boy who moves to a
city in his own nation, and shows great ability in business and complete respectability in his personal behavior, he can, through time, earn

high prestige among the city's successful people. But if he is an un-educated peasant, who comes to an advanced industrial nation and walks the streets behind a pushcart selling apples, and fails to master the language and the urban habits of the host culture, then he is relegated to a low position and may well be regarded as "that stupid, dirty foreigner."

America has welcomed many foreigners. More than twenty-eight million people have come to our shores and remained here [2]. They, and to some extent their children, have found places in the class order that were influenced by their foreign traits. *The less observably foreign they were, the less influence their ethnicity had on their placement.* Thus those who arrived from countries of origin with races and cultures most like our own, and those who learned most quickly to think and act like Americans were least affected by their ethnic membership (we use this term to cover all groups whose racial or cultural characteristics make them distinguishable from the generalized body of native white Americans). With such an enormous record of immigration, our strat-ification system must have been much affected, and the problem of this chapter is to explore the major interrelations between social classes and ethnic groups.

WHO WERE THE IMMIGRANTS?

By the time of the founding of the republic, something like half a million white persons and a quarter of a million Negroes had migrated to the United States. Eighty per cent of the white people had come from Great Britain and Ireland, 7 per cent from Germany, and 3 per cent from the Netherlands [3]. Their rate of natural increase was phenome-nal; although immigration continued to contribute a part, the major growth from 1790 to 1840 was due to an excess of births over deaths. Consequently, the population just before the Civil War consisted primarily of the descendants of the English, Scotch, and Irish, with a sprinkling of Germans and Dutch, and, of course, with a large block of Negro slaves in the South.

The government began to collect yearly statistics on immigration in 1820. These figures show that immigration was in the hundreds of thousands every decade up to 1840; then it increased to the millions. Almost two million arrived in the forties, about two and a half million each decade in the fifties, the sixties, and the seventies, and five million in the eighties. Roughly speaking, the country absorbed an influx every decade equal to almost ten per cent of the total population [4]. During this period the immigrants came primarily from Germany, Ireland, and Great Britain, in that order. Sweden and Norway also contributed a sizable number. Many settled in the cities (especially the Irish), but most moved into the Middle-Western farm belt.

Why did all these people migrate? Primarily to escape from poor economic conditions at home, and to take advantage of economic growth in America. The Irish were suffering from overpopulation; the potato famine in the forties only brought to a head a long-term decay in Irish agriculture. In England and Germany fundamental changes in society led to rural depression, complicated in Germany by political upheaval. At the same time, the United States had vast unsettled areas with practically free farms available; and we were actively promoting immigration in order to supply farmers and, after the Civil War, factory workers. When times were good in America, the incoming tide increased proportionately.

1890 is a bench mark in American history. The frontier was finally settled, and the new opportunities were in factories rather than on farms. Simultaneously, conditions changed in Europe; England, Germany, and Scandinavia had industrialized to the point where they could absorb their own excess rural population, and the countries of southern and eastern Europe were beginning to experience rural poverty and overpopulation at the same time that they were being penetrated by modern communications which made it easier to move. The agents of the steamship companies (a very potent force in stimulating migration) moved south and east. Before 1890 over three quarters of the newcomers came from northern and western Europe, but in the nineties slightly more than half came from the south and east. Soon after, over three quarters of the immigrants were from the southeastern areas—and the size of the influx increased to a peak of almost nine million in the first decade of this century (still at a rate of almost 10 per cent of the population).

This so-called "new" immigration was dominated by peasants from Italy, Austria-Hungary, and Russia. They were less educated than the typical "old" immigrant; their cultures were more divergent from the English traditions that formed the United States; they were mostly Catholics; and although four fifths were peasants, most went either to the cities or to the mines where their agricultural backgrounds were of little use in helping them master their new environments.

Because of their lack of industrial experience, these new immigrants began as unskilled laborers. Their standard of living was low; they would accept wages somewhat below those of the natives. They had nothing to offer but strong backs. Many employers took advantage of this situation; for example, to combat the unionism of the miners, the railroads that controlled the coal mines of Pennsylvania brought in various groups of Slavs in such numbers that by 1900 they dominated the industry. Of course, the union and the newcomers eventually woke up to the fact that their long-run interest was a common one, and once the Slavs were welcomed into the ranks of organized labor, they became devoted adherents to the cause.

The movement of large groups from the same European country into a given region or industry was quite common. An employer would take on additional hands from a group with which he was familiar; a straw boss or foreman would hire his cousins. The recent arrivals would send home news and money that brought more people of their village to them.

The immigrants centered particularly in the expanding industrial cities. For example, in 1890, 41 per cent of the people of Chicago were foreign-born, and three quarters were either foreign-born or the children of immigrants. This clustering in the cities made the immigrants more noticeable than when they were scattered amongst the prairie farms; it made possible the development of immigrant institutions, like newspapers, that seemed to indicate a perpetuation of the foreign tongue and the foreign culture. Many Americans became alarmed that the nation was being overrun with a type of immigrant who would not be so easy to assimilate into the national life. There was also much talk of biological inferiority in the new strains; supposedly, the people closest to the Anglo-Saxon were the best, and the population was being "diluted" by inferior stock. The craft unions joined this movement, desiring to protect high wages from immigrant competition.

The First World War brought the issue to a head. Five million people in the country could not speak, read, or write English. More than half of the adult immigrants had failed to become citizens. The cities were teeming with huge colonies of foreigners who formed cities within cities, with their own newspapers, churches, and social institutions. Also, it finally seemed that the country was populated at an adequate level. There was no more free farm land, and the cities appeared to have an excess of unskilled laborers. These conditions, plus the nationalism of war, produced a mood that called for restricted immigration, particularly from the countries of southern and eastern Europe.

Congress changed the traditional open-door policy in 1917, excluding illiterates. In 1921, and finally in the permanent act of 1924 (taking full effect by 1929), the quota system was applied. The entire quota per year was only 150,000, and this was to be apportioned among different countries according to the relative proportion of the American population in 1920 that was descended from stock originating in those countries. This gave 80 per cent of the total allowable immigration to northwestern Europe, 20 per cent to southeastern Europe. Furthermore, preferences were set up within the quotas favoring farmers, and some

nonquota immigrants were permitted beyond the fixed quotas, especially spouses of Americans, and citizens of Western Hemisphere nations. Asiatics and Africans were practically excluded.

Since these laws were passed, the quotas from northwestern Europe
have never been filled. There was almost no immigration during the
early thirties when we suffered from the great depression. Since then
we have amended the law to admit many refugees—first from Hitler,
later from the effects of war, and finally from Stalin—but in no year
has the influx exceeded two hundred thousand. Many of the recent immigrants have been nonquota Mexicans and Canadians. The act of 1952
slightly facilitated the immigration of refugees by allowing countries to
increase current admissions temporarily by mortgaging their quotas
into future years. But we are now down to a rate of inflow that is less
than one per cent of our population each decade, as compared to the
former ten per cent. And the occupations of these recent immigrants are
higher on the scale; in 1954 we admitted 35,000 white-collar workers,
55,000 blue-collar workers, and only 5,000 farmers. There were more
professionals than common laborers, and as many clerks as operatives [5].

## CURRENT ETHNIC COMPOSITION

Given this record of immigration, what is the ethnic complexion of
the country today?

The population is 90 per cent white, 10 per cent colored. Almost 7
per cent of the total population are foreign-born, and another 16 per cent
have one or both parents who were foreign-born [6]. Thus almost one
quarter of the population are identifiably ethnic in terms of foreign
birth or parentage, and another tenth are colored. (In 1910 the proportion of foreign-born was almost 15 per cent, and those with at least one
foreign-born parent were another 20 per cent.)

In some parts of the country religion is sufficient to mark a man as
"different" and to affect his stratification position. Almost one fifth of
our people are Catholic, almost 4 per cent are Jewish [7].

In New York City there is a huge block of recent arrivals from
Puerto Rico—technically, they are not immigrants but American citizens
who have changed their place of residence. But they arrived speaking
Spanish and without industrial skills, and they entered the stratification
order at the bottom. In the Southwest there are many Mexicans; some
are descendants of people who were there when we annexed Texas before the Civil War; others are more recent arrivals. They add up to almost two million, and constitute over half the population in parts of
New Mexico and Texas [8].

There are more than a quarter of a million foreign-born French Canadians, and many more who are French speaking (usually bilingual). They are concentrated in New England, and the Westerner who travels in that part of the country expecting to find it peopled by descendants of the Pilgrims gets a rude shock: many country villages are more than half French Canadian, and the big cities often see a struggle for political control between the newer Italians and the older Irish, with the still older Yankees impotent bystanders.

## STEREOTYPES AND PREJUDICES

Through the years there has accumulated a body of standardized beliefs about the various ethnic groups; these beliefs are part of our popular culture, and many studies prove that individuals learn them regardless of whether or not they have any personal contact with members of the ethnic groups concerned. These beliefs are stereotypes, simplified pictures of entire groups that do not encompass individual differences within the groups. The stereotypes are loaded with prejudice or prejudgments of goodness and badness that are applied in advance of observation, with little attempt to alter the generalizations to fit actual behavior. Indeed, belief in these stereotypes serves to bolster the self-image of many persons by making them feel superior to others, and consequently they have psychological motivation to close their eyes purposely to any facts that might weaken their beliefs [9].

Social scientists have been studying ethnic stereotypes for more than thirty years, and they have found great consistency in the ranking of groups. For example, Daniel Katz and Kenneth W. Braly found in 1935 that the order of preference of Princeton students was as follows [10]:

> Americans
> English
> Germans
> Irish
> Italians
> Japanese
> Jews
> Chinese
> Turks
> Negroes

The same students characterized Americans as "industrious, intelligent, materialistic, ambitious, and progressive." Negroes, on the other hand, were supposed to be "superstitious, lazy, happy-go-lucky, ignorant, and musical."

When these beliefs are probed further, it is found that Americans desire various degrees of "social distance" between themselves and these groups. For example, most American Protestants express themselves as being willing to marry an English person, to have a German as a neighbor, or to hire an Italian. But they would not want the Italian as a spouse or a Negro as a neighbor. Business relationships are the least exclusive; neighborhood relations somewhat more so; and intimate interaction that involves eating together in the home or the possibilities of marriage are the most exclusive [11].

It is obvious that this range of preferred interaction parallels the attitudes held about interaction with members of social classes below one's own. An upper-class person is most insistent about having his children marry "their own kind"; he is not too upset about a well-behaved upper-middle-class family's moving into his neighborhood; and he is quite willing to do business with anybody who offers him a profit. But let any of these permitted interactions begin to encompass a more intimate familiarity, and he begins to stiffen his back.

Indeed, there is a considerable relationship between the place of an ethnic group in the rank order of stereotypes and the average stratification position of its members. This relationship is a loose one, for there is much variation from one part of the country to another, and much individual mobility that raises many persons above the average for their group. But the tendency is clear. The English and Germans, for instance, are descendants of early immigrants. They came with cultural values not very dissimilar to the official American norms. They assimilated easily, and many have risen to high positions in the stratification order. The Italians are more recent arrivals; on the average, they are clustered in the blue-collar occupations in the big cities. Negroes are the least educated and the lowest skilled group in the country.

Of course, the causal relationships work both ways; not only is ethnic group reputation a reflection of average stratification position, but individual placement is influenced by group reputation. A Negro finds that prejudice and discrimination make it harder for him to rise in the occupational world, to move to a better neighborhood, to educate his children in the better schools. There is a strong tendency to rationalize the present state of things; because Negroes are lower in the scale, they are thought to be fundamentally inferior, and thus incapable of rising. This makes it harder for them to rise; they are caught in a vicious circle. In all stratification systems, people of high status explain their advantages through rationalizations about their innate superiority over others.

The particular stereotypes applied to people at the bottom have a consistency, regardless of which ethnic group occupies the position.

These phrases express the opposite of those values that the successful people cling to as explanations for their success. The middle-class virtues involve hard work, steadiness and reliability, education, thrift, honesty (extending to family and sex relations as well as business interactions), cleanliness (and all the associated values of keeping up a good public appearance). A person from a peasant background, or a confirmed lower-class urbanite who sees no chance to get ahead, is likely to care less about such virtues. Consequently, to the middle-class person his behavior appears to be motivated by laziness, ignorance, lack of ability to plan ahead, dishonesty, slovenliness, immorality. The same phrases, uttered in the same disapproving tone of voice, can be heard on the lips of respectable men describing Southern Negroes, New York Italians, San Antonio Mexicans, or Elmtown Americans who live on the wrong side of the tracks. The relationships between a position at the bottom of the stratification system and these traits of behavior were explored by Allison Davis in "The Motivation of the Underprivileged Worker," as discussed above in Chapter VII. The additional point to be made here is that much of what he says can be applied to any group occupying the bottom level, and that the reputation of the group tends to become fixed in terms of the average position of its members, which makes it difficult for individuals to climb, or at least to gain appropriate recognition and acceptance when they do climb.

## YANKEE CITY

In order to see in more detail the interrelationships between ethnic membership and the stratification order, let us turn once more to Yankee City. The third volume of the series about that city is a study of its ethnic groups that offers unusual historical perspective; it is called *The Social Systems of American Ethnic Groups*, by W. Lloyd Warner and Leo Srole.

The Irish began to arrive in Yankee City in the 1840's, just after the textile factories were established. Until the end of the Civil War, the factories drew their workers primarily from the native Yankee population (especially the middle classes), and the incoming Irish had no choice but to accept unskilled jobs as stevedores, hod carriers, and domestics. After the war factory wages and prestige went down, and the Irish moved into the factories in the wake of the natives who moved out. In later years the Irish diversified; some of their younger members learned higher skills and entered the business and professional worlds; others became skilled craftsmen. But this process took time and the passage of the generations. Warner and Srole measured it by a simple and useful index. They assigned the following weights to the basic categories of occupation [12]:

Unskilled labor      1
Skilled factory      2
Skilled craft        2.5
Management aid       3
Management           4
Professions          6

Using old town records, they looked up the occupations of every member of the Irish group in various years, assigned the proper weights, then struck an average for the whole group. Thereby the progress of the Irish up the occupational ladder was readily shown; in 1860 their average occupational index was 1.62; by 1893 it had risen to 1.84; by 1933 it was 2.52.

The French Canadians arrived in substantial numbers in the nineties, and started with an average occupational index of 1.95 (apparently they were able to go immediately into the factories without the preceding unskilled stage). The Jews arrived after the turn of the century, and were different from all other immigrant groups, for they were the only ones who did not come predominantly from tiny peasant villages in the old country. They were mostly from small towns, and were artisans (tailors, carpenters, etc.) and petty tradesmen. Their skills were immediately usable in the new country, and they started with an occupational index of 3.10. The Russians were the most recent arrivals, and once more we see the restriction of a peasant background. In the first decade of settlement, their index was only 1.95. By 1933 the ranks of these groups were as follows (for simplification, I have omitted some of the ethnic groups in Yankee City) [13]:

Irish                2.52
French Canadians     2.24
Jews                 3.32
Russians             1.95

All ethnics          2.42
All natives          2.56

Warner and Srole emphasize that in a town that has remained essentially stable in size and economic opportunity for a long time, this progression of ethnics could not have occurred if many natives had not moved to the bigger cities. Indeed, young people of high education and ambition found Yankee City restricted, and many left. By 1933 this was true of some educated ethnics as well as Yankees. Furthermore, the Yankee birth rate was smaller than that of the ethnics, giving the latter a chance to occupy many new positions each generation.

As people achieve some success in their occupations, they seek a better way of life, and a new house is likely to be their first desire. All the ethnic groups first entered town and took apartments in the cheapest area, along the river front. When their numbers were great enough, they clustered together in little communities that offered association and support. But then, when they could afford it, they sought a better style of housing and moved into the intermediate zone of town (called the side-street area). This was done by individual families, although often small clusters ended up near each other. Their success in moving depended not only on their money, but also on the strength of the resistance of the old homeowners who usually objected to the influx of foreigners. After a few newcomers had penetrated successfully, however, some old-timers would give up and move away, thus making room for more newcomers. A lowering of property values usually accompanied this process. Eventually some successful ethnics were able to move to the best part of town along Hill Street, and they made room for others to move into their vacated homes in the side streets.

This process of continued residential change (or invasion and succession, as the ecological textbooks rather dramatically term it) was also measured by an index. Giving values ranging from 1 for the river front to 6 for Hill Street, Warner and Srole checked the residential history of all the ethnic groups. The movement was very similar to the occupational change, as would be expected. By 1933 the residential indexes were as follows [14]:

|                  |      |
|------------------|------|
| Irish            | 2.85 |
| French Canadians | 2.43 |
| Jews             | 2.77 |
| Russians         | 1.32 |

Notice that the Jews were lower in average residential status than the Irish, but higher in occupational status. This probably indicates the greater degree of prejudice against the Jews which made it harder for them to buy desirable property.

Now let us trace the final step: achievement of a place in the prestige order and interaction networks of Yankee City (what Warner and Srole call the "class system"). The authors write [15]:

Upon first establishing himself in Yankee City, the ethnic finds himself in the anomalous position of "belonging" to no social class and having the identification only of "foreigner." He has brought with him little or no property; he has little familiarity, unless he is Jewish, with the type of economic system represented in Yankee City; he conforms hardly at all to the American behavioral modes—in short, the deviations in his social personality are so marked as to preclude relations with the natives except those of an impersonal economic type. Even in the religious aspects, all ethnic groups . . . are variants from Yankee City's solid, native Protestantism.

By establishing themselves in the occupational and residential systems, the immigrants became known. They learned American ways, soon had

American friends. They joined some American clubs and associations (such as labor unions). Within twenty or thirty years the original immigrants had established a place in the prestige and interaction hierarchies; although still identifiably ethnic, they also had become known as "good solid workers" or "steady shopkeepers."

To the extent that outside prejudice or their own institutions (such as churches and beneficent societies) keep any group apart, they remain a special sort of subgroup; to the degree that their occupational and community life puts them in contact with natives, they take on positions in the general prestige order. Ethnic children, educated in American schools, are less ethnic in behavior and reputation than their parents, but usually maintain some identification with the ancestral group. If a group is big enough to maintain many institutions of its own, and if the prejudice against them is great, they might continue to have much of their informal interaction with their own kind for several generations; in such circumstances they would develop a prestige order *within* their own group that would not be known nor recognized to any great extent by the majority group—this is the case with Negro communities, and we shall study it below.

Returning to the data on Yankee City, we learn that by 1933 there had been considerable movement up the prestige ladder. Although the upper-upper class was entirely Yankee, .31 per cent of the Irish families had achieved recognition and acceptance as lower-upper-class people (as compared to 2.78 per cent of the Yankee families). Almost 6 per cent of the Irish were upper-middle (compared to 16 per cent of the Yankees), 28 per cent were lower-middle (compared to 35 per cent), 54 per cent were upper-lower (compared to 23 per cent), and 13 per cent were lower-lower (compared to 20 per cent). The Jews were almost evenly divided between the lower-middle and the upper-lower, although a few had reached into the upper-middle. The French Canadians were predominantly lower class, as were the Russians. Each generation of ethnics had climbed higher than its predecessor.

At first the immigrants saved their money and invested it in savings accounts or property. But as they (and their children) became more secure, and as they learned more about the opportunities in the Yankee City social world, they spent more for conspicuous consumption. As they did so, they became more American and more accepted by Americans.

The most ambitious people gained social acceptance by deliberately cultivating interaction. If they had the necessary minimum of money and social graces, they could, by becoming "joiners," meet a great many prominent natives. If they used these contacts with skill, they could dissipate much prejudice about their foreignness and gain considerable personal acceptance. Warner and Srole tell about one successful Jew who arrived penniless, worked his way up in the business world, and by the age of forty was a member of Rotary, was the only Jew in the Yankee City golf club, was chairman of a committee of the Republican party, and was on the board of directors of two banks, a manufacturing company, and the public library. To do this, he needed not only money, but great personal skill in adapting his behavior to the local norms.

Acceptance cannot be earned if the superior group withholds it, and they generally try to do just that in order to keep their own symbols of prestige purer, scarcer, and thus more valuable. Given our system, they cannot prevent a man from making money, but they can keep him out of clubs and organizations that wield community power, and they can keep him outside the range of intimate associations. But after a generation or two this becomes difficult. The children go to the same schools; the money of the ethnic fathers is useful for local causes, and is solicited (and to get it, the solicitor must not snub the donor); fellow businessmen and fellow professionals and fellow operatives have interests in common that must be protected by joint action that includes successful ethnics of the same occupational level. In other words, the very dynamics of the stratification order break down ethnic isolation, both in terms of the ambitions of the newcomers and the needs of the old-timers.

The adaptation to local norms, of course, goes on constantly, and not merely for the purpose of gaining acceptance. The family structure, the food eaten, the style of house furnishing, the recreational habits—all of these slowly but persistently adjust to American ways of doing things. Warner and Srole give much fascinating detail on this process of acculturation that we cannot reproduce here.

As an ethnic group becomes differentiated into social classes, its internal solidarity breaks down. The class interest often overcomes the ethnic interest. The lower-class Irish feel snubbed by and in return sneer at the lace-curtain Irish. The lace-curtain Irish often feel more of a bond with fellow businessmen than fellow Irishmen. Indeed, business interests and desires for acceptance often make people wish they were not identifiably ethnic, and some successfully cover up their ancestry and their old religion (especially through intermarriage).

Warner and Srole summarize their data in this way [16]:

A. Factors that retard status mobility:

   1. Original migration with intention of temporary settlement.
   2. Family structure with patterns of maintaining customary status and parental determination of status.
   3. Order of a group's appearance in the city, both because the earliest group encounters local conditions which no longer operate, and be-

cause they reduced resistance that made it easier for others.

4. Large group size, a condition increasing resistance to acceptance.
5. Proximity to homeland, which slows acculturation.

B. Factors that accelerate status mobility:

1. Similarities between ethnic ancestral society and local one.
2. Similarities in religion.

However, there is often an additional step that is not discussed by Warner and Srole. The complete loss of ethnic identity becomes painful for many; American life is so rootless and lacking in firm group ties that the ethnic affiliation retains importance as a base of security. Especially when large numbers within the group have been sufficiently mobile to feel no longer that ethnic membership automatically categorizes them as lower-class persons, they begin to look on their ancestral bonds as cultural connections worthy of respect and maintenance. Middle-class Italians of the second or third generation, for instance, can cultivate Italian cuisine and Italian opera without feeling less American or less middle class. The foremost historian of American immigrants, Oscar Handlin, writes [17]:

They desired a sense of identity that would explain why they were different from "One Man's Family." They wished to belong to a group. To be, with their children, a meaningful part of the succession of generations would give a purpose to their striving, supply it with the security of a source and a goal. . . . For some now religion became the focal point of their affiliation. Men were not drawn back to the churches by the attractiveness of theological doctrine, however; the trend toward secularism was not reversed. . . . But the most powerful magnet was the round of practices and social connections capable of giving order to life in American society. Through its institutions, the church supplied a place where children came to learn who they were, where the right boys met the right girls, where men and women in their groups found satisfying diversion. In this respect, all sects were now Americanized. . . .

Religious identifications however rested not on the acceptance of defined articles of faith, but on social choices shaped by ethnic antecedents. Creedal differences still divided Americans into more than two hundred and fifty distinct sects. But those differences now faded in importance. Increasingly religious activities fell into a fundamental tripartite division that had begun to take form earlier in the century. Men were Catholics, Protestants, or Jews, categories based less on theological than on social distinctions.

## NEGROES: OCCUPATION, EDUCATION, AND INCOME

At the very time that Congress restricted foreign immigration, there began another movement of people as dramatic, and as full of human problems, as the older inflow: the movement of Southern Negroes from the farms to the cities of both the South and the North. In 1910, 55 per cent of American Negroes were farmers, and 89 per cent lived in the South. By 1950 only 25 per cent were farmers, and only 71 per cent lived in the South. The Negro population in the North increased from a little over one million in 1910 to 4,267,000 in 1950. In the North almost all Negroes lived in cities, and by 1950 half the Southern Negroes were also urbanites. Many city Negroes served as unskilled laborers, doing various chores such as keeping the stores and the streets clean, but a great many went into the factories. The working women became domestic servants and factory workers [18].

It is typical of the Negro situation that the major advances—to the cities and into the factories—came during the two World Wars when the labor shortage forced employers and unions to accept colored workers. It is expected in our society that white immigrants will go into the factories, and that they, or more likely their children, will advance in the occupational hierarchy as fast as their skills and their educations permit. Although they suffer some handicap in some economic situations if they are identifiably ethnic, this disadvantage is minor and it is temporary. Negroes have not been treated in the same way. In the South they were deliberately denied education and occupational opportunity; successful Negroes were feared and despised by most whites, instead of honored. The traditions of white supremacy were such that jobs were divided into "white men's jobs" and "Negroes' jobs," and the black man was supposed to stay "in his place." In the North the situation was less rigid, but for years no department store would hire a Negro to serve a white public, no factory would promote a Negro to be a foreman over white workers. However, the war years brought much change; the labor shortage, plus the growing realization that racial discrimination was not compatible with our war ideals, plus the growing strength of the Negro demand, all these opened new opportunities in both North and South.

By 1950 the occupational distributions for Negro men and white men compared as follows [19]:

|  | Negro Men | White Men |
|---|---|---|
| Professional persons | 2.2% | 7.9% |
| Proprietors, managers, officials: |  |  |
| Farm | 13.5 | 10.5 |
| Nonfarm | 2.0 | 11.6 |
| Salesmen | 1.5 | 6.6 |
| Clerical workers | 3.4 | 6.8 |
| Craftsmen & foremen | 7.6 | 19.3 |
| Operatives | 20.8 | 20.0 |

|                          | Negro Men | White Men |
|--------------------------|-----------|-----------|
| Service workers:         |           |           |
| Not private household    | 12.5      | 4.9       |
| Private household        | .8        | .1        |
| Laborers:                |           |           |
| Farm & mine              | 11.3      | 4.4       |
| Nonfarm                  | 23.1      | 6.6       |
| Not reported             | 1.3       | 1.2       |
| TOTAL                    | 100.0%    | 100.0%    |

Notice that the proportions of factory operatives are almost identical; the proportions who are farm owners are similar. But the Negroes are far behind in the proportions of those who have climbed into the upper positions in the urban world, for they have few professionals, proprietors, salesmen, clerks, or craftsmen. Instead, they are greatly overrepresented in the categories of service workers and laborers.

Compared to the white population the Negroes are badly off, but compared to their own past they have made enormous advances. As long as they remained on the Southern farms, they had no chance to get an education or to advance occupationally; whether classed as farm owners or laborers, they existed on a bare subsistence level. Furthermore, they lived in a society that effectively segregated them to second-class citizenship; they had difficulty in protecting their property or personal rights in the courts; they could not vote; they were segregated into second-class public schools, and had very little opportunity for higher education. But once they started moving to the cities, especially the Northern cities, they began to break the hold of a slave past. Although discriminated against at every turn, they slowly made their way into the factories. They often had the chance to go to the same public schools as white children; they could go to college. They began to vote and gain power. The progression was similar to that of foreign immigrants, although much slower: first on the streets as laborers, then into the factories as operatives, then into the crafts and professions.

Negro proprietors mostly serve their own people in residentially segregated sections of the cities. They have not been able (as have many immigrants) to become storekeepers to the community at large, nor have they become manufacturers. Similarly, the Negro professionals have mainly a Negro clientele. As long as these barriers exist, there will be a block to Negro advancement qualitatively different from that which faces other ethnic groups. Regardless of antidiscrimination legislation or Supreme Court decisions, a prejudiced public cannot be forced to patronize Negro storekeepers or physicians. Consequently, the Ne-

groes' best chances of climbing into the top occupations occur within
large bureaucratic structures that have adopted policies against discrimination: the Federal government and some corporations and universities. Progress here is slow, but it continues.

The median family income of Negroes in 1952 was $1987, whereas
white family income was $3668. Several factors combined to keep Ne-
gro income considerably below that of whites. As was discussed above
in Chapter IV, the South is the poorest section of the country, partly
because it has a high proportion of farmers (and marginal ones at that),
partly because its industrial wages lag behind those of the rest of the
country—and more than two thirds of the Negroes still live in the
South. Furthermore, the lines of discrimination in all parts of the country
concentrate Negroes into lower-level industrial jobs. Finally, partly because of discrimination and partly because of their own lack of traditions, they do not enter to any great extent into the professional and
business positions that bring high income. The results are clearly shown
in the following figures, which compare the distributions of Negro and
white incomes for families and unrelated individuals in 1952 [20]:

|              | Negroes | Whites |
|--------------|---------|--------|
| Under $1000  | 24.7%   | 13.3%  |
| 1000–1999    | 25.6    | 11.1   |
| 2000–2999    | 22.7    | 13.4   |
| 3000–3999    | 14.6    | 17.7   |
| 4000–4999    | 4.6     | 14.5   |
| Over 5000    | 7.8     | 30.0   |
| TOTAL        | 100.0%  | 100.0% |

Three quarters of the Negro families earned less than $3000 in cash in-
come (remember the problems discussed earlier of measuring farm
noncash income), whereas two thirds of the white families earned more
than $3000.

We have emphasized in many places that in the long run education is
one of the main routes to high occupation, income, and prestige. Actually this is less true for Negroes than for whites, as many Negroes
have achieved an education that fits them for jobs which the white
world denies them on account of their race. Traditionally, Pullman
porters and railroad redcaps are often college men. Nevertheless, education is a prerequisite for occupational success, and as they achieve it,
Negroes' demands for the right to compete for higher jobs gain in
potency.

The educational achievement of the Negro people in the last fifty
years has been phenomenal [21]. At the turn of the century almost half
of them were illiterate. By 1950 the illiteracy rate was approaching 10

per cent. In 1950 more Negroes graduated from college than had graduated from high school in 1920; indeed, the rate of increase in Negro college enrollments during this period was six times that of the whites. Nevertheless, although the Negroes are fast catching up to white educational levels, they started with a great handicap which still marks them. As of 1950, over a third of the total white population, but only 13 per cent of the Negroes had graduated from high school. Thirteen per cent of the whites had gone to college for a while, but only 5 per cent of the Negroes had entered ivy halls. And the quality of Negro education is still deficient; the Negro colleges are held back by the poor quality of preparation in Southern Negro high schools. Only recently have the gates of white colleges been opened in significant degree to colored students, and they will be at a disadvantage there as long as high schools are unequal. The Supreme Court decision outlawing segregation should vastly speed the improvement of the quality of Negro education, for only in the states that have integrated schools do the expenditures for the education of Negro pupils match those for whites. But if the Southern states succeed in outmaneuvering the decision by abolishing the public schools, then the Negroes will be set back a generation or more in progress, for they will be unable to afford good private schools even if there is a partial state subsidy.

In short, in the basic areas of job, income, and schooling, Negroes as a group stand considerably behind whites, but their rate of advance is faster, so they are catching up. This does not necessarily imply that in the near future they will achieve equality, for discrimination may find a new line to hold. Negroes are on the verge of complete equality in the Northern factories as operatives and foremen (which will be enforced by new union rules, for the industrial unions, led by the CIO, have become champions of equality); they have begun to penetrate the white-collar occupations. But prejudice may be more resistant and more subtle in the white-collar world; Negroes may well find it harder to expand and consolidate their war-won gains. Progress does not move smoothly, but in spurts, as situations change and relative balances of power are upset.

BLACK METROPOLIS

Fortunately, we have a major study of a Northern, urban Negro community, so that we can see how the above generalizations apply in a specific instance. Just as Gunnar Myrdal's *An American Dilemma* serves as an unparalleled reference on Negro life in all of America, *Black Metropolis* by St. Clair Drake and Horace R. Cayton offers much useful information and analysis about Negro society in Chicago [22].

Most of the research was done in the middle thirties, but inasmuch as the book was not published until 1945, some wartime changes were included. However, the mood of the book is a depression mood, and great changes have been taking place in more recent years. It should also be noted that the research was in part inspired and guided by W. Lloyd Warner, so that if we encounter familiar concepts, we should not be too surprised.

The job situation in Chicago fits the pattern already described. Negroes are "the last to be hired and the first to be fired." Even in 1940, when the war boom had begun, one fifth of the Negro men were unemployed, about twice as large a proportion as among white men. Five years earlier half the Negroes had been on relief or WPA projects.

By 1940 the Negro men reported that when they worked, their usual occupations were as follows: 54 per cent were unskilled or service workers (compared to 17 per cent of the white men in Chicago), and only 16 per cent were white-collar workers (compared to 40 per cent of the white men). Only in semiskilled factory labor did they find work in the same proportion as whites (about 20 per cent). Thus it was clear that Negroes were doing a large share of the hard and dirty work that kept Chicago humming, and consequently they were making it possible for many white men to work at clean and well-paid jobs.

Drake and Cayton give many details concerning the working of the "job ceiling." It operated as a generalized notion as to the types of jobs that it was practical to offer to Negroes. Nobody questioned their right to be porters or bootblacks or ditchdiggers, but when one applied for a job as a bookkeeper, the employer usually felt that his other office workers (or his customers) would object. In fact, they often did, and in many of the craft trades the unions that had tight closed-shop contracts kept Negroes out of the trade by denying them membership in the union by constitutional provision. Yet when the war emergency created a labor shortage, it was discovered in one firm after another that after a Negro was hired there was less objection than in discussions about it beforehand. Particularly if the union and the management got together and made it plain that Negroes were going to be hired and that any white worker who objected could go ahead and quit, then individual workers usually accepted the change as beyond their control, and after a while adjusted to it without complaint. In some mass-production industries, particularly the great meat-packing plants, the integration had gone on for many years, and by 1940 was so complete that unions championed equality all along the line: for workers, foremen, and union officers. Similarly, it was accepted that Negroes could compete for jobs at all levels of the city government.

It seems that instead of a single over-all set of beliefs about Negroes, there existed a number of separate sets of beliefs, one for each industry according to its own traditions. Once stabilized, these beliefs made it hard for Negroes to advance. But well-organized pressure (such as in politics) or strong demand for workers (such as in the meat-packing plants) could change the definition of the situation, often suddenly, and open up new realms where Negroes were admitted into individual competition with whites for jobs. One of the major differences between this situation and that in Southern cities was the lack in Chicago of an organized set of values that covered all situations and indicated that any changes anywhere threatened the entire social order and must be stopped by action of the total white community, whether or not the people taking action had any direct concern in the industry under discussion. In Chicago the mass of the whites were uninterested, and were quite willing to have Negroes make advances and change the level of the job ceiling, until they as individuals were personally affected.

*Black Metropolis* shows that next to job restrictions, Negroes were most affected by residential segregation. When Negroes first moved into the city, they were scattered all over it. But as the Negro group grew in size, its members concentrated in the "Black Belt," a strip of land that by 1940 contained over 90 per cent of the city's Negro population. It was a narrow strip that started close to the downtown area and extended south to the middle-class residential part of town. The section close to the center of the city contained the worst slums in town (and was being partly rebuilt with Federal housing projects). The section farther south approximated white middle-class housing in physical quality, but it was crowded and small.

The major fact about Negro housing was this: The area was hemmed in by white districts that fought every attempt by Negroes to expand their section. Until the Supreme Court recently outlawed them, "restrictive covenants" were used as a legal device to stop black-belt expansion. These were clauses put into the deeds of property preventing current or future owners from selling or renting to Negroes. Thus, the desire of white residents to keep their neighborhoods "pure" kept Negroes from equal competition for housing space. The result can easily be predicted: terrible overcrowding, the subdivision of apartments into "kitchenettes" (one room and a hot plate for an entire family), and very high rents due to the excess of demand over supply. Thus the poorest people in the city had to pay the highest rents. Much of the friction between Negroes and whites in the city occurred in areas adjacent to the black belt, where the pressure for housing was causing Negroes to seek space.

## STRATA IN BRONZEVILLE

The cultural values in Chicago kept interaction between Negroes and whites to a minimum. In some occupations they worked together; in a few unions they voted together and occasionally shared a picnic or a dance; but they rarely lived side by side, and they rarely worshiped together or exchanged house visits. They hardly ever intermarried. As a result, Negroes developed a society of their own, called "Bronzeville," a world wherein people played and prayed and made love and reared children. It was a nighttime and weekend world, as distinct from the daytime world of work which took Negroes out of the black belt to the white men's factories and stores and homes.

The natural processes of interaction that we have examined in earlier chapters were at work in Bronzeville, and a prestige structure emerged. People of like values associated together and reinforced their similarities. However, because of its segregation, the Negro prestige structure did not take exactly the same shape as usually occurs in a white community: it was smaller at the top and larger at the bottom, for Negroes were not adequately represented in the economic activities that brought high incomes and permitted the higher types of consumption.

Drake and Cayton tell the history of the emergence of this prestige structure in Chicago. We shall limit our attention to its nature in 1940, as revealed primarily by interviews but buttressed by some systematic statistical analysis. They write [23]:

> Everybody in Bronzeville recognizes the existence of social classes, whether called that or not. People with slight education, small incomes and few of the social graces are always referring to the more affluent and successful as "dicties," "stuck-ups," "muckti-mucks," "high-toned folks," "tony folks." The "strainers" and "strivers" are well-recognized social types, people whose whole lives are dominated by the drive to get ahead and who show it by conspicuous consumption and a persistent effort to be seen with the right people and in the right places. People at the top of the various pyramids that we have described are apt to characterize people below them as "low-class," "trash," "riff-raff," "shiftless."

Drake and Cayton estimate that one thousand families recognized each other as "upper class"—"an articulate social world of doctors, lawyers, schoolteachers, executives, successful business people, and the frugal and fortunate of other occupational groups who have climbed with difficulty and now cling precariously to a social position consonant with what money, education, and power the city and the castelike controls allow them [24]." As a whole, this group is much poorer than the white upper class in Chicago, although it does contain a very few wealthy individuals. And of course it is newer, since the Negroes have not had enough time in Chicago to form dynasties. Because there is much less chance to earn big money, attention tends to be concentrated on education as the mark of a successful and worthy man—the mere achievement of a college degree (rather than what it will earn) is a mark of distinction in Bronzeville. It is usually associated with a great desire for family respectability, for graceful living, and for interaction with other persons of similar tastes. The most common focus of interaction seems to be bridge parties. The upper-class consumption values and styles of life are modeled primarily upon those of successful white people. As Americans they desire to live like those who have mastered the rules of American economic competition. But these people interact for more than mutual amusement: their education and their occupational achievements make them community or "race" leaders. They are a power within Bronzeville, and also the main channel of communication between the masses of Bronzeville and the powers of the white world.

On the fringe of this upper class is a small group of very rich men who have made their money in the policy racket and other shady enterprises. They are adopting many of the consumption values of the respectable upper class, and their money and power make them hard to ignore. Some of them have become race leaders. They are invited to some upper-class functions, but do not entirely belong.

But despite much in their lives that is very similar to successful whites, Bronzeville's upper class is different because it is intensely race-conscious. Many of its members realize that their income and position are due to segregation; without it, they would lose clientele and power. Furthermore, they interact with the white leaders on various community projects, and are constantly made aware of differences in prestige and power. Consequently [25]:

The attitude of the upper class toward the lower is ambivalent. As people whose standards of behavior approximate those of the white middle class, the members of Bronzeville's upper class resent the tendency of outsiders to "judge us all by what ignorant Negroes do." They emphasize their *differentness*. But, as Race Leaders, the upper class must identify itself psychologically with "The Race," and The Race includes a lot of people who would never be accepted socially.

Although this group may be an upper class from the perspective of the Negro community, its income, occupations, and values are more similar to the white upper-middle class. They are successful, self-made men, not wealthy capitalists. If education, occupation, and rents are used as indexes (rather than the interaction within the most select group of elite Negro families), then the Bronzeville upper class includes about 5 per cent of the community, whereas on similar terms, the white upper and upper-middle group is more than twice the size.

The Negro middle class is similar to what we have called above the white lower-middle class. It is distinguished from the upper group by its lesser education and income; it is separated from the lower group by its intense desire for moral respectability and its acceptance of the values of striving and getting ahead. Some are white-collar workers, most conspicuously the postal employees. But many are steady blue-collar workers, whose values and family-centered lives mark them off from the mass of manual workers. Drake and Cayton comment [26]: "Life to them has stability and order; expectations for their children and for their own future can be predominantly this-worldly; and the individual psyche is given form by the church and associations whose dues they are able to pay with some regularity and from whose functions they are not barred by inadequate clothing or by lack of education, formal or informal."

The middle-class family desires a good home, but they have trouble getting it. Overcrowding makes rents high, and consequently they often have to take in boarders or relatives in order to meet the payments. The middle-class groups have been unable to organize neighborhoods of similar people, as the demand for space is so great that lower-class people are always moving in, and dividing previously respectable buildings into kitchenettes. Consequently, the middle class emphasizes organizations wherein they can associate with their own kind and display their superior accomplishments in education, dress, and manners. They are joiners.

There is much tension in the middle-class pattern [27]: "The drive to get ahead, to 'lay a little something by,' to prepare for the education of children, and at the same time to keep up 'front' by wearing the right kind of clothes, having a 'nice home,' and belonging to the proper organizations—the pursuit of these goals brings into being definite social types which Bronzeville calls 'strivers' and 'strainers.' " These people are struggling to maintain a style of life that is extremely difficult in terms of their limited incomes and limited hopes for future advancement. They have adopted the white middle-class values, but are denied white middle-class opportunities.

Drake and Cayton estimate that 30 per cent of Bronzeville follows the middle-class pattern, whereas 65 per cent do not seek such respectability. The latter live as they can from day to day, expecting to be on relief for long stretches between jobs, seeking pleasures from relatively uninhibited sex, gambling, and fighting. Respectable Negroes shun them; they in turn look with disgust (tinged with a bit of envy) at the strivers who think they are better than other people. Lower-class men are wanderers, having moved from plantations to Southern cities to Chicago, searching for jobs. This movement has led to unstable family patterns, and the mother usually ends up with responsibility for the children. Marriage is expensive and inconvenient; informal liaisons are much easier. The children grow up with little supervision; if there is a man in the house, he is unlikely to be the father, and the mother is off working as a maid. The areas they inhabit are marked by the highest rates of delinquency and disease in the city.

Perhaps a third of the lower class (predominantly women) are active in "the old-time religion"—evangelical, emotional, hell-and-damnation sects. Such religion offers an emotional outlet for pent-up feelings, and a promise of better things to come in the next world. It also offers standards of moral conduct that are for some an anchor in an environment of chaos. Some of the religiously minded are striving to rear their children with enough direction and education to enable them to climb into the middle class.

## ETHNIC GROUP, CASTE, AND RACE

In his "methodological note" to *Black Metropolis*, W. Lloyd Warner makes the following distinctions between the concepts of social class and color caste. He quotes himself, and gives the definition of class that emerged from the Yankee City research. Social classes are [28]:

. . . two or more orders of people who are believed to be, and are accordingly ranked by the members of the community, in socially superior and inferior positions. Members of a class tend to marry within their own order, but the values of the society permit marriage up and down. A class system also provides that children are born in the same status as their parents. A class society distributes rights and privileges, duties and obligations, unequally among its inferior and superior grades. A system of classes, unlike a system of castes, provides by its own values for movement up and down the social ladder . . . a social class is to be thought of as the largest group of people whose members have intimate access to one another.

Warner goes on to say that when his research team moved to the city written up as Deep South, they realized that whites and Negroes constituted two separate groups ranked as superior and inferior, but that the division was more than a class or ethnic distinction [29]:

Negroes and whites cannot intermarry; members of two classes can. Negroes cannot rise out of the lower to the higher white levels; members of a lower white class are able to do this. Unlike the ethnic individual, the Negro individual's symbols of inferiority cannot be removed; they stay with him until death. . . .

There were a large number of ethnic groups [studied in the *Yankee City Series*]. Each of them had had members who had climbed up the class ladder and out of the group entirely. The cultural stigmata of the ethnic origin rapidly disappeared and left the members of the group free to try to move to higher levels.

Consequently, Warner adopted the definition used by many anthropologists, and said that a system of prestige distinctions between groups that prevented mobility and intermarriage was a system of "caste." The ethnic groups in Yankee City had some castelike characteristics insofar as members were identified and treated as belonging to minority groups that were different from ordinary people and consequently subjected to limitations on mobility and intermarriage. But their inferiorities were recognized by the majority society to be cultural; as soon as ethnic individuals learned the culture of the dominant society, they lost their stigmata and were able to compete without distinction in the class order. In other words, European ethnicity is a temporary phenomenon, and each succeeding generation in this country is less ethnic than its predecessor. But a black skin does not get lighter through time; Negroes remain Negroes, and although they have *as a group* won increasing advantages in our society, entering new levels of education and occupation, they remain identified as a separate group, and *individuals within it* cannot take advantage of their increasing culture to become less Negro.

In ordinary parlance, Negroes are a race. But anthropologists are often reluctant to use this term because the popular definition of a Negro is social rather than biological, and race is a biological concept. A person with white skin and blue eyes who is known to have a Negro great-grandfather is popularly classified as Negro. He can become socially white only by going to a new community that sees his skin but does not know about his great-grandfather. However, caste is a term that comes from India, and the Indian social system is a very complicated one that involves much more than immobility and endogamy. It involves a system of sub-societies, each connected with an occupation, a division into many castes (some of which, although distinct, are socially equal in prestige), and a religious sanction for the entire system. Furthermore, caste is not based on racial divisions. Oliver Cox has written a detailed study of this system in *Class, Caste, and Race,* and he makes a sufficient case for the uniqueness of Indian caste to make it of doubtful utility to call our Negro-white division one of caste [30].

Indeed, we lose sight of the fundamental distinction if we deny that our society is divided by race. True, individuals are put into one or the other race according to social rather than purely biological criteria, but the social criteria are cultural definitions of a biological race, and the fact that they stretch a point for those who have more white than Negro blood does not negate their biological assumptions. In other words, Negroes are people whom the popular (not scientific) culture considers to be members of the Negro race, and that involves popular beliefs about racial characteristics. Negroes are denied mobility for two reasons: (1) their skin makes them readily identifiable (with a few minor exceptions), and (2) the popular culture assumes that race is an unalterable biological fact that makes a great difference in social life. As long as the assumption of difference and inferiority persists, and the ready identification is available, Negroes are not just another ethnic group.

Robert E. Park, W. Lloyd Warner, and others have made a useful distinction between the caste (or better, race or color) line and the class lines [31]. They suggest that we can visualize the race line as a diagonal, and the class lines as horizontals, as shown in the accompanying chart. As the definition of Negro inferiority becomes weakened, and the race makes educational and occupational progress, the color line tilts more toward the vertical, and the size of the upper and middle classes among Negroes increases. Some Southern whites claim that segregation is designed to produce "separate but equal" societies in which the color line would be a completely vertical division, but this ignores the fact that if the two groups were actually thought of as equal, nobody would bother to try to keep them separate.

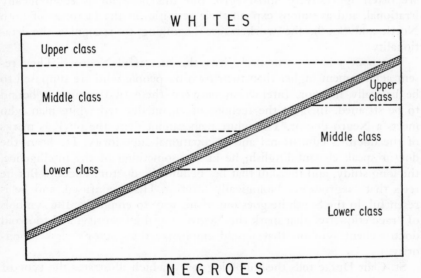

Figure 1. Class and Race Lines [32]

The chart calls our attention to one of the most interesting forms of interaction in America: between persons of equal class but unequal race. Generally speaking, our traditions about Negro-white interaction have grown out of a situation of contact between upper- or middle-class whites and lower-class Negroes (field hands, house servants, and such). This is the type of situation that is relatively stable and comfortable, for the class difference reinforces the race difference, and the usual behavior between superiors and inferiors is appropriate. But the situation becomes ill-defined and uncomfortable when the class and race differences do not reinforce each other. For example, lower-class whites and lower-class Negroes have many class interests in common; these are not so noticeable in Southern rural areas, but when the people are gathered in cities, it becomes increasingly apparent that economic interests tend to pull these people together. An industrial union cannot be effective in raising wages if it does not include all the workers; otherwise, one group is played off against the other by the employers. The upper classes in the South understand this fact and have traditionally encouraged the lower-class whites to turn against Negroes. This is not hard to do, for the emotions of the poor whites need a scapegoat in order to relieve their own frustrations concerning lack of success. Consequently, the poor whites are often aggressively anti-Negro. But this behavior is economically irrational, and as unions expand their activities in the factories of both North and South, the workers are beginning to recognize the irrationality.

The poor whites particularly hate the successful Negroes. They resent achievement higher than their own by people who are supposed to be basically inferior. Interaction between these two groups is bound to be strained. Imagine the feelings of an uneducated white man who meets a Negro doctor. The white man cannot deny the obvious marks of the doctor's educational and occupational superiority. He hears the doctor speak elegant English; he knows something of the intelligence, the long study, and the skill that lies behind the doctor's success. But he feels that Negroes are biologically inferior. He is confused, and he is resentful. In the South he goes out of his way to emphasize the symbols of "race etiquette" that mark the Negro's racial inferiority, and to avoid doctor-client symbols that would emphasize the doctor's class superiority.

St. Clair Drake tells the following story which illustrates the type of interaction that occurs when color and class symbols are in conflict [33]:

A Negro was driving through the Deep South; his car went dead in a small town late one afternoon. The white constable came up and said: "Boy, why you stoppin' traffic? You better get a move on; no niggers allowed in this town at night." The Negro replied, "My motor died; I'm having trouble getting it started again." At this point the constable noticed some books in the back seat, and asked: "You a communist or agitator?" "No." "Preacher?" "No." "Teacher?" "Yes, a college teacher." Then the constable said: "Boy, I ain't heard you say 'sir' to me yet." The Negro replied: "Well, sir, I'm just trying to get my car started so I can move on." At that point the constable hollered to two Negroes sitting on the curb in front of a gas station: "Hey, you niggers, come help this colored gentleman get his car started!"

Most middle-class white people find interaction with middle- and upper-class Negroes to be uncomfortable. They are used to Negroes as servants. When they meet one who is obviously not a servant, but who in education and occupation and general cultural accomplishments is similar to themselves, they do not know how to behave. They do not want to deny the legitimacy of the symbols of class superiority, for that would weaken their own values about themselves. As a result, such interaction is usually marked by rather excessive formality, and is kept to a minimum.

CONCLUSIONS

Although Americans put many limitations on the behavior of white ethnic individuals in economic competition and social interaction, they expect that eventually ethnic differences will disappear as the various streams of European immigrants adapt to American culture. Indeed, Americans cut off large-scale immigration precisely because they did not like to have large groups of strange people in the country. The dominant cultural values all stress eventual assimilation. The good immigrant or son of an immigrant is the fellow who learns how to become "100 per cent American."

Americans usually make exactly the opposite assumption about Negroes. They do not want them to assimilate to the point of social equality, intermarriage, and absorption into the white majority. As Myrdal repeatedly emphasizes, this is the basic premise behind most white reactions to Negroes. Southerners, who are more afraid of assimilation, erect every possible barrier to Negro educational and occupational progress because they believe that such progress implies that the day of assimilation is brought closer, and the purity of the white race is, for them, a supreme goal in life. Northerners are less afraid of assimilation; there are fewer Negroes among them, and the Northern whites seem more ready to believe in the possibility of a biracial society in which Negroes can achieve high occupations without demanding intermarriage. Ecological segregation in the cities seems to most Northerners adequate protection.

Thus, the dynamics of the stratification variables hasten the assimilation of white ethnics, whereas they work in contradictory ways with respect to the assimilation of Negroes, for the economic variables are improving their position, whereas the interaction variables are holding them apart. In the sphere of values, whites are caught up in the contradiction. It is Myrdal's central thesis that although the values of many Americans concerning their personal integrity and self-enhancement lead to segregation, the values of the American creed emphasize equality of opportunity for all individuals.

The vast European immigration, and more recently the urbanization of the Negro, have had great effects upon class structure. They have provided every generation of Americans with a new group coming into the urban stratification order at the bottom. This pushed up the older residents, allowing them to don white collars while they directed the labor of the newcomers. Furthermore, the newcomers have provided lower-class old-timers with a group they could look down upon and thus gain a feeling of superiority. Finally, the second generation of immigrant children could always remember how far they had advanced over their foreign parents. All these factors together have caused great actual mobility and even greater perceptions of mobility among Americans [34].

### REFERENCES

[1] Reprinted by permission of the publishers from Oscar Handlin, *The American People in the Twentieth Century* (Cambridge, Mass.: Harvard University Press, Copyright, 1954, by The President and Fellows of Harvard College), p. 88.

[2] The estimate for 1820 to 1930 is by Professor Wilcox of the National Bureau of Economic Research, reported in Maurice R. Davie, *World Immigration* (New York: Macmillan, 1936), p. 12. I have added the approximately one million arrivals since 1930, and the one million before 1820. Davie's book is a useful source with material on all the major immigrant groups to the U.S.; a more recent treatment is Donald R. Taft and Richard Robbins, *International Migrations* (New York: Ronald, 1955). An excellent shorter treatment is William S. Bernard, ed., *American Immigration Policy* (New York: Harper, 1950).

[3] Estimates based on the family names that appeared in the first census in 1790; see Davie, *World Immigration*, p. 44.

[4] *Ibid.*, p. 53. These are figures for in-migration; as many as a third of these people eventually returned to Europe.

[5] U.S. Bureau of the Census, *Statistical Abstract of the United States, 1955* (Washington: Government Printing Office, 1955), Table 109, p. 97. See also *ibid.*, Table 102, and Bernard, *American Immigration Policy*, Chap. II.

[6] *Statistical Abstract of the United States, 1955*, Table 30, p. 36.

[7] Arnold and Caroline Rose, *America Divided: Minority Group Relations in the United States* (New York: Knopf, 1948), p. 62. For other texts on ethnic groups, see R. A. Schermerhorn, *These Our People* (Boston: Heath, 1949), and George E. Simpson and J. Milton Yinger, *Racial and Cultural Minorities* (New York: Harper, 1953).

[8] Taft and Robbins, *International Migrations*, Chap. XXI.

[9] For a short treatment of this subject, see Theodore M. Newcomb, *Social Psychology* (New York: Dryden, 1950), Chap. 16. The definitive treatment is Gordon W. Allport, *The Nature of Prejudice* (Cambridge, Mass.: Addison-Wesley, 1954).

[10] Daniel Katz and Kenneth W. Braly, "Verbal Stereotypes and Racial Prejudice," in *Readings in Social Psychology*, rev. ed., Guy E. Swanson *et al.*, eds. (New York: Holt, 1952), pp. 70–71.

[11] See E. S. Bogardus, "A Social Distance Scale," *Sociology and Social Research*, XVII (1933), 265–71.

[12] W. Lloyd Warner and Leo Srole, *The Social Systems of American Ethnic Groups* (New Haven: Yale University Press, 1945), p. 59.

[13] *Ibid.*, p. 60.

[14] *Ibid.*, p. 68.

[15] *Ibid.*

[16] *Ibid.*, p. 102.

[17] Reprinted by permission of the publishers from Oscar Handlin, *The American People in the Twentieth Century* (Cambridge, Mass.: Harvard University Press, Copyright, 1954, by The President and Fellows of Harvard College), pp. 221–22. The secularization and Americanization of a religious sect are well described in Donald Wray, "The Norwegians: Sect and Ethnic Group," in *Democracy in Jonesville*, by W. Lloyd Warner *et al.* (New York: Harper, 1949).

[18] Maurice R. Davie, *Negroes in American Society* (New York: McGraw-Hill, 1949), pp. 92, 134; and Jessie P. Guzman, ed., *1952 Negro Year Book* (New York: William H. Wise, 1952), pp. 2–3. Most statistics of the Census Bureau divide the population into "white" and "nonwhite." But insofar as 96.2 per cent of nonwhites are Negroes, we can equate the two terms (except for a few regions where the Indian population is substantial).

[19] U.S. Department of Labor, *Negroes in the United States: Their Employment and Economic Status*, Bulletin 1119, December, 1952, p. 44.

[20] U.S. Bureau of the Census, *Statistical Abstract of the United States*, 1954, p. 314.

[21] The figures that follow are taken from U.S. Information Agency, *The Negro in American Life* (no date; pamphlet).

[22] Gunnar Myrdal and Associates, *An American Dilemma: The Negro Problem and Modern Democracy*, 2 vols. (New York: Harper, 1944).

St. Clair Drake and Horace R. Cayton, *Black Metropolis: A Study of Negro Life in a Northern City* (New York: Harcourt, Brace, 1945).

[23] *Ibid.*, pp. 521–22.

[24] *Ibid.*, p. 522.

[25] *Ibid.*, p. 563.

[26] *Ibid.*, p. 524.

[27] *Ibid.*, p. 668.

[28] Drake and Cayton, *Black Metropolis,* p. 772, quoting from W. Lloyd Warner and Paul S. Lunt, *The Social Life of a Modern Community* (New Haven: Yale University Press, 1941), p. 82.

[29] Drake and Cayton, *Black Metropolis,* pp. 773–74.

[30] Oliver C. Cox, *Caste, Class, and Race* (New York: Doubleday, 1948). Much of the book is dogmatic Marxist interpretation, but that does not weaken its criticism of the use of "caste" as a concept applied to American race relations.

[31] Myrdal, *An American Dilemma,* Vol. I, Chapters 31 and 32, discusses these concepts in detail, and draws various versions of the chart.

[32] Based on Allison Davis, Burleigh B. Gardner and Mary R. Gardner, *Deep South* (Chicago: University of Chicago Press, 1941), in "Introduction" by W. Lloyd Warner, p. 10.

[33] Told in a lecture at Harvard University.

[34] The psychological consequences of the fact that most Americans are the children or grandchildren of immigrants are well delineated by Margaret Mead, *And Keep Your Powder Dry* (New York: Morrow, 1942).

# IX

# Succession and Mobility: The Occupational Base

I DON'T THINK THAT THE MANAGEMENT PICKS ITS SUCCESSORS; I THINK THAT THE SUCCESSORS JUST RISE BY THEIR OWN ABILITY AND THE FORCE OF THEIR OWN PERSONALITIES. IT'S PERFECTLY OBVIOUS WHO IS COMING TO THE TOP. *An Executive*

WHAT'S THE USE OF TRYING TO GET SOMEPLACE AROUND HERE— THE BOSS IS TRAINING HIS SON TO TAKE OVER.
*A Worker* [1]

AS EACH GENERATION succeeds its predecessor, there occurs a vast sifting process that places individuals into class levels. If a society were completely "open," the forces of pure competition would sort people according to their native talent and the effort with which they used their talent. No man would get help or hindrance from his father in the competition for worldly success.

Reality does not match the logical model of the completely open society. Talent is partly inherited, and more important, perhaps, is the fact that a family greatly influences the motivation of a son and thus shapes his ambitions and his drive for success. In addition, there are limitations on the free play of competition in the market which bias the distribution of rewards. Education is necessary before talent can be properly exploited, and it is expensive in tuition and in the less obvious costs of supporting a boy while he studies and replacing the income that he might otherwise be contributing to his family. Furthermore, once he is out of school, a boy gains advantages if his father has money or connections or even a distinguished name in the community. There are limitations on free competition because the stratification variables influence one another, because occupation, money, connections, and values are interdependent, and through the family are passed on from one generation to the next. This is sufficient reason, even if there were no other, to speak of a class system instead of a collection of separate stratification variables.

251

No society is completely "open." But neither is it completely "closed," with a system in which each son inherits his father's position and no movement up and down the scale ever occurs. The latter type is most closely approached in caste systems where occupation is normally inherited and marriage is usually confined to caste equals, but even in prewar India some mobility existed.

The problem of this chapter is to measure the degree of inheritance of class position that prevails in the United States today. Inheritance from father to son will be called "succession," and movement from one class level to another between generations will be called "mobility." The relative degree of succession versus mobility will be examined in this chapter. The next one will look at some studies which explore the question of individual motivation in an effort to find out why some persons take advantage of the opportunities for mobility that exist in the system whereas others ignore them.

PROBLEMS OF MEASUREMENT

Ideally, to measure the amount of succession from one generation to the next, the research man should use a composite index of several stratification variables to indicate the class positions of a representative sample of American men and of their fathers, and compute the correlation between the two distributions.* If every son had the same position as his father, the correlation would be perfect and would be so indicated by a coefficient of unity. If a son's position were not related to that of his father, the coefficient would be zero. The actual coefficient would of course lie somewhere between zero and unity.

There are many difficulties that prevent the calculation of a correlation coefficient to measure the amount of succession that occurs. Correlation demands a numerical scale with many intermediate scores. The closest approximation to such a scale would be provided by a composite index of class position similar to the Index of Status Characteristics of Warner discussed in Chapter II. But the relative values of the items in such an index do not remain stable from one generation to the next. For example, a high-school education would be worth much more in 1920 than in 1950, but we do not know how much more because nobody studied Jonesville in 1920. Furthermore, it would be impossible to get adequate information about the older generation on many useful items that might be included in the index; for instance, how can one find out how a man's father identified himself or who his friends were? In most cases, the father of the respondent will be dead or living in an-

---

* We simplify by dealing only with men. Married women have the same class positions as their husbands. Unmarried women will here be ignored.

other town and the son will be unable to answer detailed questions about him.

The most practical procedure is to use a single measurement (rather than a complex index), and one that is simple and can be supplied by the son concerning both himself and his father. Furthermore, it should have relatively stable meaning from one generation to the next (and preferably, one country to another). Almost all researchers have used occupation, and they have grouped occupations into broad categories such as those of the social-economic levels of the U.S. Bureau of the Census discussed above in Chapter III. These broad categories tend to balance many of the fine-grain changes in prestige and income that have occurred for some occupations in recent decades, and thus can be used for intergenerational comparisons. However, it should never be forgotten that the classification is a crude one and involves many shades of meaning. For instance, in the category of proprietors, managers, and officials, the scheme puts all sorts of men together ranging from the president of the General Motors Corporation to the man who runs a peanut stand. The occupational classification treats these two gentlemen as equals, which they may be before God and the law, but not in the stratification system.*

The census figures themselves give some information regarding mobility even though they give none about the relative positions of specific fathers and specific sons. For instance, the data indicate that there were more than twice as many professional men in 1950 as in 1920. Insofar as professional men did not average two sons each, it is clear that many sons of men from lower levels had the opportunity to climb into the professional ranks. And by using a sample questionnaire for sons concerning themselves and their fathers, and combining that information with data from the census, it is possible to approximate the correlation model by constructing a table showing the proportion of men at each level who have been mobile.

If one starts with the conception of a completely closed society and then seeks to learn what factors might open it to some mobility, one discovers four causes of movement:

*a. Individual mobility.* Some people slip down and make room for others to move up.

*b. Immigration mobility.* Immigrants will cause mobility if they do not enter the system at all levels in proportion to the men already there. In Chapter VIII it was stated that in the decades close to the turn of the last century millions of immigrants came to the United States and most of them went to work as semiskilled or unskilled workers in the new

---

* It should be noted that the size of the categories influences calculations of mobility. The smaller the size and the larger the number of categories, the more the mobility.

factories in Northern cities. Because they took these low-level jobs, they made it possible for the sons of many American fathers to climb into the white-collar ranks.

   c. *Reproductive mobility.* The men at the upper levels of the system tend to have smaller families than those at the lower levels, thus making room at the top.

   d. *Technological mobility.* Technological change is constantly altering the shape of the occupational distribution by creating new jobs at the upper levels. As the industrial system becomes more complex, a higher proportion of men work as technicians and administrators and a lower proportion as unskilled laborers. This upgrading of the work force creates mobility as many sons of unskilled laborers become technicians and administrators.*

   A man who has advanced in the world as compared to his father has no idea which of the four factors made it possible for him to get ahead, and he probably would not care if he were told. But a student who looks at the system as a whole to measure the amount of mobility and ask about trends through time must examine each of the four factors separately. It is important to find out whether our society has been getting more or less rigid, and to predict the probable situation in the next generation. The only way we can study trends is to isolate each of the causes of mobility and then examine the historical forces impinging upon it. Let us consider the factors in reverse order from their listing above.

TECHNOLOGICAL MOBILITY

   The basic trends in the occupational structure were analyzed in Chapter III. From 1870 to 1950 the labor force expanded from almost 13 million to over 62 million. The proportion of women increased from 15 to 30 per cent. And the distribution of jobs changed radically. Farm jobs declined from over one half to less than one eighth of the total, whereas urban professional, business, and clerical jobs increased from one eighth to almost one half, and urban semiskilled jobs doubled from one tenth to one fifth of the available positions. During these eight decades, the life span of many a man, the country changed from a rural to a highly industrialized nation.

   It has often been said that in the nineteenth century the great undeveloped farmlands of the West kept American society open, for if a man did not like his job he could pack up and move to the frontier. The

---

* The absolute size of our society has been increasing rapidly. Immigration, differential reproduction, and technological change have distributed this increase to sons disproportionately to *their* fathers.

Table 1.  *Male Occupational Distributions,*
*Actual and Expected, 1920 and 1950*

IST ESTIMATE: OCCUPATIONAL CHANGE ONLY [2]

| SOCIAL-ECONOMIC GROUP | (1) ACTUAL, 1920 | (2) EXPECTED, 1950 | (3) ACTUAL, 1950 | (4) MOBILITY |
|---|---|---|---|---|
| Professional persons | 1,062,000 | 1,349,000 | 3,025,000 | +1,676,000 |
| Proprietors, managers, & officials: | | | | |
|   Farmers | 6,122,000 | 7,775,000 | 4,205,000 | −3,570,000 |
|   Others | 2,635,000 | 3,347,000 | 4,391,000 | +1,044,000 |
| Clerks, salespeople, & kindred | 3,491,000 | 4,434,000 | 5,345,000 | + 911,000 |
| Skilled workers & foremen | 5,469,000 | 6,946,000 | 7,917,000 | + 971,000 |
| Semiskilled workers | 4,371,000 | 5,551,000 | 9,153,000 | +3,602,000 |
| Unskilled workers: | | | | |
|   Farm laborers | 3,162,000 | 4,016,000 | 2,048,000 | −1,968,000 |
|   Others | 6,494,000 | 8,248,000 | 5,582,000 | −2,666,000 |
| TOTAL | 32,806,000 | 41,666,000 | 41,666,000 | ±8,204,000 |

farm frontier no longer exists, but instead there is a technological frontier that continually opens up new types of positions at higher levels of skill.

Let us attempt to measure the number of new openings that have been created by technical change in the space of but one generation, from 1920 to 1950. It will simplify matters to consider only men, and to take a snapshot of the situation in 1920 and compare it to that of 1950 rather than measure the constant process that went on all the time. By this procedure it is assumed that all the men in the labor force in 1920 have been replaced by their sons by 1950. If succession were complete and mobility did not exist, then all sons would have jobs at the same level as those of their fathers. We shall measure the degree to which succession is not complete, or the degree of mobility, by measuring the proportion of sons who have jobs different from their fathers *solely as a result of technological redistribution of the labor force.*

The basic figures are shown in Table 1. The first column of the table, headed "Actual, 1920," gives the approximate distribution of the male labor force in 1920 as revealed by the census of that year. By 1950 the number of men had increased from 32,806,000 to 41,666,000, a growth of 27.01 per cent. If every category had increased at the same rate, it would have been possible for every son to have the same type of job as his father. But this was not the case. For instance, the professionals almost tripled, whereas the farmers declined by about one third. The distribution that would have occurred if every category increased by 27.01 per cent is shown in Column 2, "Expected, 1950." The actual distribution revealed by the census of 1950 is shown in Column 3, "Actual, 1950." The difference between Column 3 and Column 2 is the amount of mobility that occurred, as shown in Column 4, "Mobility." This last column indicates that 1,676,000 men had to enter professional ranks even if the sons of all professionals followed in their fathers' offices. Similarly, there had to be a million new urban proprietors and managers, almost a million new clerks and salespeople, almost a million new skilled workers and foremen, and over three million new semiskilled workers. Where did they come from? Obviously, they were sons of farmers who moved to the city, and sons of unskilled workers who climbed up the hierarchy. The total of all the new workers was 8,204,000, which represented 19.7 per cent of the labor force in 1950. Thus at least 19.7 per cent of the men working in that year had changed jobs relative to their fathers as a result of technological change.

The above estimate is a minimum one, for it assumes that the sons of men whose occupations were contracting moved directly into the expanding levels. Actually, there was much more movement, for a good proportion of the change was step by step. For instance, it was not too likely that a farmer's son became a professional person; rather, a skilled worker's son may have taken the professional position, the son of a semiskilled worker thus had the chance to take over the skilled job, and a farm boy moved to the city and entered the factory at the semiskilled level. Thus, one new job at the top may have meant three mobile sons. But we cannot measure step-by-step mobility from census tables; we have to get the actual father-son comparisons from a sample of currently working men. That will be done below.

There can be little argument that the 4,634,000 urban and rural men who climbed above the unskilled level had achieved an advance in the class system. Most of them moved into the semiskilled ranks, taking over the new jobs there as well as the slots vacated by hundreds of thousands of sons of semiskilled workers who donned white collars. However, the 3,570,000 sons of farm owners may not all have advanced over their fathers by their move to the city. Many entered business and the professions and did improve their stratification position. But many became semiskilled and skilled workers; they lost the independence of the farm but usually gained in income. If we assume that all proprietors are above all workers, they slipped down; if we compare their standards of living with those of their parents, they climbed up. Here is one of the cases that is more complicated than the simple occupational hierarchy can measure.

REPRODUCTIVE MOBILITY

The discussion so far has been based on two unstated assumptions, namely, that all levels reproduced themselves at equal rates, and that there was no immigration. Let us drop the first assumption while keeping the second.

There are no adequate figures on the average number of sons of men in the various occupational levels. However, it is possible to make an estimate by using a set of net reproduction rates calculated for the year 1928 and assuming that these rates held throughout the thirty-year period from 1920 to 1950 [3]. In fact, the rates were changing in those years, so the estimate is a crude one and is offered as an indication of the general effects of differential reproduction rather than as a precise measurement of those effects.

Column 2 of Table 2 shows the estimated reproduction rates for each occupational category. Although the average number of sons for all men was 1.27, the average for professional men was only .87 whereas the average for farmers was 1.52. Obviously, many sons of farmers had the opportunity to become professionals because of differential reproduction.

### Table 2. Male Occupational Distributions, Actual and Expected, 1920 and 1950

2ND ESTIMATE: OCCUPATIONAL CHANGE AND DIFFERENTIAL REPRODUCTION [4]

| SOCIAL-ECONOMIC GROUP | (1) ACTUAL, 1920 | (2) REPRODUC- TION RATE | (3) EXPECTED, 1950 | (4) ACTUAL, 1950 | (5) MOBILITY |
|---|---|---|---|---|---|
| Professional persons | 1,062,000 | .87 | 924,000 | 3,025,000 | + 2,101,000 |
| Proprietors, managers, & officials: | | | | | |
| Farmers | 6,122,000 | 1.52 | 9,306,000 | 4,205,000 | − 5,101,000 |
| Others | 2,635,000 | .98 | 2,582,000 | 4,391,000 | + 1,809,000 |
| Clerks, salespeople, & kindred | 3,491,000 | .98 | 3,421,000 | 5,345,000 | + 1,924,000 |
| Skilled workers & foremen | 5,469,000 | 1.22 | 6,672,000 | 7,917,000 | + 1,245,000 |
| Semiskilled workers | 4,371,000 | 1.18 | 5,158,000 | 9,153,000 | + 3,995,000 |
| Unskilled workers: | | | | | |
| Farm laborers | 3,162,000 | 1.52 | 4,806,000 | 2,048,000 | − 2,758,000 |
| Others | 6,494,000 | 1.35 | 8,767,000 | 5,582,000 | − 3,185,000 |
| TOTAL | 32,806,000 | 1.27 | 41,636,000 | 41,666,000 | + 11,074,000 |

Table 2 adds the force of reproductive mobility to that of technological mobility as shown in Table 1. The expected number of sons in 1950 in each category (Column 3) is found by applying the estimated reproduction rates (Column 2) to the number of fathers at each level as shown by the census of 1920 (Column 1). These expectations are compared to the realities of the 1950 census (Column 4) and the differences indicate the mobility that occurred (Column 5).

This new calculation, which includes both technological and reproductive mobility, indicates that 11,074,000 men were mobile in the last generation, or 26.5 per cent of the labor force in 1950. Subtracting from the total the mobility caused by technological change, we arrive at the mobility caused by differential reproduction: 2,870,000 men, or 6.8 per cent of the current labor force.

Once again, this estimate is a minimum one, for it does not include step-by-step movement.


IMMIGRATION MOBILITY

From 1920 to 1950 about two million men came to the United States and remained here (immigrant aliens minus emigrant aliens). Published figures on their occupations are not fully adequate for our purposes, but once again a rough estimate can be made. Assuming that the occupational distribution for men is the same as that for men and women combined, and assuming that these men took jobs in the United States at the same level as the occupations they declared as their usual ones, then the immigrants entered the occupational hierarchy as follows [5]:

| | |
|---|---|
| Professional persons | 7.6% |
| Proprietors, managers, officials, clerks, & salesmen | 7.1 |
| Skilled & semiskilled workers | 30.3 |
| Unskilled workers | 37.6 |
| Farmers & farm laborers | 12.4 |
| Miscellaneous | 4.8 |
| TOTAL | 99.8% |

Comparing these percentages to those for all men in 1950 as shown below in Table 6, we see that immigrants entered professional ranks in the same proportion as did the native-born; thus the immigrants did not affect mobility at that level. Roughly speaking, the same is true for farmers and skilled and semiskilled workers. However, the immigrants were notably underrepresented in the ranks of businessmen and clerks and overrepresented in the ranks of unskilled workers. There were 23.9 per cent of all men in business and clerical positions in 1950; if immigrants had entered proportionately, 478,000 would have been businessmen and clerks instead of 142,000. This deficit of 336,000 was filled by native-born men. A similar calculation shows that about 464,000 more immigrants than would be expected according to proportionate entry took unskilled positions. Consequently, about one per cent of the native-born men were upgraded by immigration. (This procedure, of course, ignores the question of the mobility of the immigrants with respect to their fathers.)

In other words, in the generation preceding 1950 the effect of immigration on the mobility of the native-born was almost nil. But in earlier generations the effect was much greater for two reasons: the number of immigrants was much larger, and their skills were less developed. For instance, Elbridge Sibley computed the number of native-born men crossing from the blue-collar to the white-collar ranks in the generation preceding 1930. He estimated that on the average 415,000 men were upgraded each year: 150,000 from technological change, 160,000 from differential reproduction, and 105,000 from immigration [6]. His figures are not directly comparable to those computed here, but the relative proportions from the different causes of mobility give some indication of the decreasing importance of immigration (as well as differential reproduction) in more recent years.

TOTAL AND INDIVIDUAL MOBILITY

There is another way to study the rates of mobility besides analyzing occupational data from the census, namely, a direct questioning of adult men regarding their occupations as compared to those of their fathers. This procedure measures total mobility from all causes. There have been several studies of this type, but only two of these used a sample representative of the entire country, and we shall examine one of them [7].

In 1947 the National Opinion Research Center (NORC) did a national study of occupations, as reported above in Chapter III. Included in their questionnaire was an item about the occupation of the respondent's father. The father-son comparisons for 1334 men are shown in Table 3. Unfortunately, a sample of this size is not large enough for the number of breakdowns in the table, but, as always, we must use whatever data we have, with the usual reservations as to their adequacy.

Let us apply the NORC percentages to the census data of 1950. Table 4 shows the percentage of men who told the NORC they were *not* in the same occupation as their fathers (Column 2). This percentage is applied to the number of men in each category in 1950 (Column 1) to provide the number of men who were mobile (Column 3).

The resulting figures indicate that 27,933,000 men were mobile rela-

### Table 3. Occupations of Sons and Their Fathers
NORC SAMPLE OF 1334 MEN IN 1947 [8]

| OCCUPATIONS OF SONS | N | PER CENT OF THEIR FATHERS WHO WERE: | | | | | | | | |
|---|---|---|---|---|---|---|---|---|---|---|
| | | Profs. | Props. | Clerks | Skilled | Semisk. | Farm | Unsk. | D.K. | Total |
| Professional persons | 164 | 23 | 24 | 10 | 13 | 5 | 17 | 7 | 4 | 100 |
| Proprietors, managers, & officials, nonfarm | 219 | 4 | 31 | 9 | 18 | 8 | 25 | 5 | | 100 |
| Clerks, salespeople, & kindred | 294 | 9 | 23 | 15 | 21 | 10 | 10 | 6 | | 100 |
| Skilled workers & foremen | 175 | 3 | 7 | 4 | 30 | 14 | 29 | 12 | | 100 |
| Semiskilled workers | 224 | 2 | 11 | 6 | 19 | 19 | 32 | 10 | | 100 |
| Farmers & farm laborers | 189 | 2 | 2 | 2 | 3 | 4 | 84 | 3 | | 100 |
| Unskilled workers, nonfarm | 69 | 3 | 12 | — | 9 | 17 | 32 | 20 | | 100 |

## Table 4. *Total Mobility, 1920 to 1950*
### CALCULATED FROM TABLES 1 AND 3

| | (1) | (2) | (3) |
|---|---|---|---|
| | ACTUAL, | NORC PER | NUMBER |
| SOCIAL-ECONOMIC GROUP | 1950 | CENT MOBILE * | MOBILE |
| Professional persons | 3,025,000 | 77% | 2,329,000 |
| Proprietors, managers, & officials, nonfarm | 4,391,000 | 69 | 3,030,000 |
| Clerks, salespeople, & kindred | 5,345,000 | 85 | 4,543,000 |
| Skilled workers & foremen | 7,917,000 | 70 | 5,542,000 |
| Semiskilled workers | 9,153,000 | 81 | 7,414,000 |
| Farmer & farm laborers | 6,253,000 | 16 | 1,000,000 |
| Unskilled workers, nonfarm | 5,582,000 | 73 | 4,075,000 |
| TOTAL | 41,666,000 | | 27,933,000 |

* Those who answered "don't know" are here classed as unskilled.

tive to their fathers, or 67 per cent of the labor force in 1950. This calculation includes individual mobility, technological mobility, reproductive mobility, and step-by-step mobility, and we can call it *total mobility*. (The figure does not include the effects of immigration on the native-born, for both immigrants and their fathers are represented in the totals; however, it was shown above that immigration mobility was not significant in the last generation.) Subtraction of technological and reproductive mobility from the total indicates that 16,859,000 men, or 40.5 per cent of the labor force, were mobile because of individual mobility plus the step-by-step movements which multiply the effects of the other causes of mobility.

It is now possible to summarize the calculations to this point. Analysis of the available data (inadequate though they are) suggests that about 67 per cent of the men in the labor force in 1950 were mobile with respect to their fathers. This total can be broken into component factors as follows:

| | |
|---|---|
| Technological mobility | 19.7% of labor force |
| Reproductive mobility | 6.8 |
| Individual & step-by-step mobility | 40.5 |
| TOTAL MOBILITY | 67.0% of labor force |

Unfortunately, this method of analysis does not permit a separate computation of the step-by-step movements. However, study of the NORC data in Table 3 indicates that mobility tends to be from adjacent groups. For instance, the professional men who were mobile came predominantly from the adjacent group of proprietors, and clerks and salesmen who were mobile came from the adjacent groups of proprietors and skilled workers oftener than from levels further distant in the hierarchy. This suggests that step-by-step movements were very important, that the expansion of such levels as the professional one opened positions that were usually filled by men from intermediate levels, who in turn were replaced by men moving from farm to city or climbing out of the unskilled level. It seems fair to hazard a guess: at least half of the 40.5 per cent of individual and step-by-step mobility was a result of the step-by-step movements. If so, then individual mobility was about as important as technological mobility, and reproductive mobility was about one third as important as either of them.*

UPWARD AND DOWNWARD MOBILITY

Let us take a more detailed look at the NORC data to discern the relative rates of upward and downward movement. Assuming that each step in Table 3 represents a step in a hierarchy, and ignoring the number of steps moved by a man, the percentage of sons at each level who have moved either up or down can be calculated. The results are shown in Table 5.

These figures contain a simple pattern: between one half and three quarters of the men who are now professionals, proprietors, managers, clerks, and skilled workers have climbed above their fathers. Compared to those who have climbed, relatively few have fallen. Four per cent of proprietors and managers, 14 per cent of skilled workers, and 32 per cent of clerks and salesmen have fallen. (Actually, the figure for clerks and salesmen exaggerates the amount of downward movement, for most of their fathers were petty proprietors, and the sons often have as much income and prestige as their fathers.)

The semiskilled group is a catchall, with movement into it almost equally from above and below. The unskilled group is recruited primarily from farm owners and laborers, and secondarily from unskilled and semiskilled workers—this represents as much succession as downward mobility. *Thus, the upper levels have had many new recruits from below; the semiskilled level has had recruits from above and below; the bottom level has recruited from itself.*

It is possible to generalize even further: sons of upper-level fathers tend to remain there, but technological change and differential reproduction have made room for so many new men at upper levels that

* Note that an opening created by technological change or differential reproduction results in one mobile son (assuming no multiplication through step-by-step movements), but an opening created by individual mobility results in two mobile sons—the one who slipped down, and the one who climbed up.

### Table 5. Upward and Downward Mobility
#### CALCULATED FROM TABLE 3*

| | PER CENT WHO HAVE: † | | | |
|---|---|---|---|---|
| SOCIAL-ECONOMIC GROUP, 1950 | Moved Up | Moved Down | Remained | Total |
| Professional persons | 77 | .. | 23 | 100 |
| Proprietors, managers, & offi-cials, nonfarm | 65 | 4 | 31 | 100 |
| Clerks, salespeople, & kindred | 53 | 32 | 15 | 100 |
| Skilled workers & foremen | 56 | 14 | 30 | 100 |
| Semiskilled workers | 43 | 38 | 19 | 100 |
| Farmers & farm laborers | 3 | 13 | 84 | 100 |
| Unskilled workers, nonfarm | .. | 73 | 27 | 100 |

\* Note that it is possible to calculate percentages in the opposite direction with meaning; for example, one could compute the percentage of sons of clerical fathers who subsequently moved up or down. Computation can be made from fathers to sons, or from sons to fathers. There is a difficulty, however, when using fathers as the base for percentages: the sample is based on sons and is therefore more representative of the generation of sons than of the generation of fathers.

† Those who answered "don't know" are here classed as unskilled.

more than half of the current members are newcomers. At the same time the unskilled level has acquired most of its members from the bottom of the hierarchy. (It should be remembered that because the upper levels are smaller than the lower ones, a large proportion of newcomers at the top means that only a small proportion of men from the bottom have moved out.)

A man subjectively evaluates the fluidity of the system by comparing his own career to that of his immediate colleagues and his father. Consequently, we should expect that at the upper levels there would be a feeling of openness, for so many have climbed. At the bottom we should expect more of a sense of a closed system, for so many have remained. And the men at the semiskilled level should be confused, for there has been much movement in both directions.

### INTERNATIONAL COMPARISONS

How does mobility in the United States compare with that in other countries? Unfortunately, studies abroad have not used exactly the same occupational groupings, and so comparisons have to be gross and tentative. But there have been a number of studies in recent years, and they have recently been analyzed by Seymour M. Lipset and Natalie Rogoff [9]:

To sum up, our evidence suggests that in the United States, France and Germany, somewhere between a fifth and a quarter of those with fathers in white-collar occupations become manual workers, whereas about one-third of those whose fathers are manual workers rise to a non-manual position, and that this has been the state of affairs since before the First World War.

It seems, then, that the often-stated theory that American society is more open than others is not fully supported by the evidence. At least for urban workers, other industrialized countries appear to show about as much movement across the line from manual to nonmanual positions as does the United States. However, in the last generation there has been more rapid urbanization in the United States than in France and Germany; thus we do have more men who have changed from manual work on the farm to nonmanual work in the city.

TRENDS THROUGH TIME

Having analyzed mobility into its component factors, it is now possible to look at them one at a time to see whether rates of mobility are changing, whether American society is getting more or less open.

*a. Technological Mobility.* Let us look at the male occupational distributions as given in the censuses from 1910 to 1950. The information is in Table 6. It shows that the proportionate increase in professionals was most marked in the decades 1920 to 1930 and 1940 to 1950. The same was true for urban proprietors, managers, and officials. Thus, the two top categories in the occupational hierarchy expanded most during boom periods in the business cycle.

The increase in clerks and salesmen was greatest in the twenties, slowed down in the thirties, and reversed itself in the forties.

There is no clear over-all trend underlying changes in these white-collar positions. The professional group expanded most during the forties, the business group almost equally in the twenties and the forties; the clerks and salesmen seem to have stopped growing.

Looking at the other side of the coin, there is no clear indication that the rate of decline of unskilled workers and farmers is changing.

Consequently, we must conclude that there is no reason to expect the rate of technological redistribution of the labor force to change markedly in the immediate future. Eventually the decline in the farm group will stop, for an equilibrium will be reached between the men on the farm and those in the city whom they feed. But as automation in production becomes common there may be further spurts in the growth of the technicians and the skilled workers at the expense of the unskilled and semiskilled. Technological mobility will remain a potent social force in the next generation.

Table 6.  *Male Occupational Distributions, 1910 to 1950*
BASED ON THE U.S. CENSUS [10]

| SOCIAL-ECONOMIC GROUP | 1910 | 1920 | 1930 | 1940 | 1950 |
|---|---|---|---|---|---|
| Professional persons | 3.1% | 3.2% | 4.0% | 4.7% | 7.1% |
| Proprietors, managers & officials: | | | | | |
|   Farmers | 19.9 | 18.7 | 15.2 | 13.0 | 9.9 |
|   Others | 7.9 | 8.0 | 9.0 | 9.1 | 10.3 |
| Clerks, salespeople, & kindred | 9.2 | 10.6 | 12.8 | 13.4 | 12.6 |
| Skilled workers & foremen | 14.5 | 16.7 | 16.4 | 15.2 | 18.6 |
| Semiskilled workers | 11.2 | 13.3 | 14.4 | 18.6 | 21.5 |
| Unskilled workers: | | | | | |
|   Farm laborers | 14.0 | 9.6 | 9.5 | 8.5 | 4.8 |
|   Others | 20.2 | 19.8 | 18.8 | 17.6 | 13.1 |
| Not reported | | | | | 2.1 |
| TOTAL | 100.0% | 99.9% | 99.9% | 100.1% | 100.0% |
| NUMBER | 29,483,000 | 32,806,000 | 37,916,000 | 39,446,000 | 42,565,000 * |

* Tables 1, 2, and 4, above, omit the unreported.

*b. Reproductive Mobility.* Here the picture is different, for differential reproduction is disappearing.

The United States Bureau of the Census has published detailed fertility information for samples of women taken from the censuses of 1910 and 1940. In each instance the data are given by five-year age groups cross-classified with the occupations of the husbands. Thus it is possible to calculate the trend in differential reproduction for women who have completed their families for five-year age groups stretching from those born in 1836 to those born in 1896.

The data have been analyzed by Dennis H. Wrong of the University of Toronto [11]. He sums up his conclusions concerning native-born white women as follows:

The trend in ocupational fertility differentials between 1910 and 1940 was similar in many respects to the trend in the period before 1910. All groups continued to decline in fertility, the inverse association between fertility and socioeconomic status persisted, and the percentage divergence of the fertility rates of the two agricultural classes from the average for all classes increased. All classes declined more rapidly than in the previous period. . . . One significant change, however, is that, although the three low fertility nonmanual classes led the decline in the first period, the four classes of nonagricultural manual workers declined more rapidly than two of the nonmanual classes in the later period.

. . . In an absolute sense the size of the fertility differentials between the high, the intermediate, and the low fertility groups of classes diminished between 1910 and 1940.

Wrong's summation can be simply illustrated. Let us compare the total number of children born to 1000 wives of professional men to the number born to 1000 wives of semiskilled workers. If we take women born between 1836 and 1840, who were child-bearing wives *before* the widespread use of contraceptives and the consequent decline in family size, we note that the wives of professionals had 4714 children, and the wives of operatives 4837 children—no substantial difference between the two groups.* But a generation later the difference was marked: considering women born in the period 1861 to 1865, the professional group had only 3335 children whereas the operative group had 4556. Although both groups declined in fertility, the former group declined much more rapidly.

If we jump to the next generation, we see that for women born in 1891 to 1895 (those who had just completed fertility at the time of the 1940 census), the differences between the two groups had narrowed: wives of the professional men had 2253 children, the wives of operatives, 2983.

The trend since the Second World War is still a matter of debate, but it is probably true that the differences have narrowed still further. In recent years we have had a marked upswing in the birth rate, but the increase has been greatest among those groups who previously had the smallest families.

In general, it appears that as a country industrializes, the upper-level urban families are the first to desire smaller families, and the first to learn about effective methods of birth control. After a short period of time, both the desire and the technique are passed down to the lower levels of society, though the latter probably do not restrict their families quite so much as the upper levels. It now appears that the future pattern to be expected in the United States will be one that has three broad fertility types: urban white-collar workers, urban blue-collar workers, and farmers, with each group having slightly larger families than the preceding one (the gap between city and farm being bigger than that between white-collar and blue-collar). *Within* each group, rich couples are likely to have slightly larger families than poor ones. Thus, the simple inverse correlation of social class level and size of family will no longer exist.

Consequently, the substantial mobility that occurred in the recent past

---

* There may have been a small underreporting of working-class children due to the somewhat higher rate of mortality among their mothers compared to professional mothers.

as a result of differential fertility is not to be expected in the future. There may remain a small residue of differential fertility between the white-collar and blue-collar groups as a whole, but the effects of this on mobility will be relatively small. And within the white-collar group (and possibly the blue-collar as well) it appears that differential fertility in the future will produce downward mobility.

c. *Immigration Mobility.* Here the pattern is perfectly clear: the vast inflow of unskilled immigrants, averaging about a million a year, was stopped about 1925. Even if we continue to admit one or two hundred thousand immigrants a year, the larger size of the native population will absorb them practically without notice. Furthermore, the new immigrants are people of higher skills, and they do not all enter the occupational system at the bottom.

The recent population movement of consequence in the United States has been the migration of rural Negroes to both Southern and Northern cities. They entered industry at the unskilled and semiskilled levels, and suffered racial discrimination which slowed their ascent into the skilled and white-collar jobs. Consequently, many white workers were pushed up a notch in the hierarchy. But this type of internal migration cannot continue indefinitely as the pool of available rural Negroes will dry up. The migration of Negroes in the past forty years has softened the effects of the constriction of the European inflow, but it cannot last much longer.

d. *Individual Mobility.* Individual mobility, it will be remembered, cannot be measured from census data alone; a sampling inquiry is necessary. The procedures of public-opinion research are new, thus we have no historical comparisons available. But there is one ingenious research that contributes to our knowledge of trends in individual mobility.

Natalie Rogoff collected a sample of some 10,000 men in Indianapolis who applied for marriage licenses in 1940, and another sample of equal size for the year 1910. In each instance the men stated their occupations and those of their fathers. The resulting mobility tables automatically held constant the effects of differential fertility, for the number of fathers and the number of sons were identical. Rogoff further held constant the effects of technological change by partialing out the mobility that flowed from that cause. The final measurement was therefore one of individual mobility alone. The two samples made it possible for her to study trends through time [12].

She found that over-all rates of individual movement were about the same in 1910 as in 1940. Mobility was about 20 per cent less than would be expected under completely open or random placement. Although the over-all rates had not changed, some changes were noticed regarding movement across the line separating blue-collar from white-collar positions. In both periods this barrier was the hardest to cross. There was much more movement within each category (especially the white-collar group) than across from one category to the other. Rogoff found that upward movement across the line did not change from 1910 to 1940, but downward movement decreased—that is, it was easier for the sons of the men at the top to stay there despite the fact that upward mobility among the sons of those at the bottom remained constant. Unfortunately, Indianapolis is not representative of the nation as a whole, but we will have to accept Rogoff's conclusions as the best available national estimate.*

e. *Summary.* The available evidence suggests that technological mobility has remained relatively constant during the past generation, as has individual mobility. Reproductive mobility and immigration mobility have been steadily declining and will be unimportant in the next generation (both were most important in the generation preceding 1920). But insofar as technological and individual mobility are by far the most important factors, the over-all rates of mobility have not declined greatly in the last generation and probably will not do so in the next generation. American society is not becoming markedly more rigid.

## RECRUITMENT OF THE BUSINESS ELITE

There is especial interest in the origins of the people who are now at the very top of the occupational hierarchy, for they have power and influence that affects the entire society. Perhaps the most important group from this standpoint are the leaders of big business. If they formed a closed group that passed their positions on from one generation to the next, our society would have a new type of commercial aristocracy and would be far from the model of an open society, regardless of the amount of shifting among persons in intermediate ranks.

---

* Rogoff's method was to measure actual succession and mobility against what would be expected under the principle of random placement, holding differential reproduction and technological change constant. Mobility tables constructed on this principle lead to different conclusions from tables constructed from gross father-son comparisons that do not take into account differences in the sizes of the various groups. For instance, the NORC data in Table 3 show that 23 per cent of professionals had professional fathers, whereas 30 per cent of skilled workers had skilled fathers. But when we realize that in 1920 only 3.2 per cent of fathers were professional, compared to 16.7 per cent of skilled workers, then it becomes clear that there is relatively much more inheritance among the professional than among the skilled workers. In fact, Rogoff found succession to be greatest at the top (professionals and semiprofessionals) and at the bottom (unskilled workers), and much less at intermediate levels. The same conclusion was reached in a recent extensive study in England by D. V. Glass and associates. Incidentally, they made an attempt, with admittedly scanty data, to compare several countries. They found that individual succession appears to be about the same in England and the U.S., and slightly higher in Italy and France [13].

Fortunately, there is excellent information on this question that carries us beyond the studies already reported. In 1928, two Harvard professors, F. W. Taussig and C. S. Joslyn, sent out questionnaires to a large group of American business leaders, and received about half of them back (usable returns totaled to 7371). The respondents were chosen from a listing of executive officers, partners, and directors of all large and important companies in the United States, and form a rather good sampling of the top businessmen. In 1952, W. Lloyd Warner and James C. Abegglin repeated the operation and secured a sample very similar in size and composition. Consequently, we can compare the recruitment of the business elite in the two succeeding generations [14].

The basic facts concerning the business leaders of 1952 are shown in Table 7. Thirty-one per cent were descended from fathers who were also big businessmen. By contrast, only 5 per cent had fathers who were semiskilled or unskilled laborers. These figures indicate considerable succession at the top level of business. Indeed, the succession appears more marked when we realize that there were very few big businessmen in 1920. Thus the 31 per cent of business leaders who succeeded their fathers in the elite were recruited from only 4 per cent of all fathers in 1920. By chance expectation (assuming a completely open society, with a random relationship between the jobs of sons and fathers) only 4 per cent of the elite should have had fathers in the elite. The ratio of these two percentages is 7.75, indicating that the elite men of 1952 were recruited from elite fathers almost eight times oftener than would be expected under random placement. On the other hand, as the column of ratios in Table 7 shows, elite men were recruited from the semiskilled level only .16 as often as would occur in a fully open society (a ratio of unity indicates random placement).

Notice that these figures can be interpreted to indicate that American society is either relatively closed or relatively open, depending upon one's expectations. The statement that 69 per cent of the business elite were recruited from other levels suggests considerable openness. On the other hand, the statement that the business elite was recruited from its own level 7.75 times oftener than randomly expected suggests that American society is relatively closed.* Perhaps the most useful interpretation of the data is a repetition of a statement made above: the sons of men at upper levels of society tend to remain at the top, but technological change and differential reproduction (and some downward

---

* This ratio assumes that there had been no differential reproduction. If one measured separately the succession due to technological change and that due to differential reproduction, and subtracted them from the total so as to indicate only that succession due to rigidity in inheritance (individual succession) beyond random expectations, then one would arrive at a different ratio.

mobility) permit many sons of men from lower levels to climb into the elite.

Table 7.  Fathers of Business Leaders of 1952 [15]

| OCCUPATIONAL GROUP | FATHERS OF BUSINESS LEADERS | ALL MEN IN 1920 | RATIO |
|---|---|---|---|
| Professional men | 14% | 4% | 3.50 |
| Executives; owners of large businesses | 31 | 4 | 7.75 |
| Owners of small businesses | 18 | 5 | 3.60 |
| Farm tenants & owners | 9 | 20 | 0.45 |
| Clerks & salesmen | 8 | 10 | 0.80 |
| Foremen | 3 | 2 | 1.33 |
| Skilled workers | 10 | 16 | 0.63 |
| Semiskilled & unskilled workers | 5 | 31 | 0.16 |
| Farm laborers | 0 | 7 | 0.00 |
| Other occupations | 2 | 1 | .. |
| TOTAL | 100% | 100% | 1.00 |

When Taussig and Joslyn published their research, they measured the historical trend by comparing succession among the younger men in their sample to that among the older men. This comparison indicated that succession was increasing through time, that entry into the elite was becoming more difficult for men born in humble families. The authors predicted that this trend would soon create a closed business elite. But a broader perspective than was possible at that time indicates that their study was done at a crucial moment in corporation history and cannot be taken as an adequate description of the long-term trend. The big companies were just settling down in the nineteen twenties; they had been founded by financial promoters around the turn of the century, and a good many of those promoters handed their positions on to their sons. But as the companies matured, inheritance became more difficult. Stock ownership was spread among more people, and the control of the big corporations tended to pass out of the hands of the families of the original creators. Furthermore, the managements became more and more interested in efficiency and thus picked men for high position according to merit rather than nepotism. Insofar as the original founders of the companies could not have succeeded their fathers as corporation executives (there were practically no such persons in the generation of their fathers), obviously the trend from 1900 to 1928 was for more succession among the business elite. But this trend was reversed after 1928, as Warner and Abegglin prove [16].

Table 8 compares the ratios for the fathers of business leaders in 1928 and in 1952. It shows that recruitment from businessmen (large and small) dropped from 9.67 to 4.73, and recruitment from laborers increased from .24 to .32. Thus entry into the top levels of business management is becoming slightly more open through time. (It was necessary to condense categories to make the two researches comparable.)

*Table 8.   Recruitment of Business Leaders,*
*1928 and 1952* [17]

| OCCUPATIONAL GROUP | RATIO 1928 | RATIO 1952 |
|---|---|---|
| Professional men | 4.33 | 3.50 |
| Businessmen | 9.67 | 4.73 |
| Clerks and salesmen | 0.71 | 0.80 |
| Farmers | 0.32 | 0.33 |
| Laborers | 0.24 | 0.32 |

The material collected by Warner and Abegglin illuminates this statistical finding. They discovered that small companies are more rigid than large ones, for in the former a man can pass both ownership and executive control on to his sons, but in the latter impersonal competition is more likely to operate. Furthermore, they found that a college education is becoming more and more a prerequisite for business success, and college education has been markedly "democratized" in the last few decades. Formerly the sons of the elite were almost the only ones who went to college, but now a substantial portion of middle-class boys and a great many from the working class enter ivy halls. Once they graduate, they can enter the competition for management positions with almost as much chance for success as the sons of the elite. Consequently, the important sifting process has now become that which sends some boys to college but keeps others away. That process will be studied in detail in the following chapter.

Some incidental findings of the Warner and Abegglin study are of interest. The sons of foreign-born fathers do slightly better in the competition for elite positions than do those of native-born fathers. A man has a much better chance for success in big business if he is born in a big city and in any region of the country other than the South. Although the sons of high-level fathers generally reach success somewhat earlier in life than those of low-level fathers, direct help in the form of money from one's father is rare, and is more rare now than formerly.

## CONCLUSIONS

This chapter has explored data from the census, and from sample inquiries that obtained information about the relative occupations of fathers and sons, in order to measure the degree to which American society departs from the extremes of being completely open or completely closed [18].

The American class structure is not a completely closed one, for between one half and three quarters of the men who are in professional, business, clerical, or skilled jobs have climbed relative to their fathers. No wonder they feel that our society is open, for if they look around them they find that most of their colleagues have moved up in the occupational (and thus the class) hierarchy.

The two most important factors in creating mobility have been the technological change which redistributed the labor force, opening up many new jobs in upper levels, and the fact that some sons moved down in the hierarchy, allowing others to move up. These two forces appear to have been operating at relatively constant rates, at least for the space of the last thirty or forty years. A smaller contribution to mobility has been made by differential reproduction and (for the native-born) by immigration. These two factors have been declining in importance in recent decades. Consequently, a small decline in over-all mobility has probably been taking place. The amount of mobility that has occurred has been multiplied by the fact that most sons who move do so by only one or two steps in the hierarchy; thus one new job at the top may make it possible for two or three sons to have an advance.

Although there has been tremendous mobility, the American class structure is not completely open. Particularly at the extremes—the professional and top businessmen, the unskilled workers—there is much more succession or inheritance of position than would be the case under random placement. Indeed, the sons of men at the top of the system have from five to eight times more opportunity to succeed their fathers than would be the case if the structure were completely open.*

Except for the relatively few sons who inherit either their fathers' businesses or enough capital to buy businesses, the advantages of being born into an elite family are indirect. Such a family shapes a boy's motivations so that he seeks occupational success, and it gives him a good education. In other words, an elite family gives its son a favorable handicap, and then sends him out into the world to compete without further help. The next chapter examines the handicapping process.

REFERENCES

[1] Both quotations are from my interview files.

[2] Figures for 1920 from Alba M. Edwards, *U.S. Census of Population. 1940: Comparative Occupation Statistics, 1870–1940* (Washington: Gov-

* This statement (and the work of Rogoff and of Warner and Abegglin upon which it is based) assumes no inheritance of innate talent. Because there is some inheritance, the degree of succession relative to the model of a completely open society is less than the ratios suggest.

ernment Printing Office, 1943), p. 187. Figures for 1950 from *U.S. Census of Population, 1950*, Vol. II, *Characteristics of the Population*, Part I, U.S. Summary, Table 53 (Washington: Government Printing Office, 1953); I have eliminated 899,000 men who did not report their occupations, and have divided the "Service workers, except private household" by placing one fourth in the semiskilled category and three fourths in the unskilled category. See Chapter III for comments on the comparability of these series.

[3] The net reproduction rates are from Frank Lorimer and Frederick Osborn, *Dynamics of Population* (New York: Macmillan, 1934), p. 74— all rates were increased 15 per cent in order to make the total expected equal to the total labor force in 1950. For a similar type of reasoning, but based on even weaker evidence, see Carson McGuire, "Social Stratification and Mobility Patterns," *American Sociological Review*, XV (April, 1950), 195–204.

[4] Based on Table 1 plus Lorimer and Osborn, *Dynamics of Population*, p. 74 (see footnote 3).

[5] *Statistical Abstract of the United States*, 1940, Table 101; *ibid.*, 1955, Table 109. The many men who did not report occupations are omitted from the percentage distribution.

[6] Elbridge Sibley, "Some Demographic Clues to Stratification," *American Sociological Review*, VII (June, 1942), 322–30.

[7] The other national sample is Richard Centers, "Occupational Mobility of Urban Occupational Strata," *American Sociological Review*, XIII (April, 1948), 197–203. There is a large sample from six cities using the current "major occupation group" classification of the census reported in Herman P. Miller, *Income of the American People* (New York: Wiley, 1955), pp. 31–32. These two studies show substantially the same pattern as the NORC research (see next footnote). For local studies in California, see Percy E. Davidson and H. Dewey Anderson, *Occupational Mobility in an American Community* (Stanford University: Stanford University Press, 1937); and Reinhard Bendix, Seymour M. Lipset, and Theodore Malm, "Social Origins and Occupational Career Patterns," *Industrial and Labor Relations Review*, VII (January, 1954), 246–61. For Minneapolis, see Godfrey Hochbaum *et al.*, "Socio-economic Variables in a Large City," *American Journal of Sociology*, LXI (July, 1955), 31–38. For Indianapolis, see Rogoff, cited below.

Studies of this type are somewhat limited by the fact that men shift occupations during their careers. See Seymour M. Lipset and Reinhard Bendix, "Social Mobility and Occupational Career Patterns," *American Journal of Sociology*, LVII (January and March, 1952), 366–74 and 494–504. See also William H. Form and Delbert C. Miller, "Occupational Career Pattern as a Sociological Instrument," *American Journal of Sociology* (January, 1949), 317–29.

[8] National Opinion Research Center, "Jobs and Occupations: A Popular Evaluation," *Class, Status and Power*, Reinhard Bendix and Seymour M. Lipset, eds. (Glencoe, Ill.: The Free Press, 1953), pp. 424–25; originally published in *Opinion News*, IX (September 1, 1947). I have omitted sons who were service workers, and reclassified the relatively few fathers who were service workers into the category of unskilled workers.

[9] Seymour M. Lipset and Natalie Rogoff, "Class and Opportunity in Europe and in the United States," *Commentary*, December, 1954, p. 565.

[10] Sources: Same as footnote 2, above.

[11] Dennis H. Wrong, *Trends in Class Fertility Differentials in Western Nations* (unpublished Ph.D. thesis, Columbia University, 1956). Dr. Wrong very kindly sent me an advance draft of Chapter V which gives a detailed analysis of the American figures and makes pointed comparisons to British trends. The relevant government publication is *U.S. Census of Population, 1940: Differential Fertility in 1940 and 1910* (Washington: Government Printing Office, 1943–1947).

See also: Clyde V. Kiser, "Fertility Trends and Differentials in the United States," *Journal of the American Statistical Association*, XLVII (March, 1952), 25–48; Charles F. Westoff, "Differential Fertility in the United States," *American Sociological Review*, XIX (October, 1954), 549–61.

[12] Natalie Rogoff, *Recent Trends in Occupational Mobility* (Glencoe, Ill.: The Free Press, 1953).

[13] D. V. Glass, ed., *Social Mobility in Britain* (London: Routledge and Kegan Paul, 1954). See the technical comments on this study in several articles in *Population Studies*, IX (July, 1955).

[14] F. W. Taussig and C. S. Joslyn, *American Business Leaders* (New York: Macmillan, 1932). W. Lloyd Warner and James C. Abegglin, *Occupational Mobility in American Business and Industry* (Minneapolis: University of Minnesota Press, 1955); the same authors wrote a popular account of their research, with some additional data on motivational processes, which is cited in the next chapter.

[15] *Ibid.*, pp. 40–41.

[16] For a study of the very top business executives from 1899 to 1953, see Mabel Newcomer, *The Big Business Executive* (New York: Columbia University Press, 1955). See also William Miller, "American Historians and the Business Elite," *Journal of Economic History*, IX (November, 1949), 184–200. William Miller, "The Recruitment of the Business Elite" *Quarterly Journal of Economics*, 64 (May, 1950), 242–53. C. Wright Mills, "The American Business Elite: A Collective Portrait," *Journal of Economic History*, supplement, V (December, 1945), which indicates that the recruitment of the elite does not seem to have changed much since colonial times.

For labor leaders, see C. Wright Mills, *The New Men of Power: America's Labor Leaders* (New York: Harcourt, Brace, 1948). For civil servants, see Reinhard Bendix, *Higher Civil Servants in American Society* (Boulder: University of Colorado Press, 1949).

[17] Warner and Abegglin, *Occupational Mobility*, p. 48.

[18] Two recent articles evaluate the same subject in a superior manner: William Petersen, "Is America Still the Land of Opportunity?" *Commentary*, XVI (November, 1953), 477–86. Ely Chinoy, "Social Mobility Trends in the United States," *American Sociological Review*, XX (April, 1955), 180–85.

# X

# Succession and Mobility: Motivation and Education

MEN OF MY OWN AGE GROUP (AMONG THE EXECUTIVES), I WOULD SAY THAT ABOUT FIFTY-FIFTY ARE COLLEGE OR NON-COLLEGE. THE MEN IN THE AGE GROUP STARTING OUT NOW ARE PROBABLY NINETY PER CENT COLLEGE. . . . IT'S THE ATTITUDE OF TOP MANAGEMENT; THEY HAVE FELT, OR PERHAPS LEARNED, OVER THE YEARS, THAT FROM A DOLLARS AND CENTS STANDPOINT IT IS AN ASSET TO THE COMPANY, FOR THE COLLEGE-TRAINED MAN IS A BETTER RISK FOR PROMOTION AND ADVANCEMENT. THE MORTALITY IS NOT AS HIGH. PROVIDING THEY HAVE A WELL-ROUNDED AND BALANCED PERSONALITY. THAT'S THE ESSENTIAL THING, OF COURSE. YOU'VE GOT TO HAVE A WELL-BALANCED MAN WHO GETS ALONG WITH PEOPLE, WHICH IS THE FIRST ESSENTIAL.

*An Executive* [1]

IN THE PREVIOUS CHAPTER it was learned that about two thirds of the men now working are in jobs at different levels from those of their fathers; they had to make some deliberate decisions about their careers and could not automatically follow along after their parents. But it was also pointed out above that in a modern industrial system it is difficult for a father to pass his job on to his son. Actually, the major influence of a family over a son is to shape his thinking in the direction of a certain level in the occupational hierarchy: to train him to aim toward a professional career, or extol the virtues of a skilled trade, or simply to assume that he is the type of fellow who will take any job that comes along, which usually means a semiskilled position that does not demand much specific training.

Every society has organized channels for training people in various ways and for placing them into positions according to their training. In farming societies a boy learns by working alongside his father. In circles dominated by military or religious orders, formal training outside the family prepares men for roles in the governing groups. In simple commercial societies, business acumen and accumulated capital

276

are more useful than a formal education which goes beyond the necessary rudiments of reading and writing. And a successful trader or owner of a small manufacturing establishment is very likely to train his sons in the business. They may go away to college for a while, but they study classical subjects that are not supposed to have much direct connection with affairs of business—for until recently, college was designed to develop the "whole man" through the liberal arts, and anything that was practical was suspect. Only for the small number of men preparing directly for the professions of law, the ministry, or medicine was college highly practical, although not absolutely necessary, for one could train for the professions through apprenticeship [2].

Nowadays the major part of the production and distribution of goods is handled by large corporations, and ambitious young men are more likely to seek corporate careers than to start their own firms. The managements of the large corporations have become bureaucratized, and the path to an executive position professionalized; for the most part, a man starts with college training in a technical field like engineering or the newly created field of business administration. It is true that we still have many independent entrepreneurs. However, they are either the owner-operators of very tiny businesses like the classic gasoline station, in which case the entrepreneur does not expect to get rich but is only struggling to exist and stay out of a factory, or they are men who are much influenced by the trends created by large corporations and are almost as likely as are the big companies to prefer college-educated assistants. The sons of corporate executives are not likely to learn about business by working for their fathers; nepotism is difficult and inefficient in big companies. Instead of hiring their sons, executives aid them by giving them expensive, high-quality educations that automatically provide a good start in any high occupation. The combination of a complicated scientific technology and large bureaucratic organizations has made higher education necessary for success in most fields of business (and of government). Only in entertainment, art, and sport can talented individuals make headway without being asked, "Do you have a bachelor's degree?"

The bachelor's degree is becoming the ticket of admission into the occupations that provide an upper-middle-class way of life. But the educational system sorts people into other levels of the hierarchy as well. High-school graduation (often with some additional technical training) is now common amongst the technicians and white-collar workers of the lower-middle class. And the fellow who quits high school is most likely to become a semiskilled operative where special training is not necessary. The data from the 1950 census, as analyzed by Paul C. Glick, are pictured in Figure 1. It shows the job distributions for men

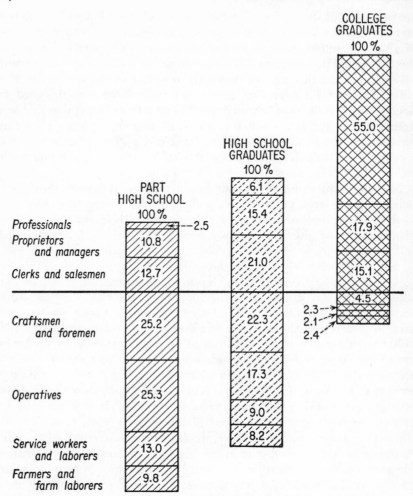

*Figure 1. School and Jobs* [3]

who have gone part way through high school, for those who have graduated from high school, and for men who have graduated from college. In monetary terms, Glick estimates that the part-high-school man will earn in his lifetime about $135,000; the high-school graduate will earn about $165,000; and the college graduate will earn $268,000 [4].*

The last chapter measured the amount of mobility that occurred and showed that our occupational system is one in which father-son succession was the exception rather than the rule. But simply demon-

---

* It makes a difference which college a man attends, for Ivy League graduates do better than others, regardless of family background [5].

strating the amount of mobility does not answer the question, "Who takes advantage of the opportunities for success, and how does he go about it?" This chapter will examine the process by which an individual boy gets placed on the path that leads to a given level in the occupational hierarchy. The emphasis will be on the distinctions between boys who choose college and those who do not, although to a considerable extent the same selection forces are at work within each of these two large groups.

## THE AMERICAN COLLEGE SYSTEM

The great changes that have taken place in our collegiate system are summarized by Dael Wolfle [6]:

In 1900, one youth out of every 60 graduated from college; now 1 in 8 [or 10] does. . . . In 1900 nearly half of the college graduates had trained for law, medicine, dentistry, or the ministry; now only 8 per cent of the new graduates have prepared for careers in these traditional professions. In 1900 professional schools of education and of business were practically unknown; now more students graduate with specialized training in these fields than in any others.

Let us make a brief comparison of our educational system with that of England as of 1950 (before the major reforms of the postwar Labor Government had time to take effect and "Americanize" the English schools). James Bryant Conant, past president of Harvard University, made the contrast effectively in a little book called *Education and Liberty*. He pointed out that in both England and the United States almost all children get universal primary education: over 98 per cent of the boys and girls fourteen years of age and under are in school. But age fourteen is the dividing line; in England that is the legal limit for compulsory schooling, and only 31 per cent of the boys and girls are still in school a year later, and only 16 per cent at age sixteen. But in the United States, about 90 per cent of the fifteen-year-olds, and about 80 per cent of the sixteen-year-olds are still in school on a full-time basis [7].

Since the Second World War, about 80 per cent of American youth start high school, and about 55 per cent graduate; some 20 per cent of our young people start college, and 10 per cent graduate [8]. In England only 3 per cent start college, and almost all of them graduate. Their training tends to be professional, as was true of our colleges fifty years ago.

Our colleges and our secondary schools have undergone a tremendous revolution in half a century. They used to be institutions with two purposes: to educate the sons and some of the daughters of rich families in the liberal arts, and to prepare some of those sons, plus the sons of some middle-class families, for the learned professions. Now they are transformed into institutions for "all the people," and are supposed to give general education plus vocational training to everybody who wants to attend. Training for the learned professions (law, medicine, scientific research) is reserved for postgraduate schools.

The high schools must now serve the majority of young people in their communities. In the last century they existed primarily to prepare students for college, and college meant classical liberal arts; three quarters of the high-school graduates continued their educations. Thus, there was agreement about the purposes and the curriculums of both secondary and higher institutions. Now only a third of the high-school graduates continue, and they go on to college courses of great diversity. Consequently, there is confusion and poor articulation between the two levels. There has been a shift away from the classical subjects like Latin and mathematics in favor of more "practical" subjects like shopwork and citizenship.

Many high schools struggle to maintain a separate curriculum of college-preparatory work that retains a traditional emphasis on language, literature, and science, alongside a modernized curriculum designed to keep boys and girls in high school who are not interested in college. But there is always the difficulty of keeping the two paths sufficiently alike for a youth who changes his mind to be able to shift his curriculum. And many do change their minds; not only in high school, but even after reaching college. We do not hurry our young people; we encourage them to grow up experimentally, to taste a number of areas of life, and then to choose their careers. Byron S. Hollinshead points out that this approach is a direct reflection of our attitudes about our social-class system [9]:

Our [educational] structure is concrete evidence of the deep concern among Americans for a fluid, casteless society, in which it should be made possible for everyone to proceed as far as his perseverance and abilities will carry him. We do not, therefore, accept the notion that students can be sorted early and then trained for the niche in life that is right for them. . . . American tradition requires similar opportunities for all, while educational efficiency would gain, at least to some degree and depending upon the educational level, by differentiation.

It was pointed out earlier in this book that the long-term trend in the distribution of income is to put more people in the middle, to reduce the numbers at the extremes of rich and poor. The same is true of education. We are approaching a system in which some high school is universal, and some college very common. Americans usually take this for granted, but for those who travel to Europe, or even just below the border to Mexico, the contrast becomes immediately apparent. Our school system creates an atmosphere of equality and an ease of communication that blurs economic disparities. It is probably the most important single factor in creating the American feeling that social-class differences are not very important.

A monopoly on learning is an ancient device to protect the prerogatives of a ruling class. Learning gives tremendous advantages in terms of occupational and political power and also in terms of the social graces which legitimize power and produce prestige. Even his cultured accent gives an educated Englishman an advantage over his Cockney cousin. By contrast, widespread diffusion of education is vital to the kind of open society we value. But we must find ways of guarding against the dilution of quality that tends to accompany diffusion of availability.

## WHO GOES TO COLLEGE?

College preparation is now required for most managerial and professional positions, and consequently for entry into the upper and upper-middle classes. To simplify our problem, once again we will concentrate on boys; furthermore, we will examine the specific factors that explain how a boy makes up his mind whether or not he will go to college. In terms of his future career this is the most important decision of his life, for later he may well change his mind about the *specific* occupation he likes, but the *level* in the occupational hierarchy that he occupies will primarily be determined by his choice between going to college and going directly to work.

First of all, it makes a difference in what part of the country a boy lives. One in Utah has three times the chance of going to college of one in South Carolina. This partly reflects another variable, race; for the data examined above in Chapter VIII indicate that Negroes get less education than whites. Similarly, Jews get more than Protestants, who get more than Catholics. Also, urban boys are slightly more educated than rural boys. These variables reflect the cultural environment of the community; areas of the country with many colleges and with traditions of college going, and ethnic groups with traditions of higher education influence more sons to aspire to the higher learning [10]. But let us look at the more personal factors that differentiate between two boys who live in the same town, or even between two brothers in the same family.

Obviously, a certain degree of intelligence is required. Most boys do not know their I.Q. score, but they do know how well they perform in grammar school, and that performance is determined by intelligence more than by any other single variable. The average I.Q. score for the general population is 100; the average for those who graduate from high school is 110; for those who enter college, 115; for those who graduate from college, 121. Thus, there is a selection according to intelligence at every level [11].

It is interesting to speculate about the question of the percentage of the population that has the minimum of intelligence necessary to complete college. The average I.Q. of graduates is 121, and about 15 per cent of the population are that intelligent. But about half the boys who get through college have an I.Q. lower than 121. President Truman appointed a commission to study the whole question of higher education, and they estimated that about a third of the population had the intelligence to profit from a college education, with perhaps half of the population smart enough to benefit from two years in junior college. Many educators have considered this estimate to be a little on the generous side; perhaps 20 to 25 per cent is a better estimate for good college material. Of course, if half the population actually did have at least some college training, the advantage of having it would decline in value as a guarantor of a high-level job [12].

As a result of good school performance based on high intelligence, the higher his I.Q., the more chance a boy has of graduating from college, regardless of other circumstances. The student himself, his teachers, and his parents all feel that a very bright boy ought to keep on in school. Consequently, if he has intelligence that scores 147 or higher on standard I.Q. scales, which puts him in the top 1 per cent of his classmates, he has about a 60 per cent chance of getting a college diploma. If he is in the top 10 per cent (126 and higher), his chance is 42 per cent. But if he is in the top 20 per cent (117 or higher), his chances fall to one in three [13]. Actually, a boy's high-school grades predict his college chances a little better than his I.Q. score, for they reflect his motivation as well as his intelligence.

Notice that for the top 20 per cent in intelligence—and everybody agrees that these boys are smart enough for good college work—two boys out of three never get a college diploma. This is the group often pointed to as "wasted talent," boys who for their own and for society's benefit should be getting more education than they do. Perhaps not all need college training to help them fully develop their talents, but certainly more than one third do.

Intelligence thus predicts the amount of education a boy will get, but far from perfectly. Especially as one gets into the level of smart-but-not-brilliant, it is clear that more boys stay outside ivy halls than study in them. Why?

Statistically, the major explaining variable is the social-class level of the boy's family, although such a statement still leaves much unexplained about the way social class operates as a motivating force in an individual boy's life. But let us glance at the statistics before we become clinical. The higher the family's status, the greater the boy's chances of getting through college. If the father is a professional or semiprofessional man, the son has a 43 per cent chance of a diploma. If the father is a business-man, the son has a 19 per cent chance. If the father is a salesman or clerk, the son has a 15 per cent chance. But if the father is a blue-collar worker (skilled, semiskilled, or unskilled), the son's chances fall to 8 per cent [14].

However, there is a statistical problem to be faced: intelligence of sons and social-class level of parents are correlated. Higher level parents have smarter children. The psychologist Lewis M. Terman, for in-stance, gives the rough estimate that an I.Q. of 110 to 120 is about five times more common among children of "superior" social class than among those of "inferior" social class. But inasmuch as there are so many more inferior families, their children make up at least half of the total number of bright youngsters [15].

It is necessary to examine figures that handle social class and intel-ligence simultaneously in order to see their separate influence. For this purpose we can use a study of more than 3000 public-school boys in cities surrounding Boston conducted at Harvard by Samuel A. Stouffer, Talcott Parsons, and Florence R. Kluckhohn. The data are shown in Table 1. They indicate the percentage of high-school boys of various types who intended to go to college (and a later follow-up showed that most actually did go). These figures are different from the ones al-ready given in this chapter, for the sample consisted of boys in the sophomore and junior years of high school, and thus did not include many of low intelligence and/or low social status who had already left

Table 1.   Percentage of Boys Who Expected to Go to College,
by I.Q. and Father's Occupation

BOSTON AREA, 1950—3348 BOYS [16]

| | I.Q. QUINTILE (BOYS) | | | | | |
| | (Low) | | | (High) | | All |
| FATHER'S OCCUPATION | 1 | 2 | 3 | 4 | 5 | Quintiles |
|---|---|---|---|---|---|---|
| Major white collar | 56% | 72% | 79% | 82% | 89% | 80% |
| Middle white collar | 28 | 36 | 47 | 53 | 76 | 52 |
| Minor white collar | 12 | 20 | 22 | 29 | 55 | 26 |
| Skilled labor & service | 4 | 15 | 19 | 22 | 40 | 19 |
| Other labor & service | 9 | 6 | 10 | 14 | 29 | 12 |
| ALL OCCUPATIONS | 11% | 17% | 24% | 30% | 52% | 27% |

school; and the percentages refer to those who expected to start college, not to those who graduated.

Notice that the combination of I.Q. and social class successfully predicted college aspiration at the extremes, for a boy with a Major White-Collar father (lawyer, doctor, executive) who was in the top quintile or top 20 per cent of intelligence had an 89 per cent chance of wanting to go to college, whereas a boy with an Other Labor and Service father (semiskilled or unskilled) who was in the bottom quintile in intelligence had only a 9 per cent chance. The proportion seeking college from low to high occupation increased from 12 to 80 per cent; the proportion from low to high intelligence ran from 11 to 52 per cent.

Fortunately, the Boston study had depth in time, for it collected statistics on the performance of the boys from the first grade in grammar school up to the time they answered the questionnaire in the middle of high school. Boys with high I.Q. scores usually had good marks starting with the first grade, but even more, those with low I.Q. scores had poor marks. Father's occupation did not affect school performance in the earlier grades, but it began to take effect in the fourth grade, and by the time of junior high school was slightly more important than I.Q. in predicting performance.

The pattern is clear: in the earliest years in school a boy performs according to his native talent and, probably, his general emotional adjustment to the classroom situation: if he is bright, he enjoys giving the right answers; if he is dull, he learns to keep quiet. But as he grows older, he begins to shape his performance according to certain values that he learns from his family and his friends. Upper-status boys learn that good, or at least adequate, performance in school is necessary, that they are expected to do well enough in secondary school to get admitted to college. Furthermore, they learn certain attitudes of cooperation with and respect for the teachers that aid their school performance. And they enjoy school, for they have enough money to go to parties; they become leaders in extracurricular activities; they have no economic problems that act as disturbing pressures.

By contrast, a boy from a lower-status home is taught that college is either "not for his kind," or at best is a matter of indifference to his parents. The boy's friends are not interested in college nor in high school; they are, on the average, not "good at books," and they are more concerned with prowess at sports and with girls than in the joys of learning. Consequently, even a bright boy among them gets discouraged; he hasn't the money or the prestige to be a social leader at school; he is often forced to work to earn money after school hours; he doesn't want to appear to be a sissy to his friends. The average tendency is for his school aspiration to be brought down to the level of that of his status equals. Indeed, somewhere in the middle of his high-school career he realizes that he now can quit school and go to work and earn almost as much money as his father does. He can be independent. School leads nowhere he is interested in going, so in more instances than not, he quits. The reader will recall that in Elmtown 89 per cent of the lower-lower class adolescents (but none of the upper-middle) quit high school before graduation [17].

What has been said so far concerns boys at the extremes of Table 1; that is, boys with high intelligence and high social status versus those with low intelligence and low social status. Also, it concerns the many boys of high intelligence but low status whose aspirations are kept down by family indifference and peer pressure.

However, *some* boys of high intelligence and low status do head toward college, even though it be a minority of this group (29 per cent of the boys in the highest quintile of intelligence from Other Labor and Service homes). Furthermore, if we look again at Table 1, we can notice that boys from Minor White-Collar or Skilled-Labor homes who have high intelligence have almost a fifty-fifty chance of heading toward college. What differentiates boys in these groups who are interested in college from the majority of their friends who are not?

To explore this problem, twenty-four boys and their parents were interviewed by myself and colleagues on the Harvard project. All had I.Q. scores in the top quintile; all had petty white-collar, skilled or semiskilled fathers. Yet almost half were college oriented, the rest were not [18].

School and the possibility of college were viewed by all the boys solely as steps to jobs. None was interested in learning for the subtle pleasures it can offer; none craved intellectual understanding for its own sake. The most common phrase in the entire body of interviews was "Nowadays you need a high-school diploma (or a college education) to get a good job." Often a distinction was drawn between the diploma and the education it symbolized; the boys wanted the parchment, not the learning. In this pragmatic approach toward schooling, the boys reflected the views of their parents (and of most of their teachers).

All the boys who were convinced that a college degree was the basic essential for a job were seeking upper-middle-class jobs. Often they had a specific occupation in mind, such as engineering or accounting. Sometimes they knew only the level of job that they wanted, and talked more about the style of life that the income would buy than the details of the work itself. By contrast, the boys who were not aiming toward college occasionally had a specific lower-middle- or working-class job as their goal, but more often had no firm goal at all—they would "take anything that comes along."

It was not always clear which came first: the job ambition or the school performance. Often the desire for the job did seem to be the base for the school motivation, yet sometimes a boy who did well in school became slowly convinced that he was good enough to think of a middle-class job and sought one that would be suitable without knowing in advance what it might be. Here are two contrasting examples: One boy had always wanted to be an architect. His hobby was drawing, and he proudly showed me the plans for many homes he had designed in his spare time. He wanted to go to the Massachusetts Institute of Technology, and was taking the technical college-preparatory course. Another boy, who had always done very well in school, planned to be a high-school teacher because everybody told him that a boy who did well with books would be a good teacher—but he had no special subject in mind and wasn't sure he would like teaching.

Boys tended to shift their peer-group affiliations to match their school aspirations. If one kept his schoolwork up while his neighborhood friends did not, he shifted into another peer group with higher ambitions.

The boys could be divided into two groups, each reflecting to a remarkable degree the values about life held by their parents: those who believed in "getting by" and those who believed in "getting ahead." This basic split showed in their more specific attitudes toward the details of schoolwork, after-school recreation, and jobs. The boys who believed in just getting by generally were bored with school, anticipated some sort of low-level job, and found peer-group activity to be the most important thing in life. They were gayer than those who felt an ambition to be successful. These latter boys who were striving to get ahead took schoolwork more seriously than recreational affairs. Both groups noticed the differences: the nonstrivers said the others "didn't know how to have any fun," whereas the strivers said the others were "irresponsible; didn't know what was good for them."

Two quotations from interviews with parents will show how these contrasting attitudes of the boys were reflections of the values about life, work, and school held by their parents.

CASE A.  The father is a bread salesman; he has five children. He is a high school graduate.

"I was never a bright one myself, I must say. The one thing I've had in mind is making enough to live on from day to day; I've never had much hope of a lot of it piling up. However, I'd rather see my son make an improvement over what I'm doing and I'm peddling bread. . . . I think he's lazy. Maybe I am too, but I gotta get out and hustle. . . . I don't keep after him. I have five kiddos. When you have a flock like that it is quite a job to keep your finger on this and the other thing. . . . I really don't know what he would like to do. Of course, no matter what I would like him to do, it isn't my job to say so as he may not be qualified. I tried to tell him where he isn't going to be a doctor or lawyer or anything like that, I told him he should learn English and learn to meet people. Then he could go out and sell something worth while where a sale would amount to something for him. That is the only suggestion that I'd make to him. . . . I suppose there are some kids who set their mind to some goal and plug at it, but the majority of kids I have talked to take what comes. Just get along. . . . I don't think a high school diploma is so important. I mean only in so far as you might apply for a job and if you can say, 'I have a diploma,' it might help get the job, but other than that I don't see it ever did me any good."

CASE B.  The father is a foreman in a factory with about 20 men under him. He had three years of high school and is convinced that he would have gotten further ahead if he had had more education.

"Down at the shop we see a lot of men come in and try to make their way. The ones with the college education seem to succeed better. They seem better able to handle jobs of different sorts. They may not know any more than the other fellows but they know how to learn. Somehow they've learned how to learn more easily. . . . If they get a job and see that they aren't going to get anywhere they know enough to get out of it or to switch. They know enough to quit. . . . So that's why I hope my boy will go to college. . . . The college men seem also better able to handle themselves socially. They seem smoother in getting along with people and more adaptable to new situations. I think that I would have gotten along a lot better myself if I had had that sort of an education."

In most instances the parents who believed in getting ahead were somewhat frustrated in their own degree of success: father had not reached the place in the hierarchy that he had expected and desired. *He blamed his failure on insufficient education, and was determined that his son would do better.* By contrast, the parents who believed in merely getting by were adjusted to their way of life and saw no reason to influence their sons to live differently.

The research pointed to a general conclusion: upper-status boys aimed toward college as a matter of course, for everybody in their group did so. Lower-status boys tended to be uninterested in college. Consequently, those who did aim high were exceptions. The motivation in these exceptional cases came from four directions:

1. If a boy had done well in the early years, *and* had built up a self-conception in which good school performance was important, he would work hard to keep up his record. But an idea that school was important occurred only when that early performance was truly exceptional, or if the importance of his standing to him was reinforced by one or more of the other factors listed below.

2. A boy would sacrifice other pleasures for homework when they were not important to him. If a boy was not good at sports, if he did not have close and satisfying peer contacts, or if he had no hobby that was strongly rewarding as well as distracting, then the cost of homework was less and the balance more in its favor. In extreme cases frustrations in these alternative spheres motivated a boy to good school performance as compensation.

3. If a boy's family rewarded good school performance and punished poor performance, and the boy was not in rebellion against the family for emotional reasons, he was more likely to give up some play for homework.

4. If a boy had a rational conviction about the importance of schoolwork for his future career, he would strive to keep up his performance. But that conviction never appeared unless the parents emphasized it.

Notice how the theme of parental influence runs through three of the four categories. Indeed, the evidence showed that if the parents were pushing toward college, in eight out of nine cases the boy responded appropriately, but if the parents were indifferent about college, in eleven out of fifteen cases the boy was uninterested. It should be remembered that all of these boys had high enough intelligence for college work (though few were brilliant), and that all of the parents had roughly the same social status (lower-middle or working class).

Thus, intelligence and social status account for the major variations in college aspiration, especially at the extremes of the distributions. But in the lower-middle occupational range, and the intelligence range of smart-but-not-brilliant, the prediction is not good, for about half of such boys go to college and half stay away. For those boys the major determining factor is the attitude of the parents regarding the importance of college for occupational success, and the importance of occupational success for personal happiness. Some maintain that college is necessary for their sons to get a "decent" job; others say that their sons should "do whatever they like." Although the amount of money available for college expenses is also significant (especially for very poor families), in stable homes at the working-class level it usually happens that lack of money is more an excuse than a cause: if the parents and the boy think college is important, they usually find a way for him to go. Especially if there is a public college within commuting distance of his home, he can work his way through without too much difficulty [19].

It is probably true that ambition persists in families through the generations. Several studies have shown families who for two or three generations have had more education than was common at their status level. It is easy to picture an ambitious man who migrates to an American city, either from a surrounding farm or from Europe, and devotes himself to hard work. He gets as far as he can with the education he has, and then teaches his son that the next step up demands more education. Indeed, there is a likelihood that the son will become interested in the same type of job as his father's, only a step higher. For instance, a factory worker's son learns that the engineers are the people of prestige and income in the factory world; an office worker's son learns the possibilities of accounting as a good career. It may be the third generation before a son aspires to become a doctor or a research scientist. The way parents talk about the possibilities of different kinds of work influences the boy's thinking: the sheer information he has determines to some extent what decisions he makes. Many parents are not against college or occupations that depend upon higher education—they simply do not know or care anything about them. But in ambitious families, who believe in the old-fashioned virtues of thrift and of always wanting more than you have, the next higher level of work is a matter of concern and discussion.

## THE ACHIEVEMENT MOTIVE

So far, we have been examining the kind of motivation that a boy learns easily and automatically from the values of his parents and his friends. We have been showing how he absorbs a general point of view about work and school from his social environment. But there is a deeper kind of motivation that influences a few boys: a driving hunger for great success, a need for achievement that becomes the dominant passion of life. There is some evidence, impressionistic and clinical, yet convincing, that such men are the ones who climb to the very top. Many men, of course, are at the top because they were born there, but we must take a look at those who start from humbler levels in society (usually the lower-middle class, much more rarely the working or lower class), and manage to reach the summit of success.

W. Lloyd Warner and James C. Abegglin sketch the portraits of many men of great ambition in the same study that we noted in the last chapter for its statistics on entry into the business elite. The authors emphasize the movement involved in a pattern of success from humble origins: movement away from family, from friends, from ethnic group, from community of birth, and movement into a new world with new values and new habits of behavior. In fact, the movement is repeated many times, for each success means leaving associates and friends behind [20]:

The three-room apartment is left behind for a duplex, after which the children need to be taken to a suburb for the schools (or because the place we have is too small or because everyone we know lives in Forestdale). Each of these changes of house and neighborhood brings with it myriad changes large and small, from home furnishing to clubs, to vacation habits, to the children's schools. Mobility may be seen as a continual process of departing—arriving—departing. . . .

We know from depth psychology that one of the strongest desires of man is the need for belonging. Through history most men have desired to stay close to home, to family, to familiar people and places. What kind of man, then, is able to keep so much on the move, to sacrifice "belongingness" so many times for the chance for a new success? Remember that new success does not necessarily offer a new group to belong to which is as satisfying as the old, for despite its greater prestige, the new group is strange and will seldom emotionally encompass a man as did the old one.

Warner and Abegglin report that their interviews and projective tests indicated that most of the keenly ambitious men in their sample were not only trying to achieve, but also to escape. There was something in their home backgrounds which was distasteful, and they wanted to get away from it. Most commonly they had failures as fathers: men who were drunkards, who were unable to earn a steady living, who deserted their wives and children, or who were simply weak and uninteresting. And they had strong mothers, who taught them that it was important to be better than their fathers, and that the path was through devotion to tasks in school and on the job. Yet their mothers were not so strong that they smothered their sons and kept them tied to their apron strings; instead, they taught them to leave and go out into the big world. Notice that the fathers were inadequate as male role models, and the mothers were protecting and encouraging but not very warm and loving. Furthermore, these families were not active in kin and community activities; the sons were isolated from outsiders.

Very often the boy found a substitute for his father during adolescence—another man who offered strength and encouragement, such as an athletic coach. This pattern provided a useful learning experience, for in business the ambitious young man must become the protégé of a well-placed older one, and then eventually break away when he has achieved as much or more success than his patron [21]: "Later in life they are able to continue relating themselves easily to figures of authority, never too close for disattachment when necessary—never too far away when continuity and closeness are necessary for advancement."

Warner and Abegglin summarize as follows [22]:

The mobile man must be able to depart: that is, he must maintain a substantial emotional distance from people, and not become deeply involved with them or committed to them; and he must be an energetic person and one who can focus his energy on a single goal. There has probably been in his life a basic and deep experience of separation and loss. . . . And what of arrival? The mobile man in each of these continuing moves must, it seems, be accurate and realistic as he looks at the world around him. He must be able to select his central goals, and drive to them with a total concentration of energy. He must be an attractive person, one who appeals to other people, and one who wants, and is able, to relate to them readily (but always with the underlying reservations that permit perpetuation of his movement). He must be a man who has early been convinced of the fact that through his own efforts, and despite disadvantages, he can achieve some of the goals he sets himself.

The authors warn us against caricaturing this portrait. The highly mobile men use others for their own ends; they sacrifice recreation and artistic creativity for concentration on the job; they demand of their wives behavior that aids their careers—but they are not sadistic men who enjoy hurting others, nor immoral men who will do anything to advance themselves regardless of its effect on others.

Warner and Abegglin also give portraits of some men born into the elite. Although the evidence here is not so sharp, it appears that the son of a successful man is faced with a difficult problem: if he tries to emulate his father, he must have great self-confidence, for his father is a driving and important man. Some sons succeed, and they have business careers, often in the family firm. Many sons feel that the father is too powerful a man to compete with and seek alternative paths. The learned professions are one common alternative, for they provide esteem without demanding the driving competition of big business. A slightly more variant path is into the arts. There is also the possibility of living off inherited capital without working at all. At any rate, it is not so easy to grow up the son of a successful self-made man in a culture that expects each man to make his own way, to be a little better than his father. It is much easier to excel over a failure.

The psychologist David C. McClelland and his associates have tackled the problem of measuring the achievement motive and seeking some of its causes and effects. They use a form of the Thematic Apperception Test, a device which asks subjects to create stories about persons shown in pictures, thus projecting into the stories some of their own unconscious desires. McClelland then rates the stories according to the number of themes that appear which express achievement needs.

These researchers have discovered that the achievement motive is measurable and is related to cultural values [23]. Some cultural groups express more achievement need than others. Furthermore, boys in high school with strong achievement needs perform better at their schoolwork. And there is evidence that the achievement motive is at least partly learned as a result of the way parents, especially mothers, teach their young children habits of early independence. The child who is taught to stand on his own two feet, to feed and dress himself, to roam about the neighborhood, is likely to grow up with higher achievement drives than the one who is coddled and protected (or ignored).

It is a reasonable assumption that families or cultural groups who stress achievement will give early independence training to their children, and that children who have had such training will grow up to stress achievement as adults. The causation is circular. Middle-class parents, and working-class parents who believe in getting ahead, probably give their children more independence training than working-class parents who believe in just getting by [24].

Incidentally, McClelland gathered a bit of evidence that supports Warner and Abegglin. He asked thirty college students to rate their parents, and he found that there was an inverse relationship between the achievement needs of the sons and the following traits in their parents; friendliness-helpfulness, and cleverness-self-confidence. And there was a positive correlation between the son's perception of rejection by his father and his score on need for achievement. McClelland reports on several researches of this type; they do not all point in the same direction, so the reader should not conclude that these relationships are demonstrated [25]. The studies are mentioned here only as an indication of the kind of work that must be done in the future if we are to advance our understanding of the variations in motivation among individuals that are important in explaining differences in their career activities. We already understand the major sociological determinants; we need more investigation of the subtler psychological determinants. Although the desire for occupational success is partly a result of consciously learned social values, it also reflects deeper layers of the personality that are formed in early childhood, long before occupational success is even considered [26].

### EFFECTS OF MOBILITY

Very little is known about the psychological consequences of mobility. There is, of course, the ancient observation that a newcomer to any group, be it a religious convert or a newly successful businessman, tends to overdo his allegiance to the values and symbols of the new group in order to convince himself and his colleagues that he really belongs. In other words, insecurity breeds overreaction. Thus members of minority groups who make money wear clothes that are flashy and drive automobiles that are big and gaudy.

However, the meager statistical evidence we have concerning attitudes tends to contradict this theory, for it appears that the opinions of the newcomers tend to be intermediate between those of the group from which they originated and the one at which they have arrived. For instance, Herbert H. Hyman shows that, on the average, manual workers have values that put less stress on college education and on aspiration toward professional work than do business and professional men. Yet members of the latter groups whose fathers were manual workers express intermediate opinions. The same is true of manual workers who have been downwardly mobile from business and professional families [27]. Similarly, Patricia Salter West reports that economically successful graduates who had worked their way through college, and thus can be presumed to have come from poorer families than those who were fully supported by their parents while in school, were less likely to be Republicans. But as they grew older, they became Republicans in greater numbers, thus learning and adopting the values of those who have been in the upper brackets for a generation or more. The older and the more successful a man became, the more conservative his views became, despite his origins at humbler levels of society [28].

There is some evidence that persons who have been highly mobile, particularly those who have moved from high to low positions, express insecurity and frustration through attitudes of prejudice toward minority groups. It seems that these mobile individuals are somewhat more prone to need scapegoats than nonmobile individuals. But the evidence is not so clear-cut as to inspire much confidence [29].

CONCLUSIONS

As a result of trends toward greater technological complexity and larger organizational size, our society has become more bureaucratic both in private industry and in government. A major feature of bureaucracies is that they establish formal rules of "personnel policy." These rules define various jobs, and establish requirements of education and experience for each position. The importance of formal education grows. Before people are allowed to show what they can do, they must display diplomas that indicate what they have learned.

Consequently, the school system has become the major institution not only for training people but also for selecting and placing them. A man starts in the occupational world according to the level he has achieved in the educational world. Native intelligence plays an important role in determining the amount and type of schooling that a boy gets, although our measurements leave much to be desired. But intelligence does not, by a long way, fully account for his educational attainments, although it is a necessary prerequisite for success. A boy is also much influenced by the social status of his family. The stratification position of his parents (and thus of most of his friends) shapes his information about various jobs and determines his motivation for occupational achievement.

Indeed, the role of the family in creating the occupational outlook of its children is the major device for perpetuation of stratification position through the generations, far more important in the modern world than the amount of money that is inherited.

Beyond these major variables of intelligence and status-determined motivation, there operate subtler variables of personality that influence the strength and type of motivation. Some boys have interests and skills in science, others in art, others in salesmanship. Some crave great success and recognition and power; others prefer to avoid responsibility. And reversing the coin, a man's experiences of success and failure in turn affect his personality. Some gain contentment because they have reached their own goals; others suffer from the anxieties of a sense of inadequacy bred by failure.

In dealing with these psychological moods, we must always remember that they are relative to a person's own feeling of what an appropriate success ought to be for a man of his type. Success and failure are not absolutes, but are measured by the goals one set out to achieve. The goals in turn are related to average values within a class level. But why do some men accept the values of their class of birth, and others turn their eyes upward?

As research progresses, it is likely that we will develop better measures of the social values and the psychological traits that are characteristic of "typical" members of various status groups. Only then will we be able to discover variations from the typical that cause or result from mobility. As it now stands, our research skills have been, for the most part, devoted to discovering gross attitude differences between such large classifications as manual workers and white-collar workers. But insofar as these groups contain so many members who have been or desire to be mobile, we should not expect the groups to be homogeneous in their attitudes, even though we believe that on the average and in the long run manual workers will display different values from white-collar workers. Some data that now look confusing may turn out to be orderly once we can measure adequately both the typical for each level and the explainable variations from the typical.

REFERENCES

[1] Quoted from Chapter VII, above.

[2] For a general discussion of selection procedures in many societies, see Pitirim Sorokin, *Social Mobility* (New York: Harper, 1927), Chaps. VIII and IX.

[3] Adapted from Paul C. Glick, "Educational Attainment and Occupational Advancement," in *Transactions of the Second World Congress of Sociol-*

*ogy* (London: International Sociological Association, 1954), Vol. II, pp. 183–94, Table 1.

[4] Glick, "Educational Attainment and Occupational Advancement."

[5] See Ernest Havemann and Patricia Salter West, *They Went to College* (New York: Harper, 1952).

[6] Dael Wolfle, *America's Resources of Specialized Talent* (New York: Harper, 1954), p. 24.

[7] James Bryant Conant, *Education and Liberty* (Cambridge, Mass.: Harvard University Press, 1953), p. 3.
    I have slightly adjusted the figures for the U.S. to bring them up to 1950. Conant points out that this comparison is somewhat unfair, for it does not include the fact that part-time, after-work education is more prevalent in England than in America. The recent English reforms plan to raise the compulsory minimum to sixteen years, and by use of examinations to sort students at the age of eleven into groups that will get more or less education according to talent, with state scholarships aiding the poor but bright children.

[8] Byron S. Hollinshead, *Who Should Go to College* (New York: Columbia University Press, 1952), p. 10.
    Notice that Hollinshead estimates that 10 per cent graduate from college, whereas Wolfle, *op. cit.*, says one in eight. The difference stems from the difficulty of estimating how many veterans in college in 1950 would have been there had no war occurred. It seems that the trend toward more college attendance is such that the figures for 1955 probably approach 25 per cent starting college, and half that number graduating. The books by Hollinshead and Wolfle, both reports to commissions that studied higher education, are the best national summaries available. Wolfle gives more statistical detail. For two excellent regional studies, see R. Clyde White, *These Will Go to College* (Cleveland: The Press of Western Reserve University, 1952), and Ralph F. Berdie, *After High School—What?* (Minneapolis: University of Minnesota Press, 1954).

[9] Hollinshead, *Who Should Go to College*, pp. 6–7. Wolfle, Chap. III, documents the amount of shifting that occurs at various levels.

[10] The details are in Wolfle, *America's Resources of Specialized Talent*, Chap. VI.

[11] *Ibid.*, p. 146. Wolfle uses Army General Classification Test scores, which may run a point or two higher than most I.Q. scales. Of course, I.Q. tests are far from perfect, especially because they reflect both native ability and some learning (and the learning is class-related). For a criticism, see Kenneth W. Eells *et al.*, *Ingelligence and Cultural Differences* (Chicago: University of Chicago Press, 1951), and Allison Davis, *Social Class Influences upon Learning* (Cambridge, Mass.: Harvard University Press, 1952).

[12] President's Commission on Higher Education, *Higher Education for American Democracy* (Washington: Government Printing Press Office, 1947). Seymour E. Harris, *The Market for College Graduates* (Cambridge, Mass.: Harvard University Press, 1949), countered with a pessimistic view that we were educating too many people and that they would be unable to find the jobs for which they thought they were properly prepared. At least for the short run, he turned out to be wrong. The growth in the proportion of youths who graduate from college will eventually slow down; my own guess is that it will level off at 15 to 20 per cent of the appropriate age group.

[13] Wolfle, *America's Resources of Specialized Talent,* p. 149.

[14] *Ibid.,* p. 162.

[15] Hollinshead, *Who Should Go to College,* p. 37. If we neglect the class bias of I.Q. tests, it is possible to estimate the amount of mobility that occurs because some children are born into an occupational level that is not "appropriate" to their intelligence in terms of the average I.Q. of men at that level. This has been done in an ingenious article by C. Arnold Anderson *et al.,* "Intelligence and Occupational Mobility," *Journal of Political Economy,* LX (June, 1952), 218–39. They write that "the proportion of actual mobility that may be imputed to disparities between the intelligence of the sons and the occupational status of their fathers was estimated to be roughly 40 per cent." They add that mobility would have to be tripled before a perfect correlation between I.Q. and occupational level could be reached.

The reader must be very careful in handling such correlations. The data (based on admittedly biased I.Q. tests) indicate that high-level occupations are filled by men of high intelligence (90 per cent of professionals who went into the army had AGCT scores of 110 or more). To a much lesser degree, very low occupations are filled by men of low intelligence. But the intermediate levels which contain the greatest number of workers, such as skilled workers and petty white-collar workers, show an I.Q. distribution that approaches normality.

[16] Joseph A. Kahl, "Educational and Occupational Aspirations of 'Common Man' Boys," *Harvard Educational Review,* XXIII (Summer, 1953), 188.

[17] See the details in Hollingshead, *Elmtown's Youth,* in Chapter V, above. See also the appendix by Robert J. Havighurst and Robert R. Rodgers, "The Role of Motivation in Attendance at Post-High-School Educational Institutions" in Hollinshead, *Who Should Go to College;* it includes selections from the pertinent research literature. See also W. Lloyd Warner *et al., Who Shall Be Educated?* (New York: Harper, 1944), which gives statistical and clinical evidence on the way social pressures shape the adolescent's outlook toward school and work.

[18] The following paragraphs are adapted from Kahl, "Educational and Occupational Aspirations of 'Common Man' Boys."

[19] Lack of motivation probably dwarfs inadequate funds as the reason why so many bright boys do not go to college. Havighurst and Rodgers, in "The Role of Motivation," estimate that of these boys a scholarship program might induce a third to go. Other experts feel that such an increase in attendance would demand both money and a careful program of counseling of students and parents at the junior-high-school level. The evidence on the influence of the G.I. bill is not conclusive; some estimates say it doubled the college attendance of bright boys from poor homes, but most estimates are lower than that.

[20] W. Lloyd Warner and James C. Abegglin, *Big Business Leaders in America* (New York: Harper, 1955), p. 63. William E. Henry developed the adaptation of the Thematic Apperception Test used by Warner and Abegglin; see Henry's "The Business Executive: Psychodynamics of a Social Role," *American Journal of Sociology*, LIV (January, 1940), 286–91.

[21] Warner and Abegglin, *Big Business Leaders in America*, p. 80.

[22] *Ibid.*, pp. 81–82.

[23] David C. McClelland *et al.*, *The Achievement Motive* (New York: Appleton-Century-Crofts, 1953), esp. Chaps. II, V, VIII, IX.

[24] The evidence on the differences in child-rearing practices between middle-class and working-class mothers is contradictory; see Robert J. Havighurst and Allison Davis, "Comparison of the Chicago and Harvard Studies of Social Class Differences in Child Rearing," *American Sociological Review*, XX (August, 1955), 438–42. Contrast Kahl, "Educational and Occupational Aspirations of 'Common Man' Boys" with David F. Aberle and Kaspar D. Naegele, "Middle Class Fathers' Occupational Role and Attitudes toward Children," *American Journal of Orthopsychiatry*, XXII (April, 1952), 366–78. Some of the contradictions in the data might be resolved if it were remembered that working-class parents do not represent a homogeneous group with respect to their basic values; some accept their position, others are oriented toward getting ahead and therefore act in many ways like middle-class people. Similarly, the latter probably show less strong achievement drives the longer they have enjoyed success; paradoxically, the longer they have been in the middle class, the less they show some of the competitive values that got them there, and the more they train their children to enjoy life and to broaden their perspective beyond business. But we need attitude scales that measure class-related values before we can settle this question; I have begun to develop some, and hope in the near future to push this research.

[25] McClelland, *The Achievement Motive*, pp. 276–88.
McClelland is expanding this research; he now suggests a possible link between child-rearing practices and the values described by Max Weber as basic to the Protestant ethic, and wonders if it might be possible to use this approach in studying the current variations in rate of development among underdeveloped countries.

[26] For a full understanding of the relation of motivation to one's class of
origin and class of destination, we must investigate three types of variables simultaneously:

1. The cultural values of the parents and the sons with respect to career
—David Riesman's and Florence R. Kluckhohn's ideas are particularly
suggestive here (see his *The Lonely Crowd* [New Haven: Yale University Press, 1951], and her "Dominant and Substitute Profiles of Cultural Orientations," *Social Forces*, XXVIII [May, 1950], 376–93).

2. The constitutional energy of the son—note that Warner and Abegglin speak of the high energy of the successful man, and Charles Morris
has linked it to body type (see his "Physique and Cultural Patterns,"
in David C. McClelland, ed., *Studies in Motivation* [New York:
Appleton-Century-Crofts, 1955]).

3. The way native energy is shaped by learning into a specific achievement motive—McClelland's studies are suggestive, but we must add
that the career man channels his achievement energy into a narrow,
directed, organized path that leads directly to his success goals.

   Although the measurement tools now in use are new, the questions
are old; for example, the discussion of the "circulation of the elite,"
by Vilfredo Pareto, *The Minds and Society*, Vol. IV (New York:
Harcourt, Brace, 1935), and Plato's *Republic*.

   And there is Kinsey's interesting discovery that boys from the
working class who eventually rise in the world adopt middle-class sex
patterns in their early teens: Alfred C. Kinsey *et al.*, *Sexual Behavior
in the Human Male* (Philadelphia: Saunders, 1948).

[27] Herbert H. Hyman, "The Value Systems of Different Classes," in
*Class, Status and Power*, eds. Reinhard Bendix and Seymour M. Lipset
(Glencoe, Ill.: The Free Press, 1953), p. 441.

[28] Patricia Salter West, "Social Mobility among College Graduates," *Ibid.*,
p. 478. See also Richard Hofstadter, "The Pseudo-Conservative Revolt,"
*Perspectives*, No. 12 (Summer, 1955), pp. 10–29.

[29] Joseph Greenblum and Leonard I. Pearlin, "Vertical Mobility and
Prejudice," in Bendix and Lipset, *Class, Status and Power*. See also Bruno
Bettelheim and Morris Janowitz, *The Dynamics of Prejudice* (New
York: Harper, 1950).

# Index

Index

# Index